PRAISE FOR

But I Live

"*But I Live* is a path-breaking book that elucidates the complex relationships between story and image in Holocaust recounting. It is equally a book about relationships themselves: between the artists and the survivors and then all of us who are – literally – drawn into their vital conversations."
Henry Greenspan, author of *On Listening to Holocaust Survivors*

"In 'A Kind of Resistance', Libicki's use of wide round eyes express the innocence and terror of a small child. 'Thirteen Secrets' immediately grabbed me with Gilad Seliktar's beautiful style of artwork. There is a particular haze, the fog of memories of childhood long ago. 'But I Live' welcomed me into the story with a warm familiarity. That I know these people. That I know their stories. I know the one spoon left from everything after the war. The not wanting to remember but unable to forget. The fear left behind showing up in their walks of life, however rich and safe."
Miriam Katin, graphic novelist and author of *We Are on Our Own* and *Letting It Go*

"*But I Live* – a beautiful title – offers the stories of four survivors who shared their traumatic memories with three talented artists who have created three outstanding visual journeys. Readers discover not only the survivors' personal experiences but also the emotion of creation. Libicki, Seliktar, and Yelin take on the responsibility to continue the chain of transmission. Their graphic novels are an act of resistance against forgetting, denying, or not willing to face the truth. Too many survivors left us, taking their untold testimony to eternity. *But I Live* transforms memory into accessible, beautiful images in one of the most popular art forms."
Michel Kichka, author and illustrator of *Second Generation*

"A unique and compelling experience. These unimaginable tales of survival and loss, told through testimony, the combined narrative power of words and pictures, and historical facts, gave me an immensity of feeling – quiet, loud, raging, pensive, but most of all, true. The art is captivating, from the bright, saturated inks of 'A Kind of Resistance' to the subdued, almost mid-century modern graphics of 'Thirteen Secrets' to the rich, realistic palette and imagery that crosses the barriers of time and space in 'But I Live.' All the stories cast a spell that bridges the 'now' with the unimaginable 'then.' When you combine these narratives (in words and pictures) with the scholarship, and the humanity of all the authors, this book provides an indispensable and true way of both confronting the past and questioning the present and the future. A marvel of cross-disciplinary invention."

Ken Krimstein, Cartoonist, *New Yorker* magazine and author of *The Three Escapes of Hannah Arendt*

"*But I Live* is an essential document. Libicki, Yelin, and Seliktar masterfully use the unique narrative strengths of comics to convey survivors' experiences with sensitivity and humanity, allowing readers to experience and understand these personal accounts with appropriate empathy and urgency."

Nate Powell, artist of the *March* trilogy and *Save It for Later*

"In this beautiful, one-of-a-kind volume, Charlotte Schallié brings together three exquisitely illustrated and narrated testimonies by four child survivors of the Holocaust. Each of these graphic novellas captures the distinct memories and experiences of its child witnesses in a different style and register, all expertly hand-rendered by different graphic artists. Together with deeply insightful reflections by the artists on their process, by the child survivors as adults, and by historians of each region, *But I Live* is the most powerful collection of non-fiction graphic novellas about the Holocaust since Art Spiegelman's *Maus*."

James E. Young, author of *The Stages of Memory* and *At Memory's Edge*

But I Live

Three Stories of Child Survivors of the Holocaust

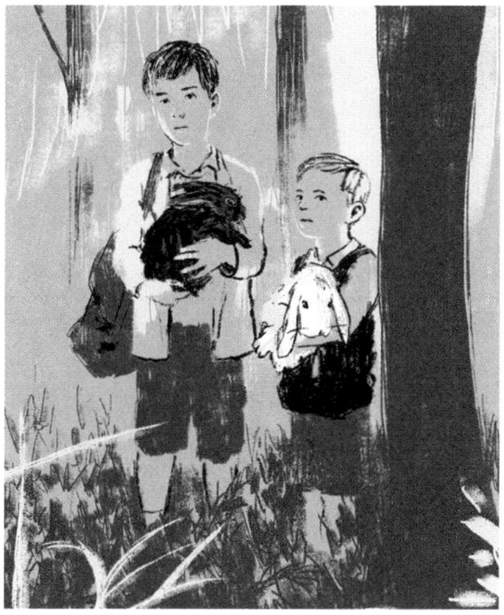

MIRIAM LIBICKI AND DAVID SCHAFFER
GILAD SELIKTAR AND NICO AND ROLF KAMP
BARBARA YELIN AND EMMIE ARBEL

Editor: Charlotte Schallié

NJP

New Jewish Press
An imprint of University of Toronto Press
Toronto Buffalo London
utorontopress.com

Library and Archives Canada Cataloguing in Publication

Title: But I live : three stories of child survivors of the Holocaust / Miriam Libicki and David Schaffer, Gilad Seliktar and Nico and Rolf Kamp, Barbara Yelin and Emmie Arbel ; editor: Charlotte Schallié.
Names: Schallié, Charlotte, editor. | Container of (work): Libicki, Miriam. Kind of resistance.
Identifiers: Canadiana (print) 20210390077 | Canadiana (ebook) 20210390190 | ISBN 9781487526849 (cloth) | ISBN 9781487526870 (EPUB) | ISBN 9781487526863 (PDF)
Subjects: LCSH: Jewish children in the Holocaust – Biography – Comic books, strips, etc. | LCSH: Hidden children (Holocaust) – Biography – Comic books, strips, etc. | LCSH: Holocaust survivors – Biography – Comic books, strips, etc. | LCSH: Holocaust, Jewish (1939–1945) – Comic books, strips, etc. | LCGFT: Graphic novels. | LCGFT: Biographies.
Classification: LCC D804.48 .B88 2022 | DDC 940.53/180922 – dc23

ISBN 978-1-4875-2684-9 (cloth)
ISBN 978-1-4875-2687-0 (EPUB)
ISBN 978-1-4875-2686-3 (PDF)

Printed in Canada

We wish to acknowledge the land on which the University of Toronto Press operates. This land is the traditional territory of the Wendat, the Anishnaabeg, the Haudenosaunee, the Métis, and the Mississaugas of the Credit First Nation.

This publication draws on research supported by the Social Sciences and Humanities Research Council.

We acknowledge the financial support of the Government of Canada, the Canada Council for the Arts, and the Ontario Arts Council, an agency of the Government of Ontario, for our publishing activities.

Canada Council for the Arts | Conseil des arts du Canada

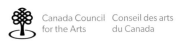

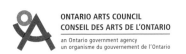

ONTARIO ARTS COUNCIL
CONSEIL DES ARTS DE L'ONTARIO
an Ontario government agency
un organisme du gouvernement de l'Ontario

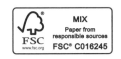

FSC www.fsc.org MIX Paper from responsible sources FSC® C016245

Social Sciences and Humanities Research Council of Canada | Conseil de recherches en sciences humaines du Canada

Canada

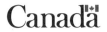

To the families of

Emmie Arbel, Nico and Rolf Kamp, and David Schaffer

CONTENTS

The Histories

In Their Own Words

PREFACE

There is an old Yiddish saying: Ink dries quickly, tears do not. It is a phrase that accompanies and underlies what I wish to express, yet my thoughts neither easily nor swiftly turn into words. And how could it be otherwise when feeling quieted and filled with great regard for *But I Live* – a deeply beautiful book, where memory and art are paired and intertwined throughout three graphic narratives, each one sensitively attuned to visualizing the testimonies of four child survivors of the Holocaust. It is a book that endows our hearts with the gift of hope.

A number of years ago, I had written and drawn a memoir about my parents and their close community of friends, all of whom were Holocaust survivors. I managed to create a footpath into their past and into the lives they made once liberated into their years forward. But now, and evermore so with aging and time's progression, almost everyone from their generation is no longer in our presence, no longer in our present. Yet, herein, with *But I Live*, the individual voices of David Schaffer, the brothers Nico and Rolf Kamp, and of Emmie Arbel join and continue the lineage of living memory. They are our moral compass that guide us through our lives, and into the world. And their voices are part of the chorus that I have heard all my life.

It is so startlingly simple: do not hate. I have found its echoing iterations among writers, philosophers, artists – the ever-expanding collective memory of response to the darkness that hatred breeds. And, as our own understandings deepen, planted within our beings, we too become responsive and responsible to its credo, to our beliefs. It is fitting, then, while being privileged to place some words on a page, I transplant a few from *But I Live* for the reader's first step:

> *My words are especially meant for you, the younger generation: Accept people who are different. And spread good in the world, not bad.*

Bernice Eisenstein

The Stories

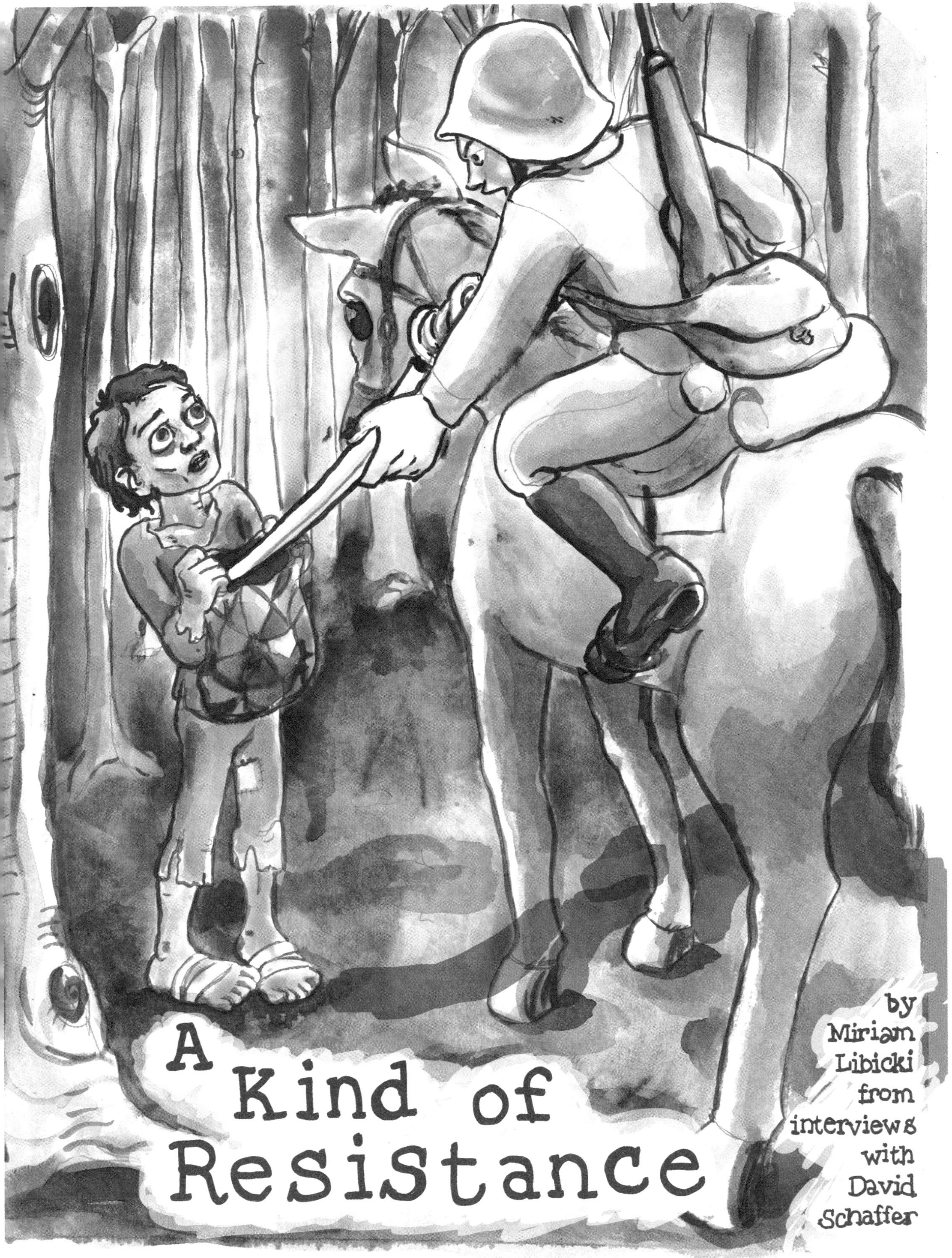
A Kind of Resistance
by Miriam Libicki from interviews with David Schaffer

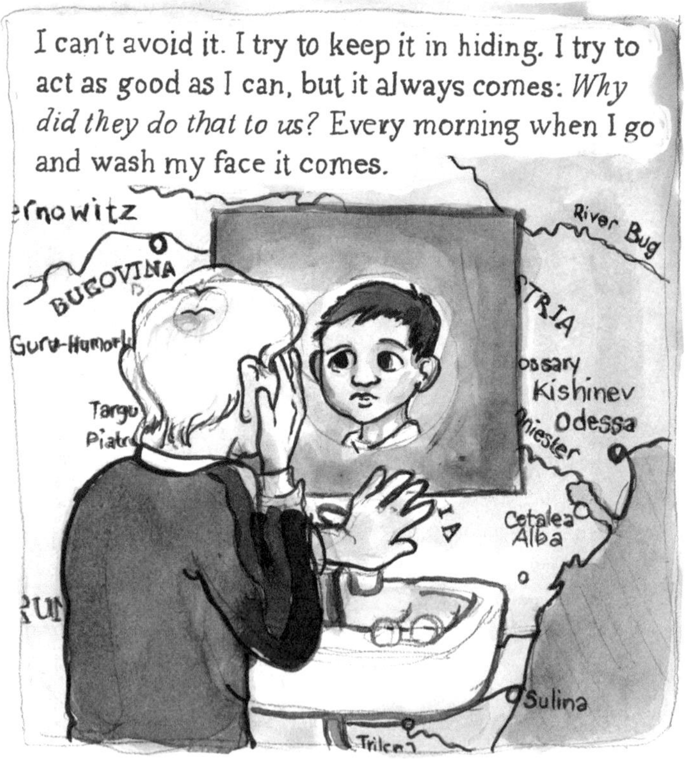
I can't avoid it. I try to keep it in hiding. I try to act as good as I can, but it always comes: *Why did they do that to us?* Every morning when I go and wash my face it comes.
BUCOVINA
River Bug
Kishinev
Odessa
Dniester
Cetalea Alba
Sulina

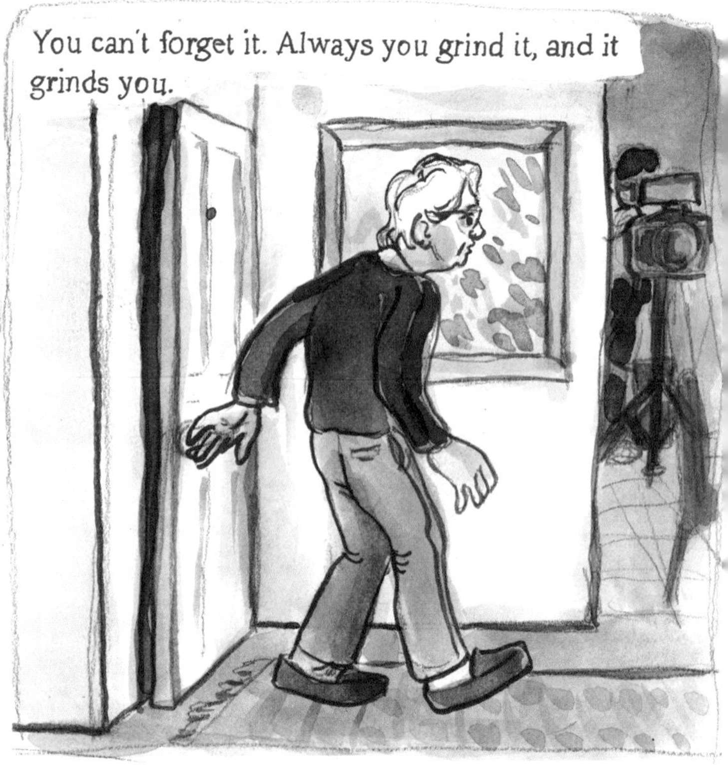
You can't forget it. Always you grind it, and it grinds you.

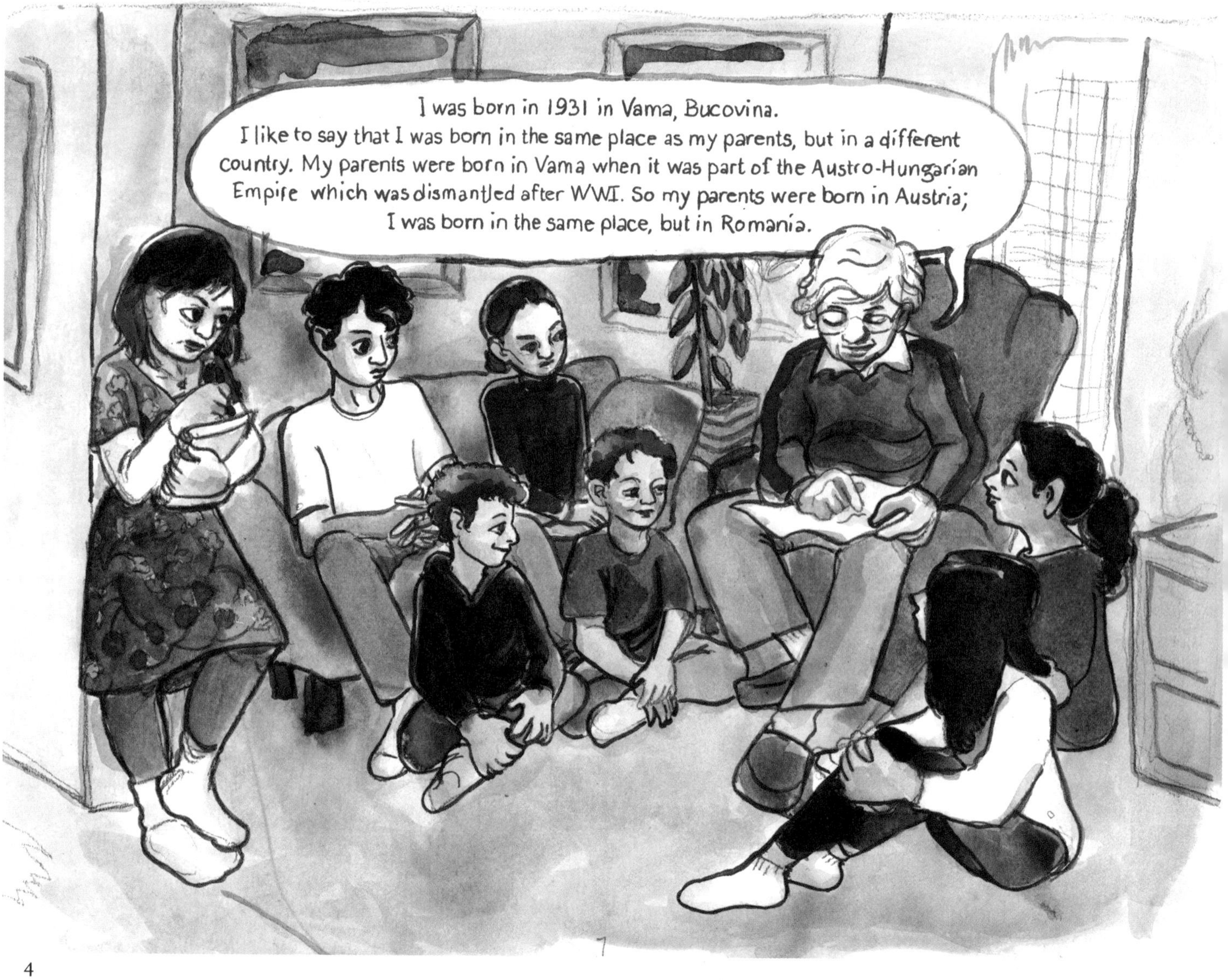
I was born in 1931 in Vama, Bucovina.
I like to say that I was born in the same place as my parents, but in a different country. My parents were born in Vama when it was part of the Austro-Hungarian Empire which was dismantled after WWI. So my parents were born in Austria; I was born in the same place, but in Romania.

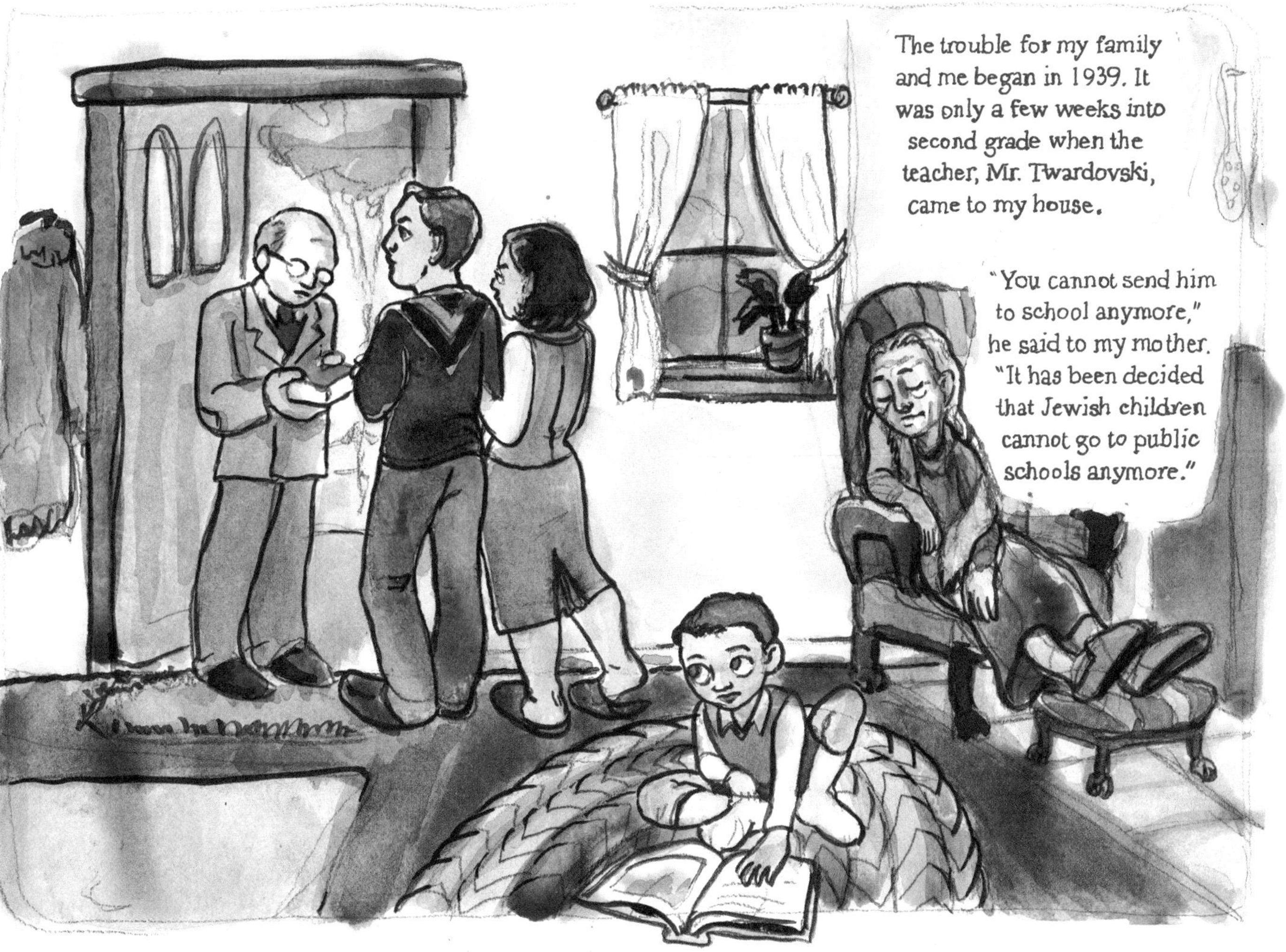
The trouble for my family and me began in 1939. It was only a few weeks into second grade when the teacher, Mr. Twardovski, came to my house.
"You cannot send him to school anymore," he said to my mother. "It has been decided that Jewish children cannot go to public schools anymore."

Mr. Twardovski didn't want to kick me out and make me feel ashamed in front of the class. So he came to my house to tell us personally.

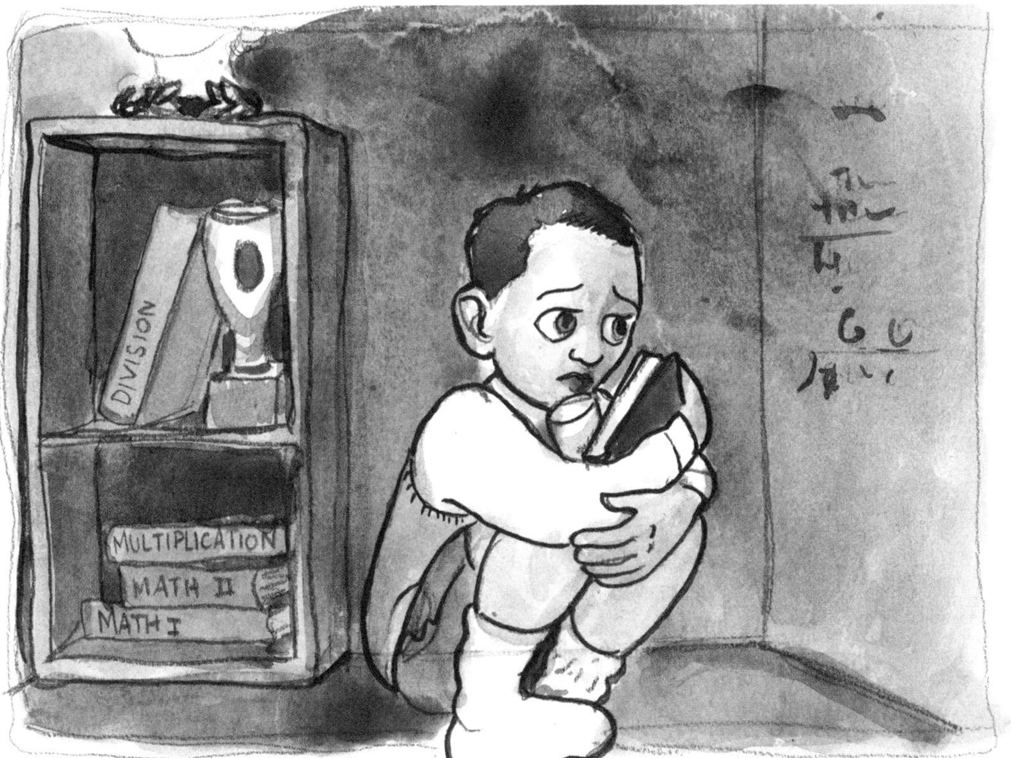
DIVISION
MULTIPLICATION
MATH II
MATH I

Despite the situation, I appreciated that gesture. The Romanian government had decreed that they were expelling Jewish students from state-run education institutions. I hadn't been expelled because I was a bad boy; being a good student and winning prizes didn't matter then.

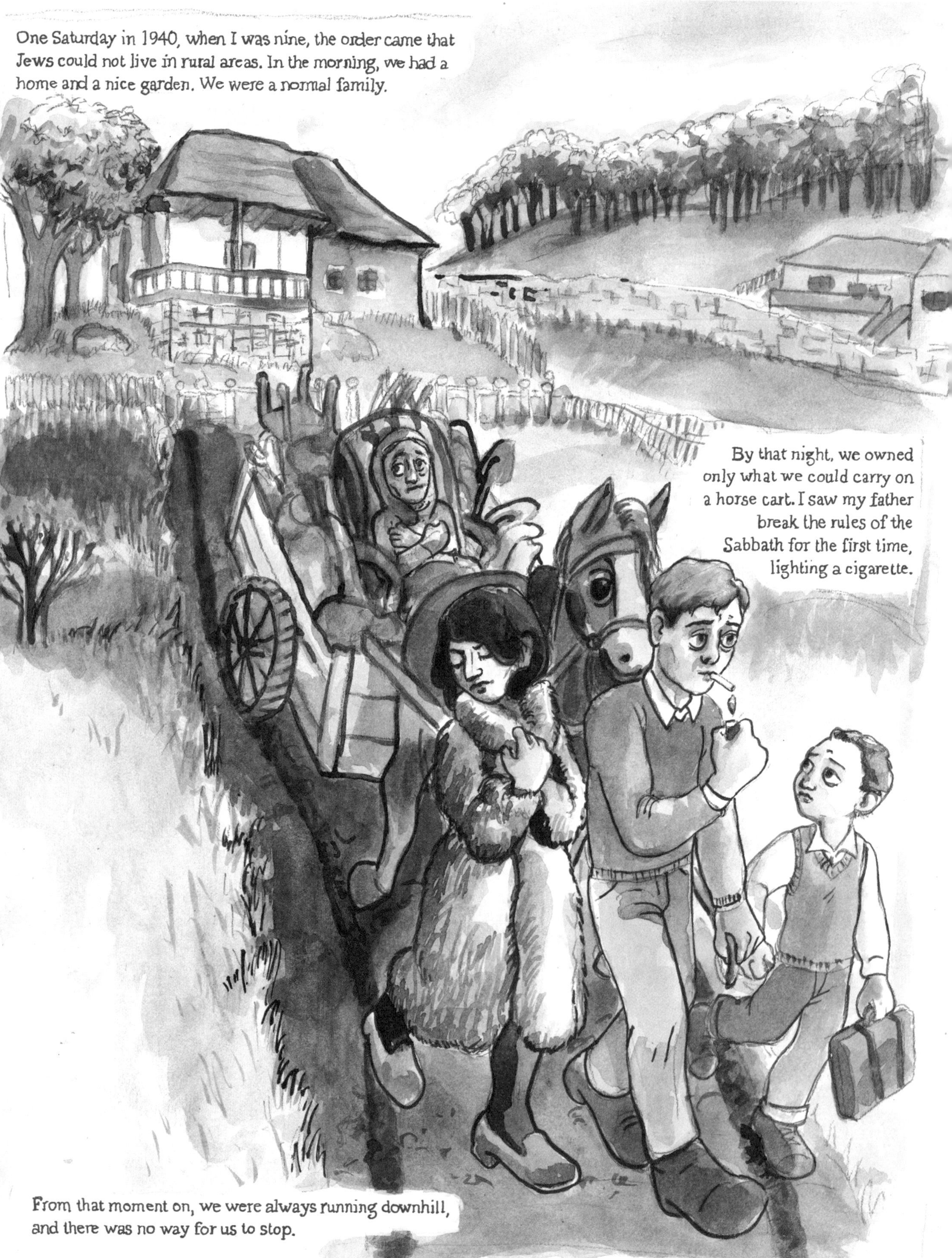
One Saturday in 1940, when I was nine, the order came that Jews could not live in rural areas. In the morning, we had a home and a nice garden. We were a normal family.
By that night, we owned only what we could carry on a horse cart. I saw my father break the rules of the Sabbath for the first time, lighting a cigarette.
From that moment on, we were always running downhill, and there was no way for us to stop.

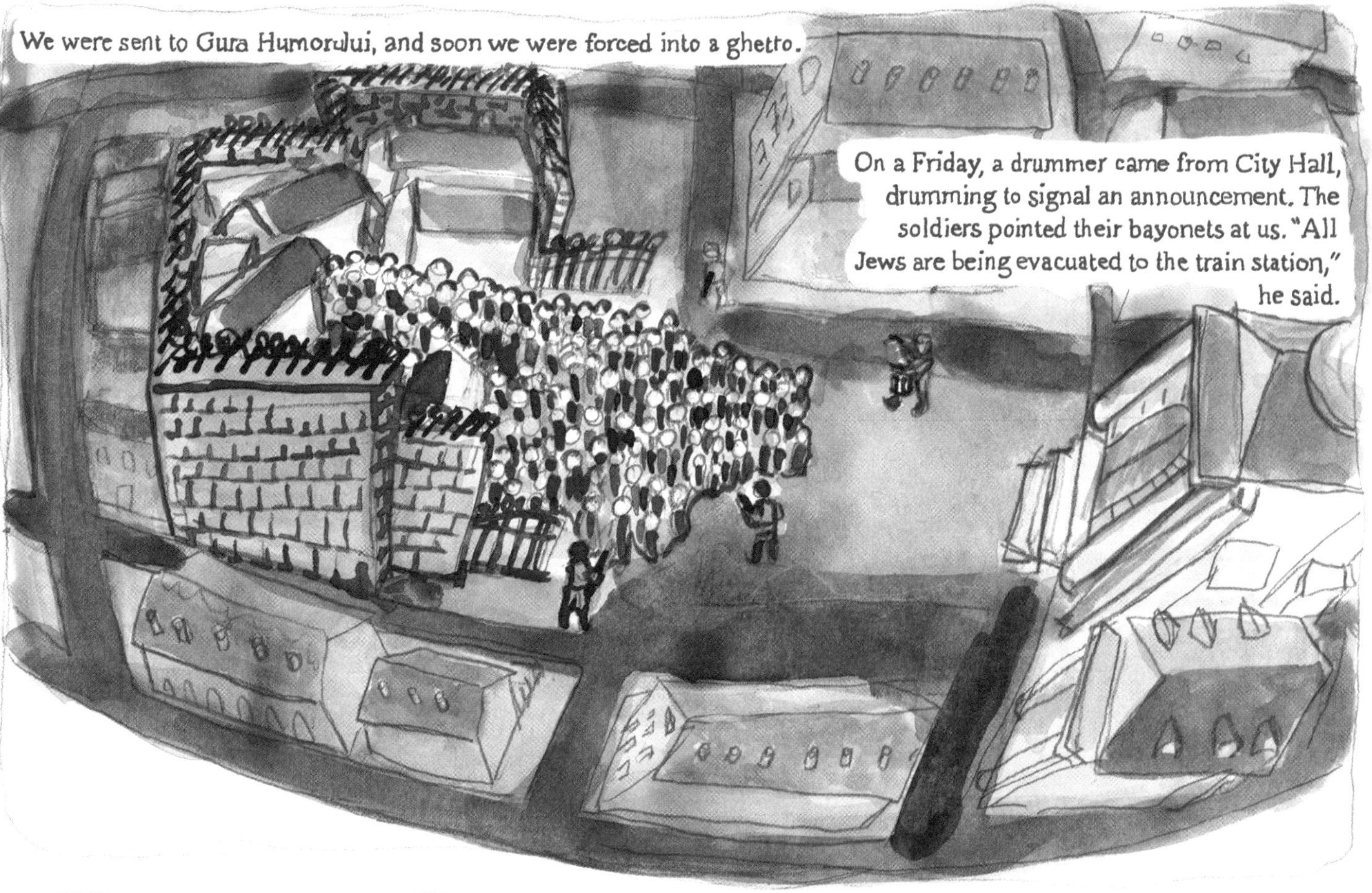
We were sent to Gura Humorului, and soon we were forced into a ghetto.
On a Friday, a drummer came from City Hall, drumming to signal an announcement. The soldiers pointed their bayonets at us. "All Jews are being evacuated to the train station," he said.

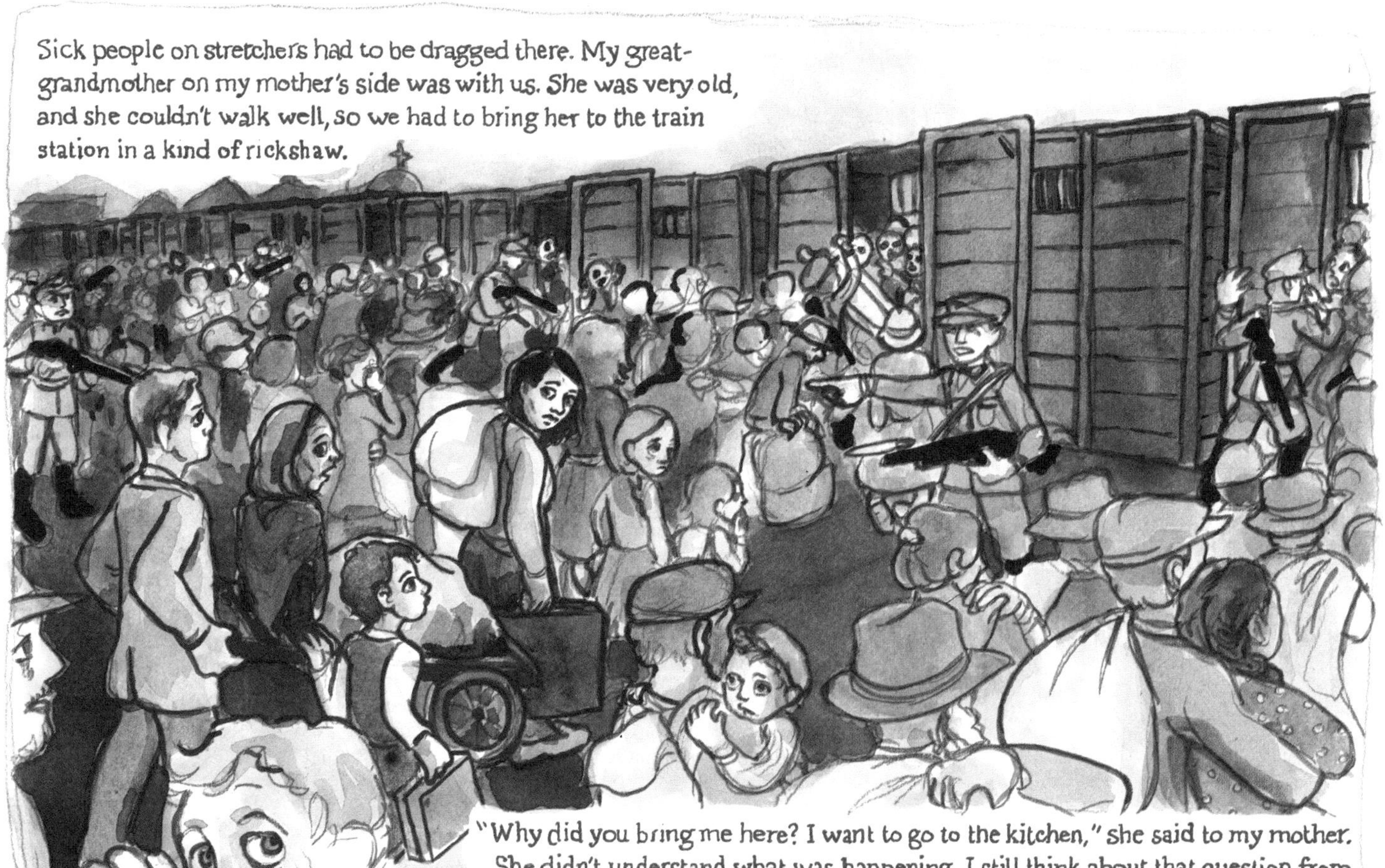
Sick people on stretchers had to be dragged there. My great-grandmother on my mother's side was with us. She was very old, and she couldn't walk well, so we had to bring her to the train station in a kind of rickshaw.
"Why did you bring me here? I want to go to the kitchen," she said to my mother. She didn't understand what was happening. I still think about that question from time to time – *Why did they bring me there?* No one has ever answered me.

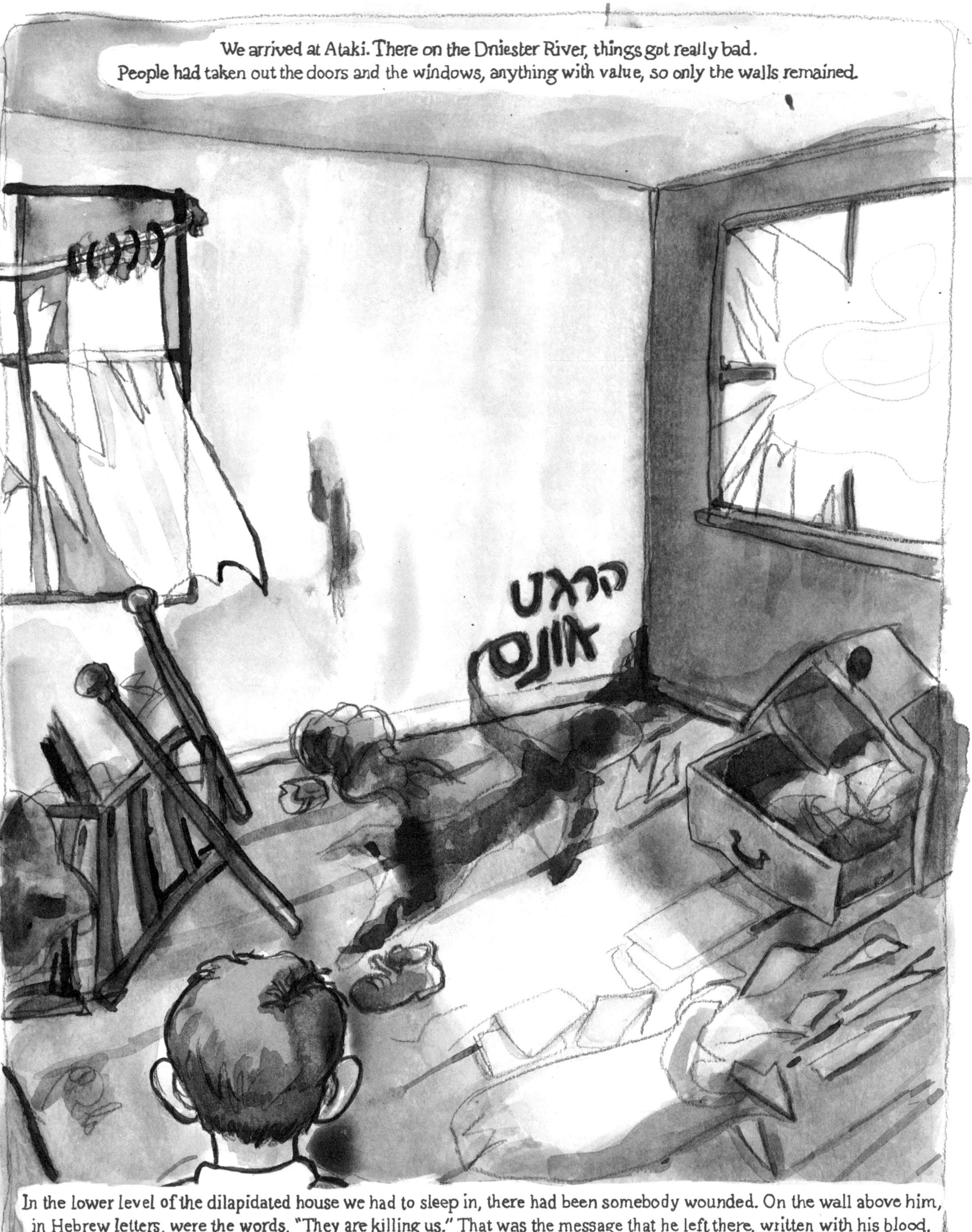
We arrived at Ataki. There on the Dniester River, things got really bad.
People had taken out the doors and the windows, anything with value, so only the walls remained.
In the lower level of the dilapidated house we had to sleep in, there had been somebody wounded. On the wall above him, in Hebrew letters, were the words, "They are killing us." That was the message that he left there, written with his blood.

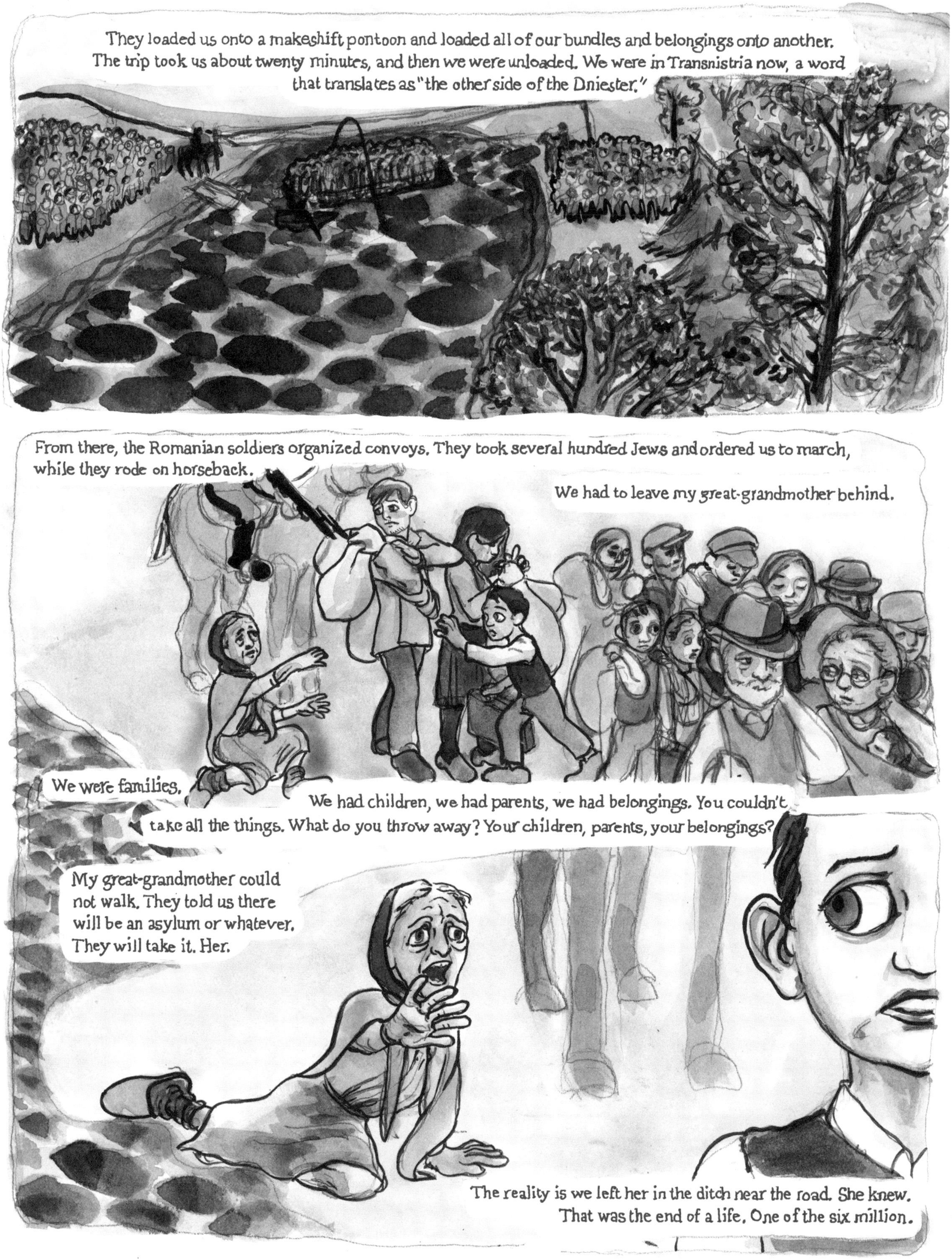
They loaded us onto a makeshift pontoon and loaded all of our bundles and belongings onto another. The trip took us about twenty minutes, and then we were unloaded. We were in Transnistria now, a word that translates as "the other side of the Dniester."
From there, the Romanian soldiers organized convoys. They took several hundred Jews and ordered us to march, while they rode on horseback.
We had to leave my great-grandmother behind.
We were families.
We had children, we had parents, we had belongings. You couldn't take all the things. What do you throw away? Your children, parents, your belongings?
My great-grandmother could not walk. They told us there will be an asylum or whatever. They will take it. Her.
The reality is we left her in the ditch near the road. She knew. That was the end of a life. One of the six million.

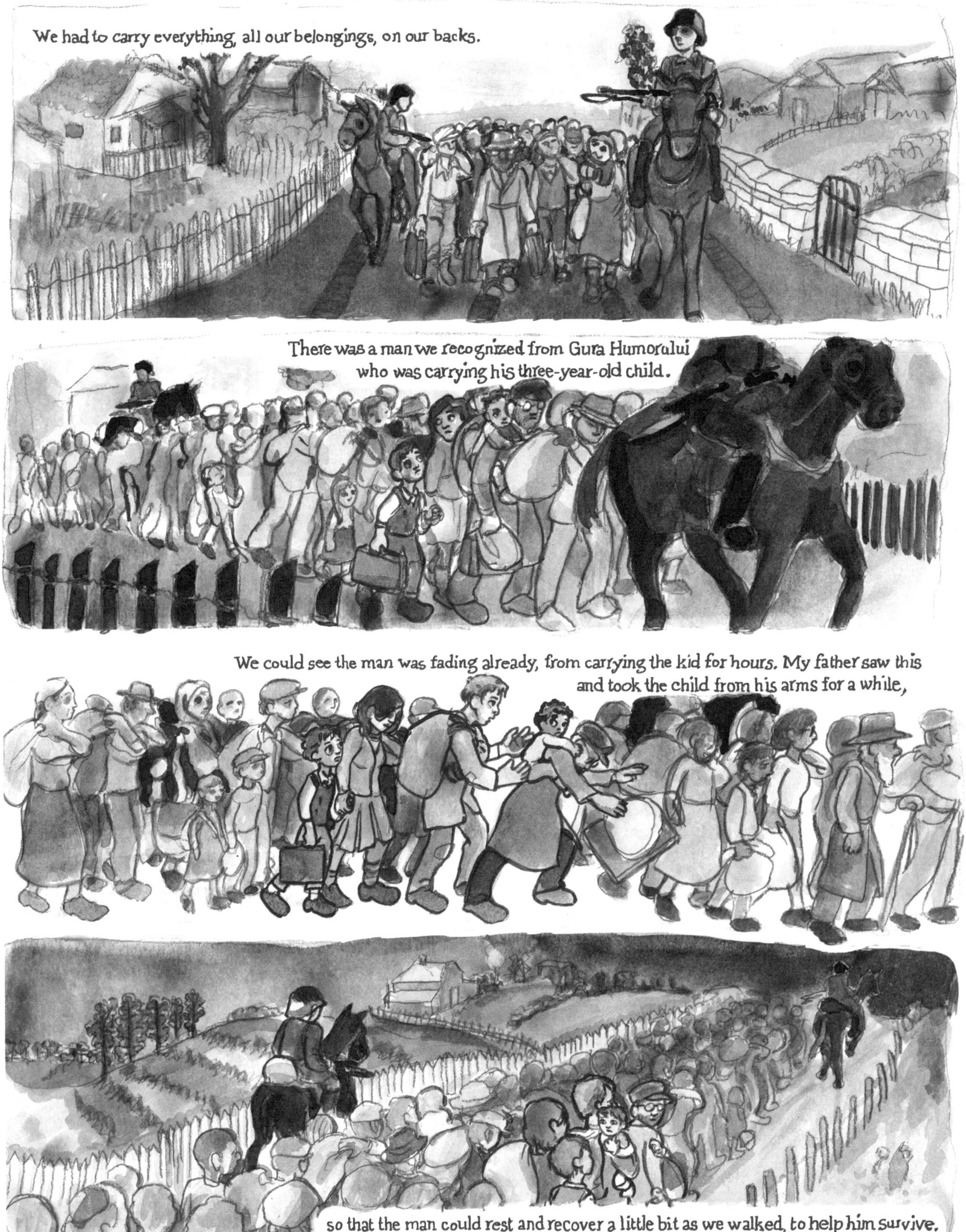
We had to carry everything, all our belongings, on our backs.
There was a man we recognized from Gura Humorului who was carrying his three-year-old child.
We could see the man was fading already, from carrying the kid for hours. My father saw this and took the child from his arms for a while,
so that the man could rest and recover a little bit as we walked, to help him survive.

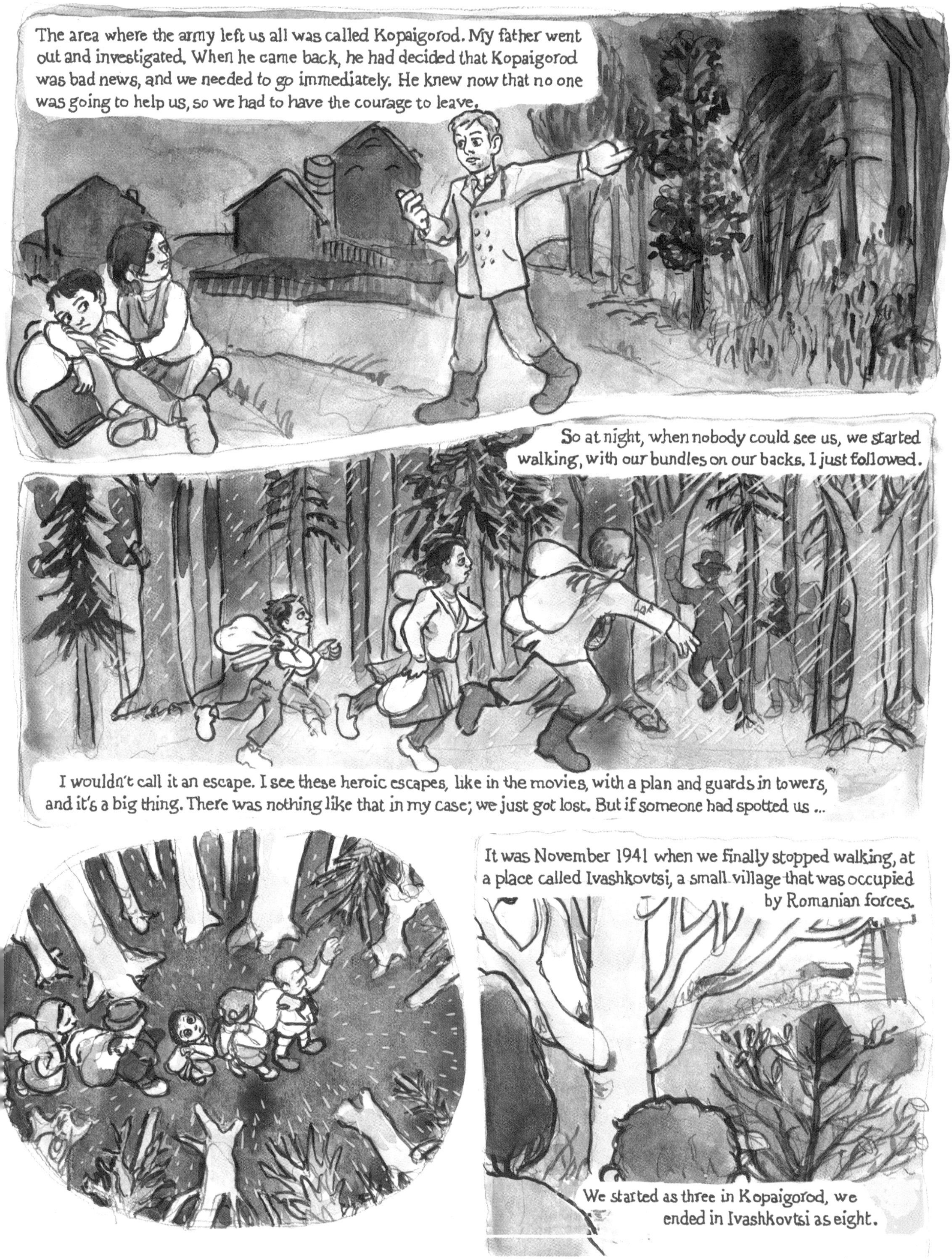
The area where the army left us all was called Kopaigorod. My father went out and investigated. When he came back, he had decided that Kopaigorod was bad news, and we needed to go immediately. He knew now that no one was going to help us, so we had to have the courage to leave.
So at night, when nobody could see us, we started walking, with our bundles on our backs. I just followed.
I wouldn't call it an escape. I see these heroic escapes, like in the movies, with a plan and guards in towers, and it's a big thing. There was nothing like that in my case; we just got lost. But if someone had spotted us ...
It was November 1941 when we finally stopped walking, at a place called Ivashkovtsi, a small village that was occupied by Romanian forces.
We started as three in Kopaigorod, we ended in Ivashkovtsi as eight.

Somewhere along the way, the Landau family joined us. They were walking in darkness, not on the road, and recognized us as Jews. There were Marcus and Nellie with their two daughters, Annie and Fritzi, and their grandmother.

Fritzi! Can you imagine, what a German name.
It couldn't help her.

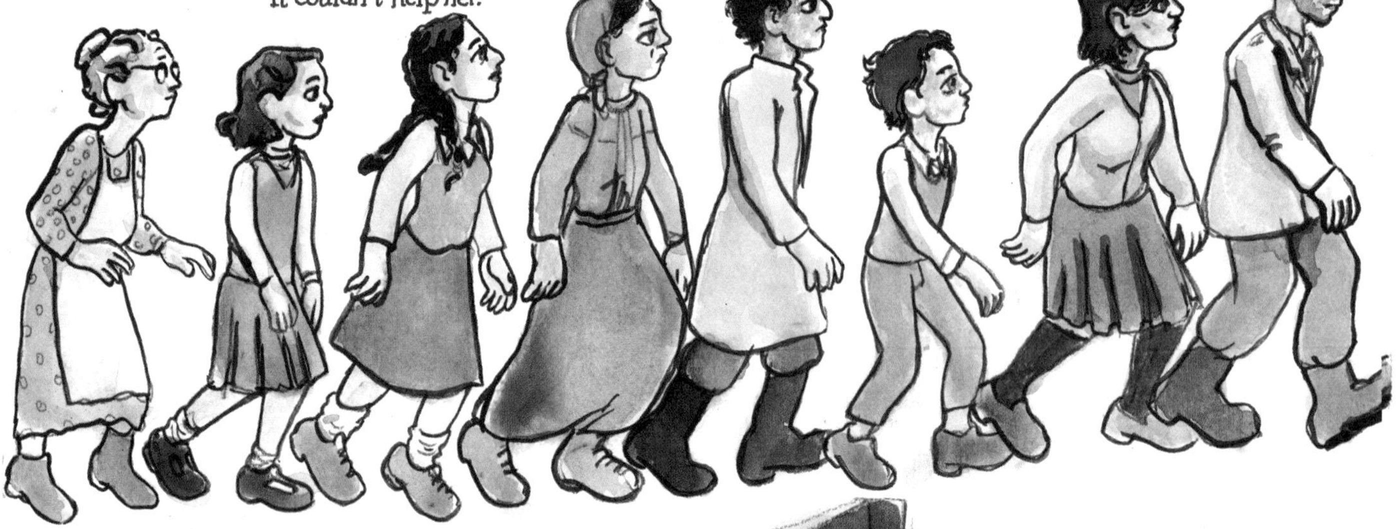

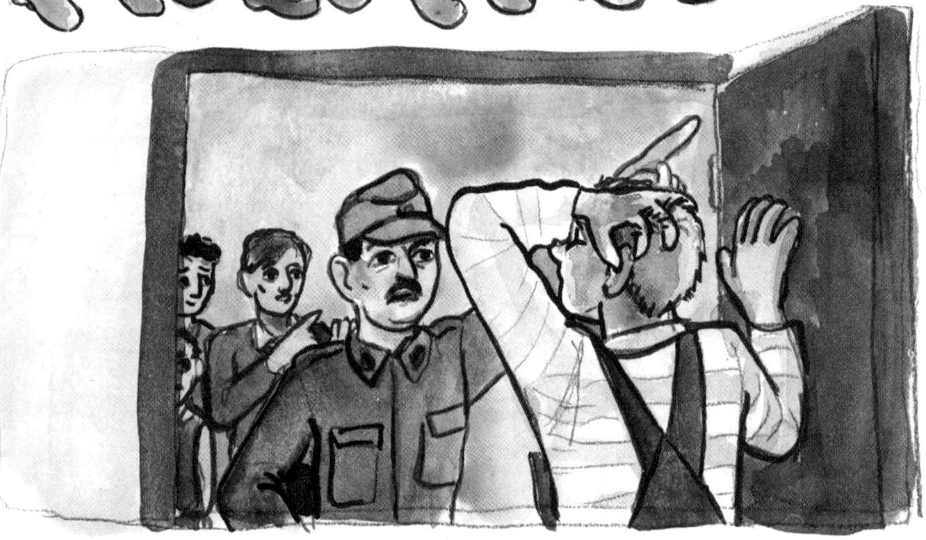

The eight of us decided to stick together. We had the advantage of being able to speak Romanian with the soldiers while the local Ukrainian population could not. Our ability to communicate gave the villagers a reason to keep us around.

In the village there was a Ukrainian family who let us stay in a summer kitchen that they didn't use, which was separate from their house.

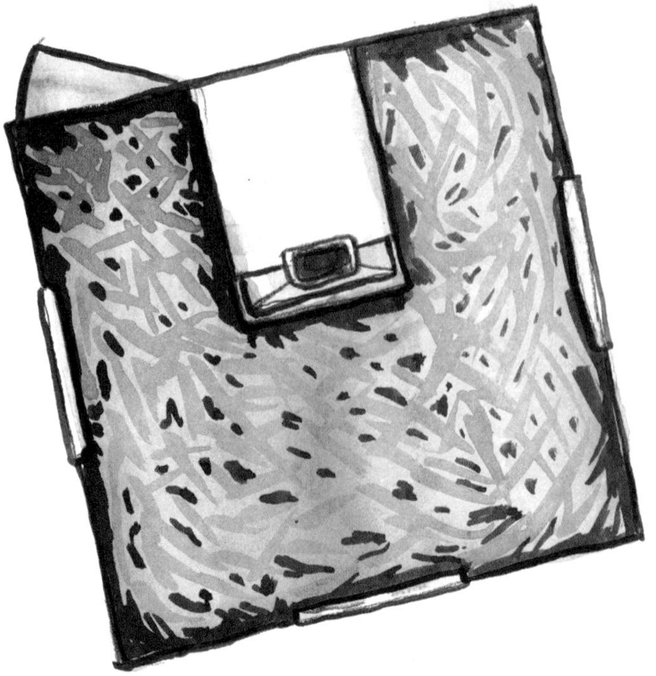

We stayed there with the Landaus.

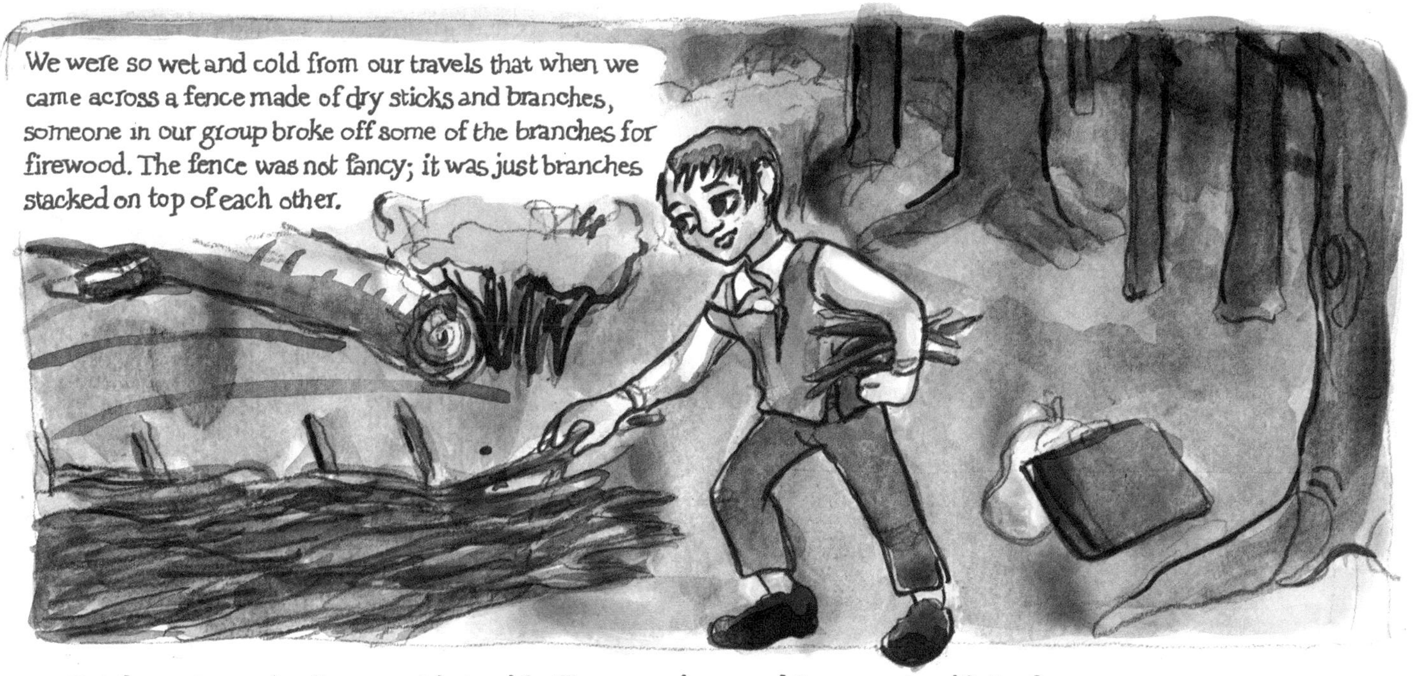
We were so wet and cold from our travels that when we came across a fence made of dry sticks and branches, someone in our group broke off some of the branches for firewood. The fence was not fancy; it was just branches stacked on top of each other.

But the next morning there was big *trouble*. The man who owned the property with the fence was very angry.

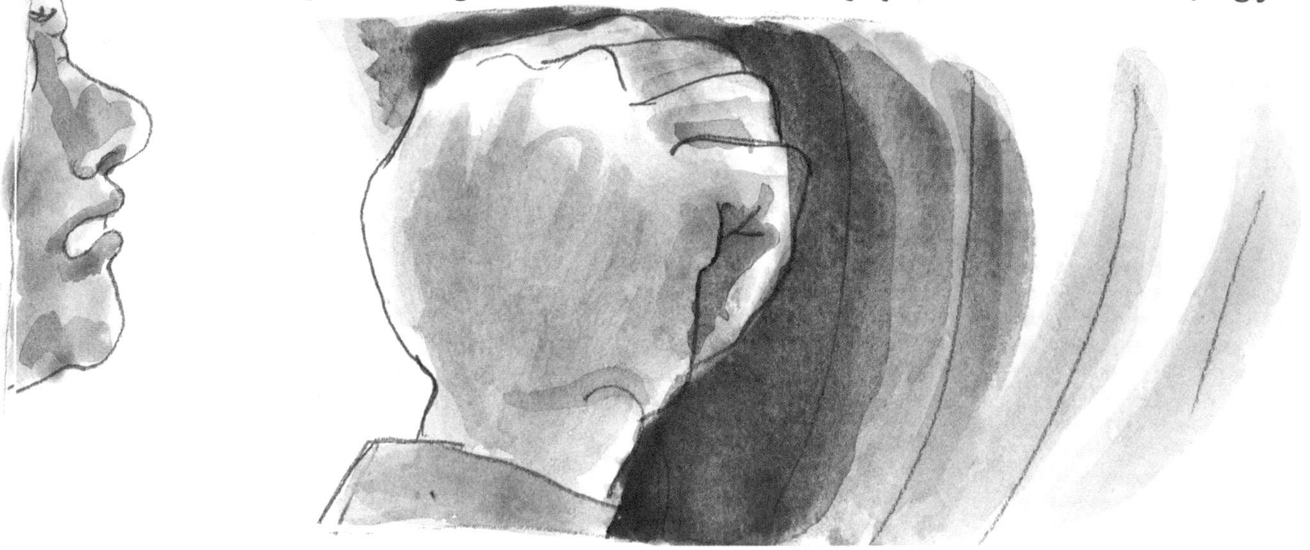

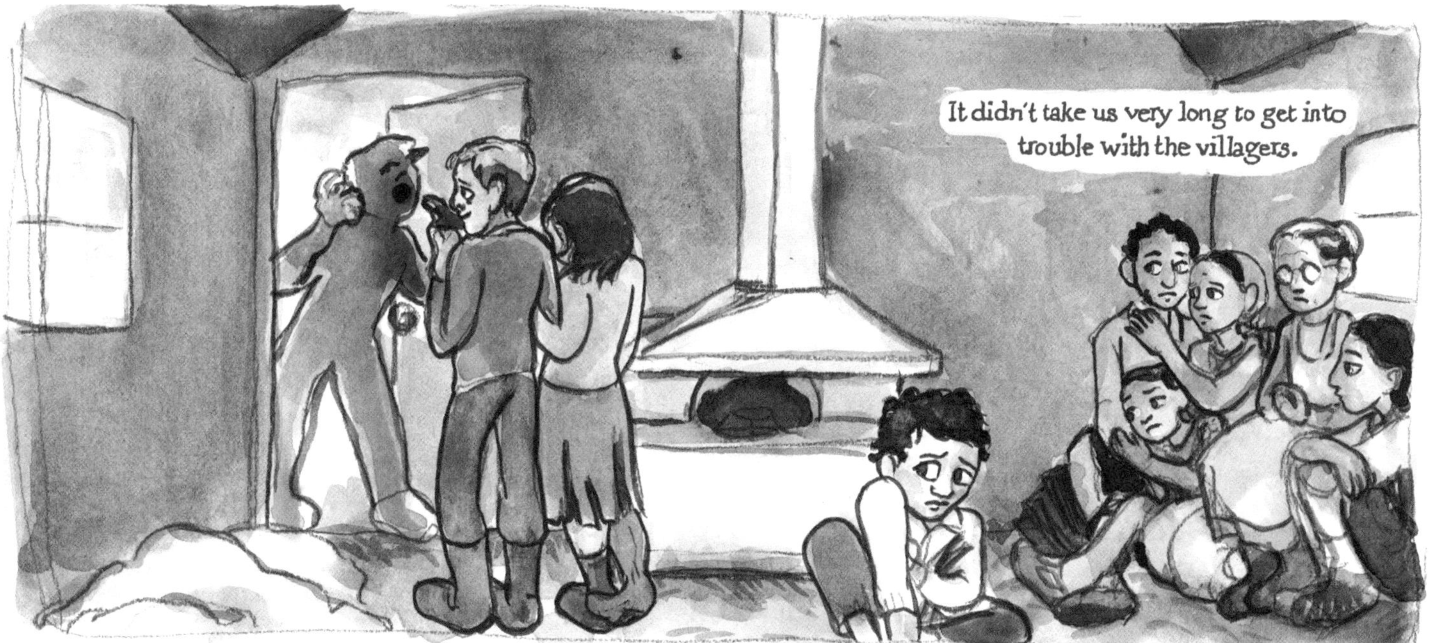
It didn't take us very long to get into trouble with the villagers.

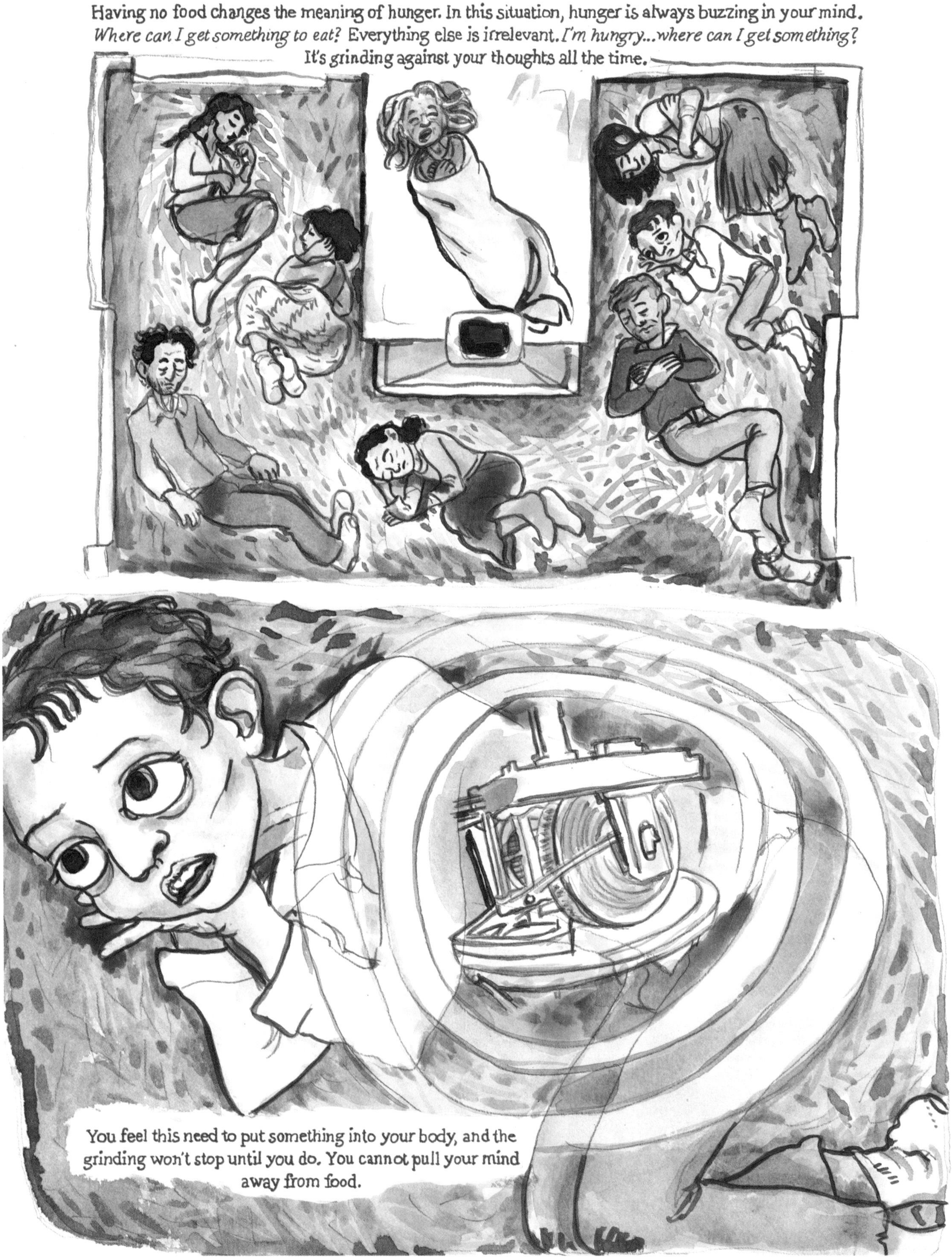
Having no food changes the meaning of hunger. In this situation, hunger is always buzzing in your mind. *Where can I get something to eat?* Everything else is irrelevant. *I'm hungry...where can I get something?* It's grinding against your thoughts all the time.
You feel this need to put something into your body, and the grinding won't stop until you do. You cannot pull your mind away from food.

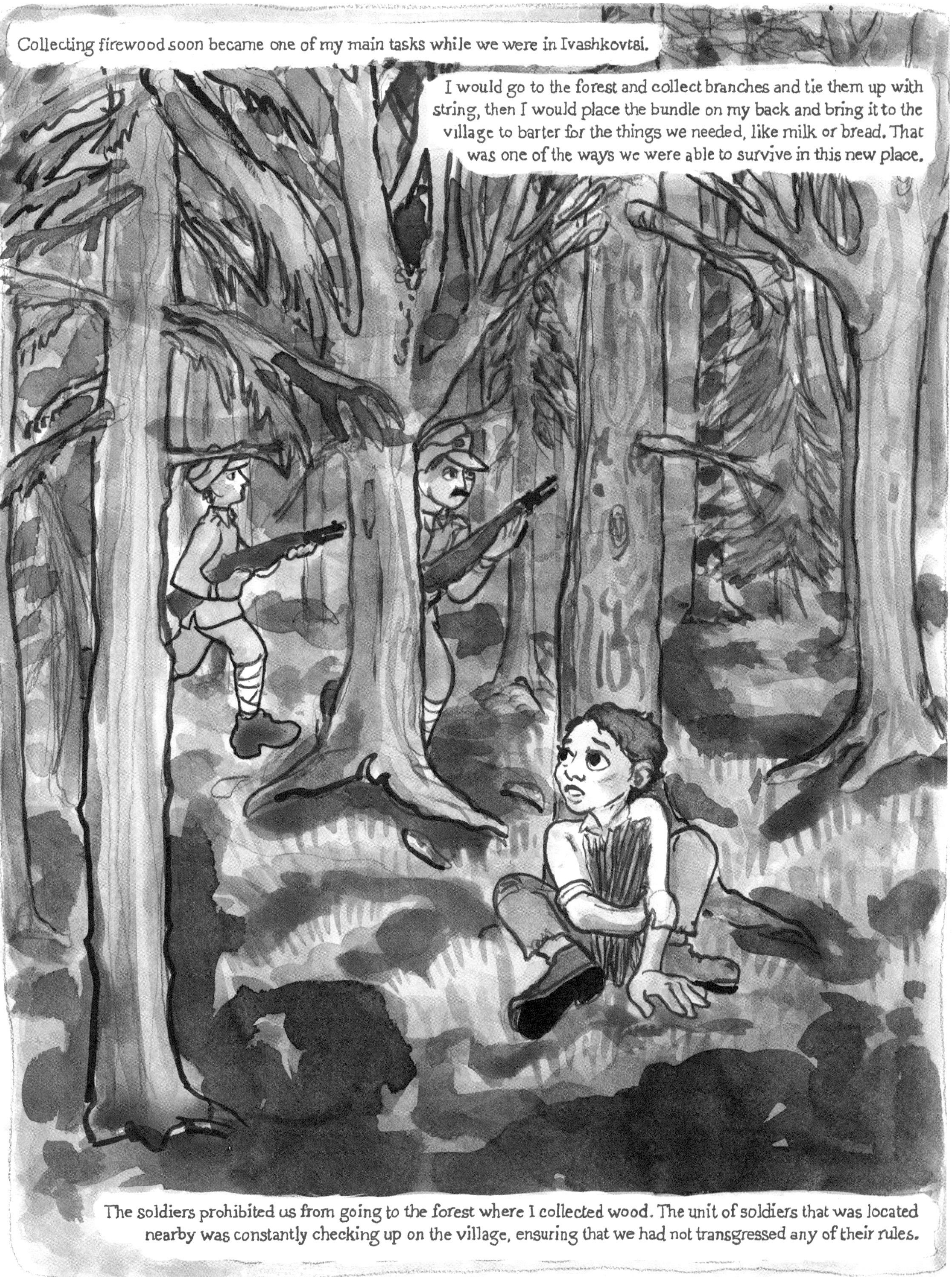
Collecting firewood soon became one of my main tasks while we were in Ivashkovtsi.
I would go to the forest and collect branches and tie them up with string, then I would place the bundle on my back and bring it to the village to barter for the things we needed, like milk or bread. That was one of the ways we were able to survive in this new place.
The soldiers prohibited us from going to the forest where I collected wood. The unit of soldiers that was located nearby was constantly checking up on the village, ensuring that we had not transgressed any of their rules.

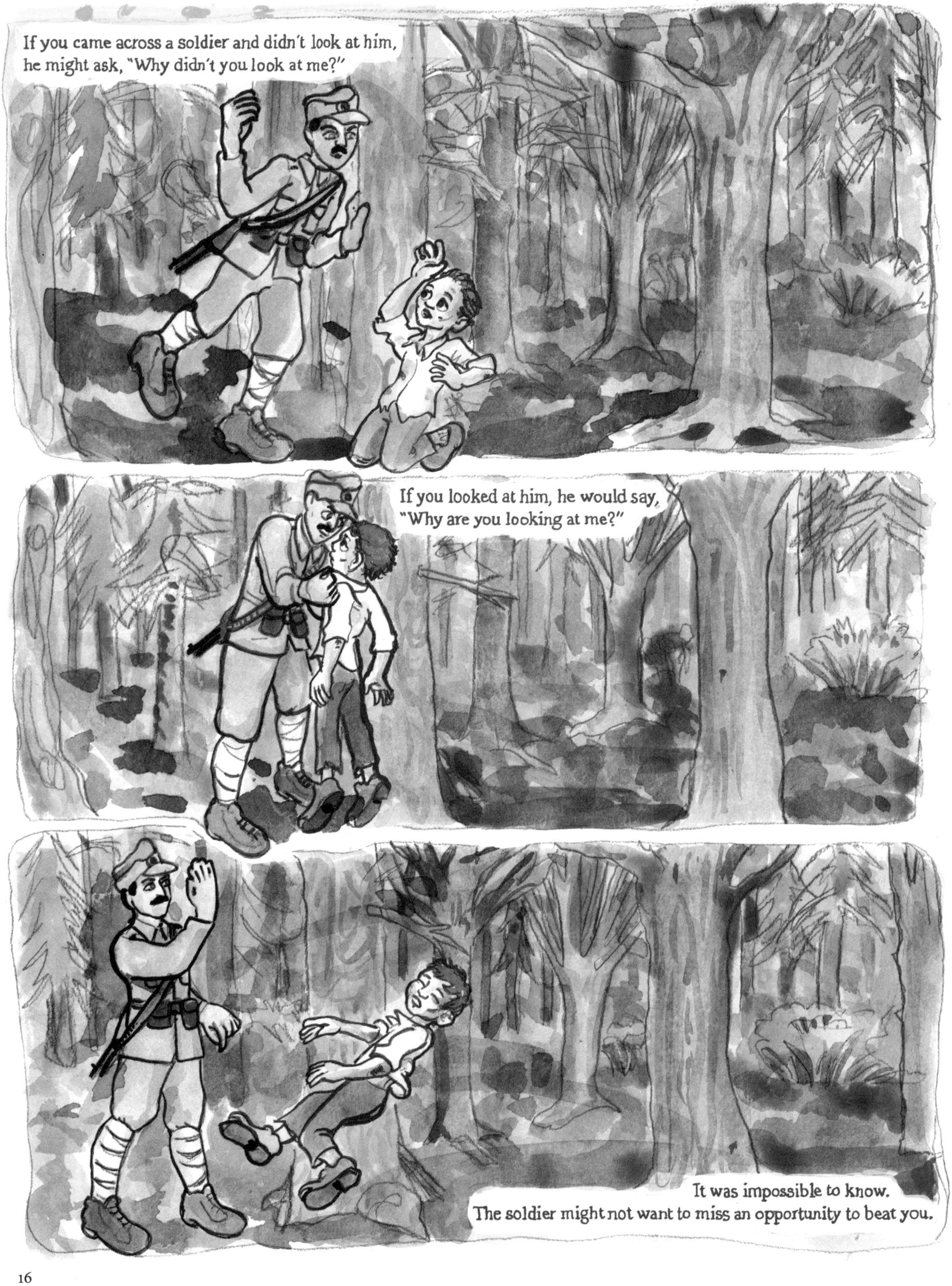
If you came across a soldier and didn't look at him, he might ask, "Why didn't you look at me?"
If you looked at him, he would say, "Why are you looking at me?"
It was impossible to know.
The soldier might not want to miss an opportunity to beat you.

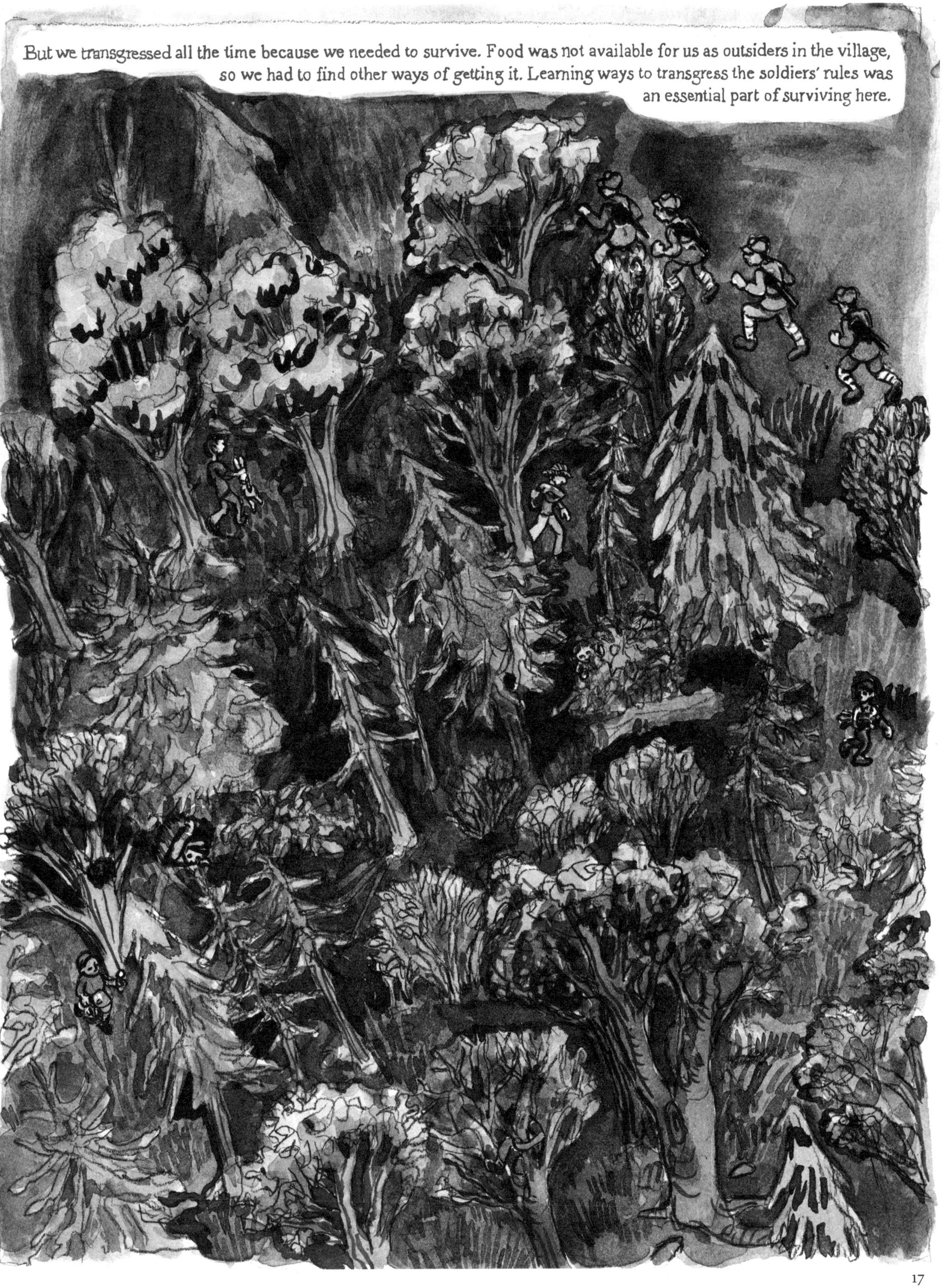
But we transgressed all the time because we needed to survive. Food was not available for us as outsiders in the village, so we had to find other ways of getting it. Learning ways to transgress the soldiers' rules was an essential part of surviving here.

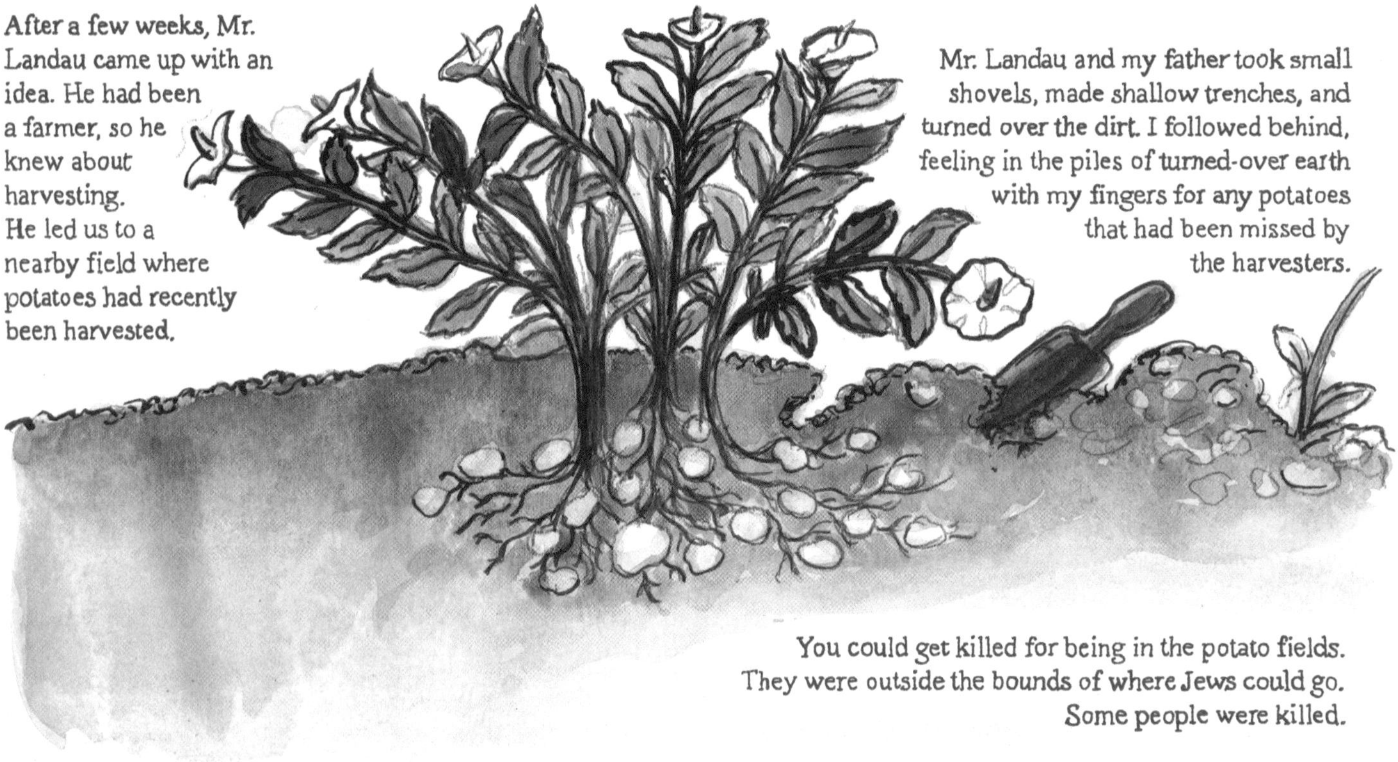
After a few weeks, Mr. Landau came up with an idea. He had been a farmer, so he knew about harvesting. He led us to a nearby field where potatoes had recently been harvested.
Mr. Landau and my father took small shovels, made shallow trenches, and turned over the dirt. I followed behind, feeling in the piles of turned-over earth with my fingers for any potatoes that had been missed by the harvesters.
You could get killed for being in the potato fields. They were outside the bounds of where Jews could go. Some people were killed.

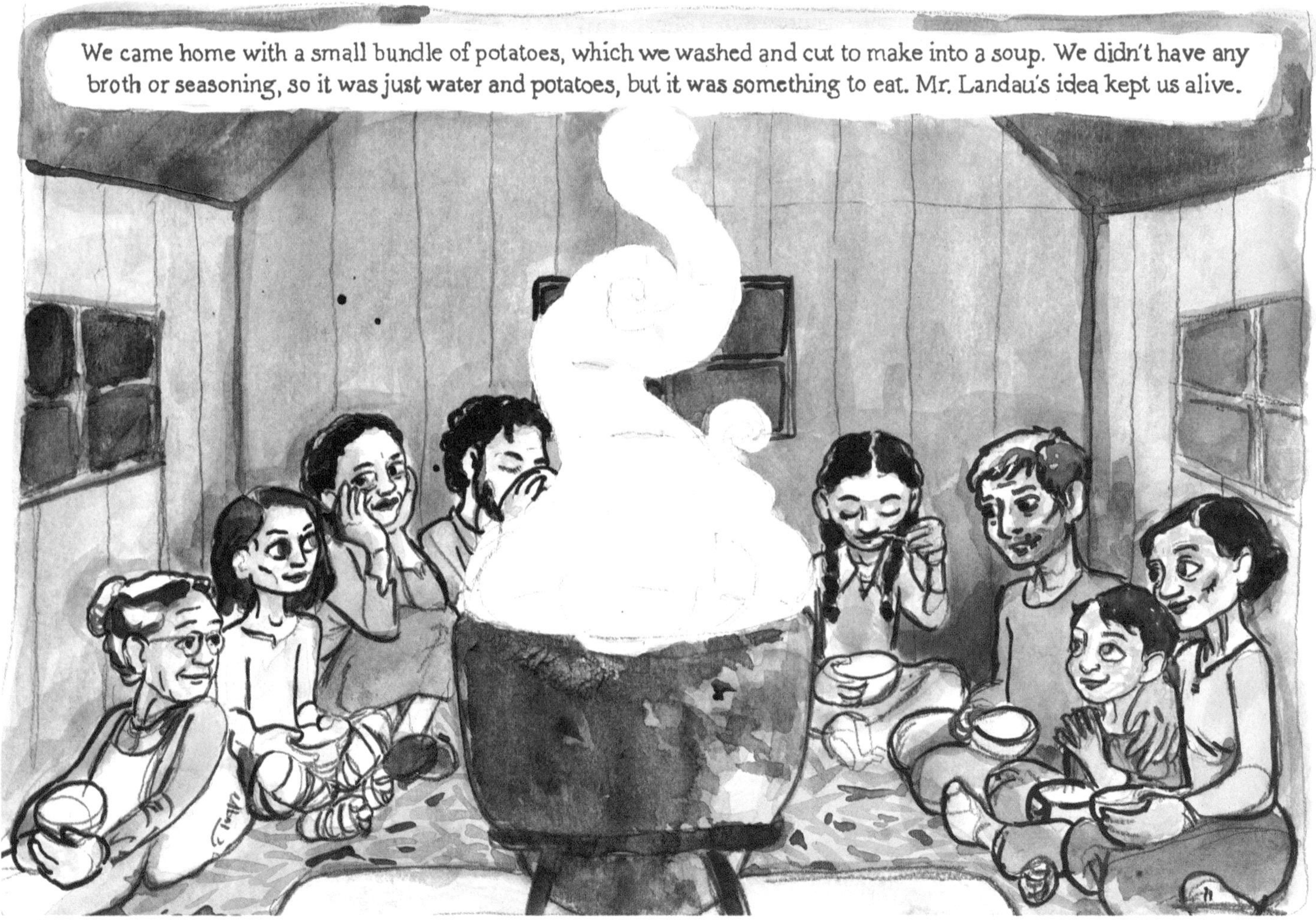
We came home with a small bundle of potatoes, which we washed and cut to make into a soup. We didn't have any broth or seasoning, so it was just water and potatoes, but it was something to eat. Mr. Landau's idea kept us alive.

One day, after a day of work somewhere, my father brought home a half-litre of oil. We would use only very small amounts at a time so that it would last us longer.

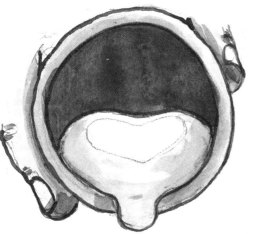

Everyone would get three drops of oil in their potato soup. My mother was the one who was pouring the oil, and I watched her very carefully. I didn't want to waste any of the oil we had. Before the oil even reached the brim of the bottle, I shouted, "Enough! Enough!"

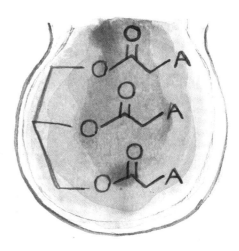

She tried to hit me, saying, "Enough from you!"
But in the end we had good soup. When you add a little bit of oil and it spreads on top …

We were doing better.

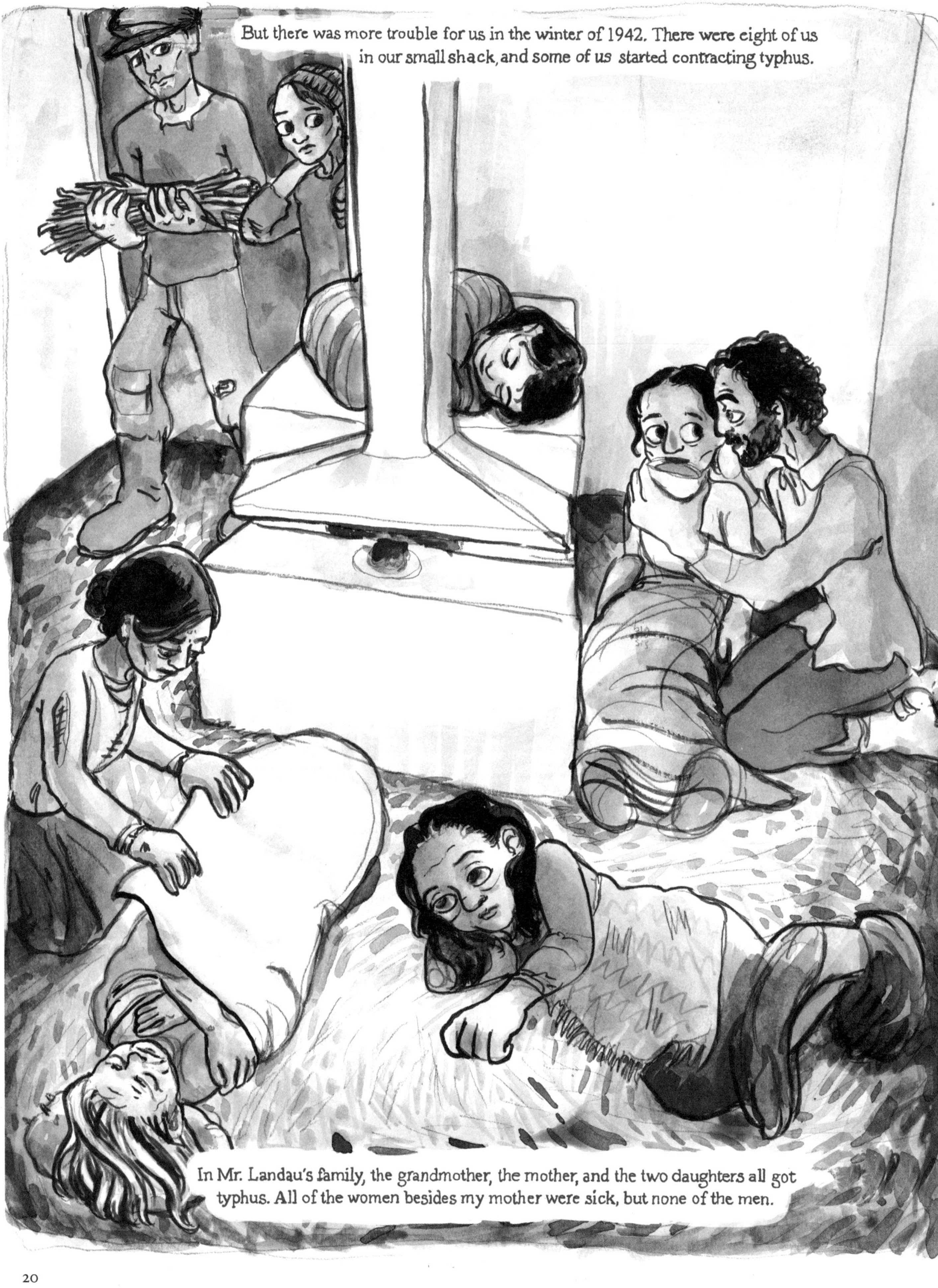
But there was more trouble for us in the winter of 1942. There were eight of us in our small shack, and some of us started contracting typhus.
In Mr. Landau's family, the grandmother, the mother, and the two daughters all got typhus. All of the women besides my mother were sick, but none of the men.

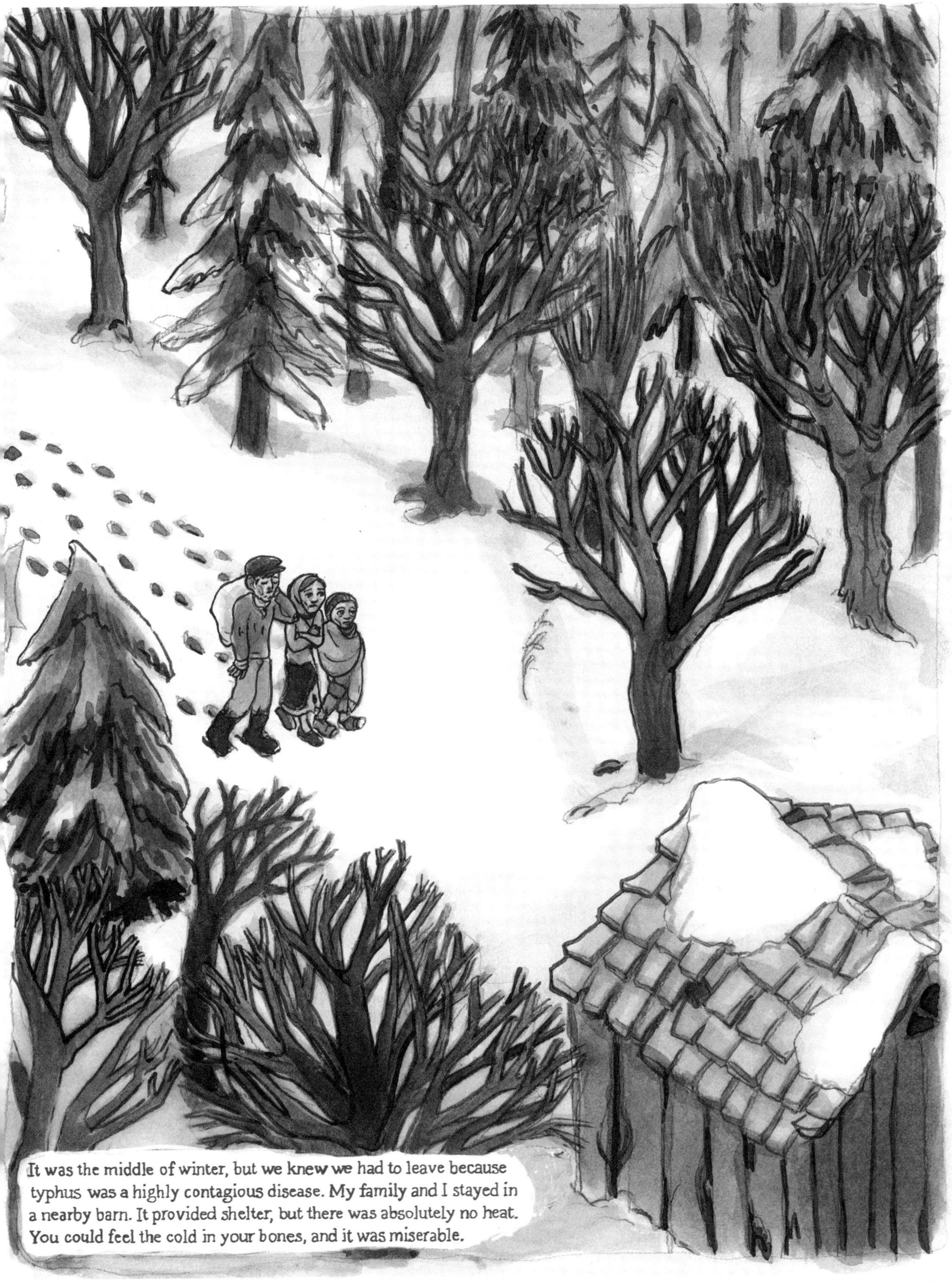
It was the middle of winter, but we knew we had to leave because typhus was a highly contagious disease. My family and I stayed in a nearby barn. It provided shelter, but there was absolutely no heat. You could feel the cold in your bones, and it was miserable.

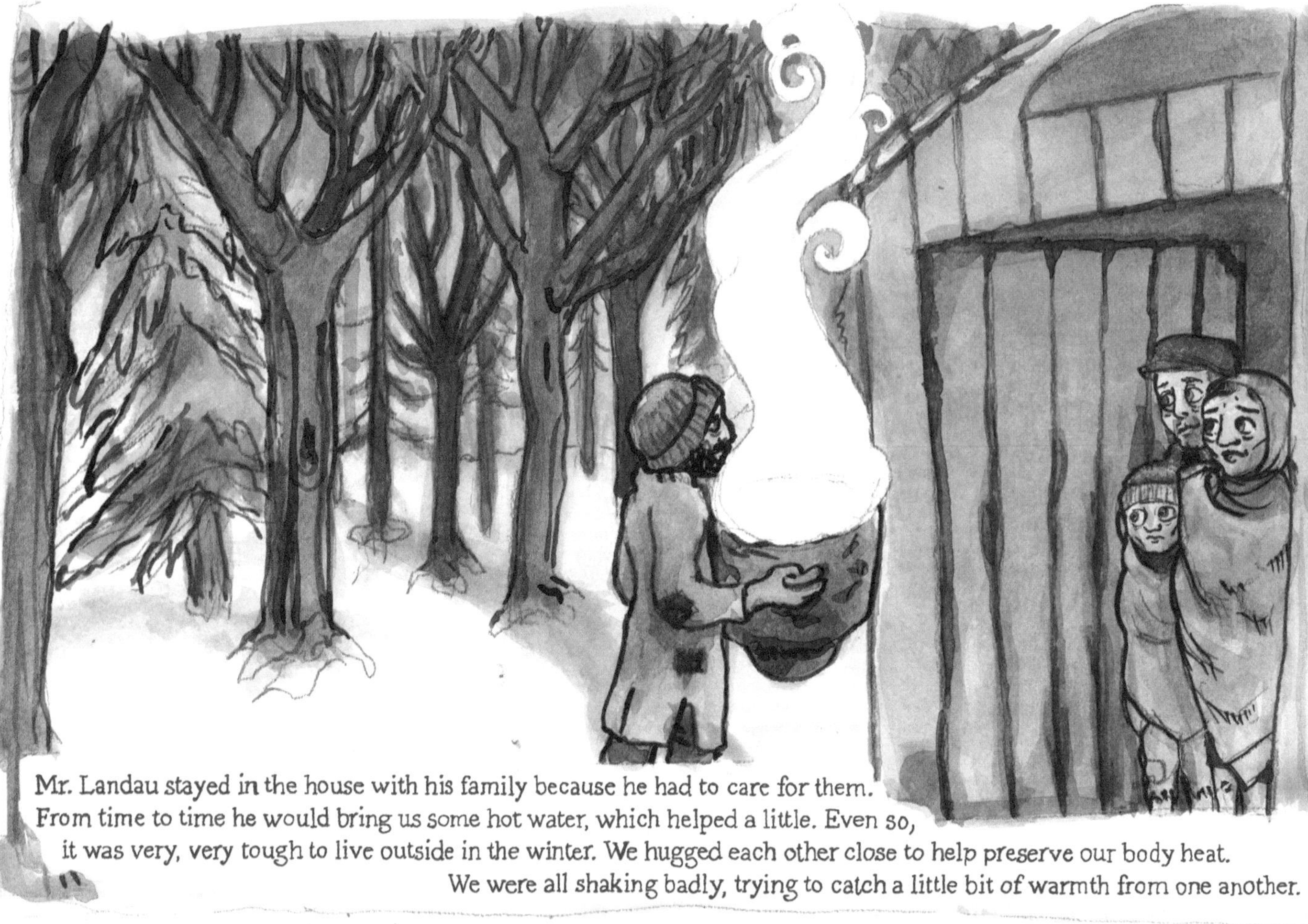
Mr. Landau stayed in the house with his family because he had to care for them.
From time to time he would bring us some hot water, which helped a little. Even so,
it was very, very tough to live outside in the winter. We hugged each other close to help preserve our body heat.
We were all shaking badly, trying to catch a little bit of warmth from one another.

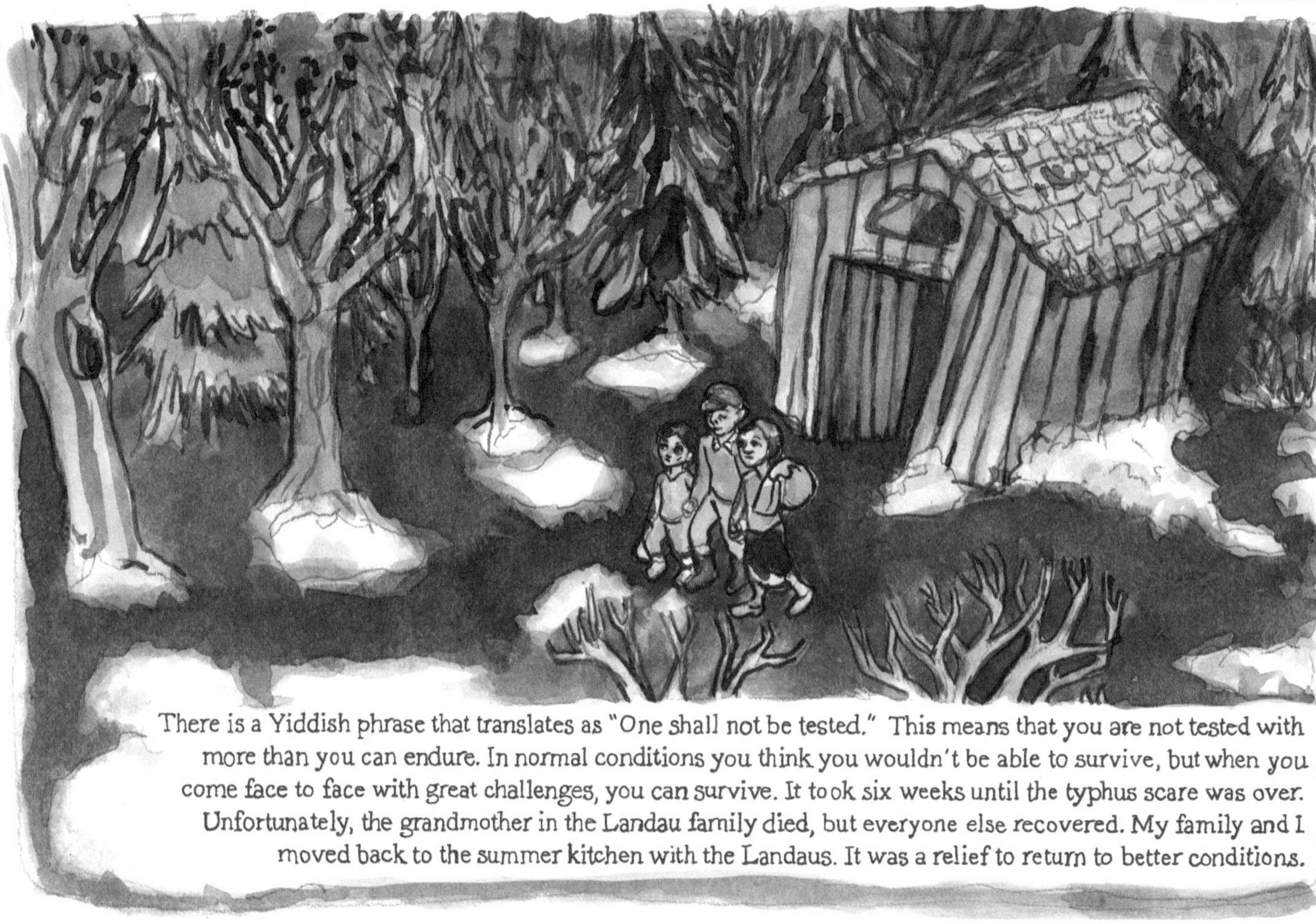
There is a Yiddish phrase that translates as "One shall not be tested." This means that you are not tested with
more than you can endure. In normal conditions you think you wouldn't be able to survive, but when you
come face to face with great challenges, you can survive. It took six weeks until the typhus scare was over.
Unfortunately, the grandmother in the Landau family died, but everyone else recovered. My family and I
moved back to the summer kitchen with the Landaus. It was a relief to return to better conditions.

My father and Mr. Landau worked when they could at the local collective farm. I helped where I could. I was too small to do the same kind of physical labor they did.

I would go to the field with a sack after the wheat harvest, and find one stalk of wheat here, another one there. When the wheat had been harvested, the straw was cut so that there were two-to-three-inch spikes left behind.

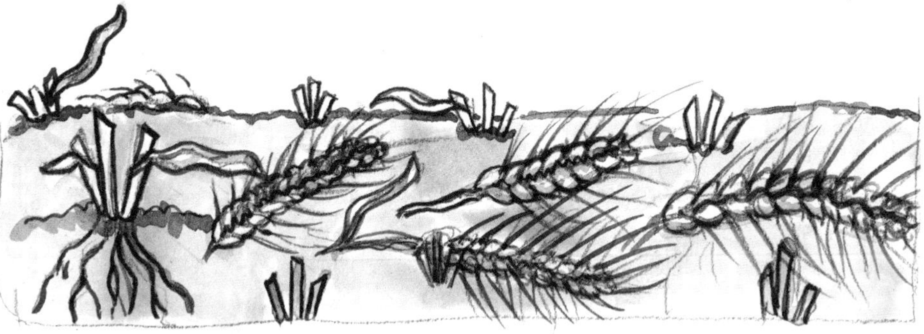

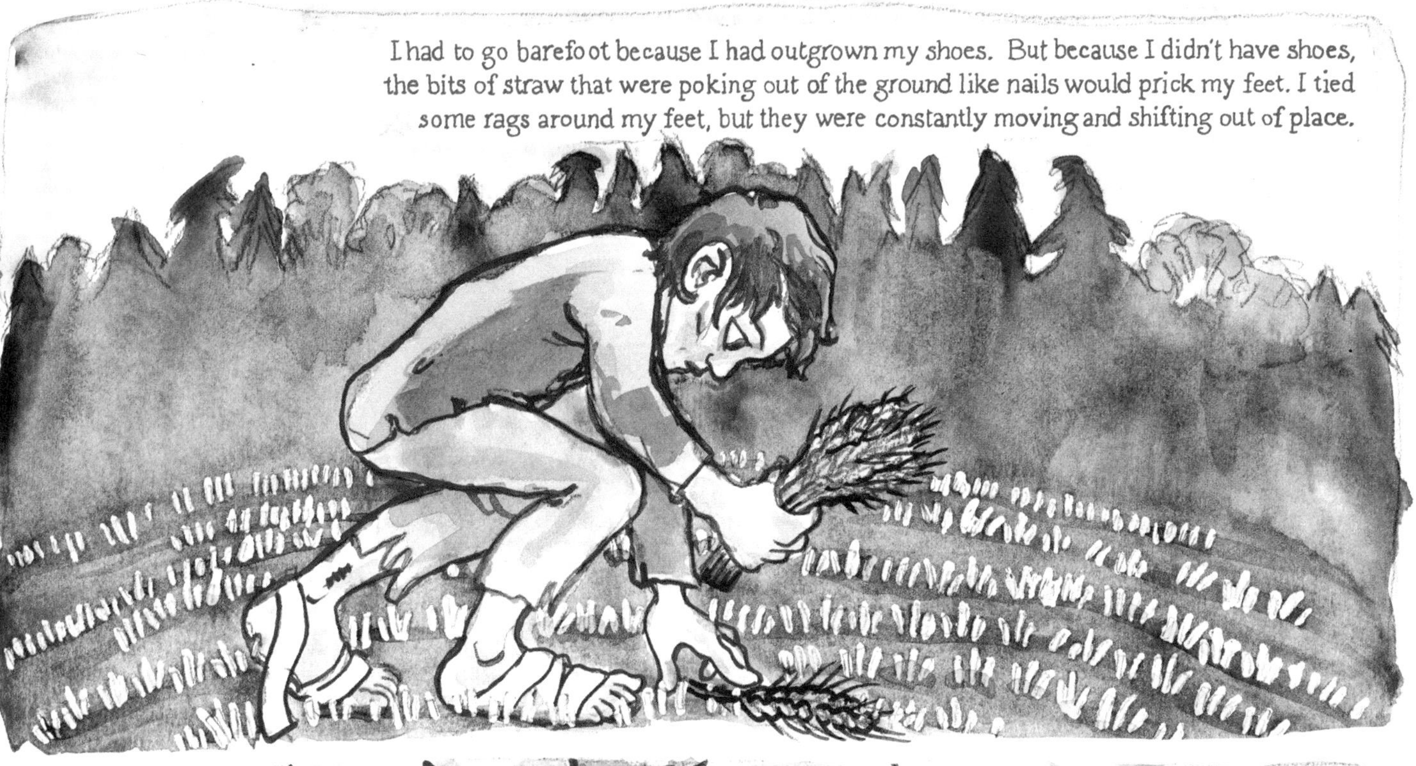
I had to go barefoot because I had outgrown my shoes. But because I didn't have shoes, the bits of straw that were poking out of the ground like nails would prick my feet. I tied some rags around my feet, but they were constantly moving and shifting out of place.

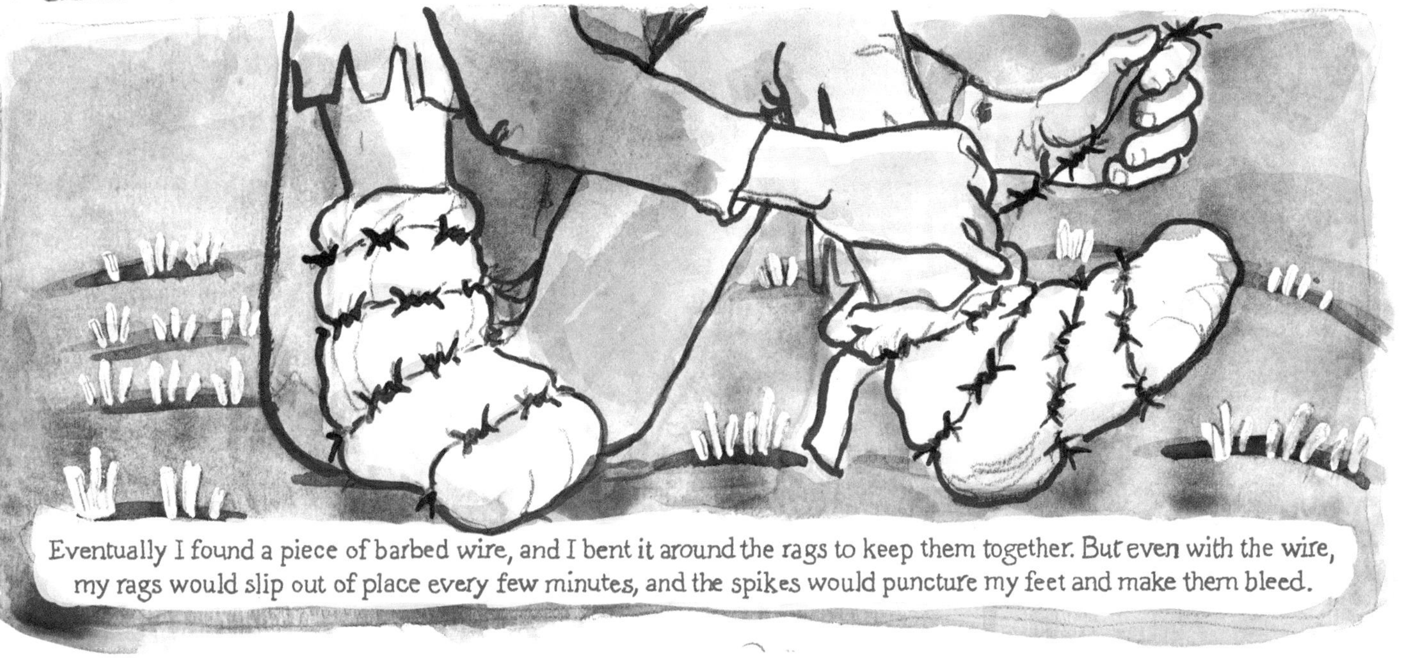
Eventually I found a piece of barbed wire, and I bent it around the rags to keep them together. But even with the wire, my rags would slip out of place every few minutes, and the spikes would puncture my feet and make them bleed.

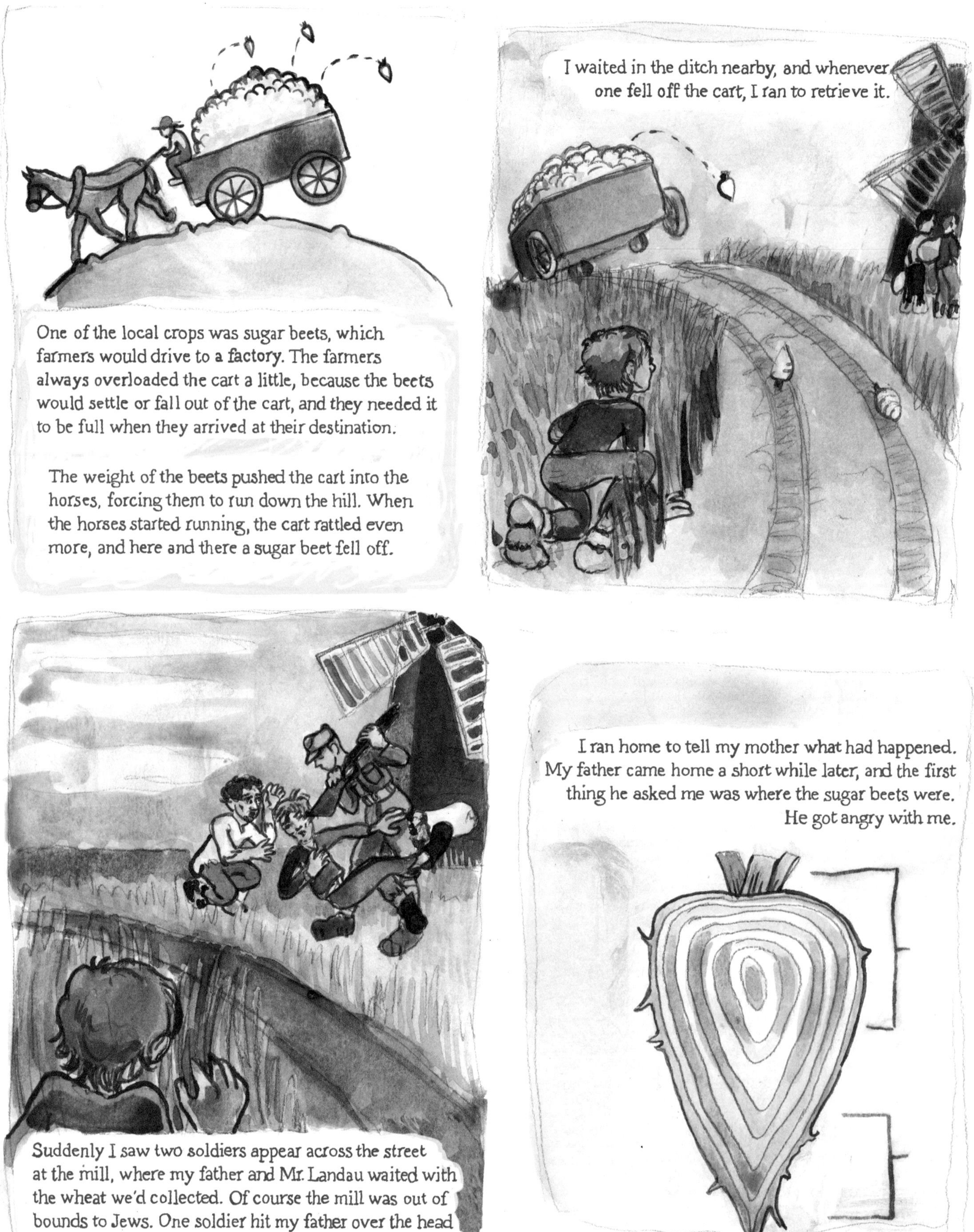
One of the local crops was sugar beets, which farmers would drive to a factory. The farmers always overloaded the cart a little, because the beets would settle or fall out of the cart, and they needed it to be full when they arrived at their destination.
The weight of the beets pushed the cart into the horses, forcing them to run down the hill. When the horses started running, the cart rattled even more, and here and there a sugar beet fell off.
I waited in the ditch nearby, and whenever one fell off the cart, I ran to retrieve it.
Suddenly I saw two soldiers appear across the street at the mill, where my father and Mr. Landau waited with the wheat we'd collected. Of course the mill was out of bounds to Jews. One soldier hit my father over the head with the butt of his rifle, splitting his ear down the middle.
I ran home to tell my mother what had happened. My father came home a short while later, and the first thing he asked me was where the sugar beets were. He got angry with me.

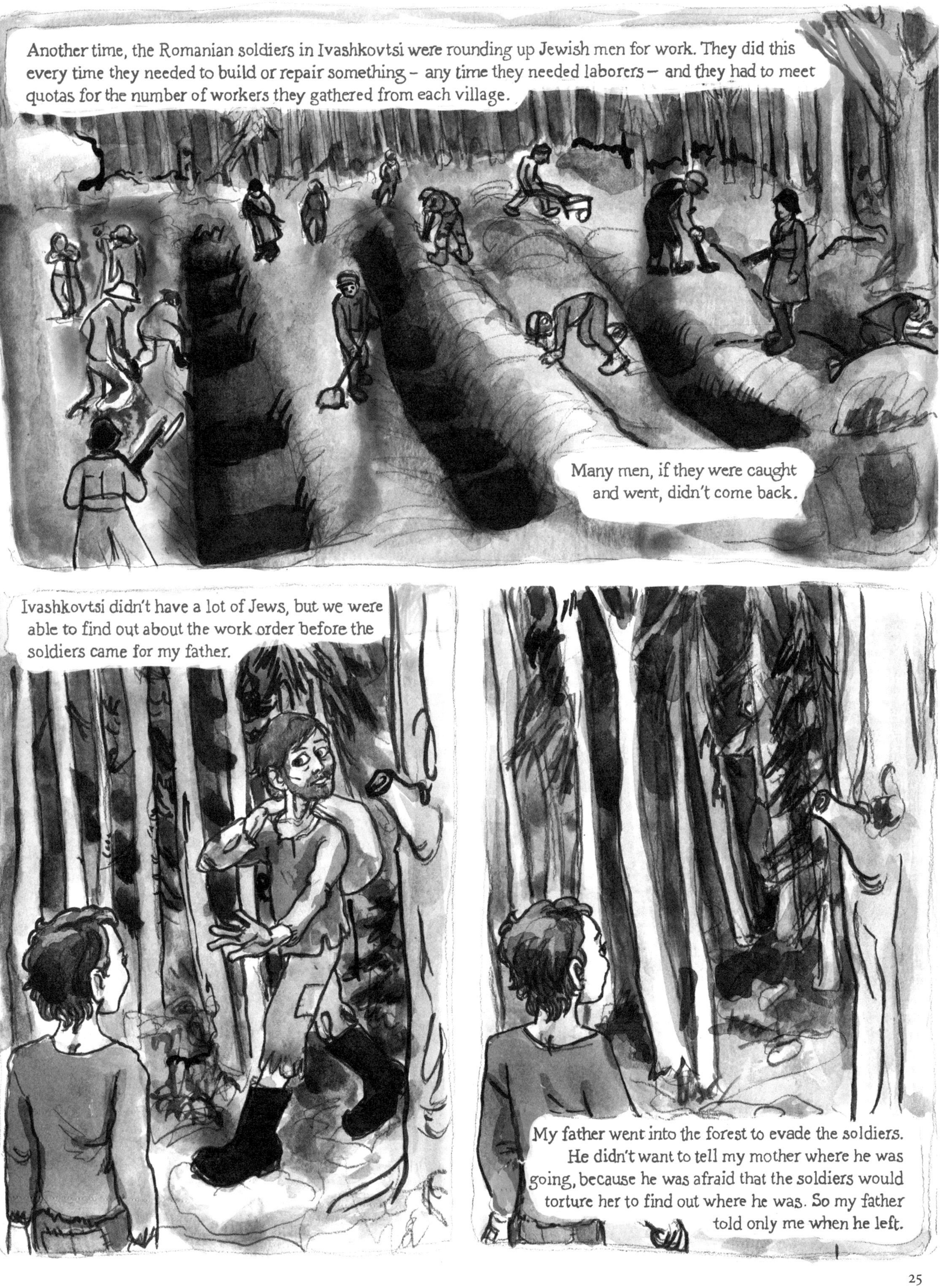
Another time, the Romanian soldiers in Ivashkovtsi were rounding up Jewish men for work. They did this every time they needed to build or repair something – any time they needed laborers – and they had to meet quotas for the number of workers they gathered from each village.
Many men, if they were caught and went, didn't come back.
Ivashkovtsi didn't have a lot of Jews, but we were able to find out about the work order before the soldiers came for my father.
My father went into the forest to evade the soldiers. He didn't want to tell my mother where he was going, because he was afraid that the soldiers would torture her to find out where he was. So my father told only me when he left.

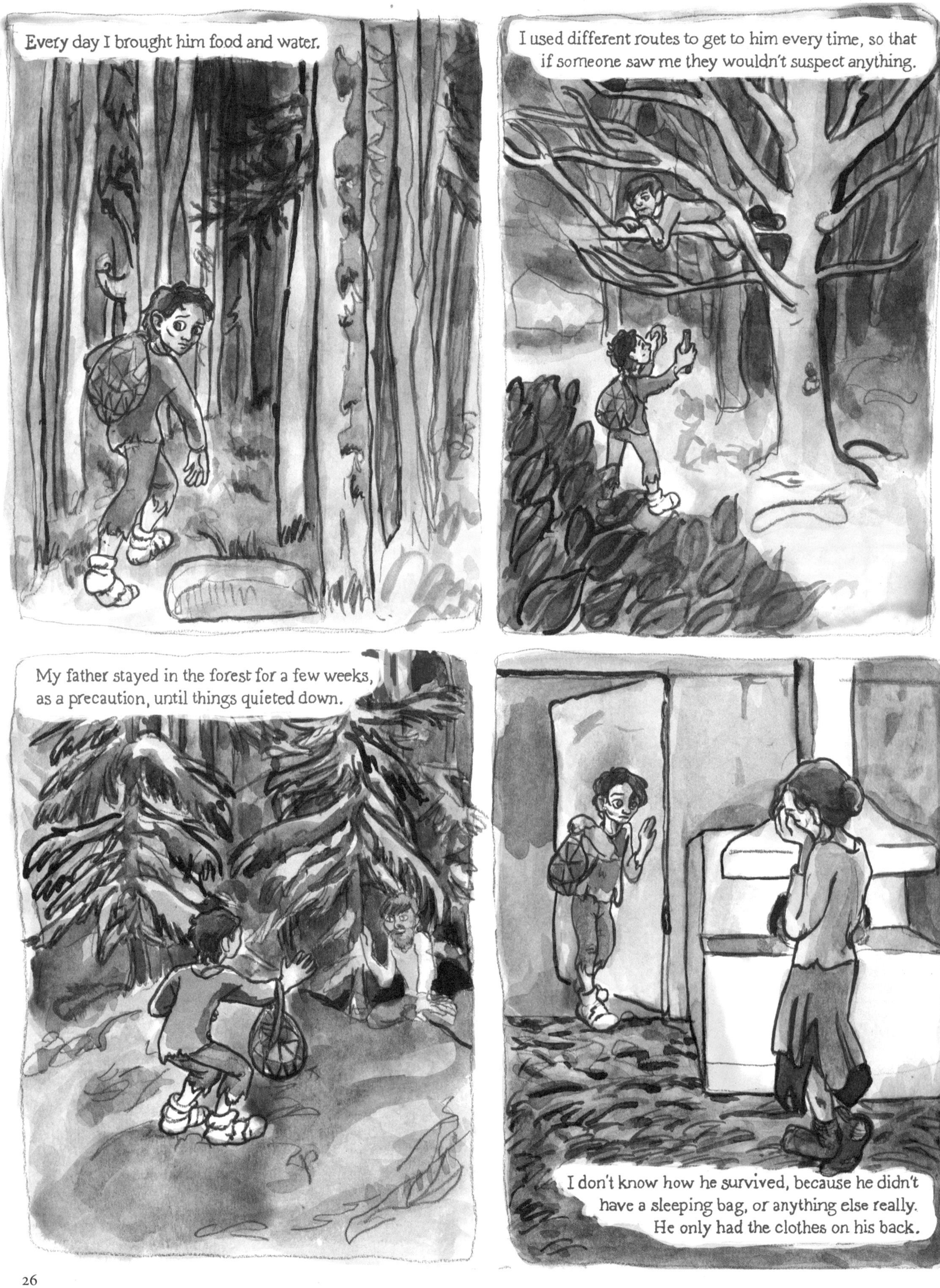
Every day I brought him food and water.
I used different routes to get to him every time, so that if someone saw me they wouldn't suspect anything.
My father stayed in the forest for a few weeks, as a precaution, until things quieted down.
I don't know how he survived, because he didn't have a sleeping bag, or anything else really. He only had the clothes on his back.

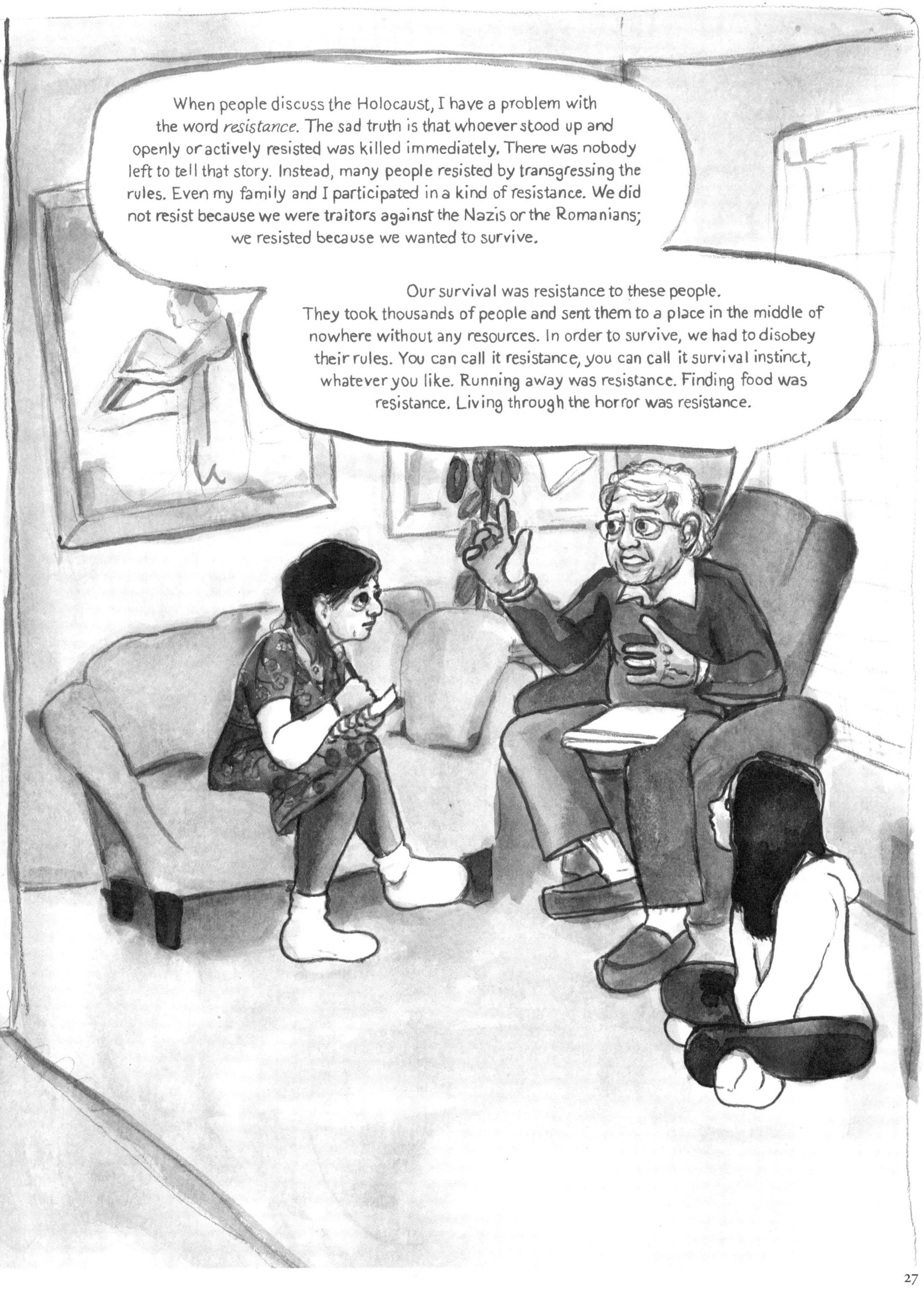
When people discuss the Holocaust, I have a problem with the word *resistance*. The sad truth is that whoever stood up and openly or actively resisted was killed immediately. There was nobody left to tell that story. Instead, many people resisted by transgressing the rules. Even my family and I participated in a kind of resistance. We did not resist because we were traitors against the Nazis or the Romanians; we resisted because we wanted to survive.
Our survival was resistance to these people. They took thousands of people and sent them to a place in the middle of nowhere without any resources. In order to survive, we had to disobey their rules. You can call it resistance, you can call it survival instinct, whatever you like. Running away was resistance. Finding food was resistance. Living through the horror was resistance.

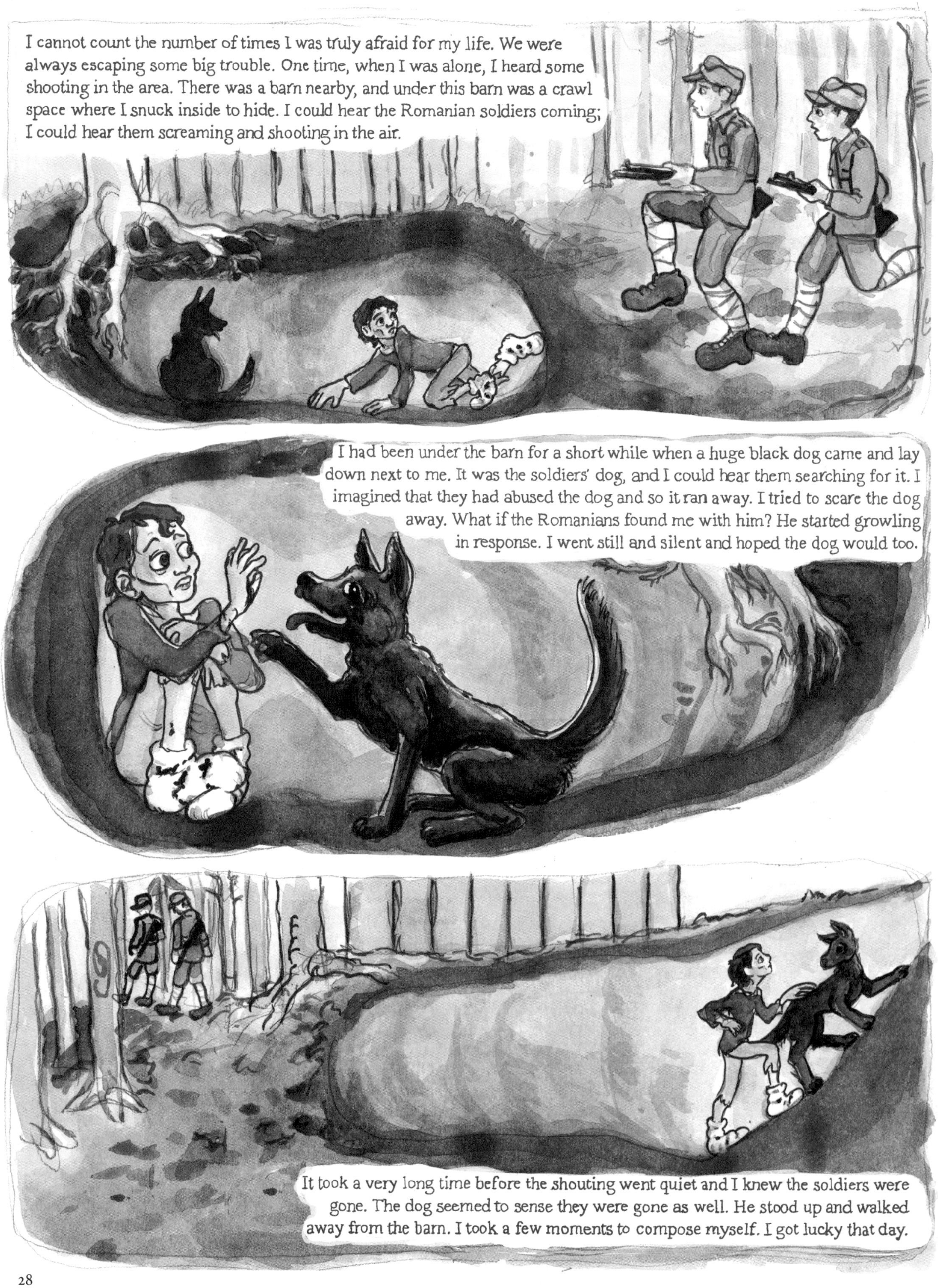
I cannot count the number of times I was truly afraid for my life. We were always escaping some big trouble. One time, when I was alone, I heard some shooting in the area. There was a barn nearby, and under this barn was a crawl space where I snuck inside to hide. I could hear the Romanian soldiers coming; I could hear them screaming and shooting in the air.
I had been under the barn for a short while when a huge black dog came and lay down next to me. It was the soldiers' dog, and I could hear them searching for it. I imagined that they had abused the dog and so it ran away. I tried to scare the dog away. What if the Romanians found me with him? He started growling in response. I went still and silent and hoped the dog would too.
It took a very long time before the shouting went quiet and I knew the soldiers were gone. The dog seemed to sense they were gone as well. He stood up and walked away from the barn. I took a few moments to compose myself. I got lucky that day.

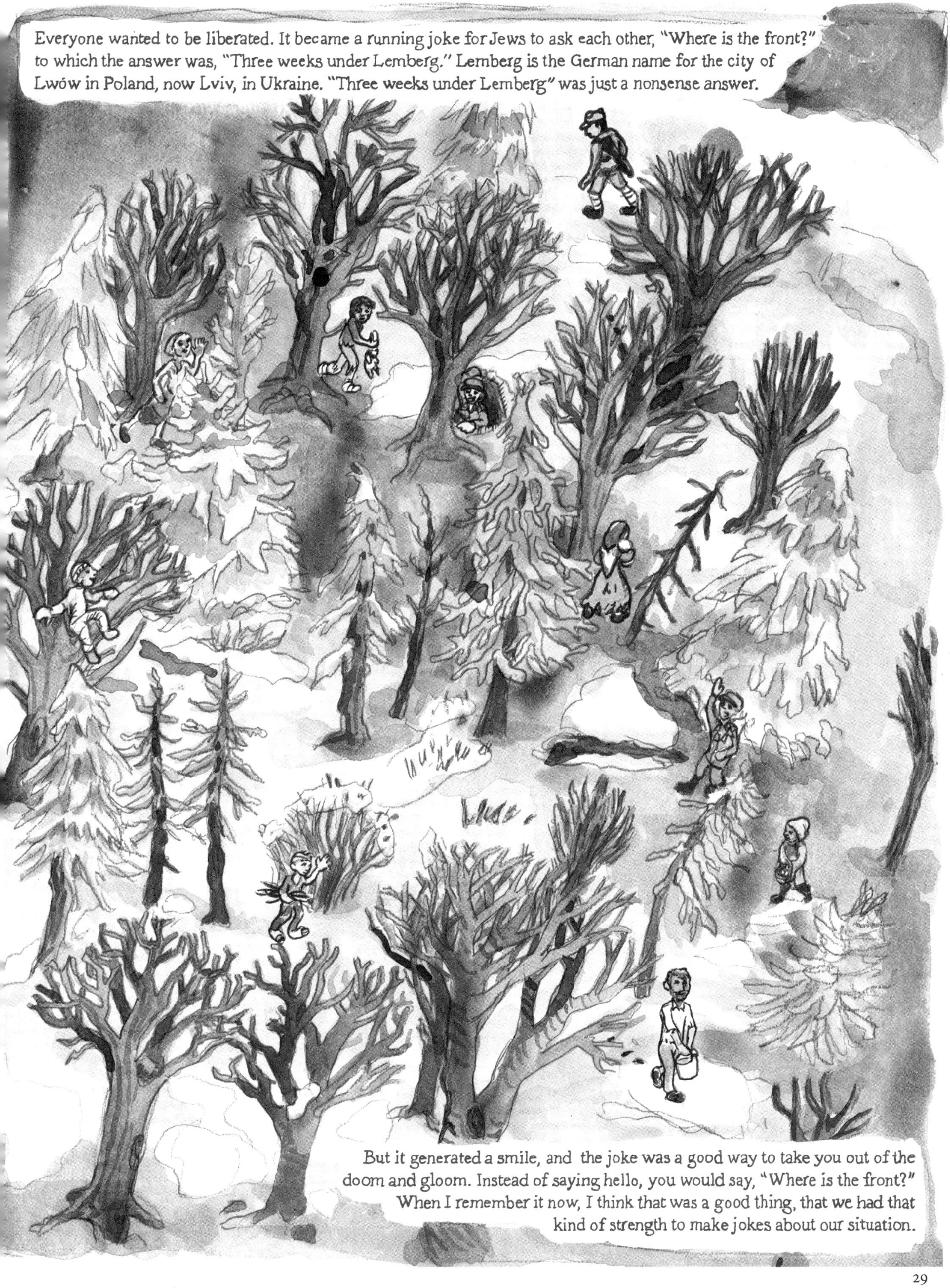
Everyone wanted to be liberated. It became a running joke for Jews to ask each other, "Where is the front?" to which the answer was, "Three weeks under Lemberg." Lemberg is the German name for the city of Lwów in Poland, now Lviv, in Ukraine. "Three weeks under Lemberg" was just a nonsense answer.
But it generated a smile, and the joke was a good way to take you out of the doom and gloom. Instead of saying hello, you would say, "Where is the front?" When I remember it now, I think that was a good thing, that we had that kind of strength to make jokes about our situation.

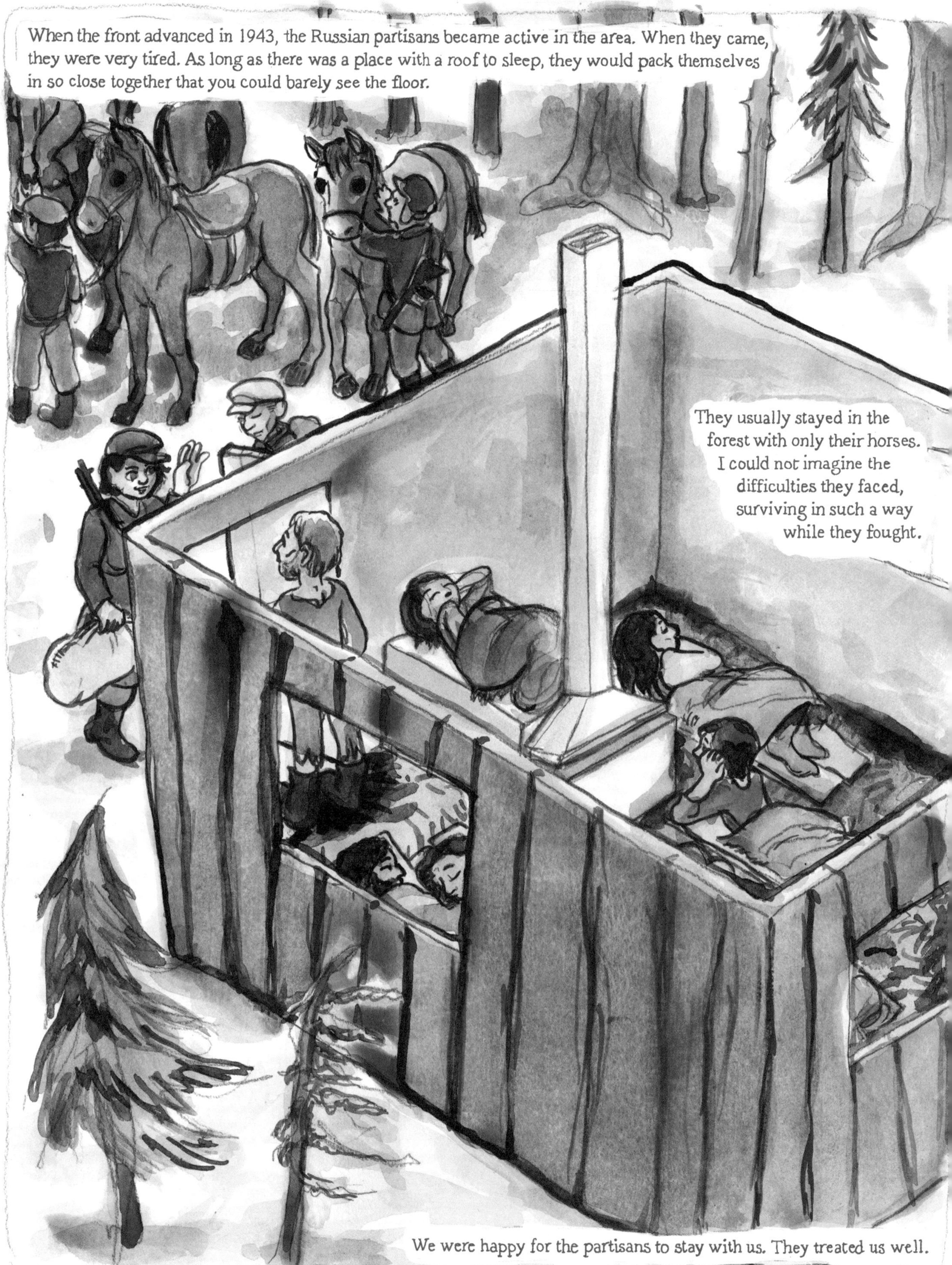
When the front advanced in 1943, the Russian partisans became active in the area. When they came, they were very tired. As long as there was a place with a roof to sleep, they would pack themselves in so close together that you could barely see the floor.
They usually stayed in the forest with only their horses. I could not imagine the difficulties they faced, surviving in such a way while they fought.
We were happy for the partisans to stay with us. They treated us well.

December of 1943. I spent one day in the forest with a bundle of wood on my back. I was walking back to the village on a mud road. The ground had completely frozen and the path was uneven, molded by the footsteps of horses and men and the tracks of carts. It was dangerous, but I had to walk on that path in order to get back.

All of a sudden, I heard a noise behind me, so I started running. After a few steps, I tripped and fell. The bundle of wood fell from my back and came down hard on my left arm. The pain was like fire; it was almost indescribable.

The bundle of wood had snapped my arm, displacing my elbow in the process. Someone brought a Ukrainian babushka from the village. She tried to reset my arm and move my elbow back into its proper place. It was unbelievably painful.

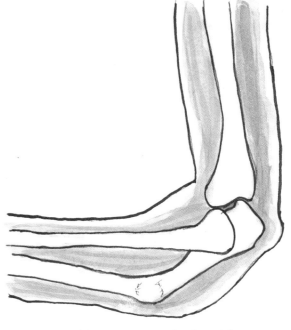

I was not able to get proper treatment for my arm. As it healed, parts of the bone grew together, and to this day I can't bend my arm all the way. That can be troublesome when I'm trying to eat with a knife and fork, because I can't reach the fork all the way to my mouth with that hand.

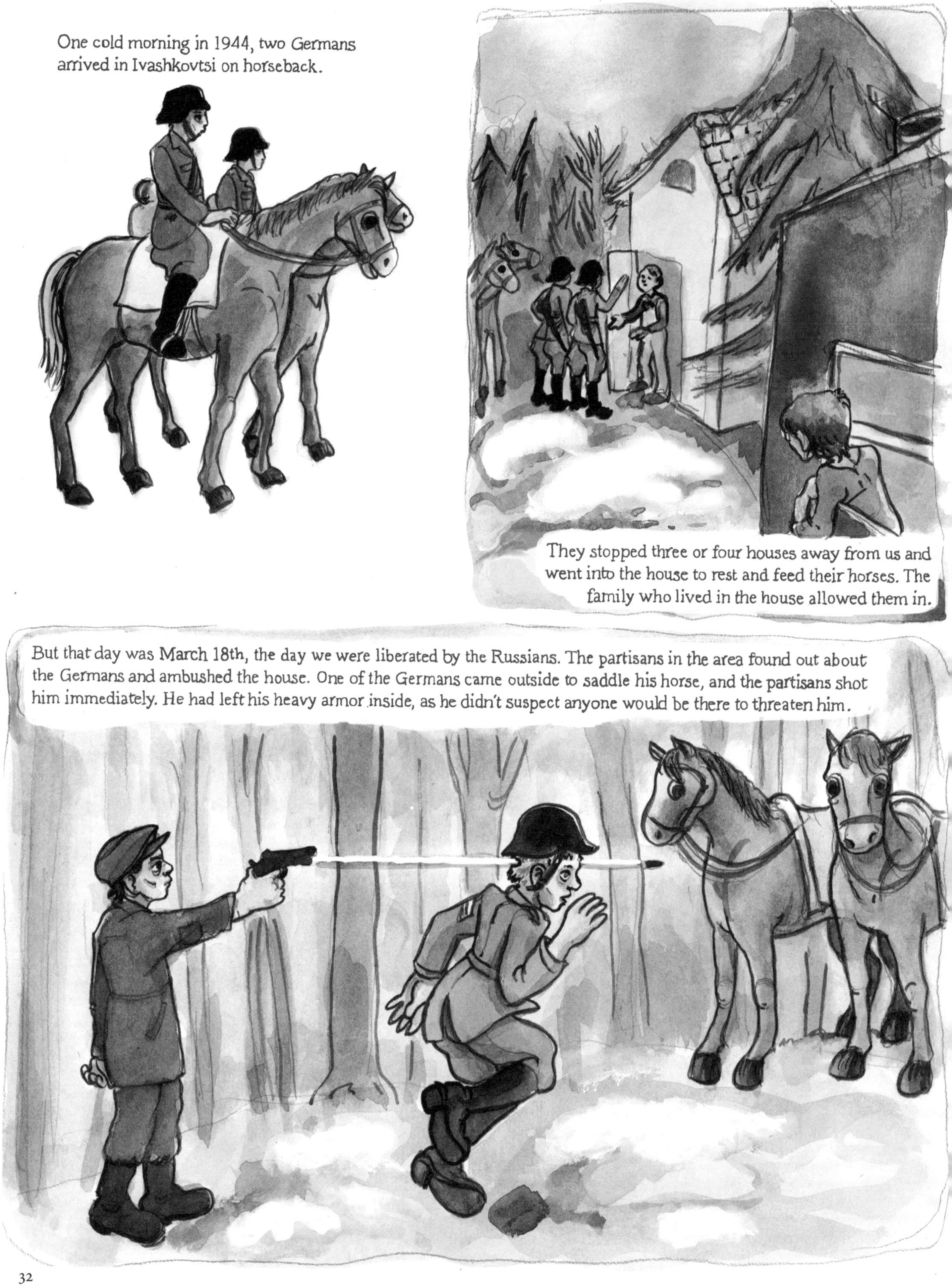
One cold morning in 1944, two Germans arrived in Ivashkovtsi on horseback.
They stopped three or four houses away from us and went into the house to rest and feed their horses. The family who lived in the house allowed them in.
But that day was March 18th, the day we were liberated by the Russians. The partisans in the area found out about the Germans and ambushed the house. One of the Germans came outside to saddle his horse, and the partisans shot him immediately. He had left his heavy armor inside, as he didn't suspect anyone would be there to threaten him.

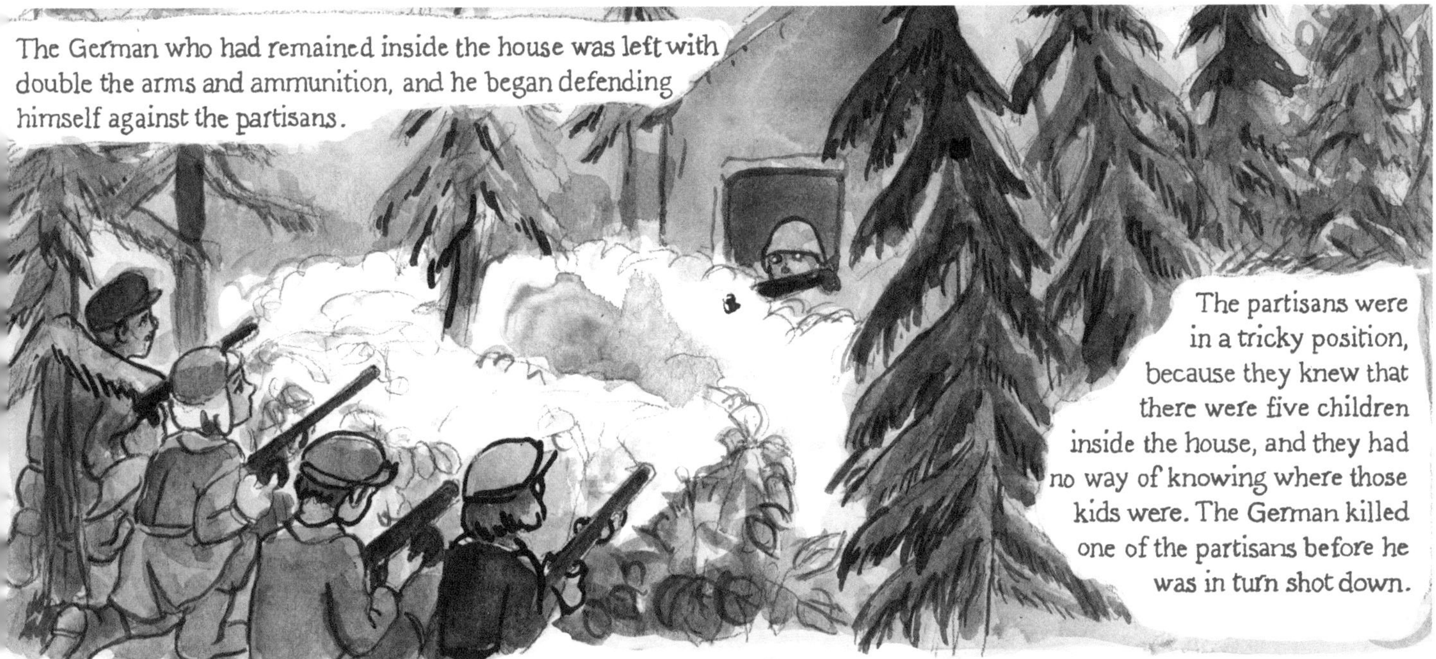
The German who had remained inside the house was left with double the arms and ammunition, and he began defending himself against the partisans.
The partisans were in a tricky position, because they knew that there were five children inside the house, and they had no way of knowing where those kids were. The German killed one of the partisans before he was in turn shot down.

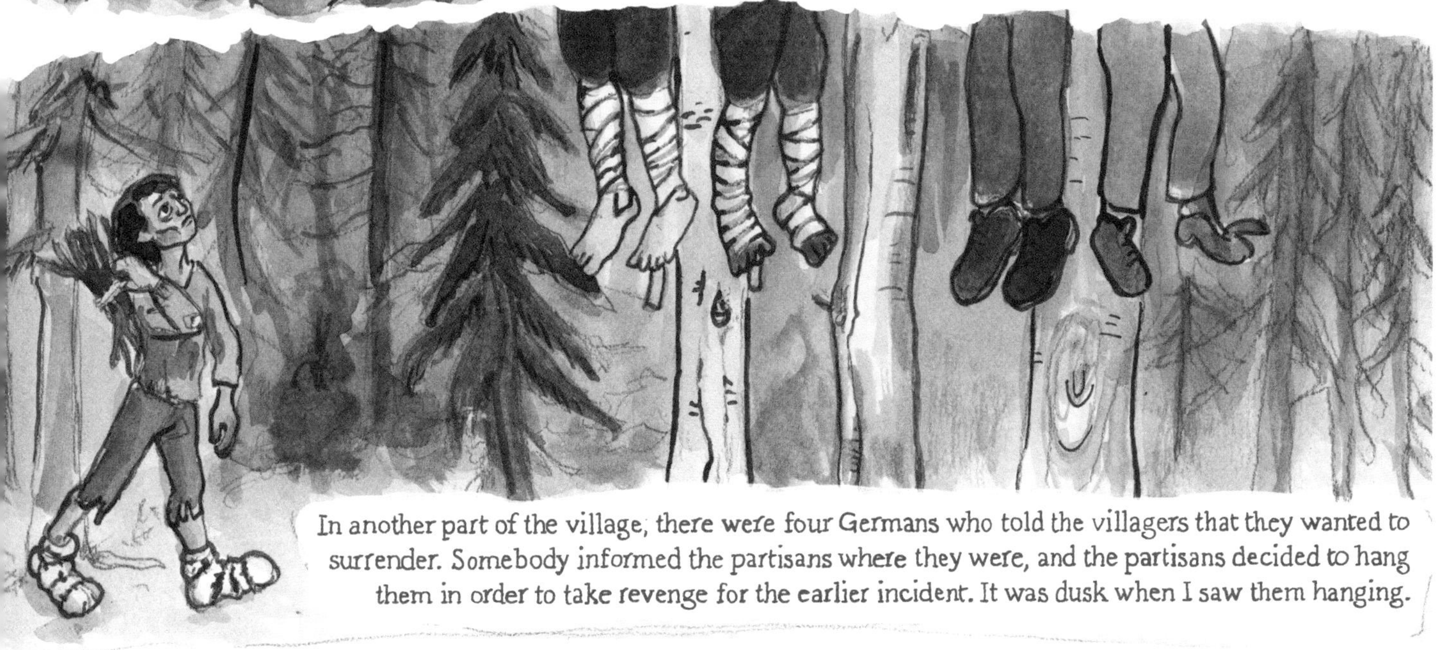
In another part of the village, there were four Germans who told the villagers that they wanted to surrender. Somebody informed the partisans where they were, and the partisans decided to hang them in order to take revenge for the earlier incident. It was dusk when I saw them hanging.

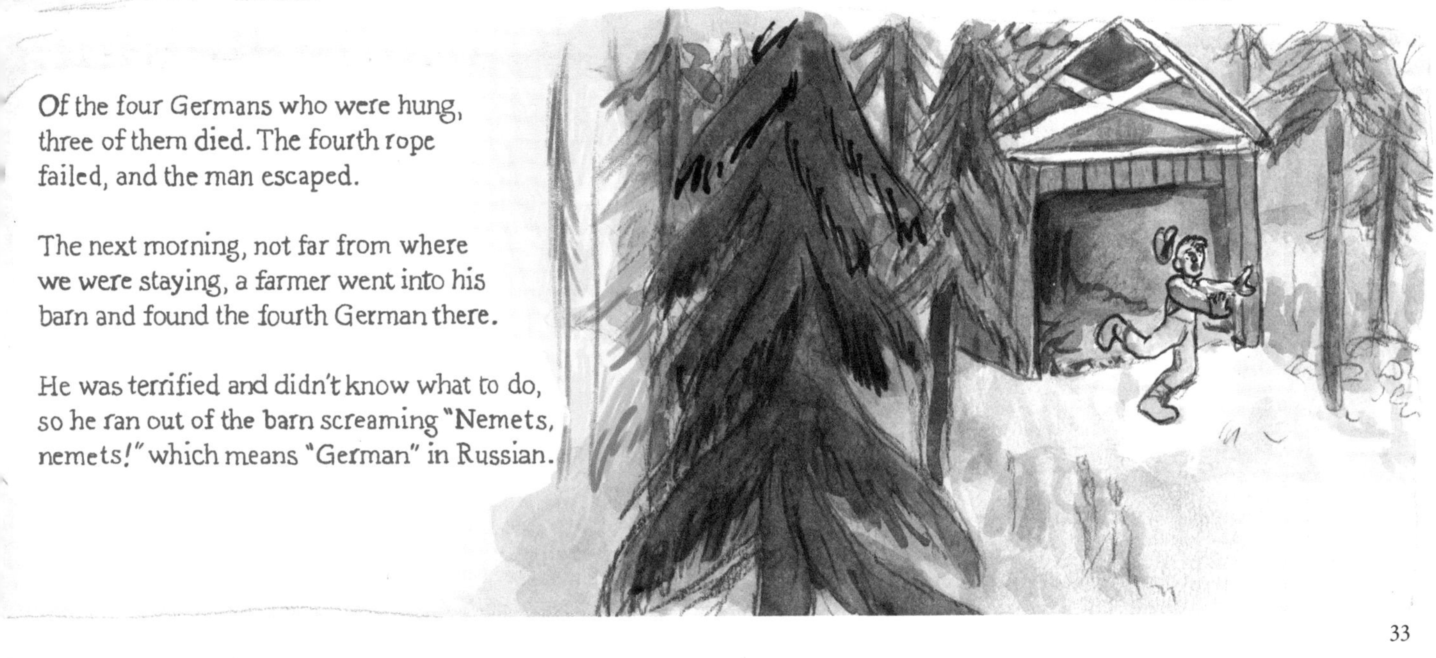
Of the four Germans who were hung, three of them died. The fourth rope failed, and the man escaped.
The next morning, not far from where we were staying, a farmer went into his barn and found the fourth German there.
He was terrified and didn't know what to do, so he ran out of the barn screaming "Nemets, nemets!" which means "German" in Russian.

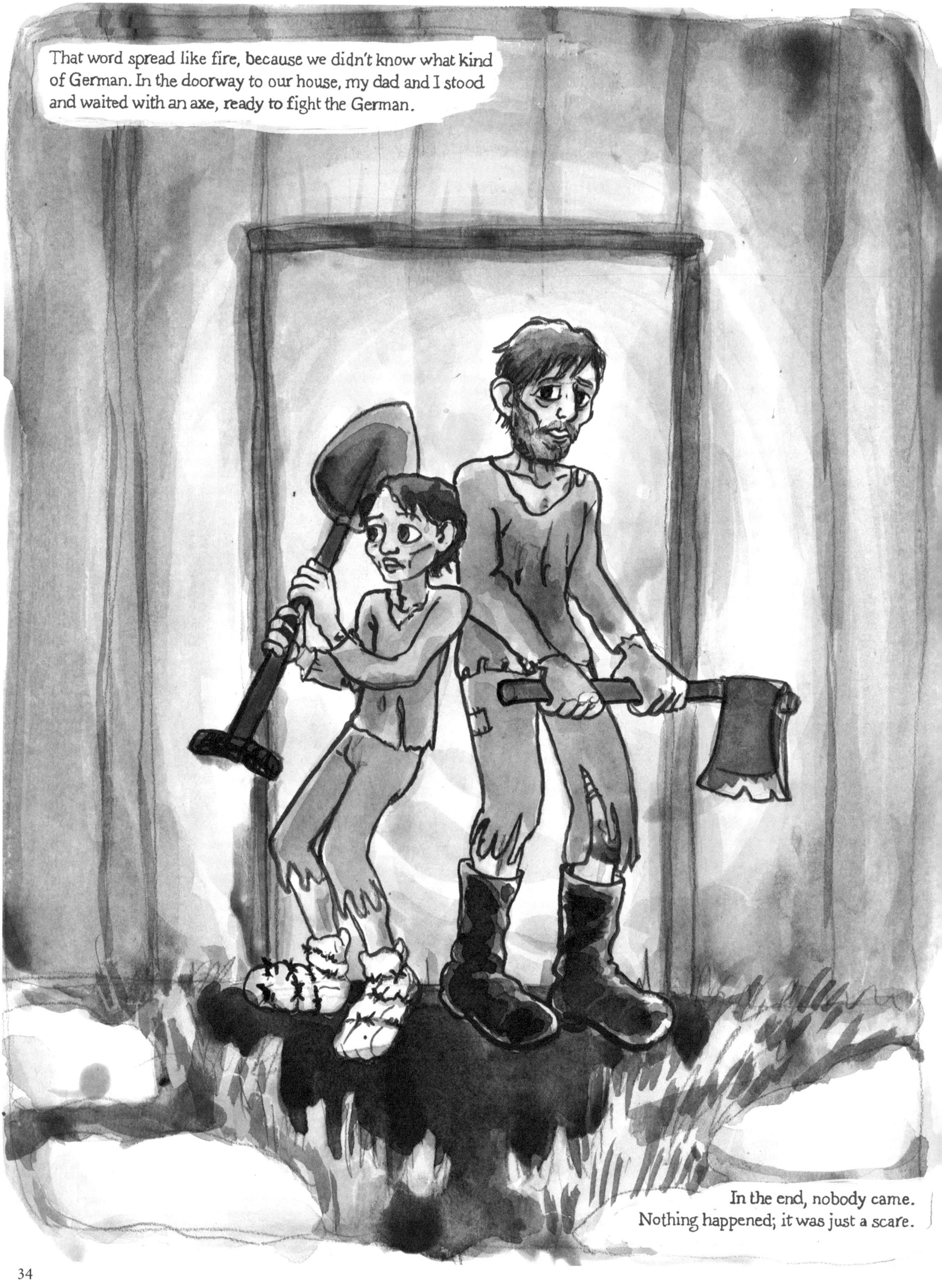
That word spread like fire, because we didn't know what kind of German. In the doorway to our house, my dad and I stood and waited with an axe, ready to fight the German.
In the end, nobody came.
Nothing happened; it was just a scare.

A few weeks after the incidents with the Germans, we decided it was safe to move towards home following the Soviets.

We went on foot because we had no other option.

I used rags around my feet for walking, but this wasn't ideal because in the winter it was freezing cold, and the rags got wet and then froze on my feet.

We would walk all through the day, and then when it became dark, we would find somewhere to sleep. It was already spring or summer by this time.

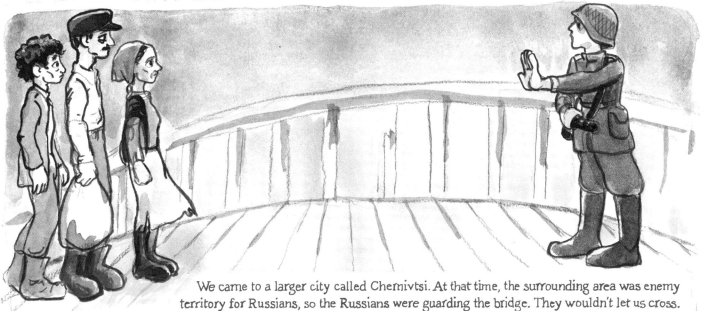

We came to a larger city called Chernivtsi. At that time, the surrounding area was enemy territory for Russians, so the Russians were guarding the bridge. They wouldn't let us cross.

Eventually a large group of peasants came along to walk across the bridge, and because I was small, I was able to sneak behind them while the Russians were checking their papers.

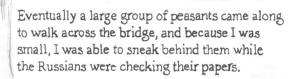

I crossed the city by myself. I walked to my uncle's address and told him that my parents were on the other side of the bridge and needed help.

We stayed in Chernivtsi with my uncle for a few weeks.

He gave us clothing because by then we only had rags. Every shirt or pair of pants I owned had either been outgrown or ripped from overuse. It was such a relief to have better clothing.

We left my uncle and continued on our journey home. We didn't have many belongings left, so there wasn't much to carry. It took quite a while, a couple months or so, for us to get back home because we had to stay behind the front, out of enemy territory. We never really knew where the front was, or how far we could walk that day. We also had to find food on the way.

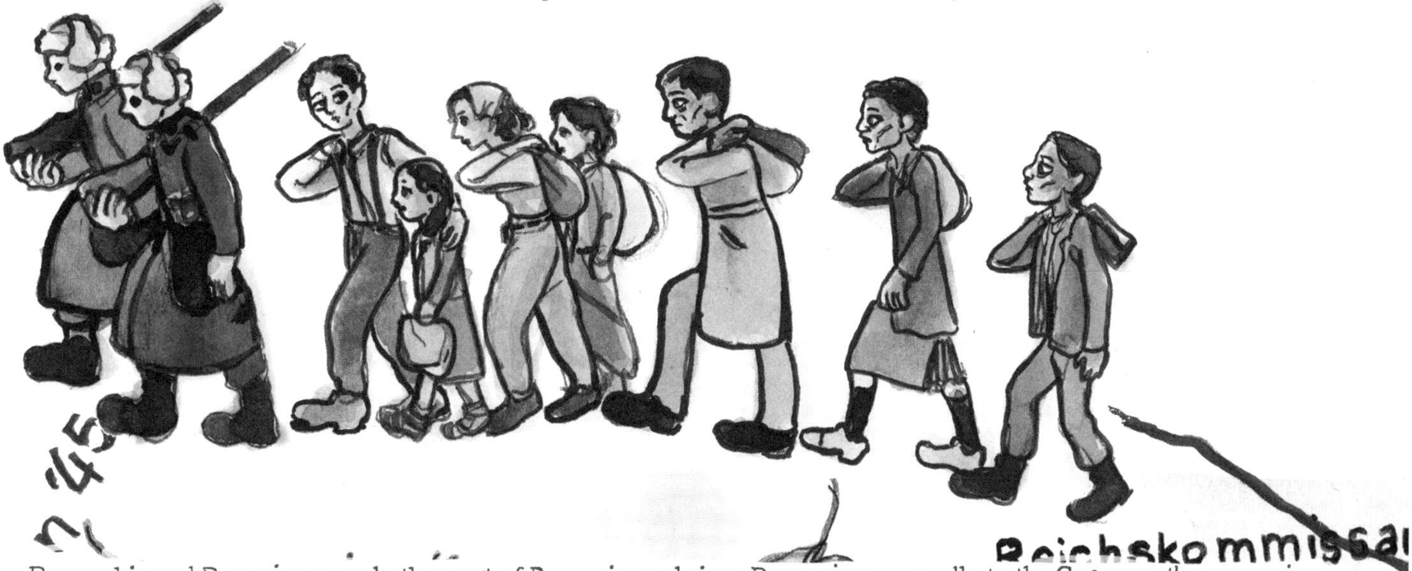

Bessarabia and Bucovina were both a part of Romania, and since Romania was an ally to the Germans, the occupying Russians considered it enemy territory. They were suspicious of everyone who was there, including us. For that reason, we didn't want to stay in Northern Bucovina, as that region had been occupied by the Russians/Ukrainians in 1939.

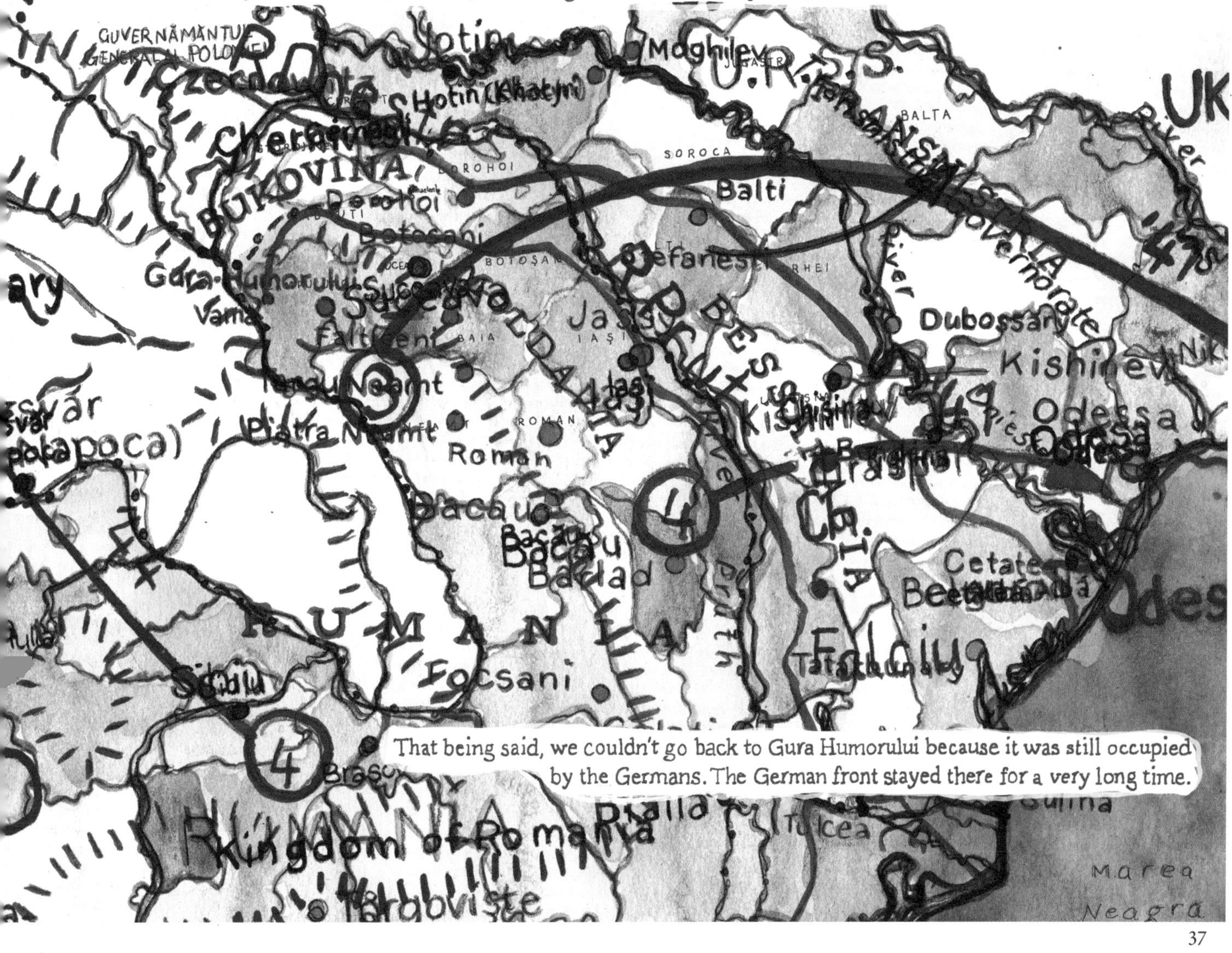
Moghilev
Hotin (Khotyn)
BALTA
SOROCA
BUKOVINA
Balti
Gura-Humorului
Vama
Dubossary
Kishinev
Odessa
Roman
Focsani
Marea
Neagra
That being said, we couldn't go back to Gura Humorului because it was still occupied by the Germans. The German front stayed there for a very long time.

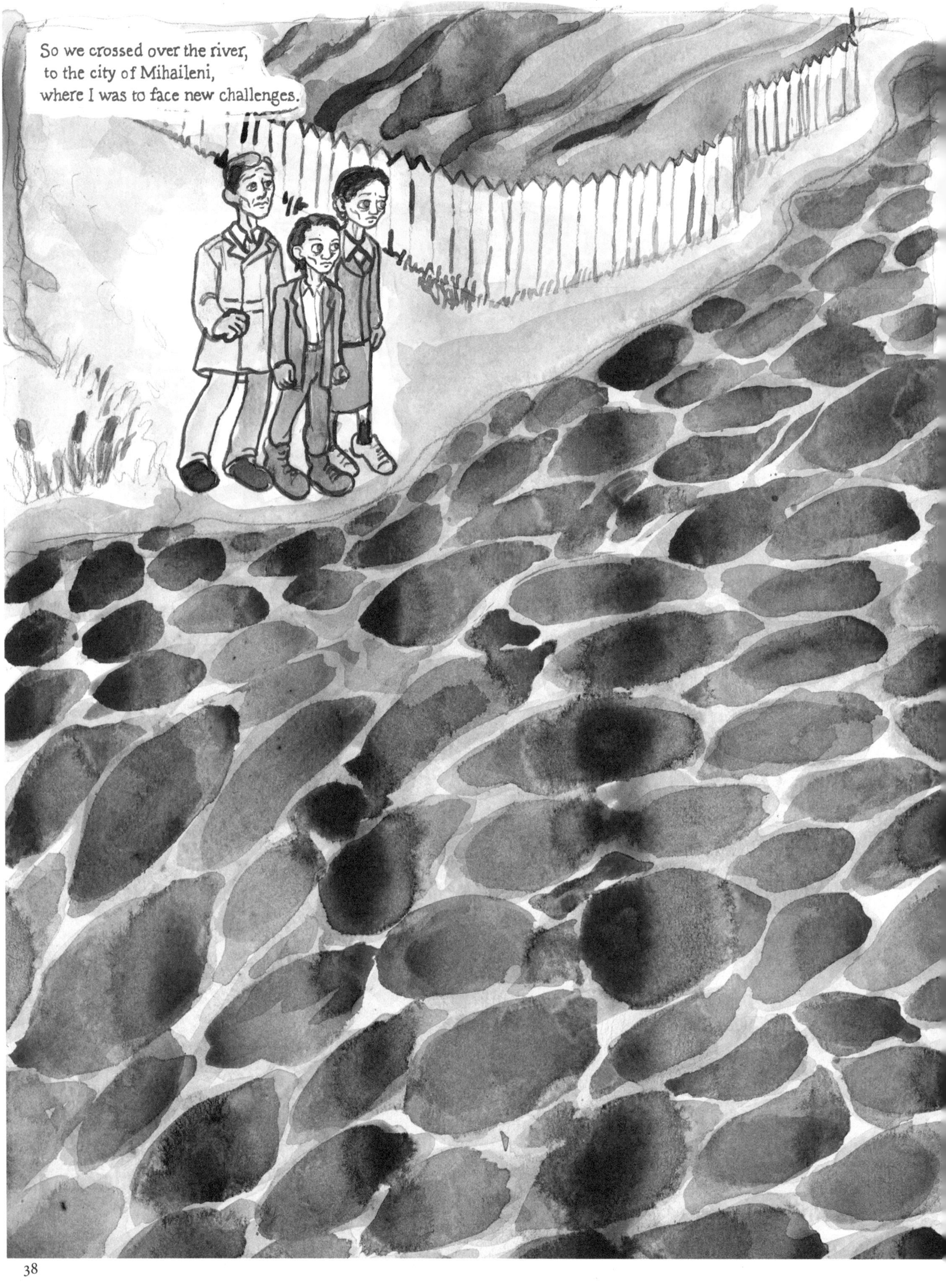
So we crossed over the river, to the city of Mihaileni, where I was to face new challenges.

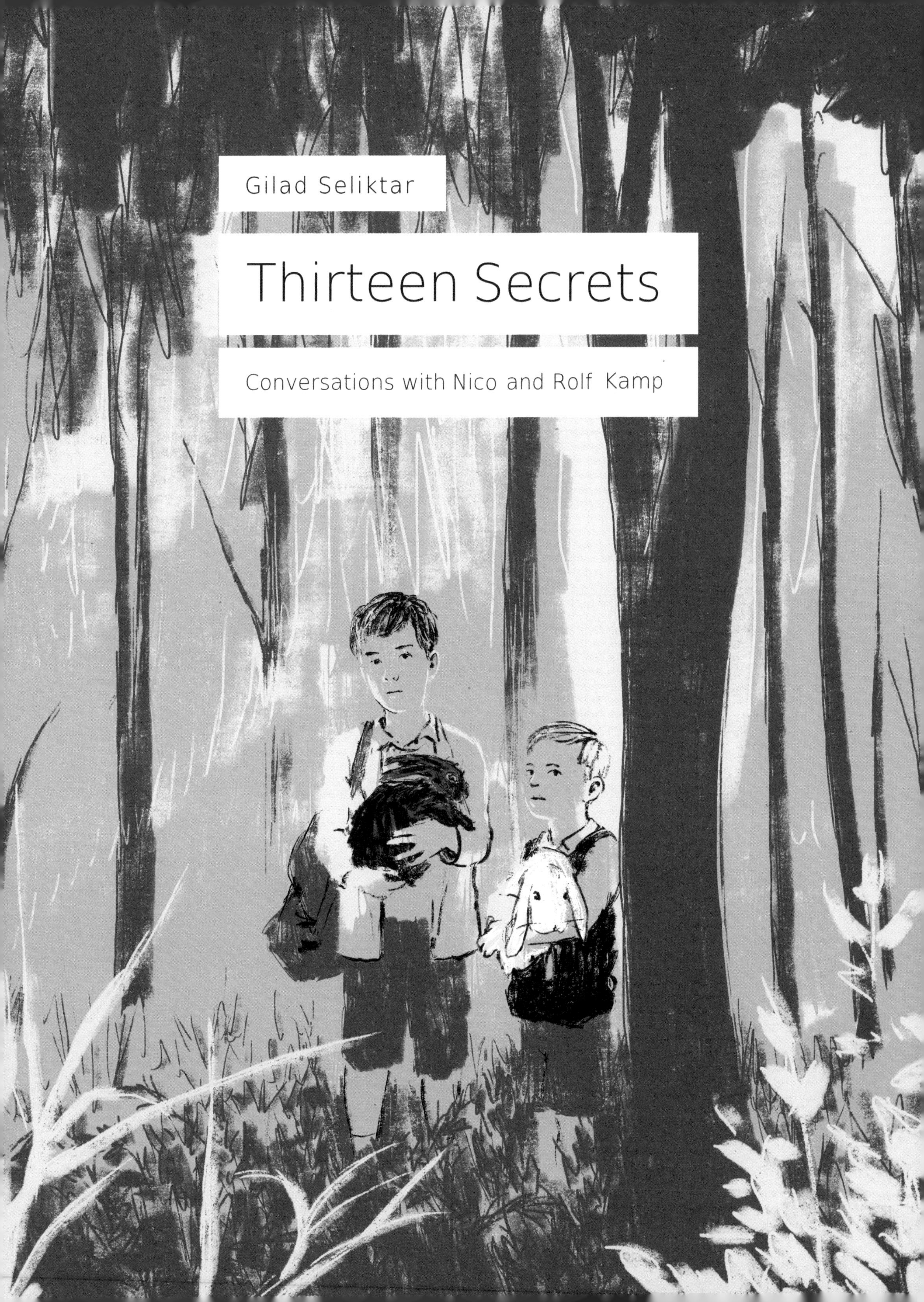
Gilad Seliktar
Thirteen Secrets
Conversations with Nico and Rolf Kamp

In December 2019, Israeli Graphic Novelist Gilad Seliktar went to Amsterdam in the Netherlands to meet Rolf and Nico Kamp, brothers and Holocaust survivors who hid from the Germans in the Netherlands during World War II. The Kamp brothers met with Gilad several times in different locations where they shared stories about their experiences during the war. As Jewish children, they were moved through thirteen hiding places. While in hiding, they had to keep their identity a secret to survive.

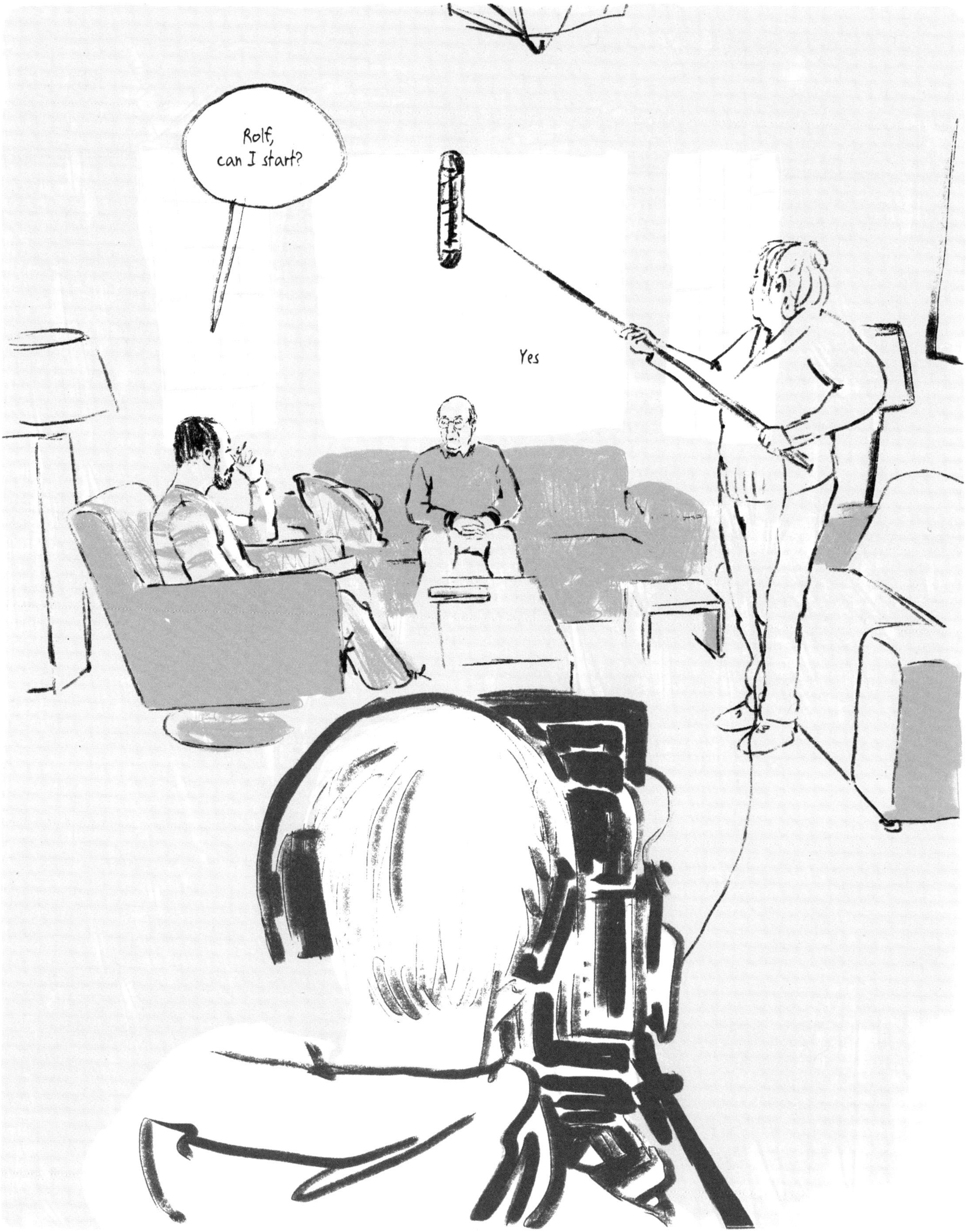
Rolf,
can I start?
Yes

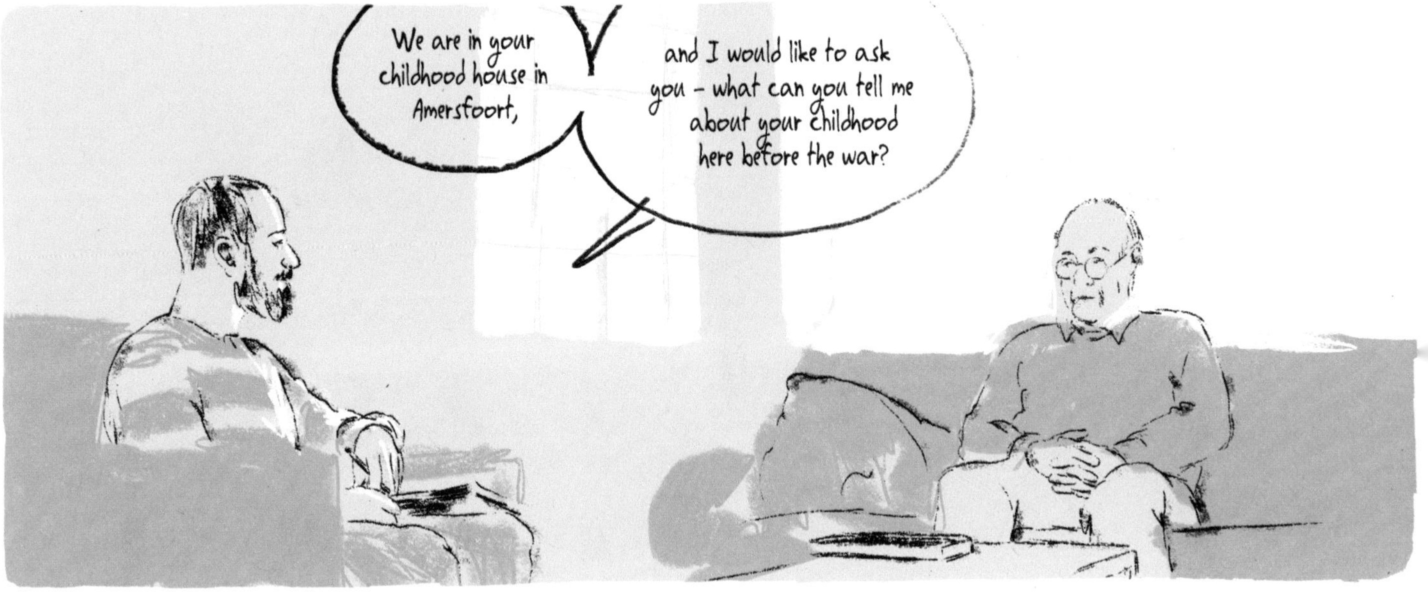
We are in your childhood house in Amersfoort,
and I would like to ask you – what can you tell me about your childhood here before the war?

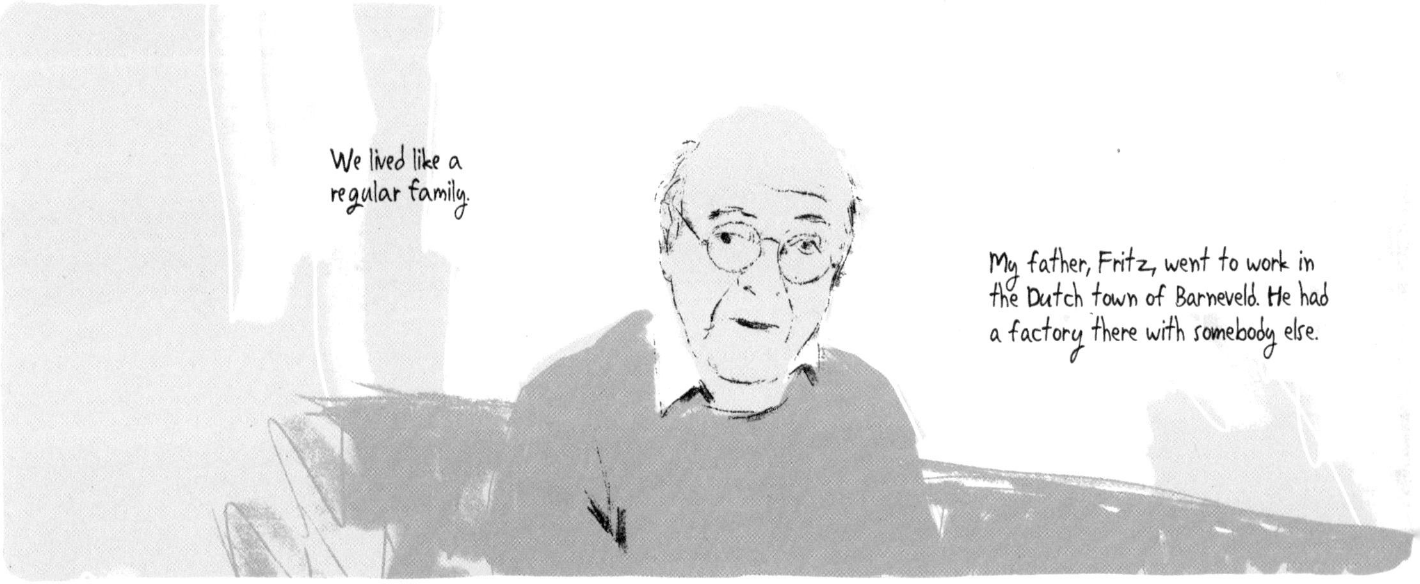
We lived like a regular family.
My father, Fritz, went to work in the Dutch town of Barneveld. He had a factory there with somebody else.

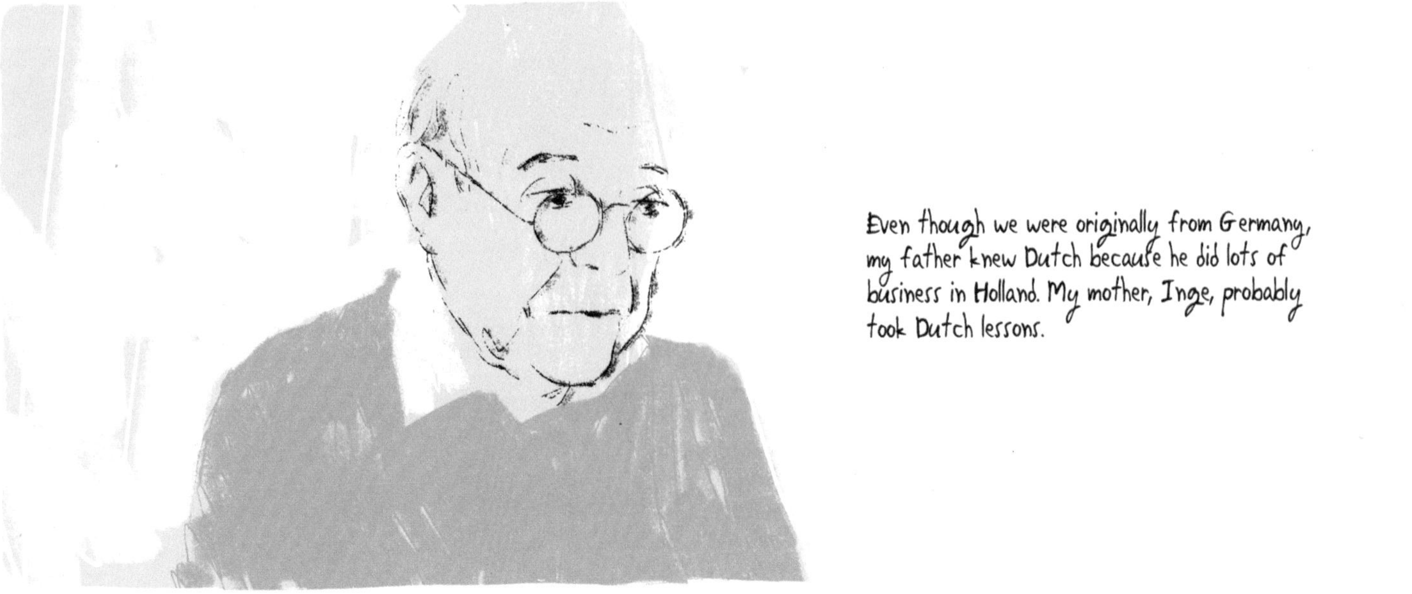
Even though we were originally from Germany, my father knew Dutch because he did lots of business in Holland. My mother, Inge, probably took Dutch lessons.

I was six years old.
My brother, Nico, was three.

My father was probably very
proud of his boys. We walked
together, holding hands. He made
grape juice for us.

When my father was putting us to bed, he took our socks and he turned them inside out with the outside bit
over the bottom part so he could easily roll them up our legs.

And I still do this today when I have
difficulty putting my socks on.

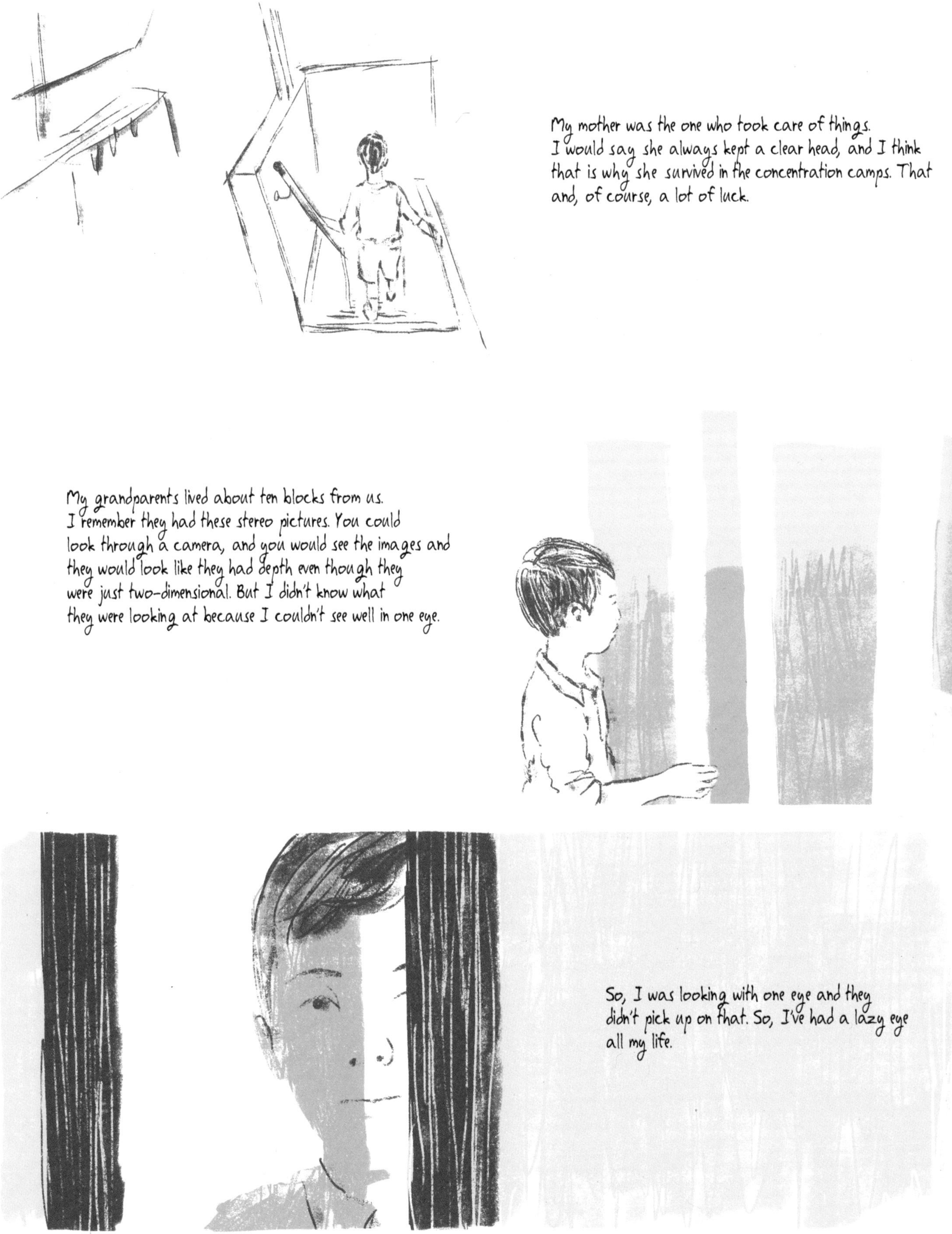
My mother was the one who took care of things. I would say she always kept a clear head, and I think that is why she survived in the concentration camps. That and, of course, a lot of luck.
My grandparents lived about ten blocks from us. I remember they had these stereo pictures. You could look through a camera, and you would see the images and they would look like they had depth even though they were just two-dimensional. But I didn't know what they were looking at because I couldn't see well in one eye.
So, I was looking with one eye and they didn't pick up on that. So, I've had a lazy eye all my life.

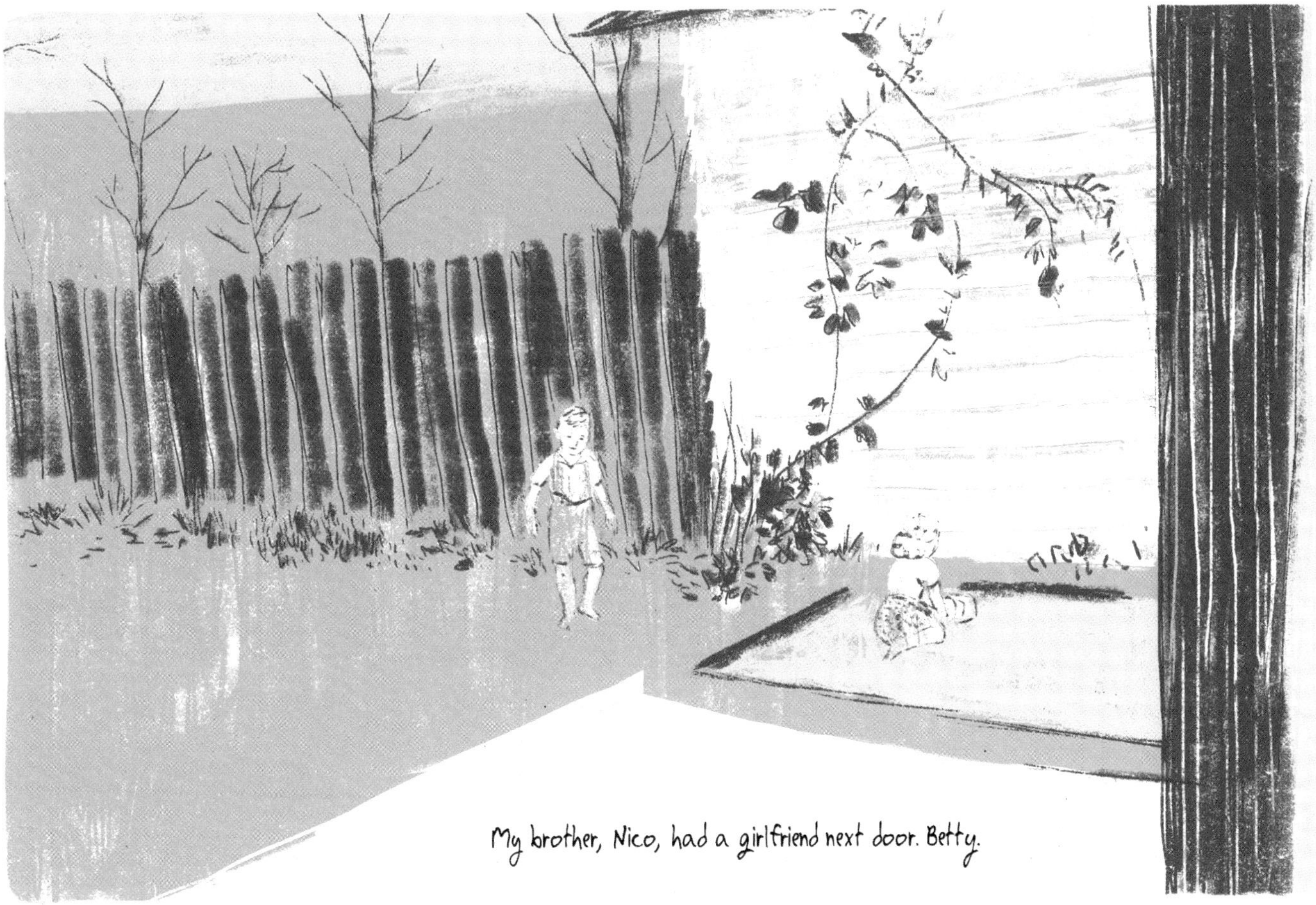
My brother, Nico, had a girlfriend next door. Betty.

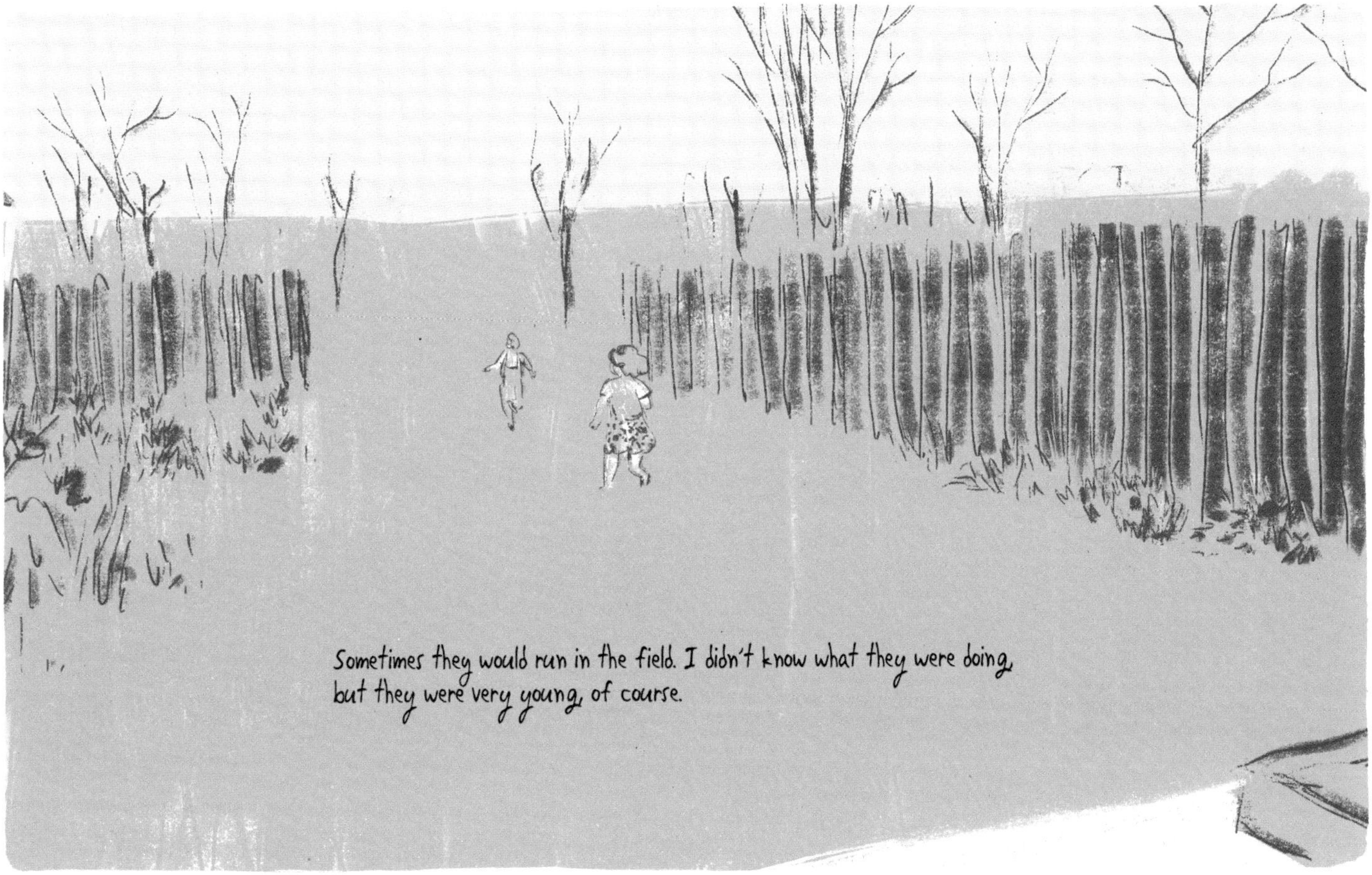
Sometimes they would run in the field. I didn't know what they were doing, but they were very young, of course.

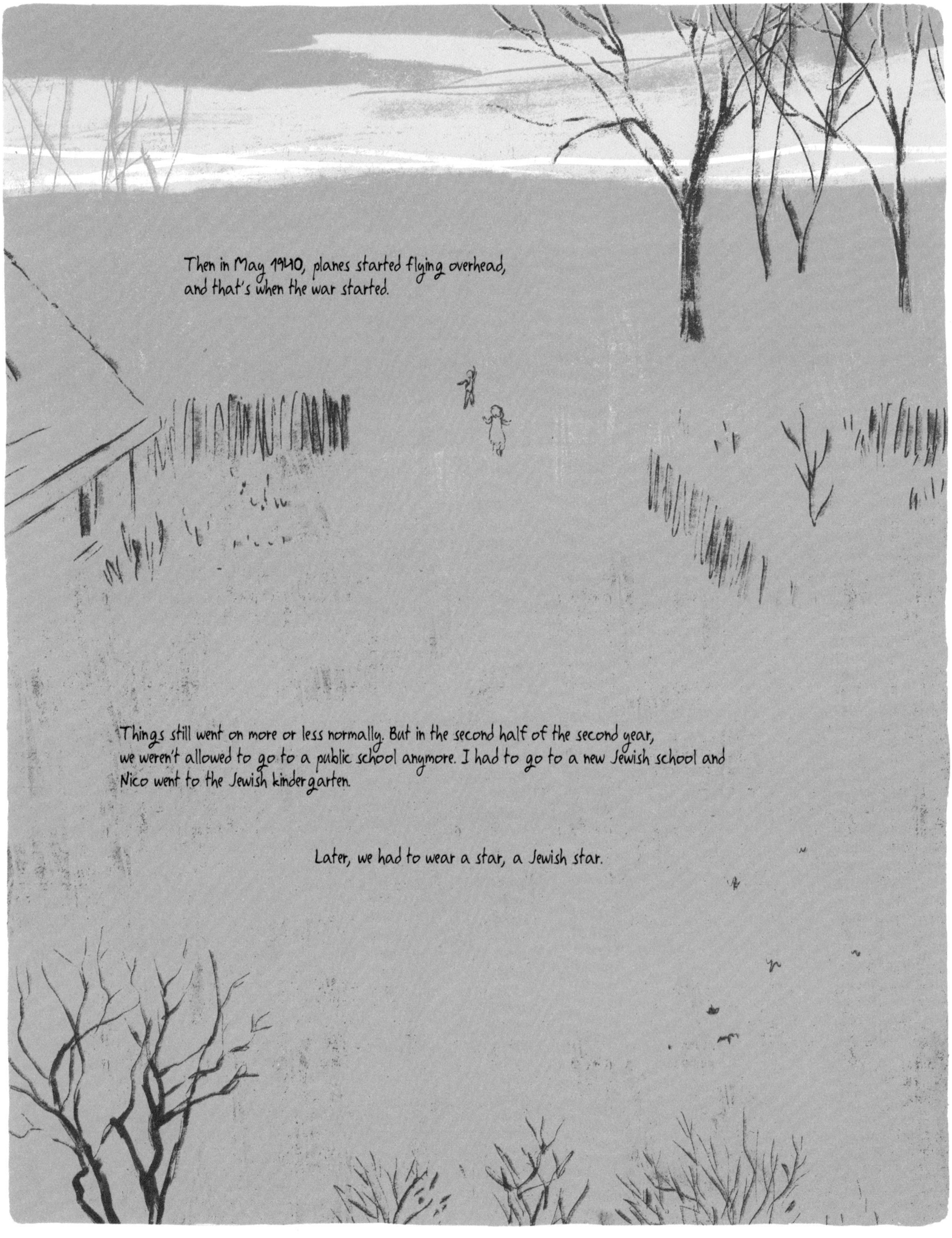
Then in May 1940, planes started flying overhead, and that's when the war started.
Things still went on more or less normally. But in the second half of the second year, we weren't allowed to go to a public school anymore. I had to go to a new Jewish school and Nico went to the Jewish kindergarten.
Later, we had to wear a star, a Jewish star.

And then one day, people I didn't know came
to take us to our first hiding place.

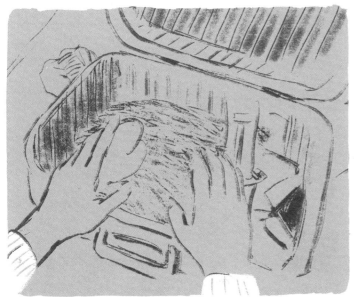

Before we went, my mother had to take the star off,
which was stitched to our clothes.

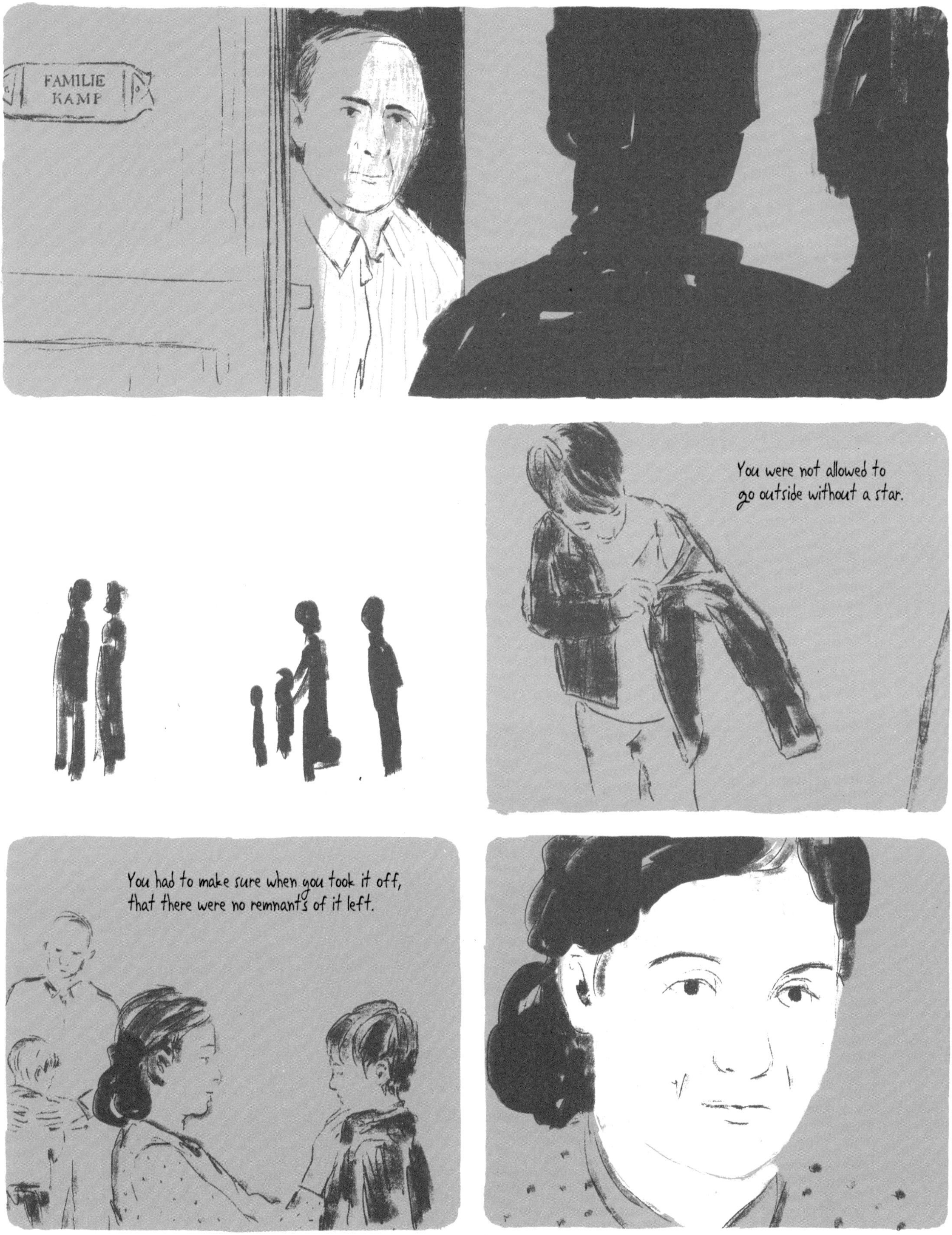
FAMILIE
KAMP
You were not allowed to go outside without a star.
You had to make sure when you took it off, that there were no remnants of it left.

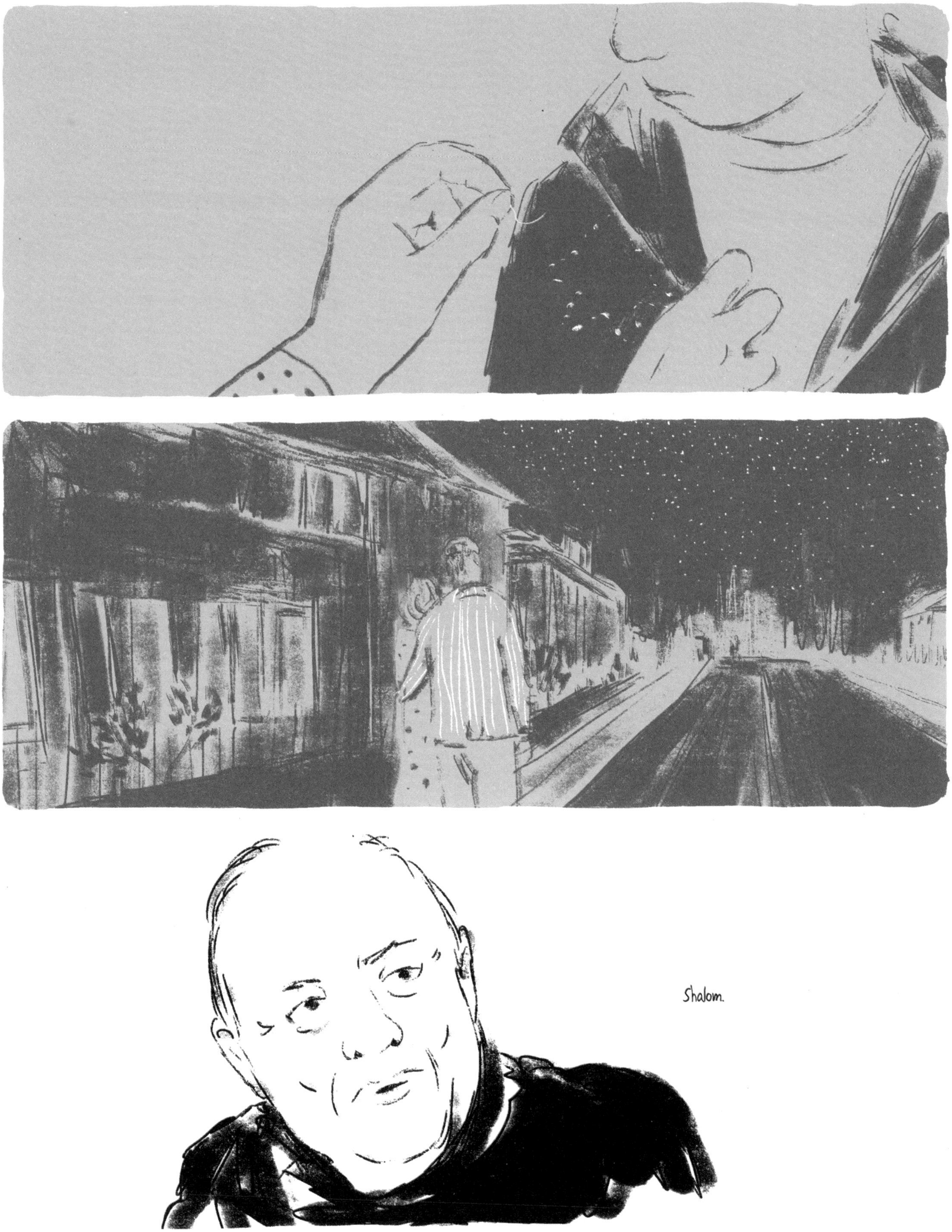
Shalom.

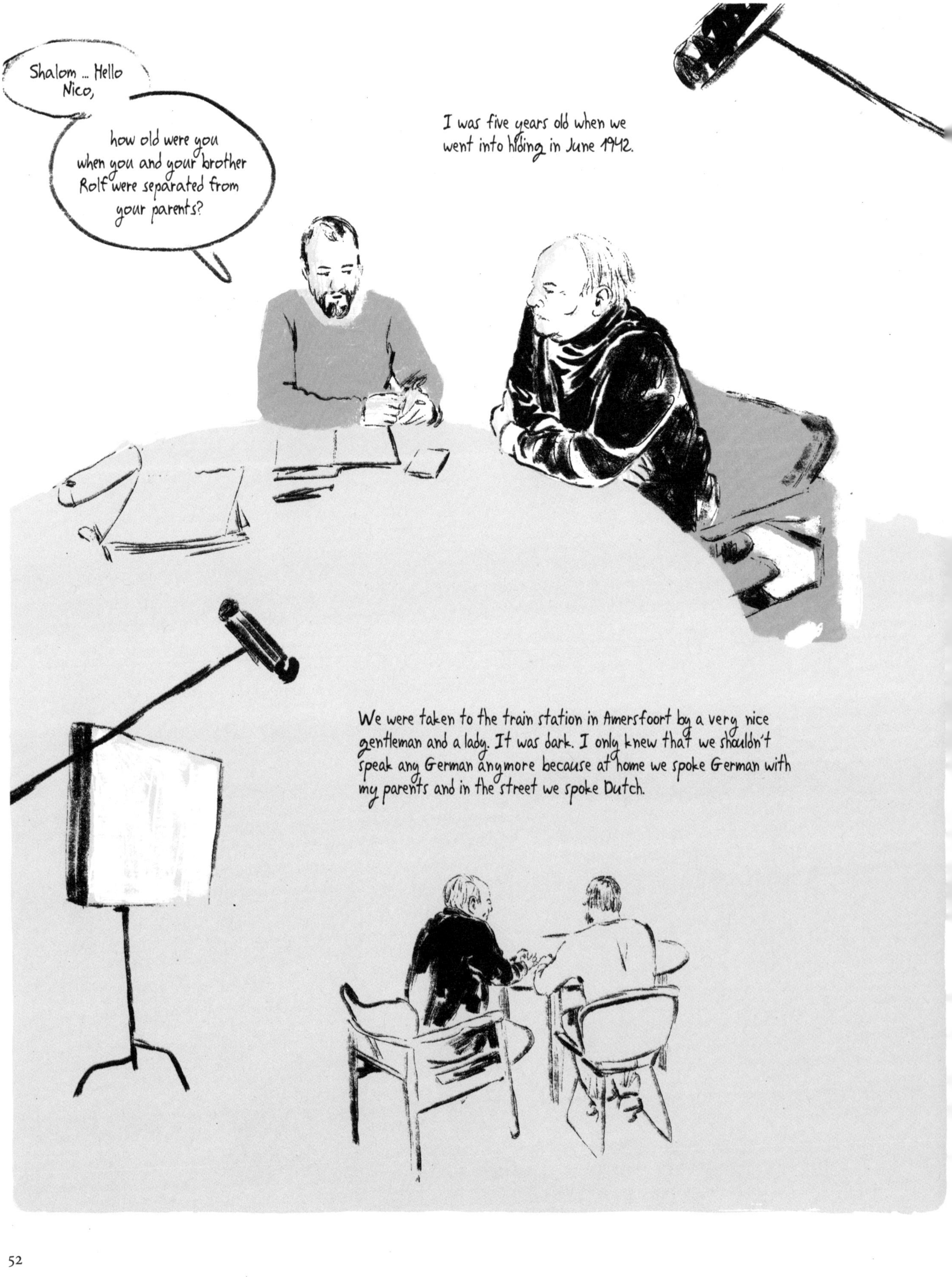
Shalom ... Hello Nico,
how old were you when you and your brother Rolf were separated from your parents?
I was five years old when we went into hiding in June 1942.
We were taken to the train station in Amersfoort by a very nice gentleman and a lady. It was dark. I only knew that we shouldn't speak any German anymore because at home we spoke German with my parents and in the street we spoke Dutch.

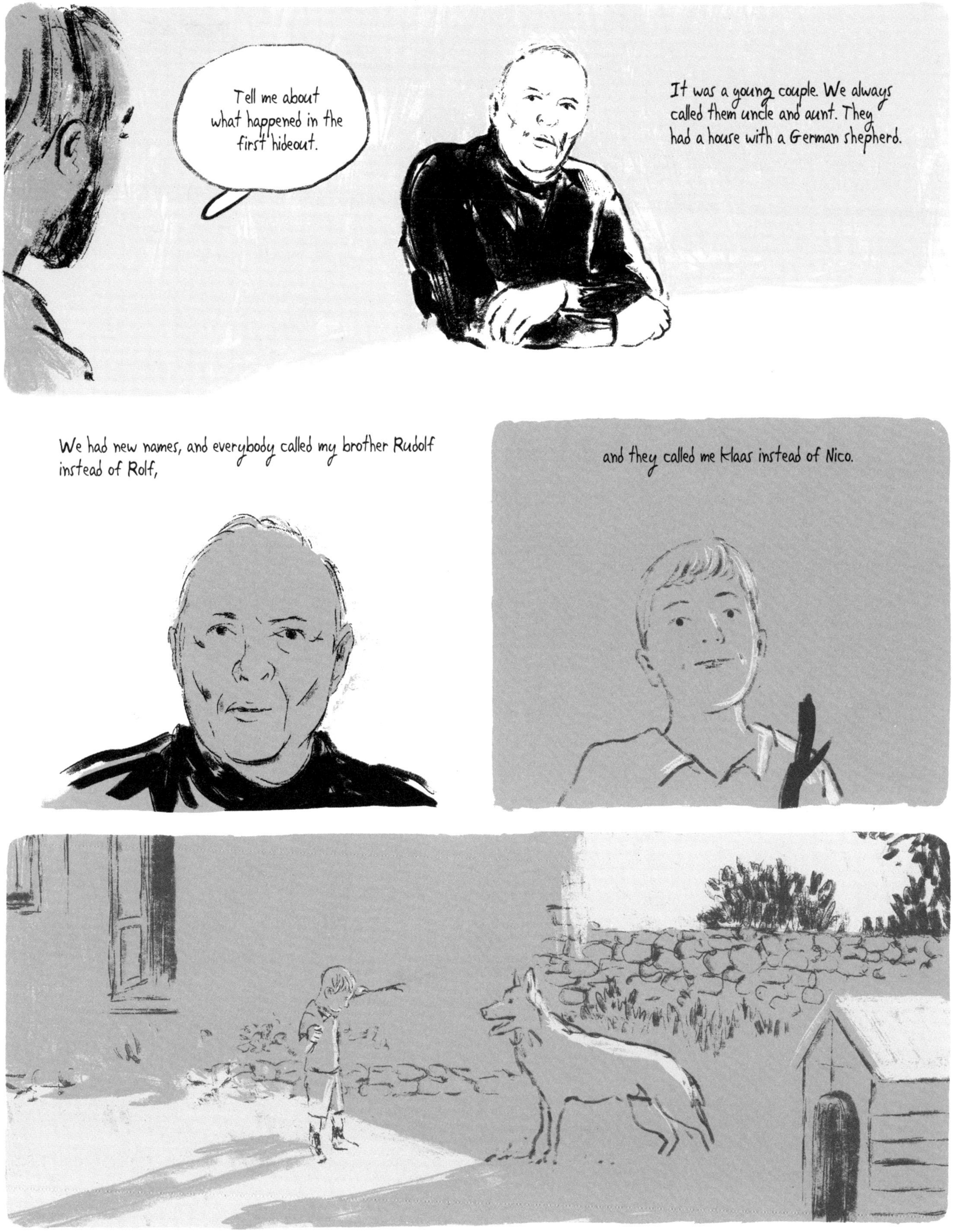
Tell me about what happened in the first hideout.
It was a young couple. We always called them uncle and aunt. They had a house with a German shepherd.
We had new names, and everybody called my brother Rudolf instead of Rolf,
and they called me Klaas instead of Nico.

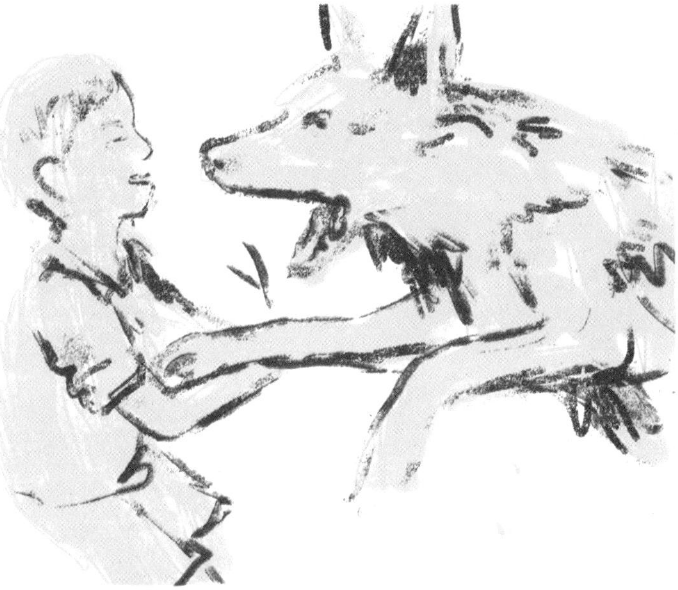

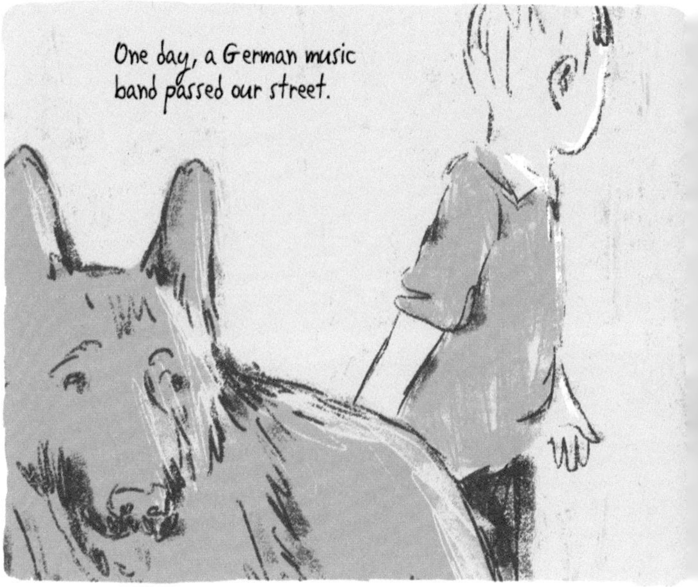
One day, a German music band passed our street.

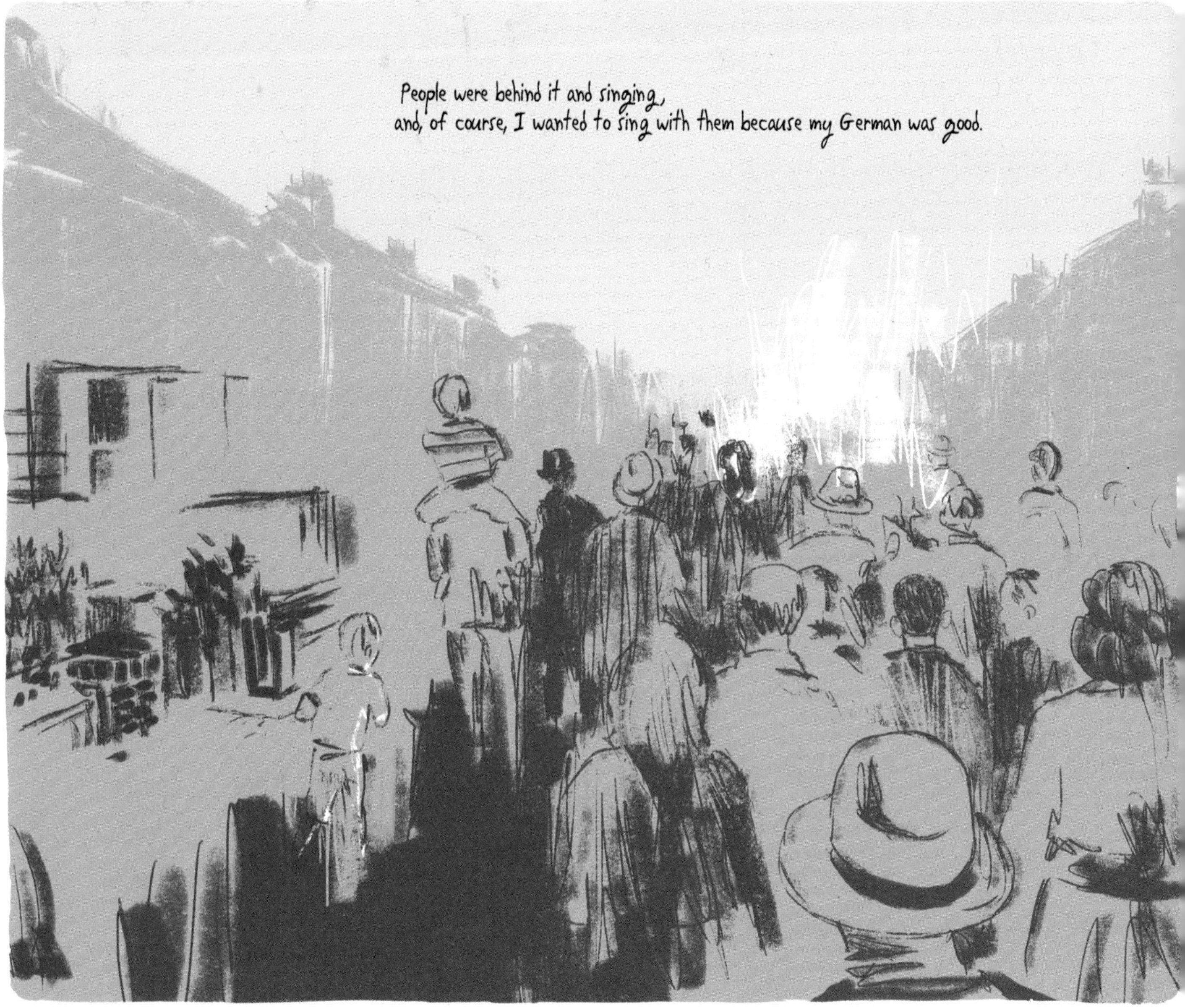
People were behind it and singing, and, of course, I wanted to sing with them because my German was good.

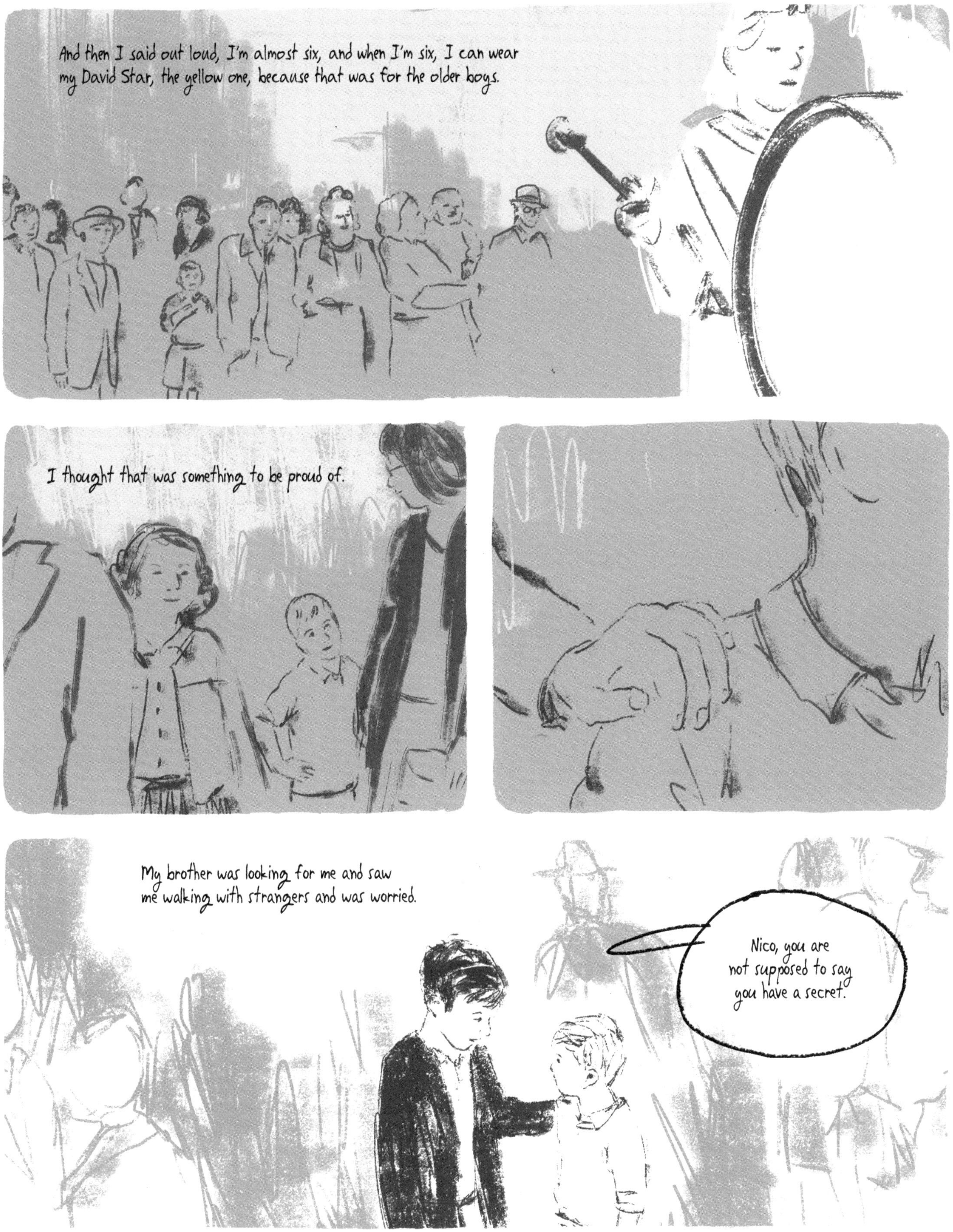
And then I said out loud, I'm almost six, and when I'm six, I can wear my David Star, the yellow one, because that was for the older boys.
I thought that was something to be proud of.
My brother was looking for me and saw me walking with strangers and was worried.
Nico, you are not supposed to say you have a secret.

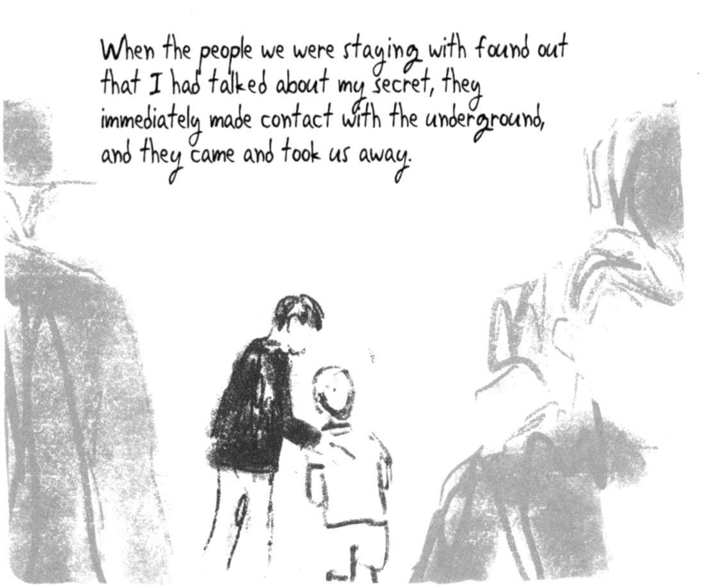
When the people we were staying with found out that I had talked about my secret, they immediately made contact with the underground, and they came and took us away.
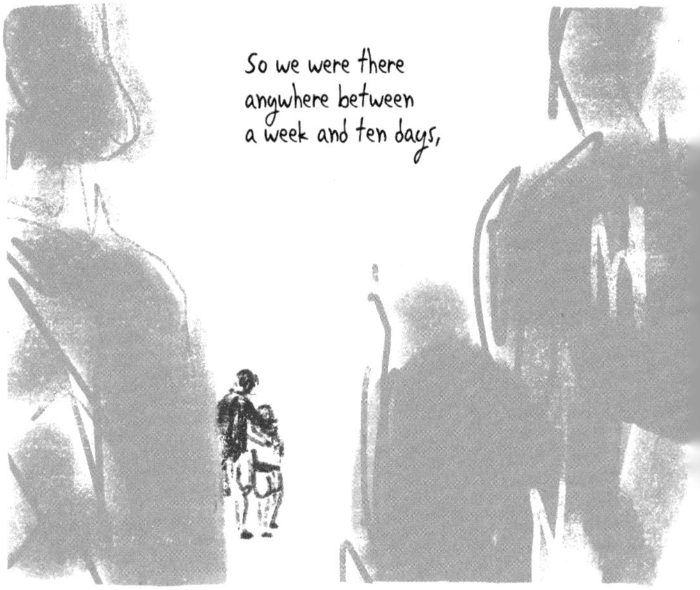
So we were there anywhere between a week and ten days,
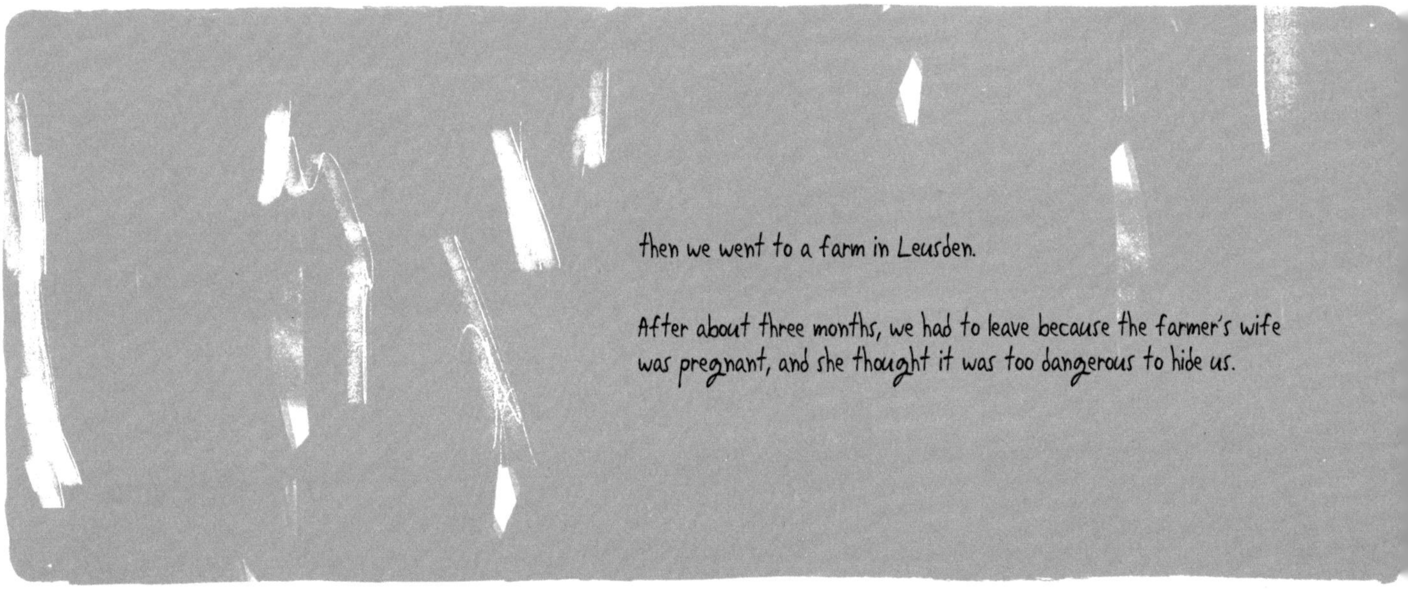
then we went to a farm in Leusden.
After about three months, we had to leave because the farmer's wife was pregnant, and she thought it was too dangerous to hide us.
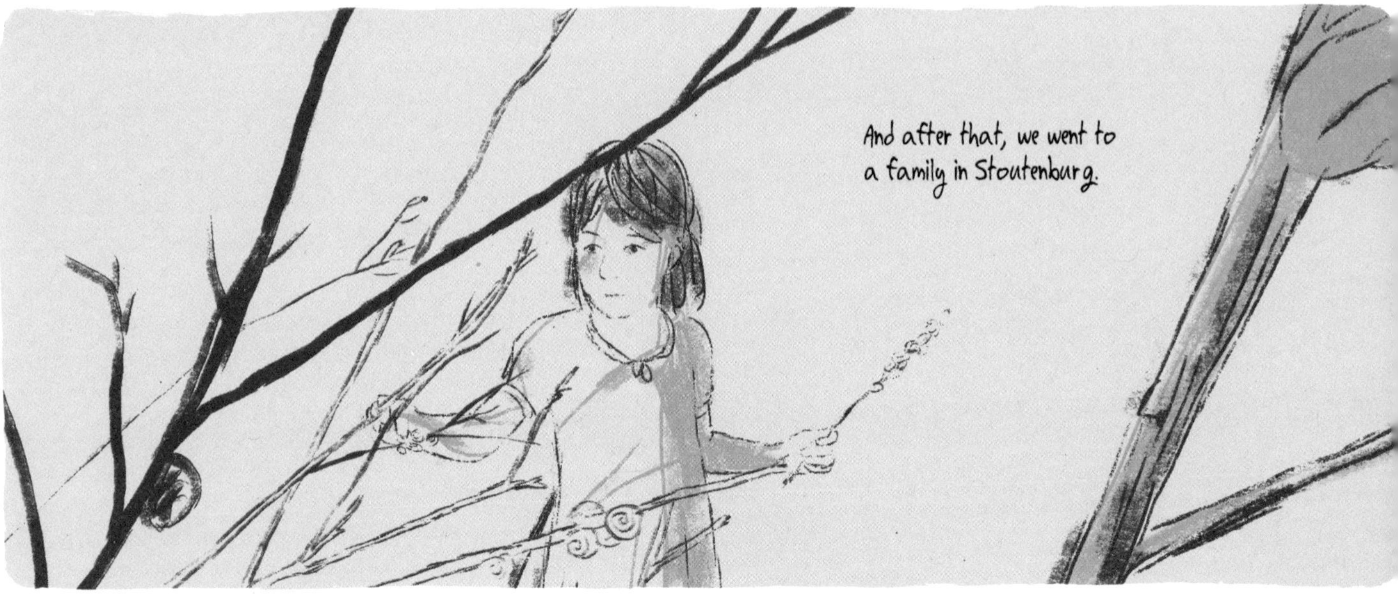
And after that, we went to a family in Stoutenburg.

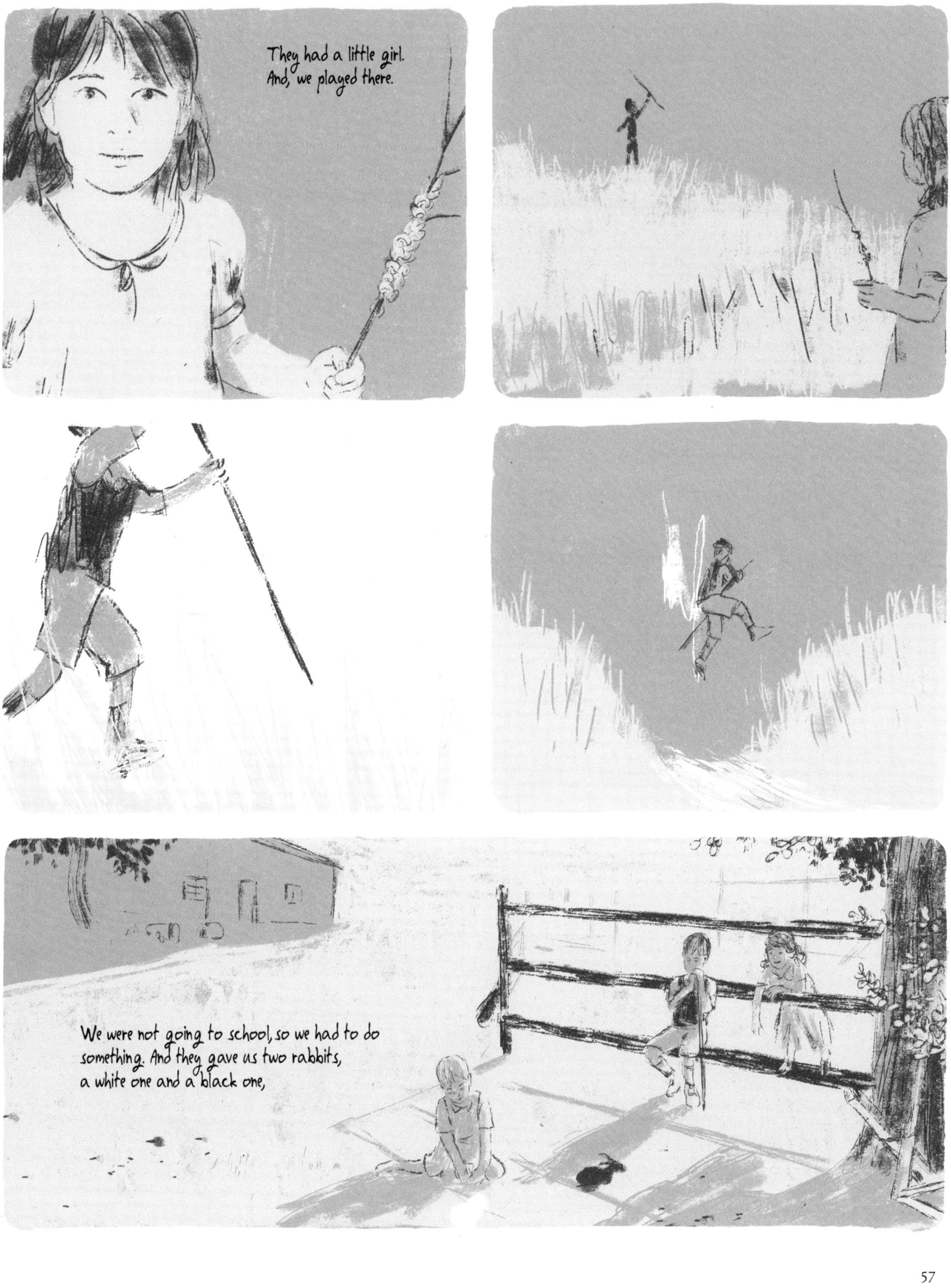
They had a little girl. And, we played there.
We were not going to school, so we had to do something. And they gave us two rabbits, a white one and a black one,

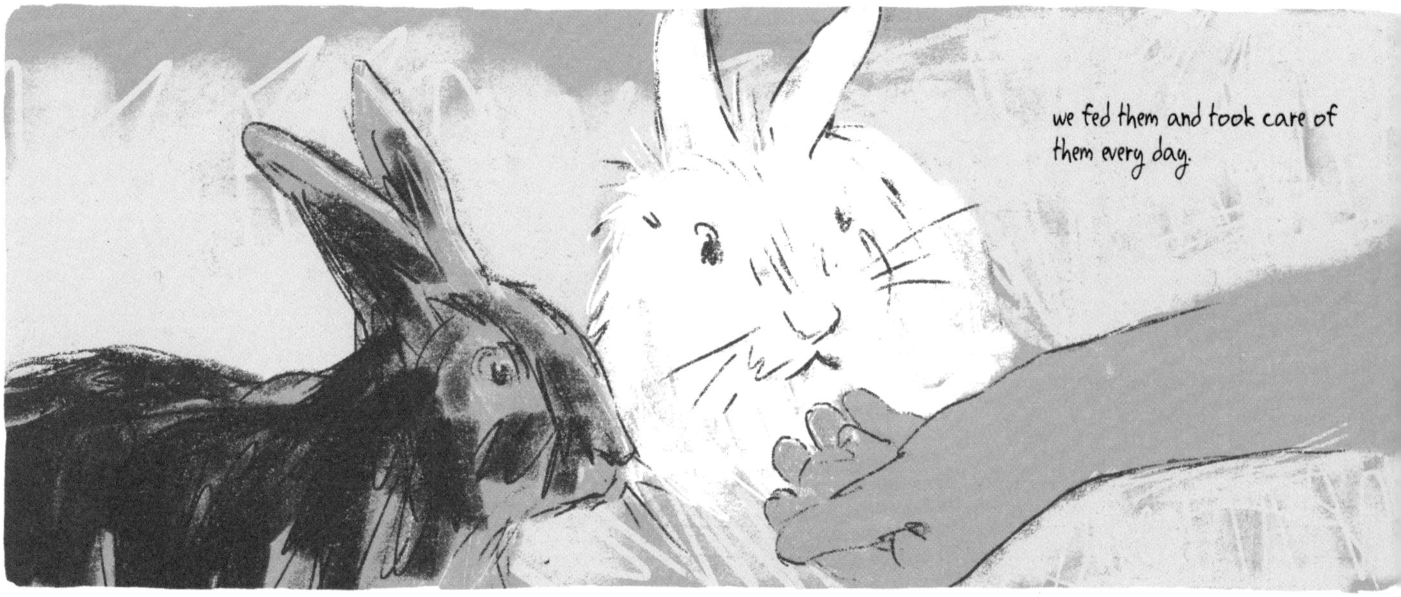
we fed them and took care of them every day.

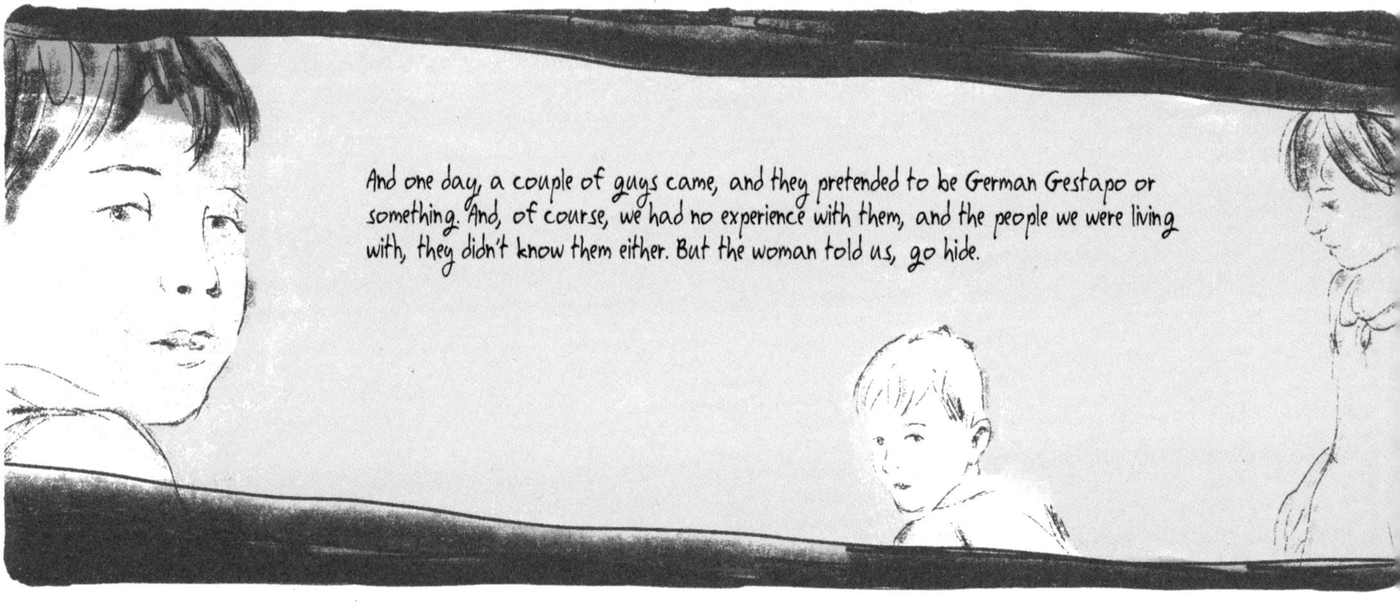
And one day, a couple of guys came, and they pretended to be German Gestapo or something. And, of course, we had no experience with them, and the people we were living with, they didn't know them either. But the woman told us, go hide.

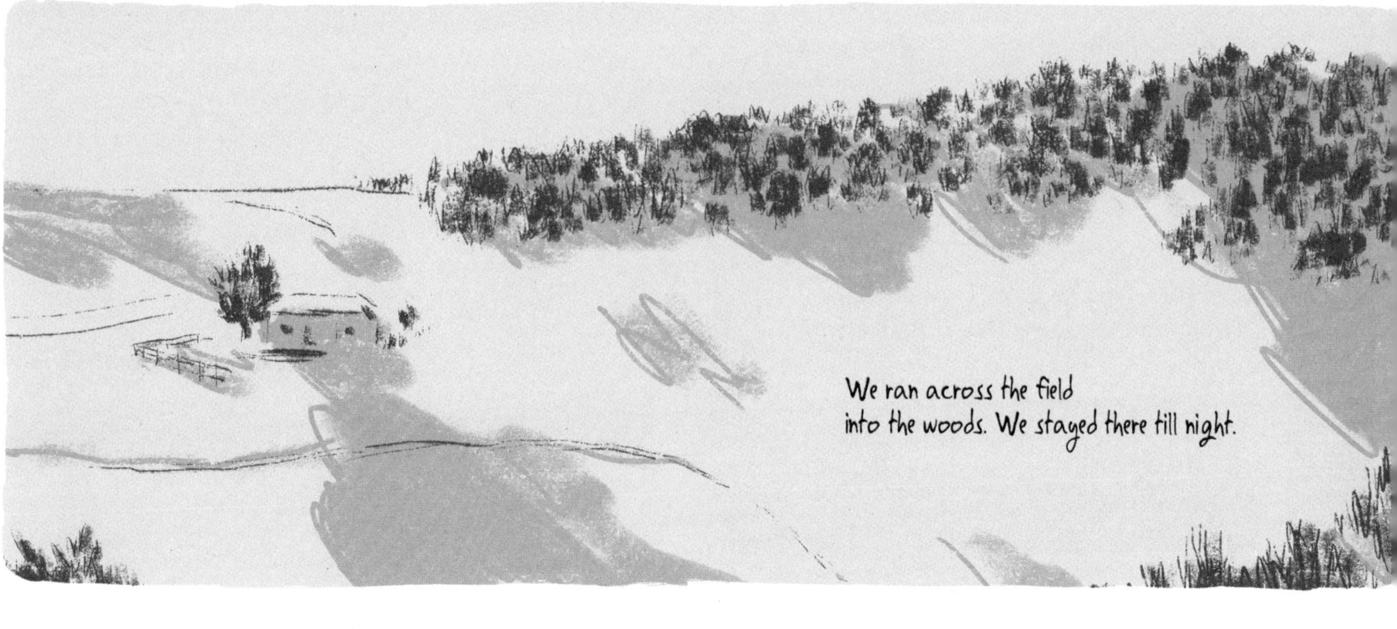
We ran across the field into the woods. We stayed there till night.

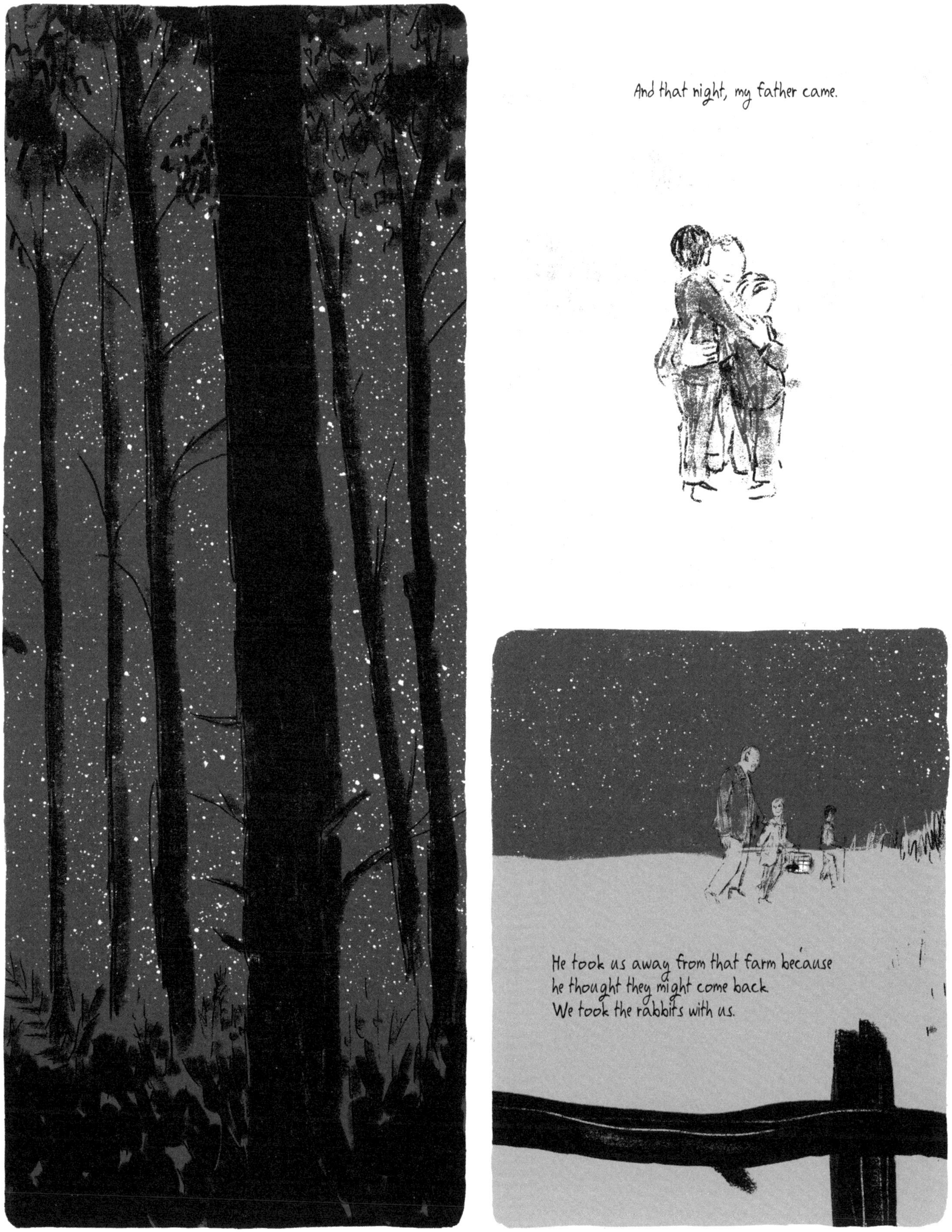
And that night, my father came.
He took us away from that farm because he thought they might come back. We took the rabbits with us.

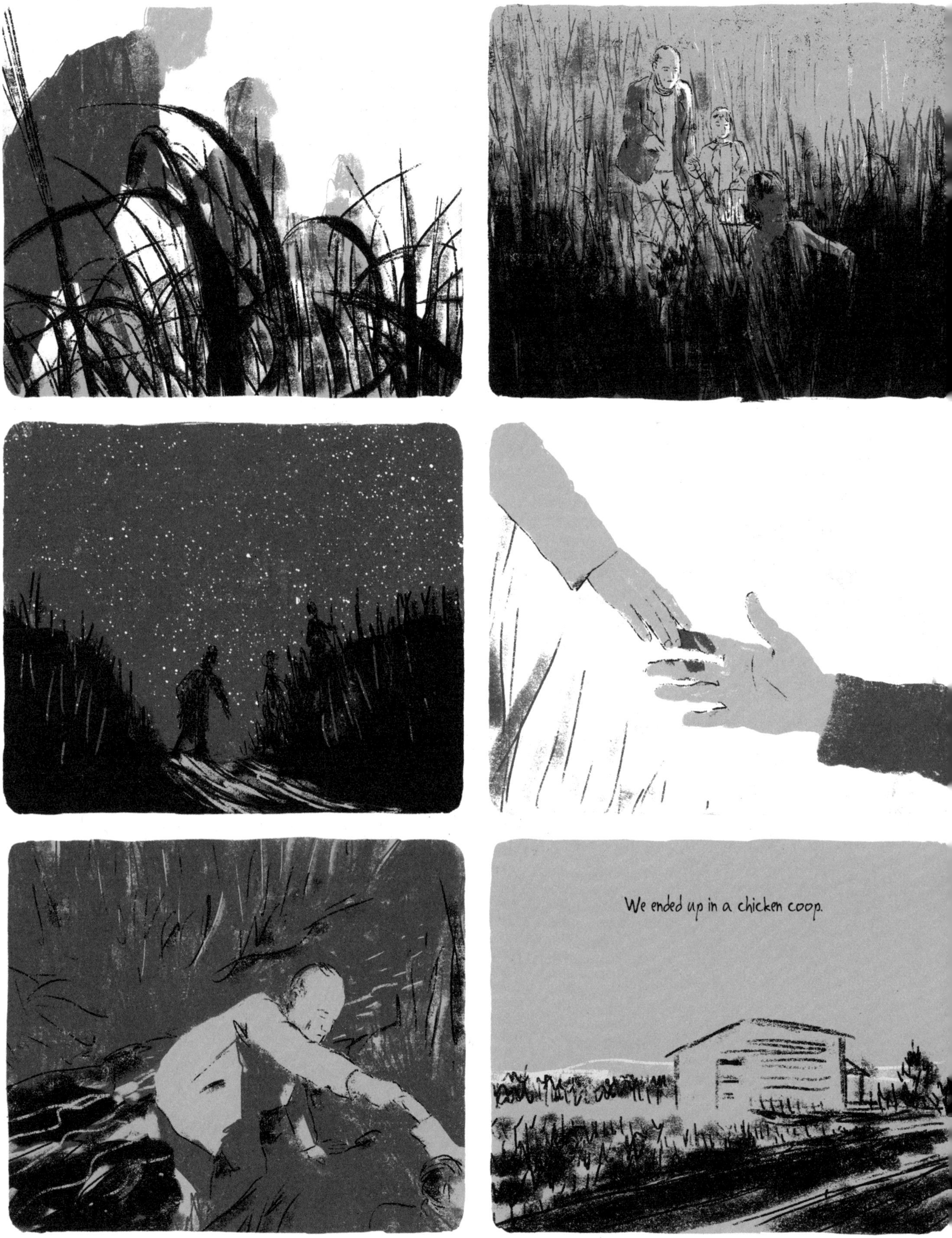
We ended up in a chicken coop.

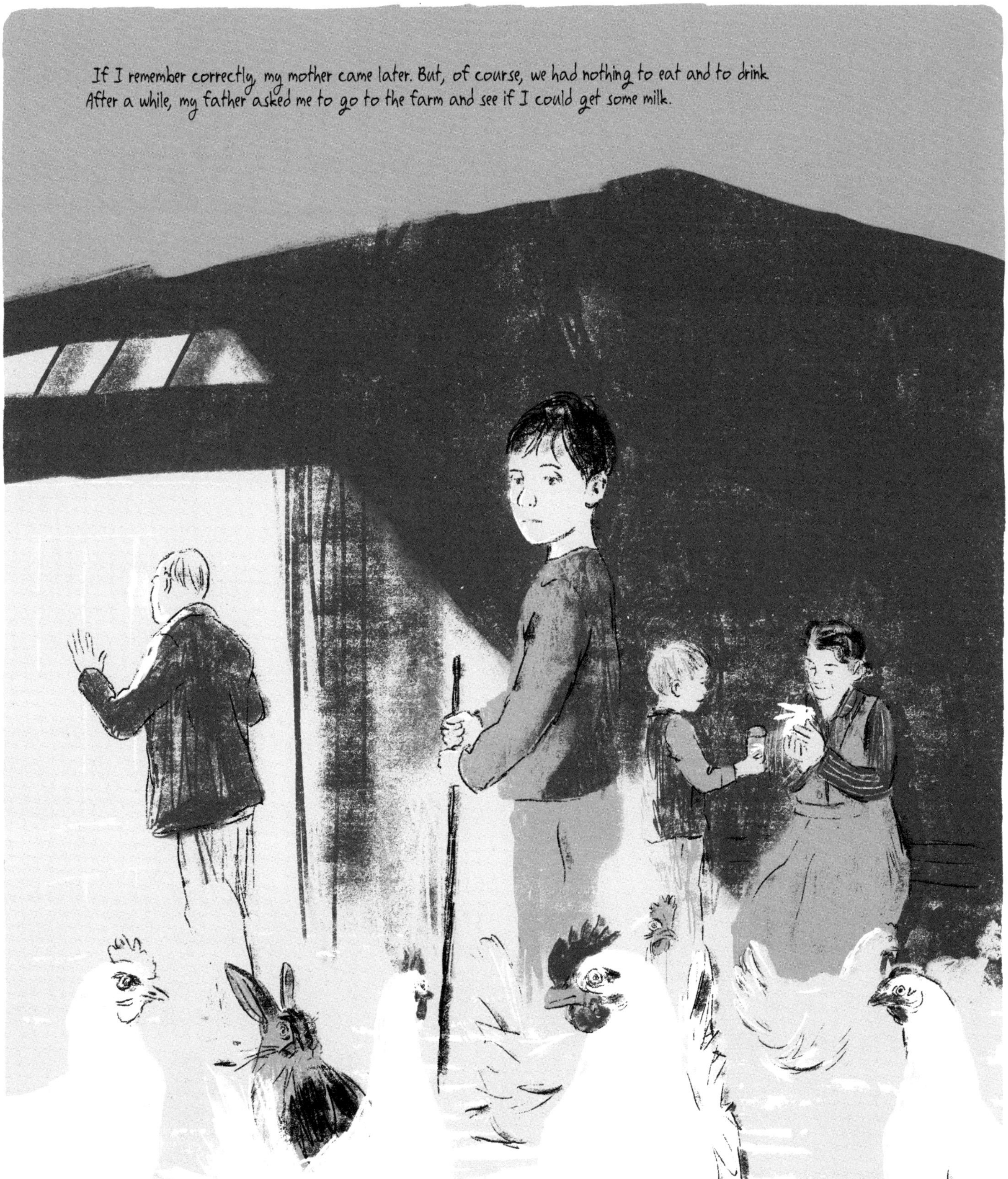
If I remember correctly, my mother came later. But, of course, we had nothing to eat and to drink.
After a while, my father asked me to go to the farm and see if I could get some milk.

I went to the farmer and I did get some milk. But he was afraid and said that we can only stay a couple of days.
In the meantime, somebody else had found a new address for us. And then we moved on.
So, in the end, we were at thirteen different addresses, including the chicken coop.

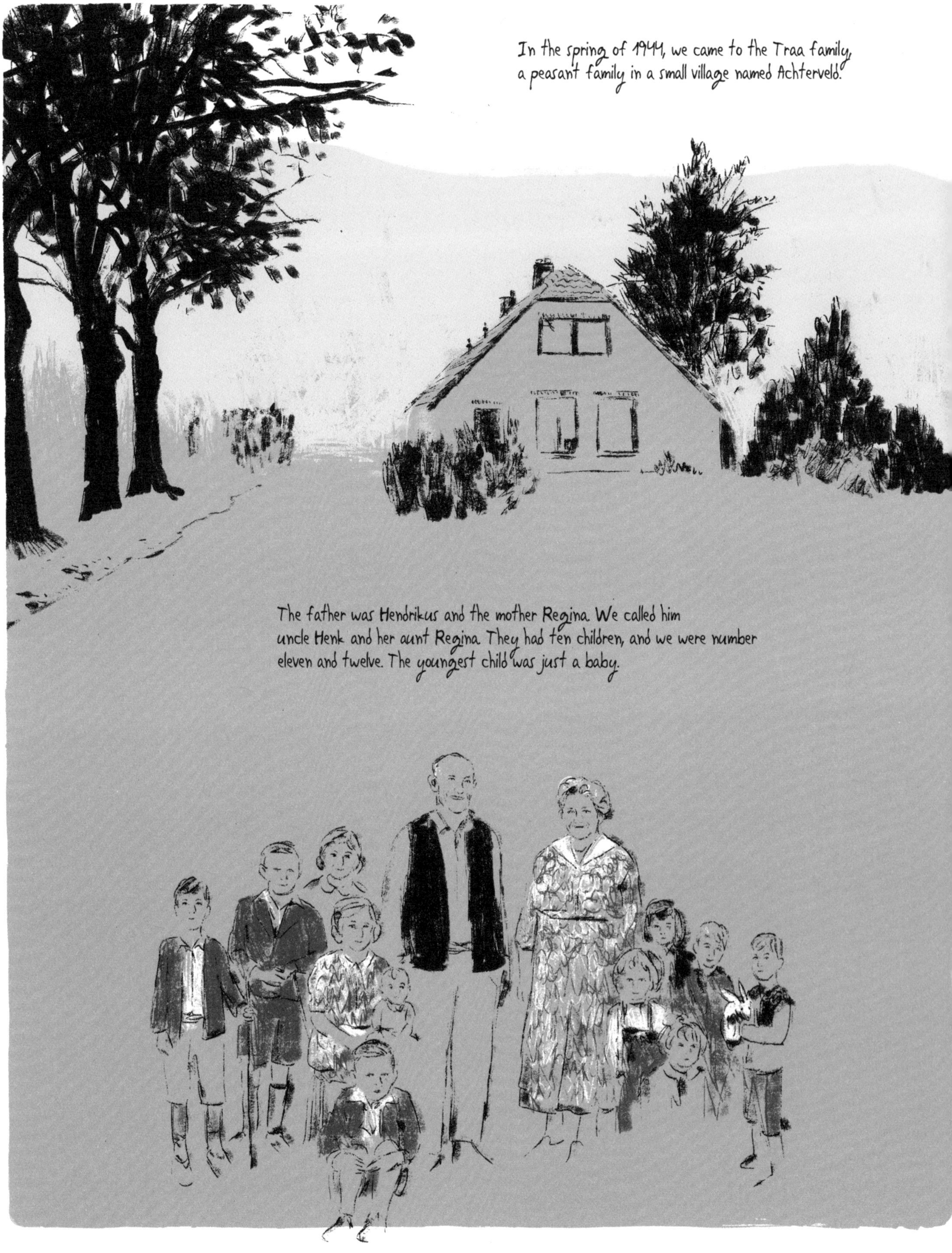
In the spring of 1944, we came to the Traa family, a peasant family in a small village named Achterveld.
The father was Hendrikus and the mother Regina. We called him uncle Henk and her aunt Regina. They had ten children, and we were number eleven and twelve. The youngest child was just a baby.

We didn't know their ways and means, and they didn't know us, so there was really culture shock on both sides. For example, at that time, many farmers didn't mind so much what was happening with hygiene. So, the baby walked in while we were eating and crawled up on the table.

We used to go to bed early because we had no electric light, and you got up early as well. We didn't go to school. But we helped on the farm. And every two weeks, we had to take a bath in a tub. For the tub, we had to take the wood, go to the kitchen, heat the water, and then pour the tub.
Luckily, we had a small running river nearby, and in the summer, we could wash ourselves there.

The family had two helpers: a fourteen-year-old girl named Phietje, and Marinus, a boy in his early twenties.
He was hiding out of fear of being sent to Germany to work in some kind of slave labor camp.
Later, Hendrik Oppenheimer, a photographer and Jew from Holland who was around thirty, came to hide.
People came and left, and by the end of the war, we were seventeen people on the farm.

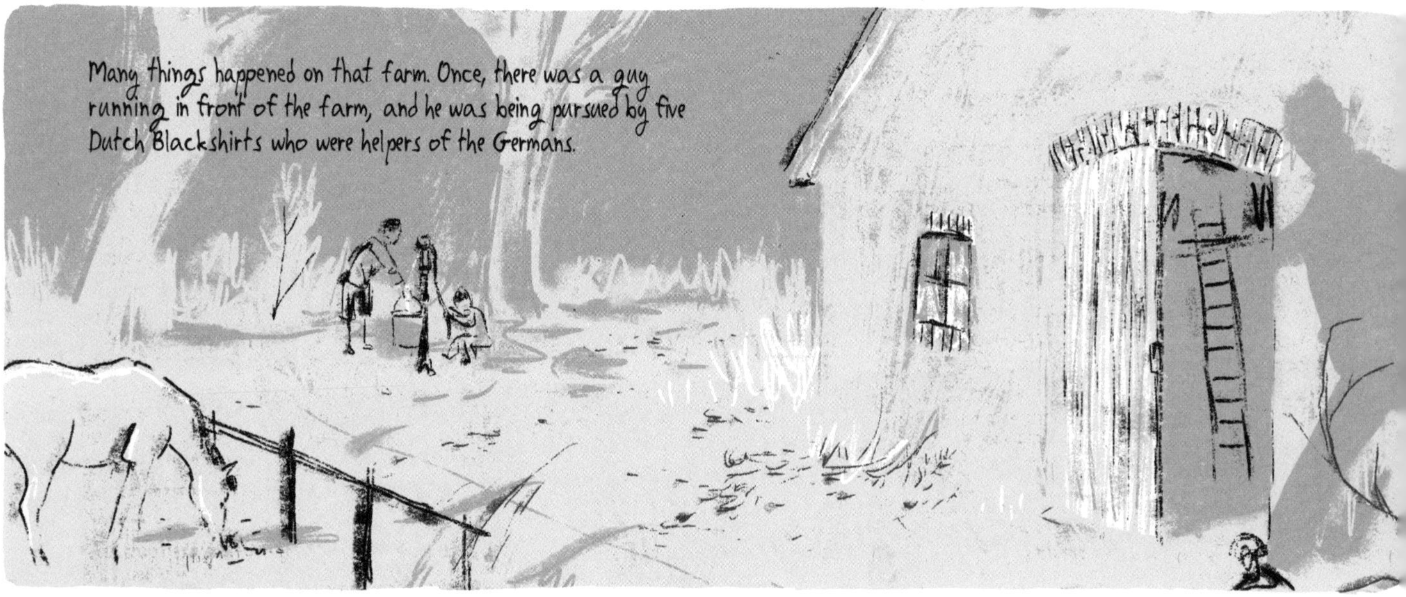
Many things happened on that farm. Once, there was a guy running in front of the farm, and he was being pursued by five Dutch Blackshirts who were helpers of the Germans.

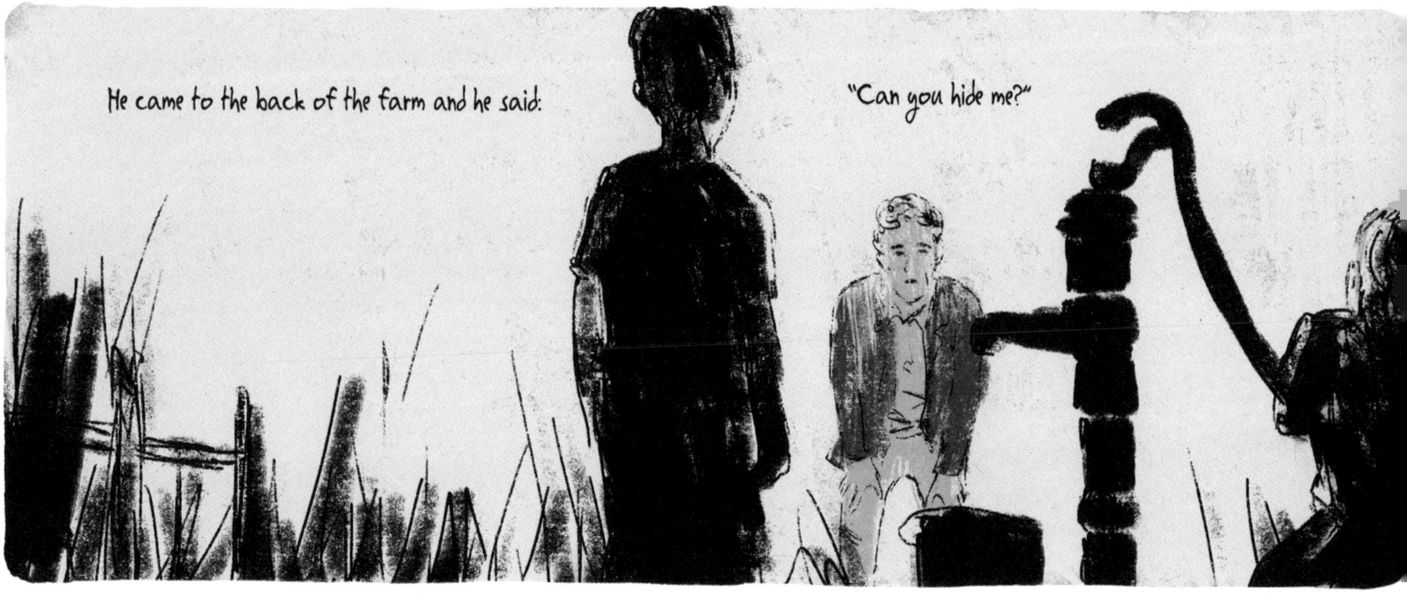
He came to the back of the farm and he said:
"Can you hide me?"

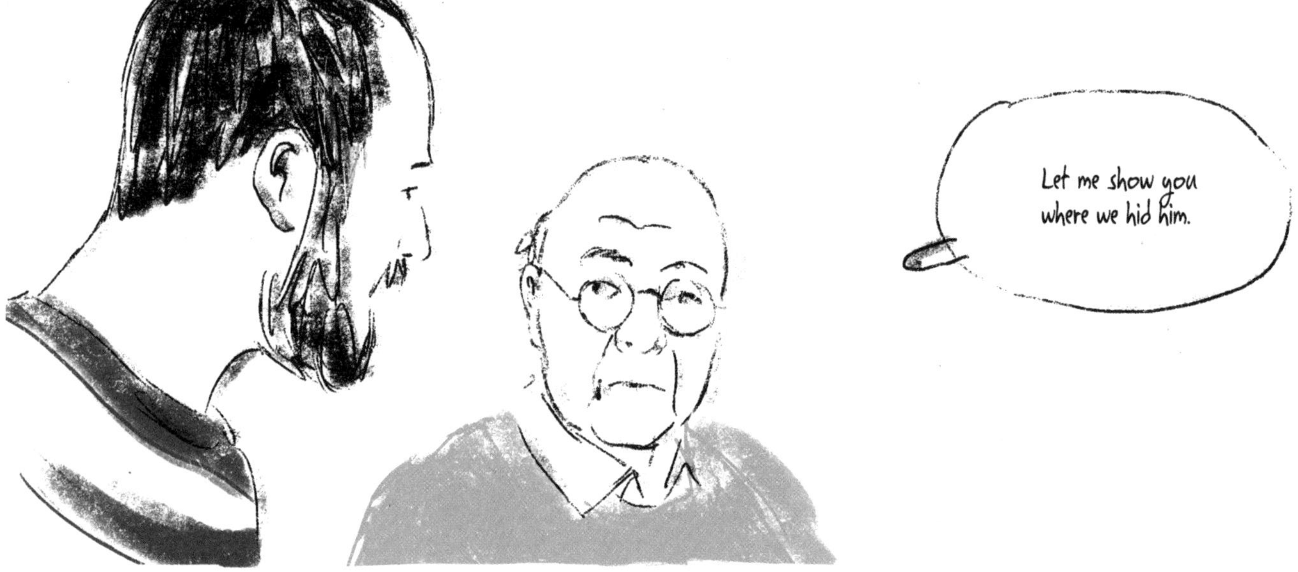
Let me show you where we hid him.

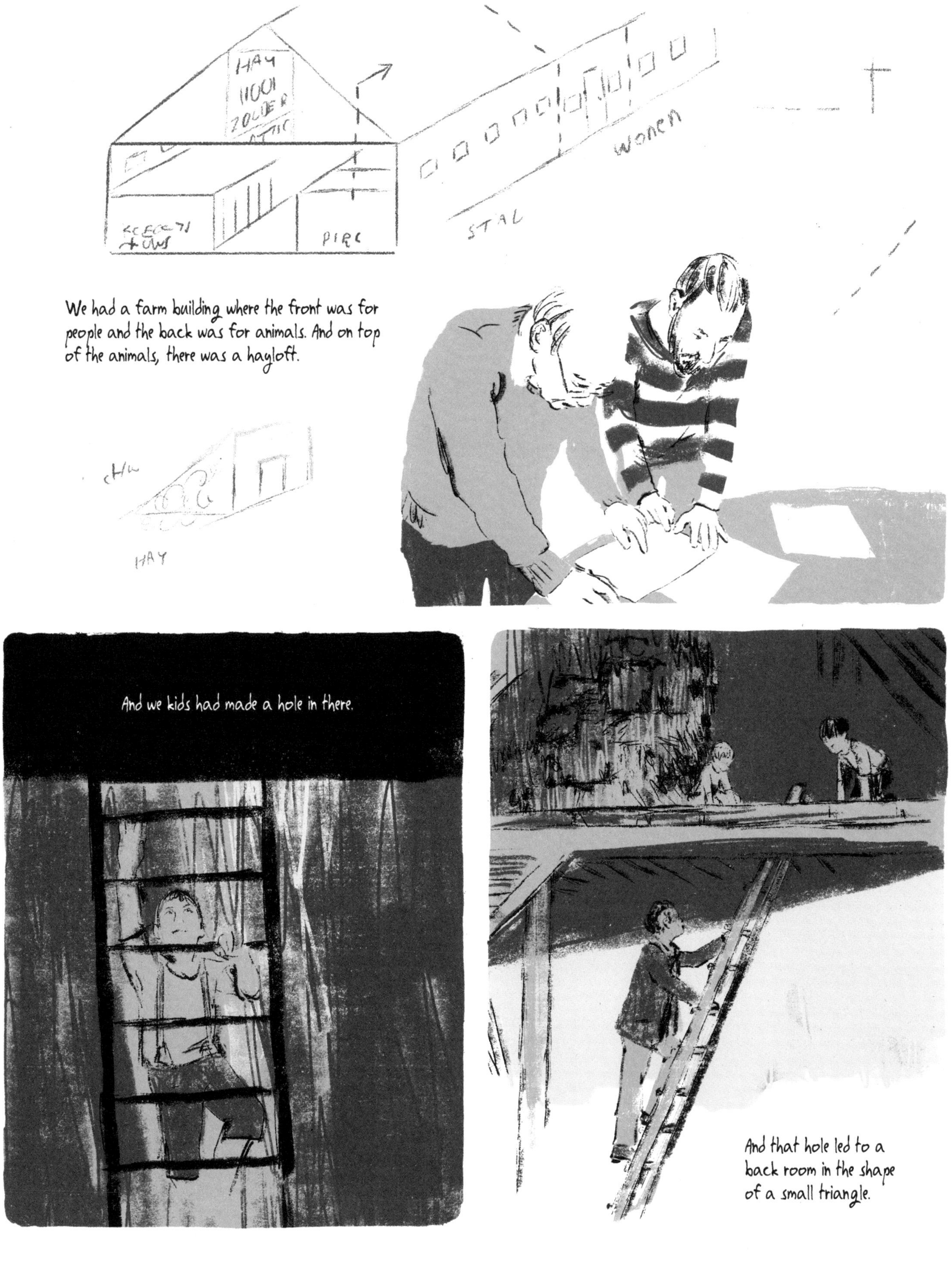
HAY
ZOLDER
WOMEN
STAL
We had a farm building where the front was for people and the back was for animals. And on top of the animals, there was a hayloft.
HAY
And we kids had made a hole in there.
And that hole led to a back room in the shape of a small triangle.

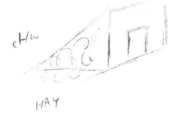

So, I said, go in there and I closed the front with hay.

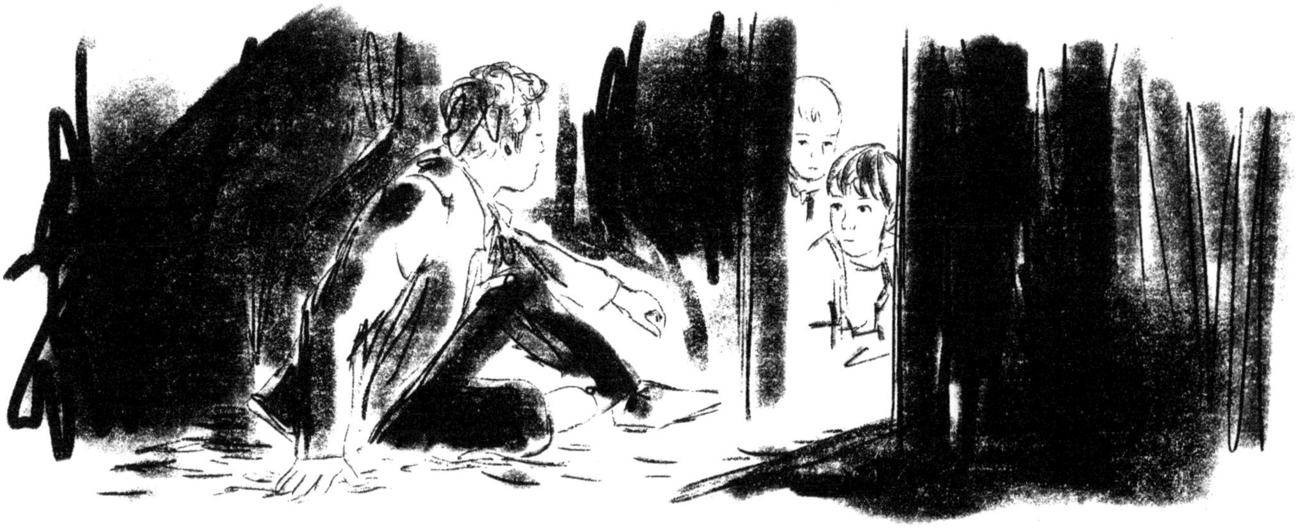

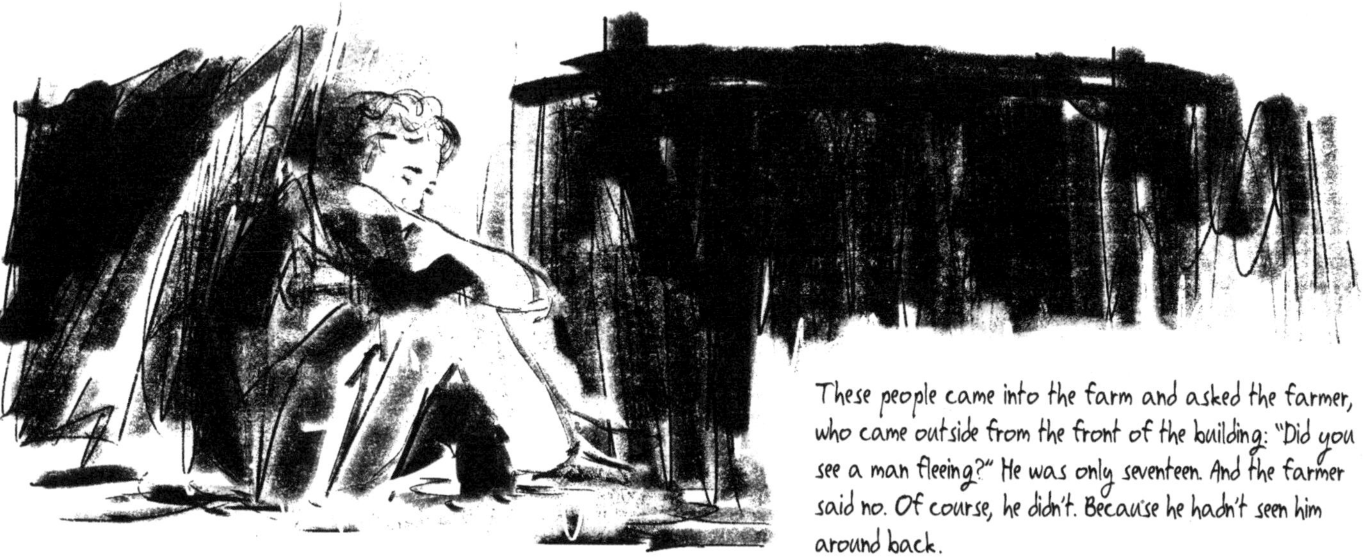

These people came into the farm and asked the farmer, who came outside from the front of the building: "Did you see a man fleeing?" He was only seventeen. And the farmer said no. Of course, he didn't. Because he hadn't seen him around back.

At night we had dinner and I said to the farmer when we were finished: "Can I have another plate of food?"

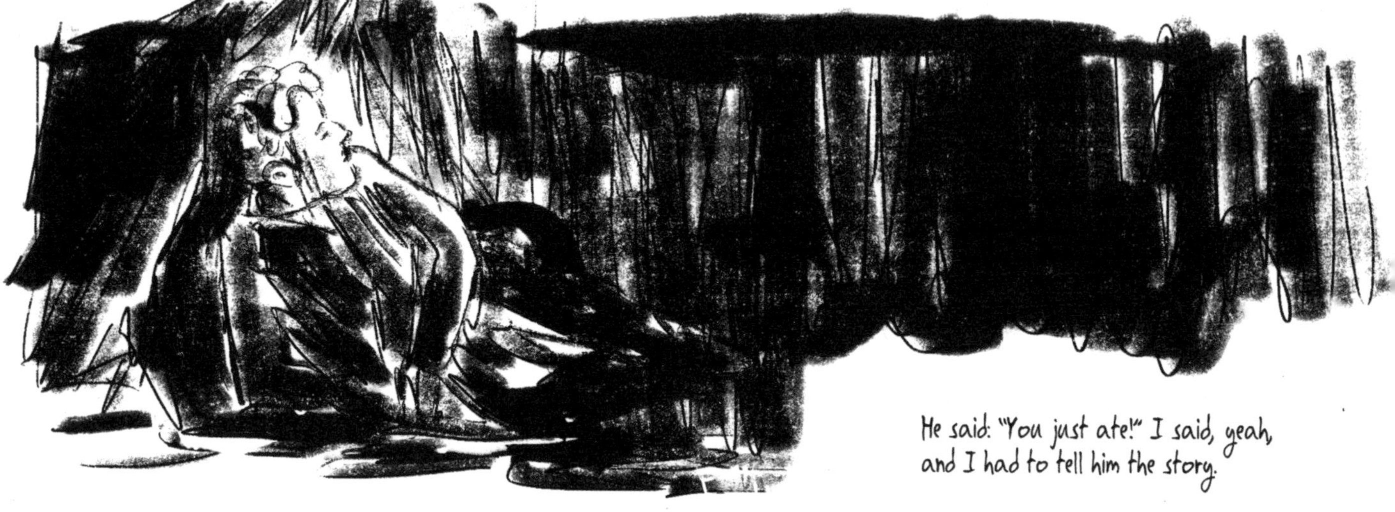

He said: "You just ate!" I said, yeah, and I had to tell him the story.

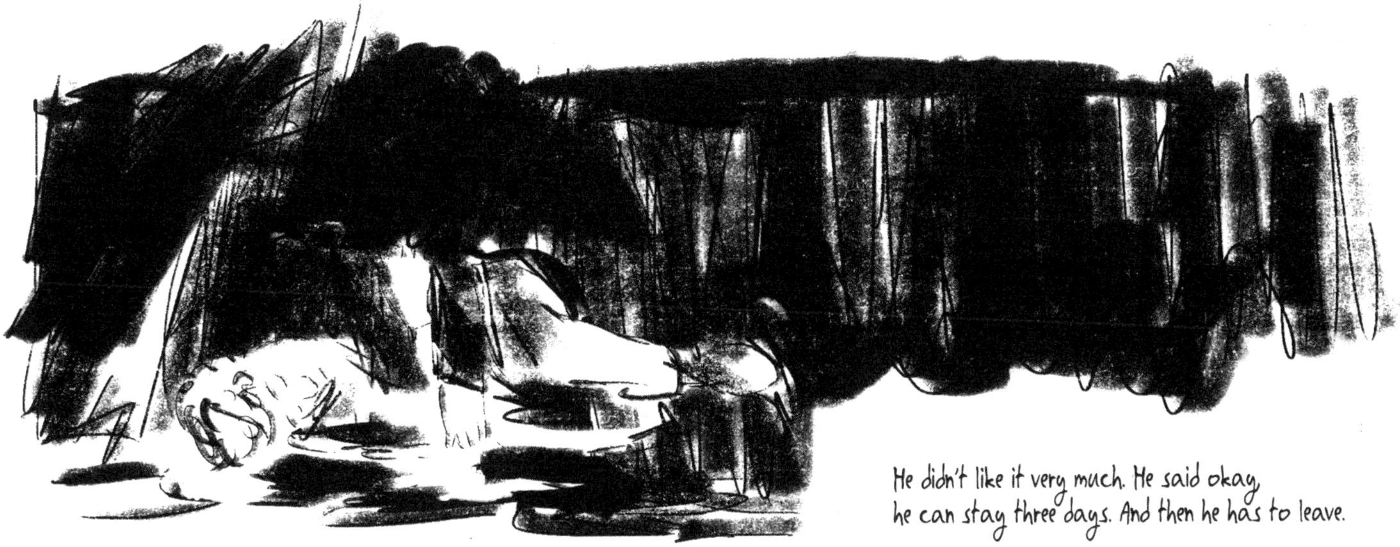
He didn't like it very much. He said okay, he can stay three days. And then he has to leave.

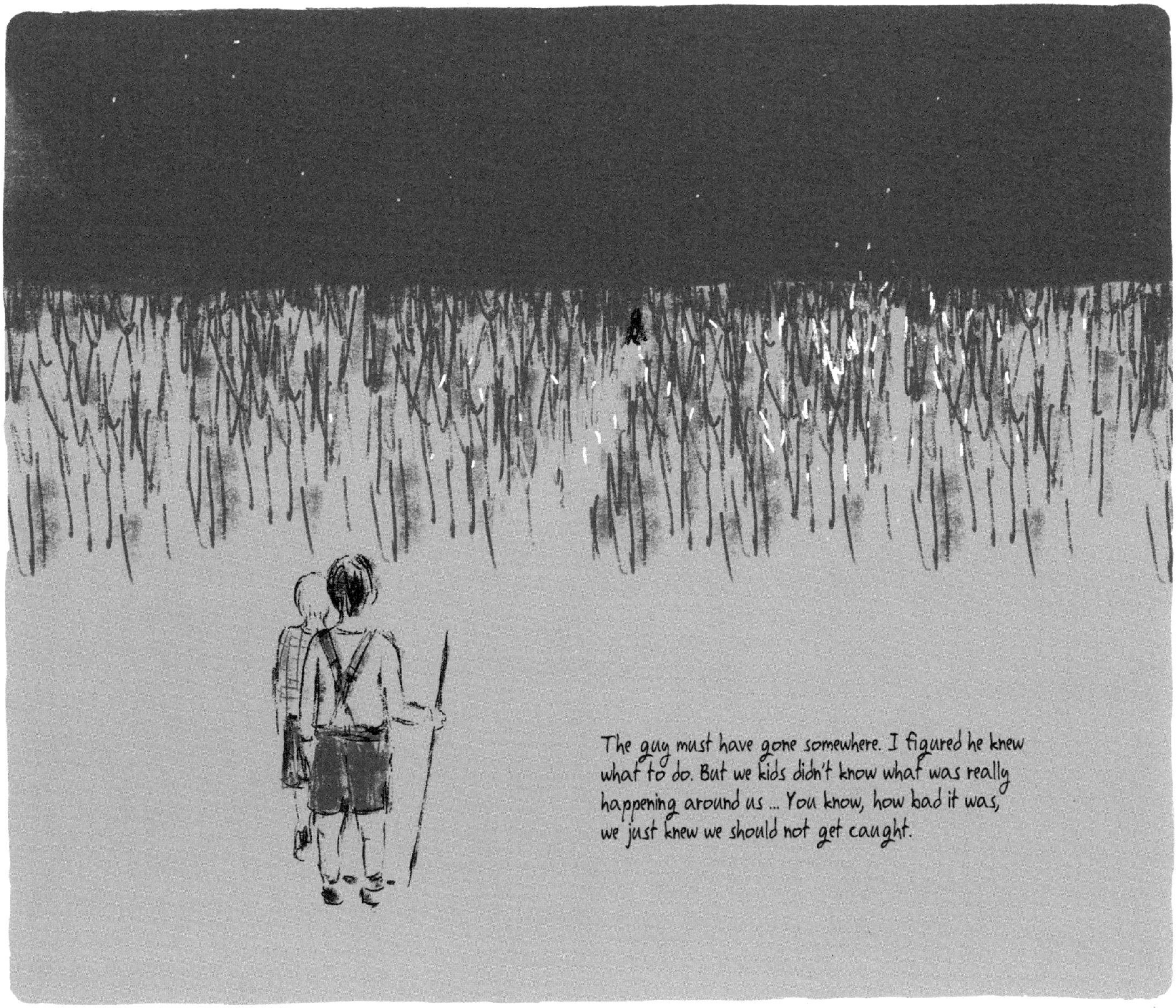
The guy must have gone somewhere. I figured he knew what to do. But we kids didn't know what was really happening around us ... You know, how bad it was, we just knew we should not get caught.

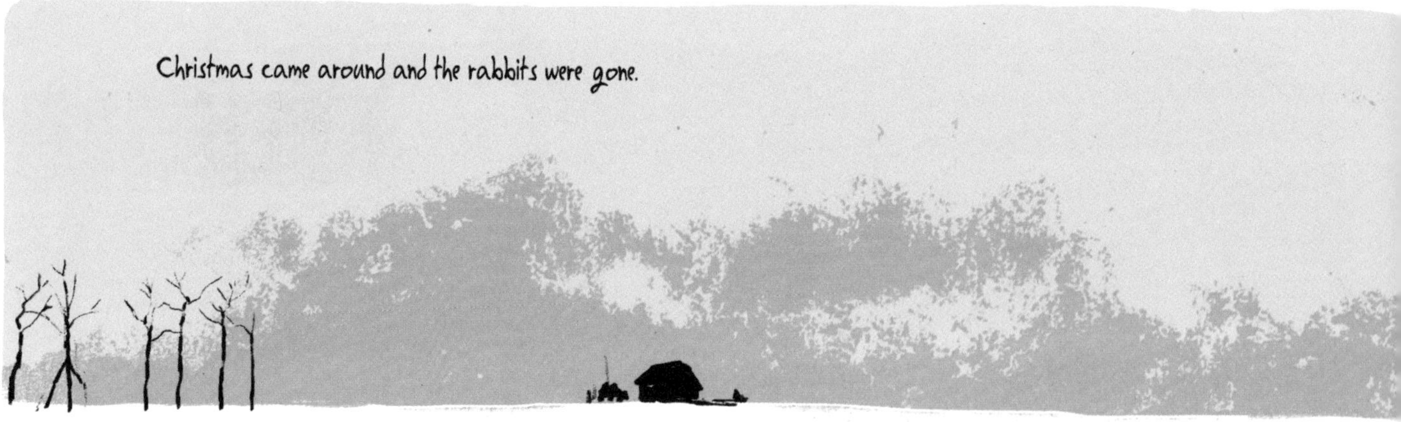
Christmas came around and the rabbits were gone.

The family said that they had escaped.

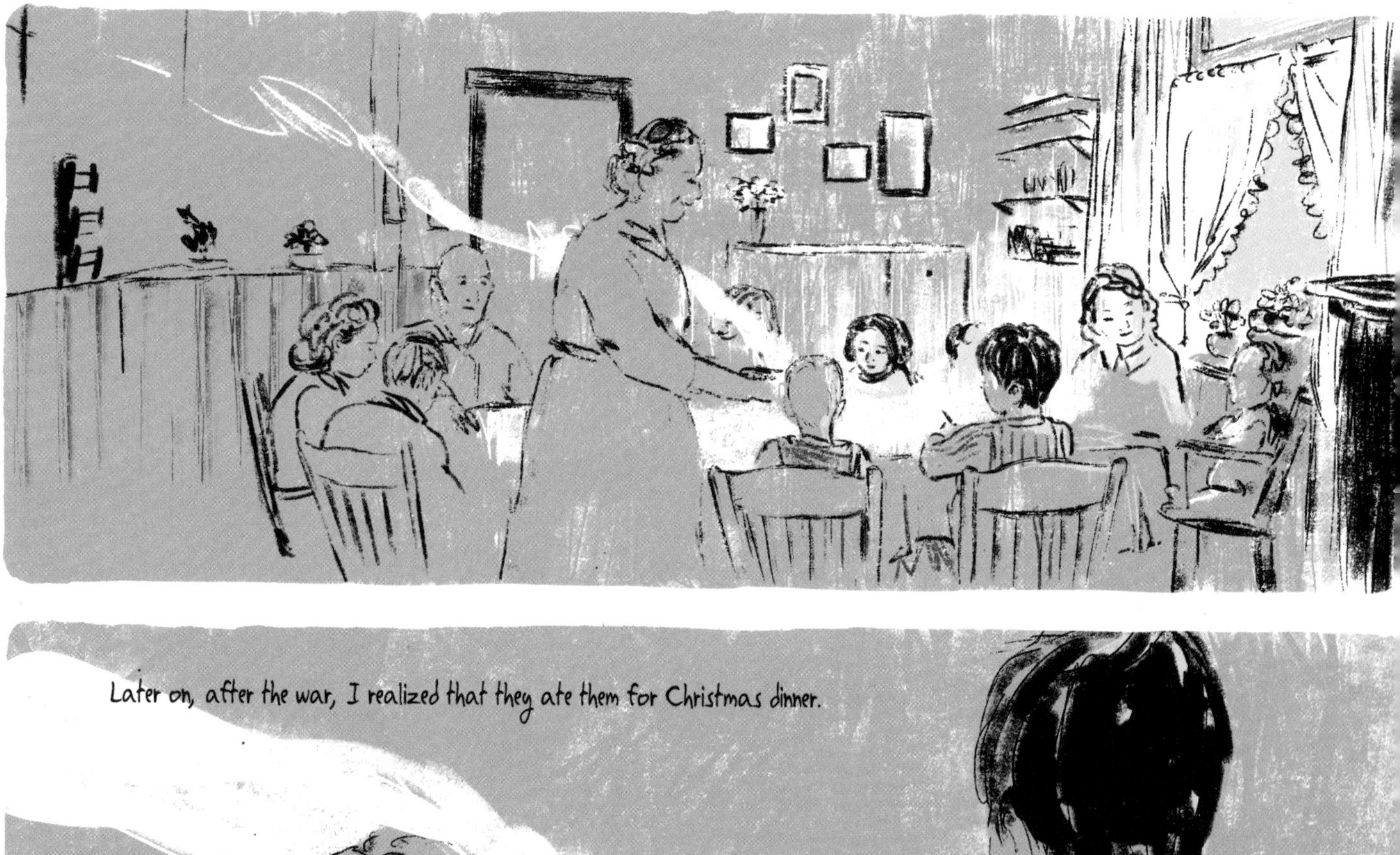

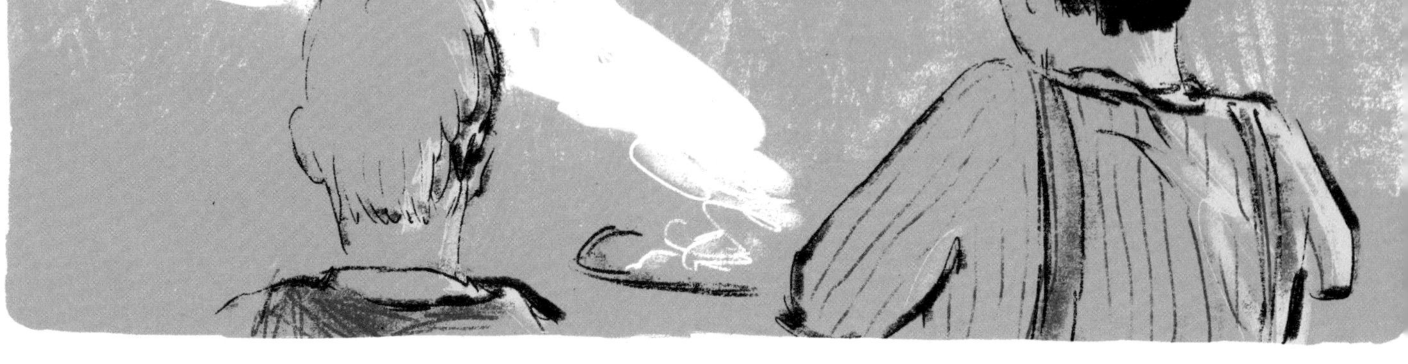
Later on, after the war, I realized that they ate them for Christmas dinner.

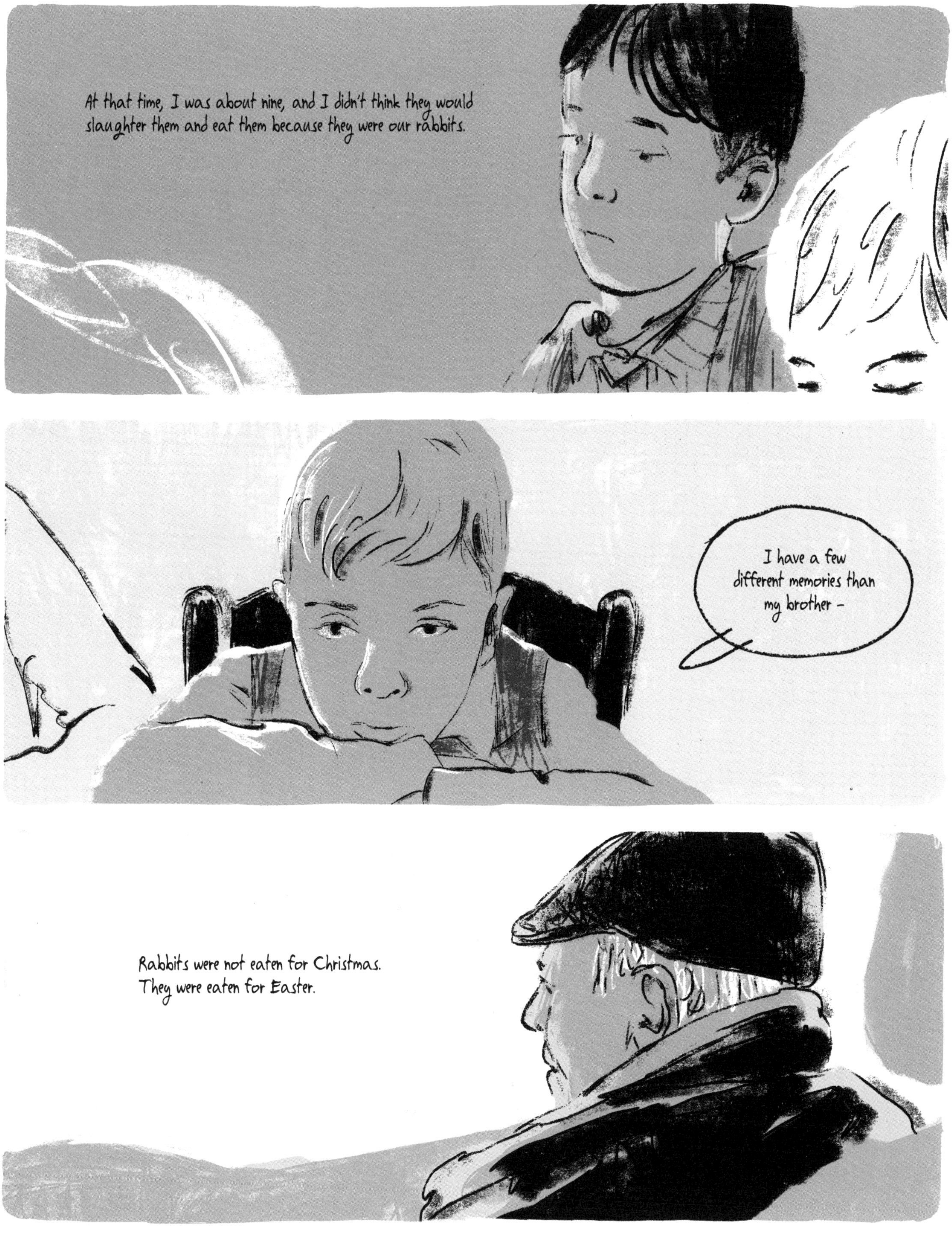
At that time, I was about nine, and I didn't think they would slaughter them and eat them because they were our rabbits.
I have a few different memories than my brother –
Rabbits were not eaten for Christmas. They were eaten for Easter.

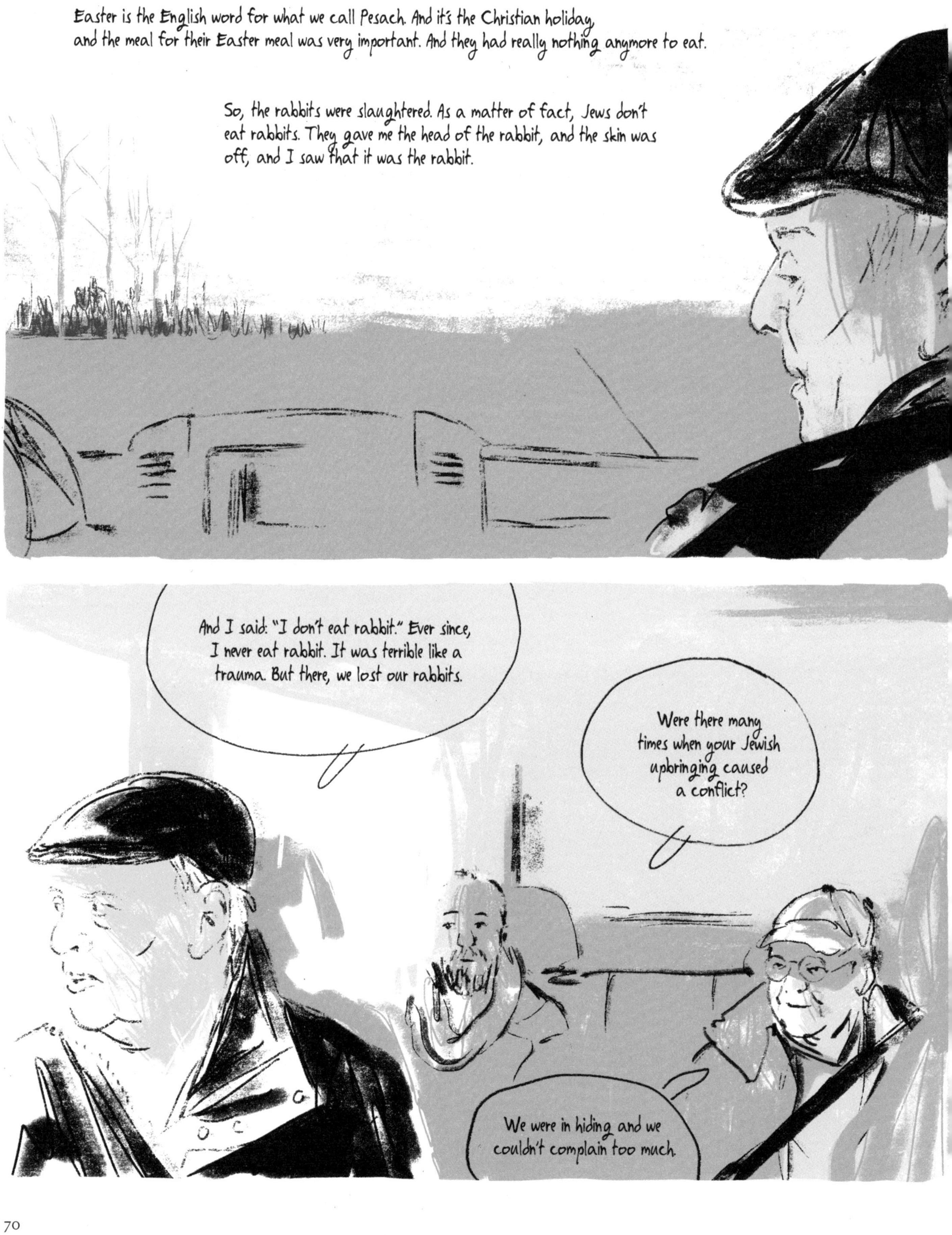
Easter is the English word for what we call Pesach. And it's the Christian holiday, and the meal for their Easter meal was very important. And they had really nothing anymore to eat.
So, the rabbits were slaughtered. As a matter of fact, Jews don't eat rabbits. They gave me the head of the rabbit, and the skin was off, and I saw that it was the rabbit.
And I said: "I don't eat rabbit." Ever since, I never eat rabbit. It was terrible like a trauma. But there, we lost our rabbits.
Were there many times when your Jewish upbringing caused a conflict?
We were in hiding and we couldn't complain too much.

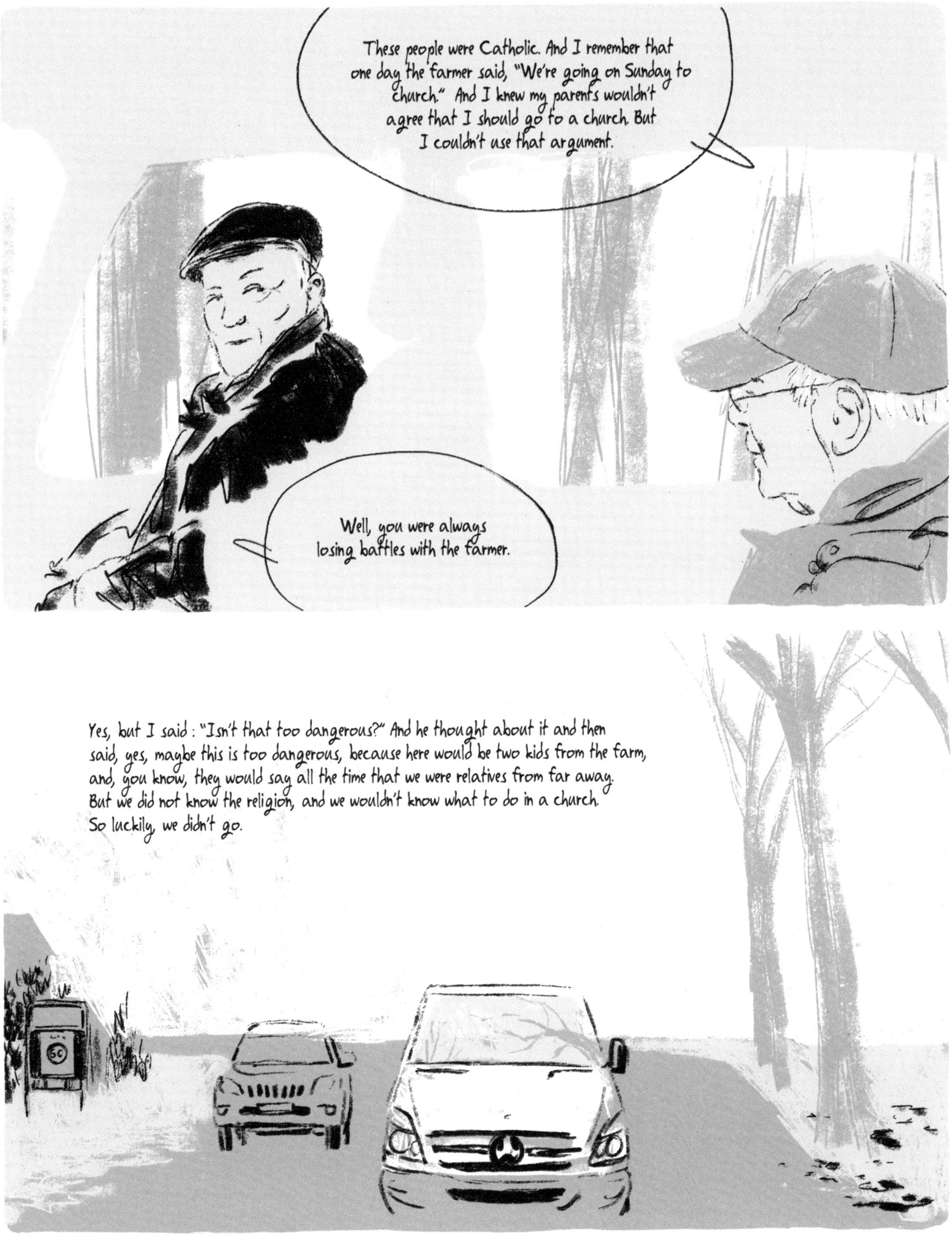
These people were Catholic. And I remember that one day the farmer said, "We're going on Sunday to church." And I knew my parents wouldn't agree that I should go to a church. But I couldn't use that argument.
Well, you were always losing battles with the farmer.
Yes, but I said: "Isn't that too dangerous?" And he thought about it and then said, yes, maybe this is too dangerous, because here would be two kids from the farm, and, you know, they would say all the time that we were relatives from far away. But we did not know the religion, and we wouldn't know what to do in a church. So luckily, we didn't go.

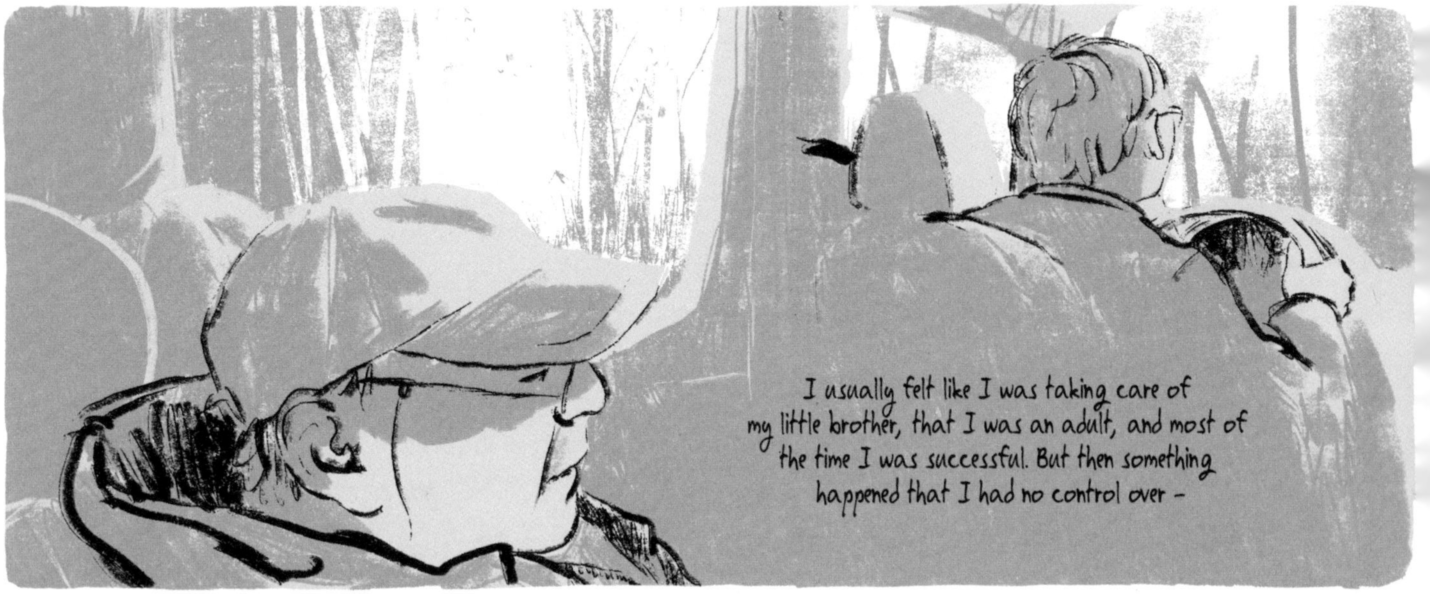
I usually felt like I was taking care of my little brother, that I was an adult, and most of the time I was successful. But then something happened that I had no control over –

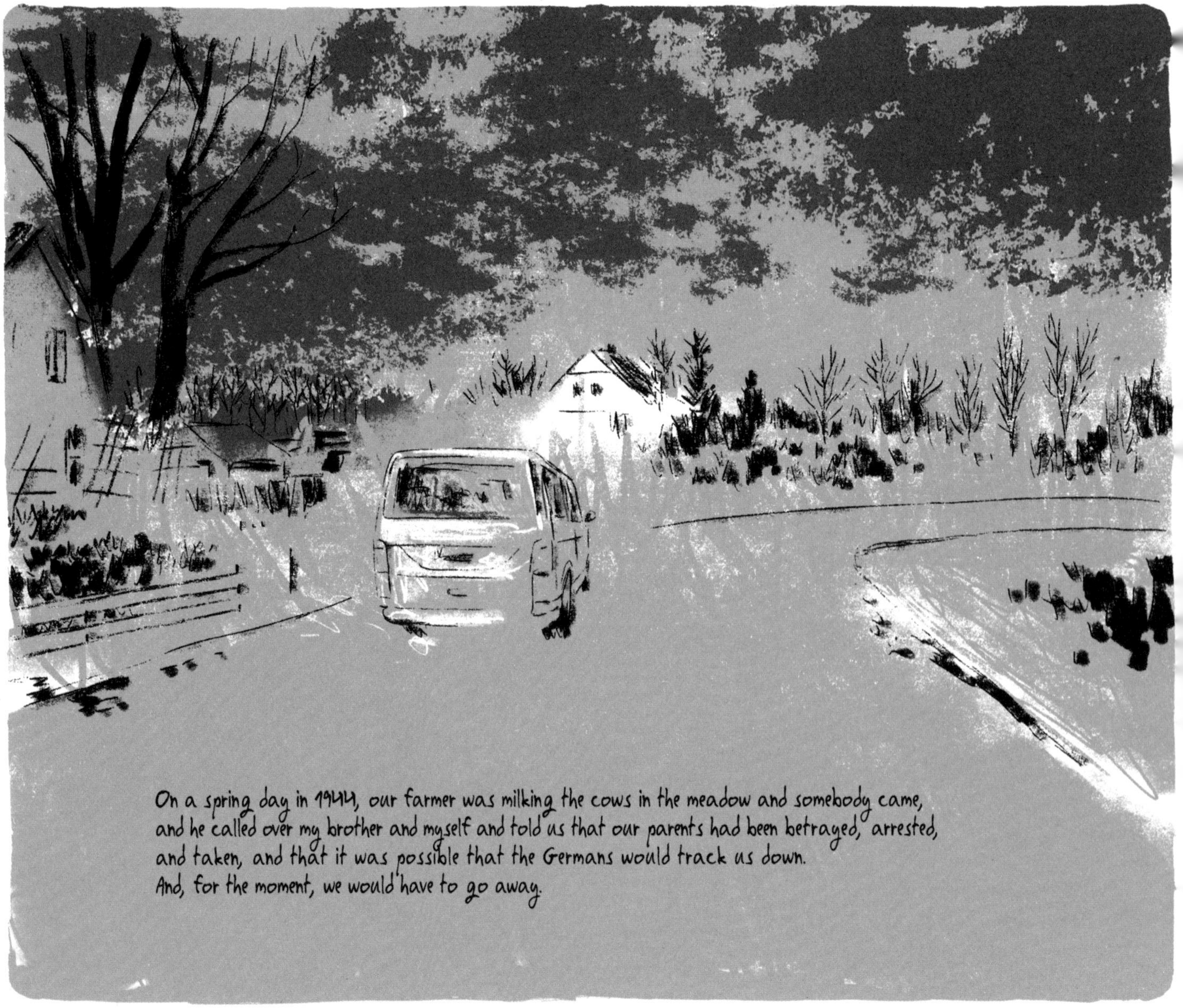
On a spring day in 1944, our farmer was milking the cows in the meadow and somebody came, and he called over my brother and myself and told us that our parents had been betrayed, arrested, and taken, and that it was possible that the Germans would track us down.
And, for the moment, we would have to go away.

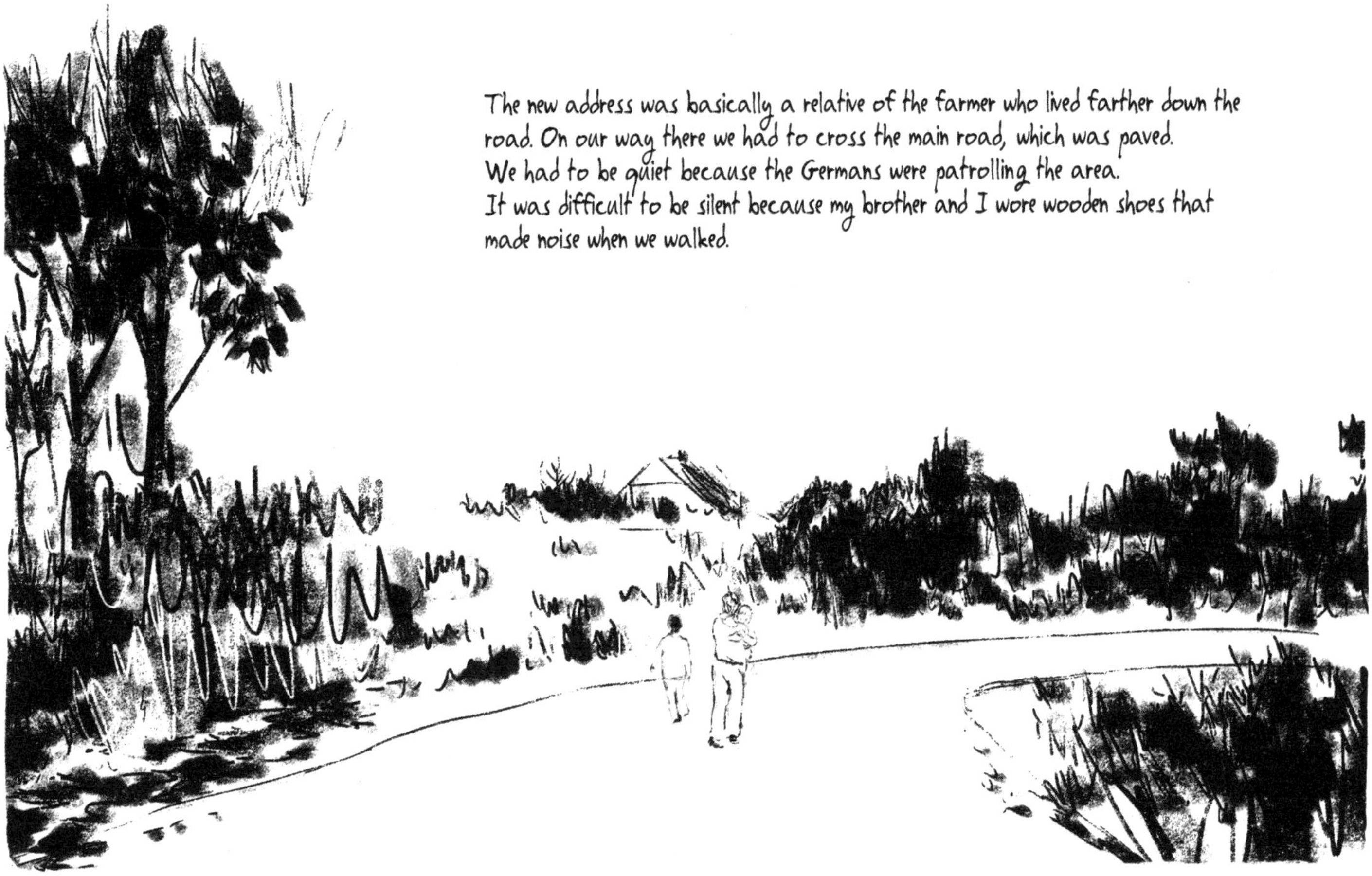
The new address was basically a relative of the farmer who lived farther down the road. On our way there we had to cross the main road, which was paved.
We had to be quiet because the Germans were patrolling the area.
It was difficult to be silent because my brother and I wore wooden shoes that made noise when we walked.

Marinus, who was also in danger himself, accompanied us there. And he took Nico under his arm.

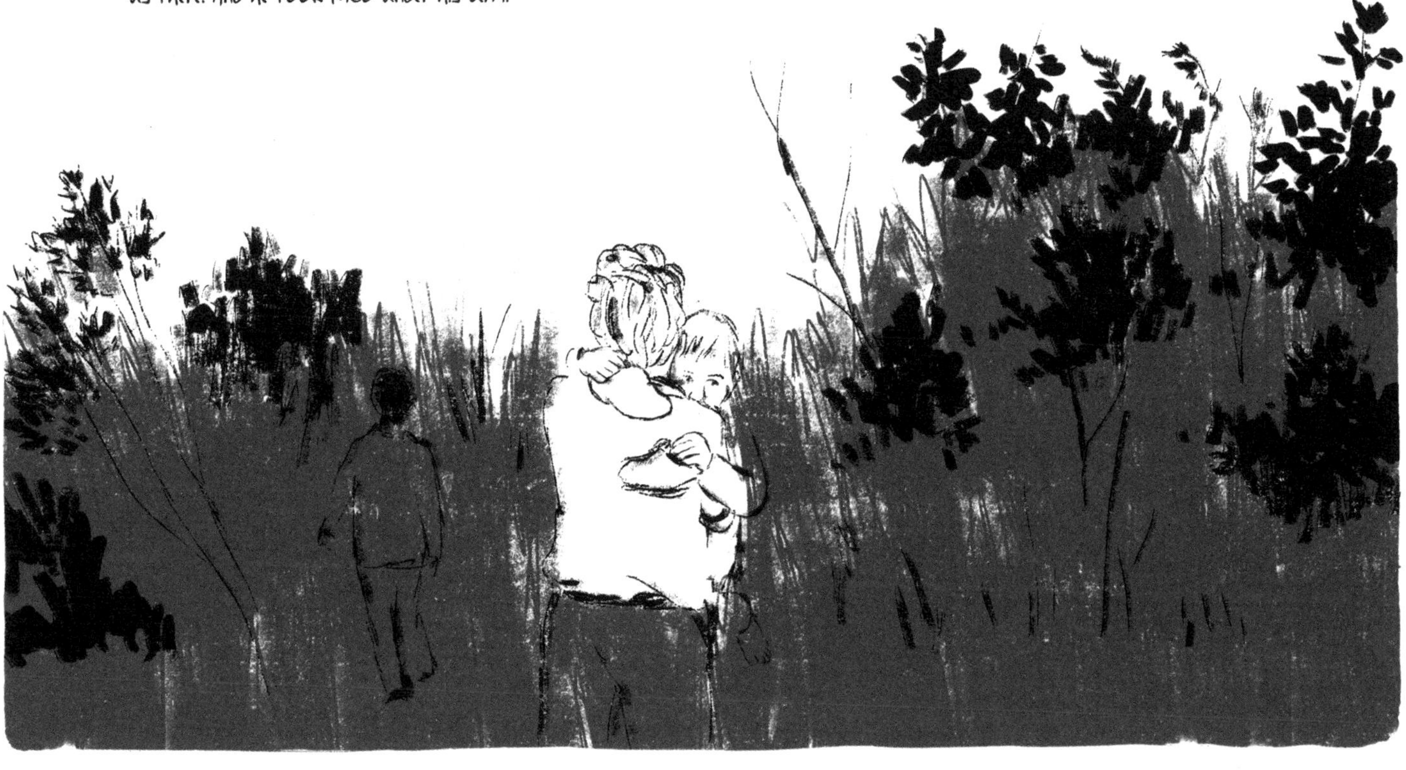

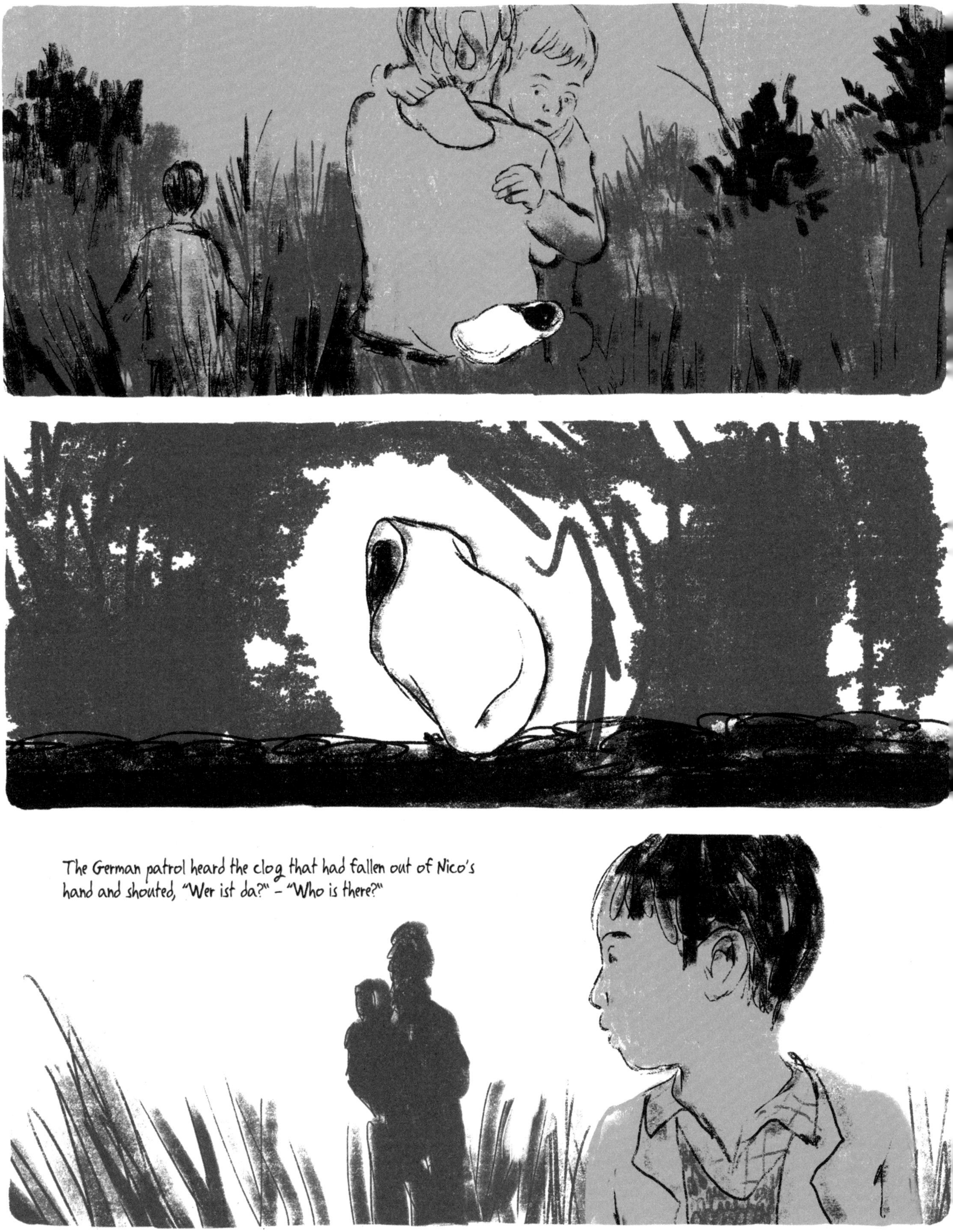
The German patrol heard the clog that had fallen out of Nico's hand and shouted, "Wer ist da?" – "Who is there?"

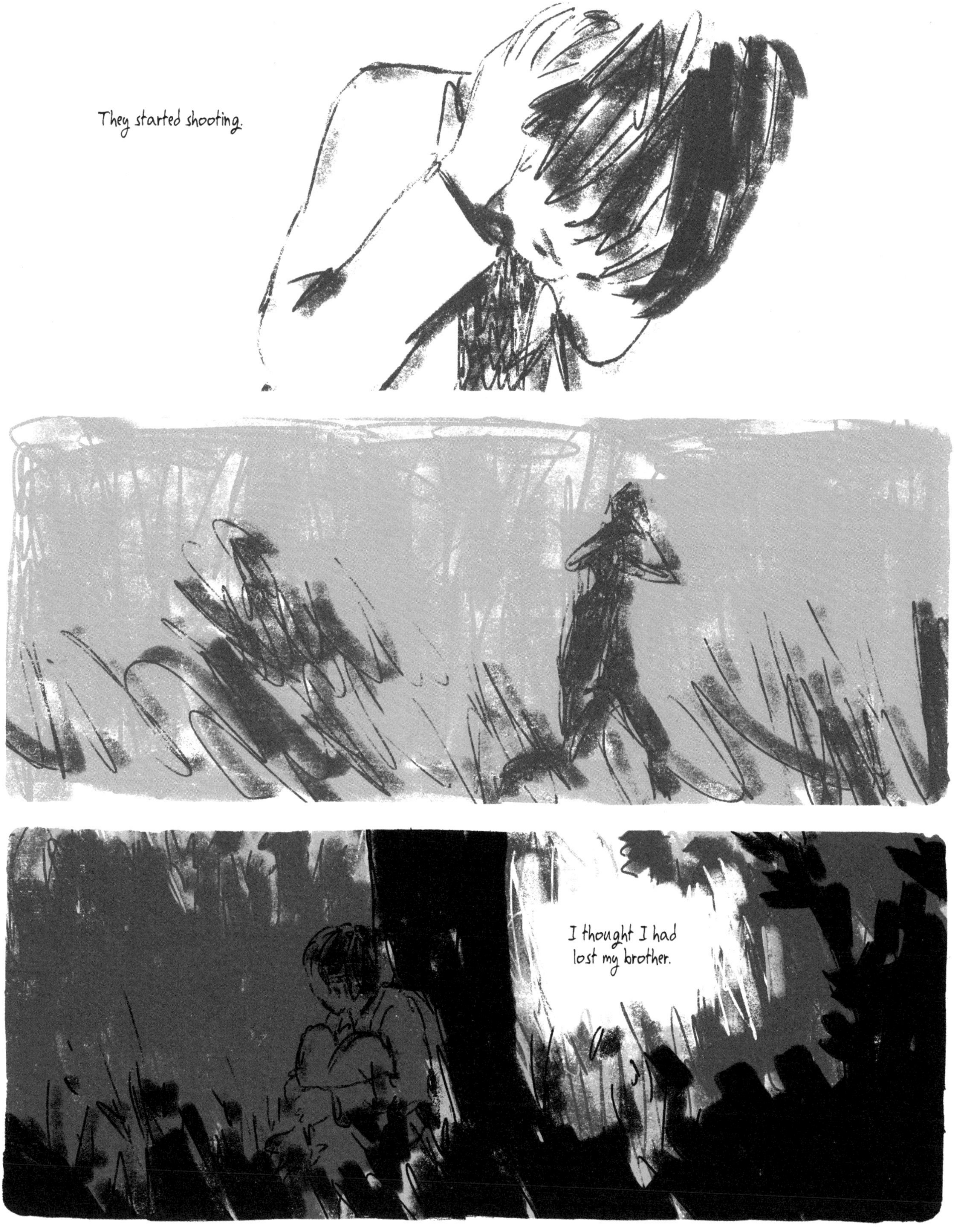
They started shooting.
I thought I had
lost my brother.

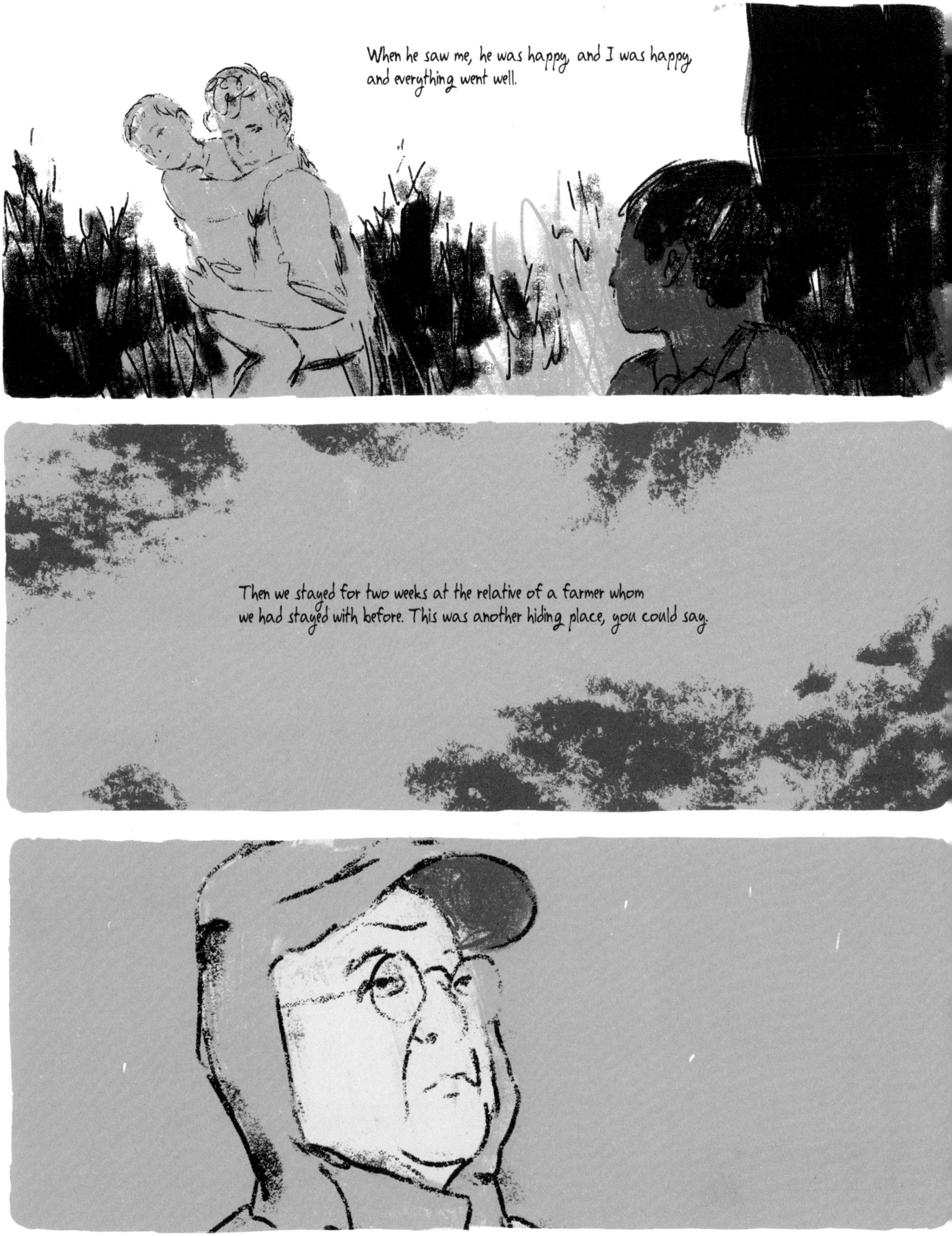
When he saw me, he was happy, and I was happy, and everything went well.
Then we stayed for two weeks at the relative of a farmer whom we had stayed with before. This was another hiding place, you could say.

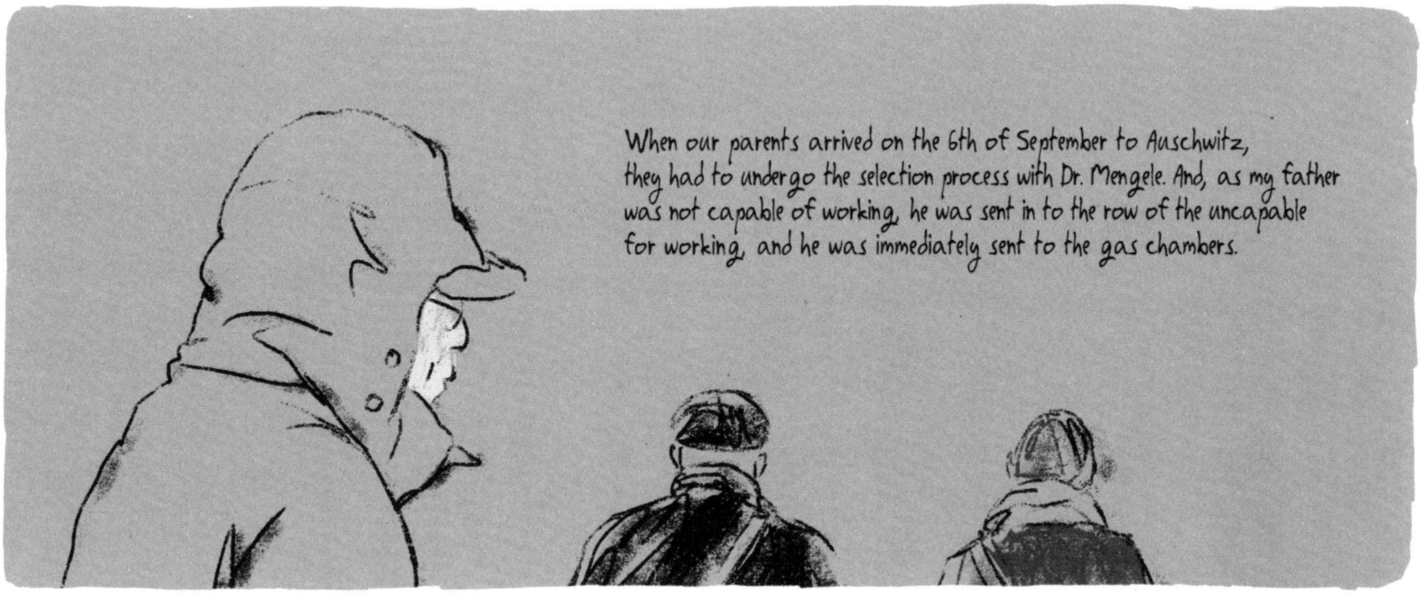
When our parents arrived on the 6th of September to Auschwitz, they had to undergo the selection process with Dr. Mengele. And, as my father was not capable of working, he was sent in to the row of the uncapable for working, and he was immediately sent to the gas chambers.

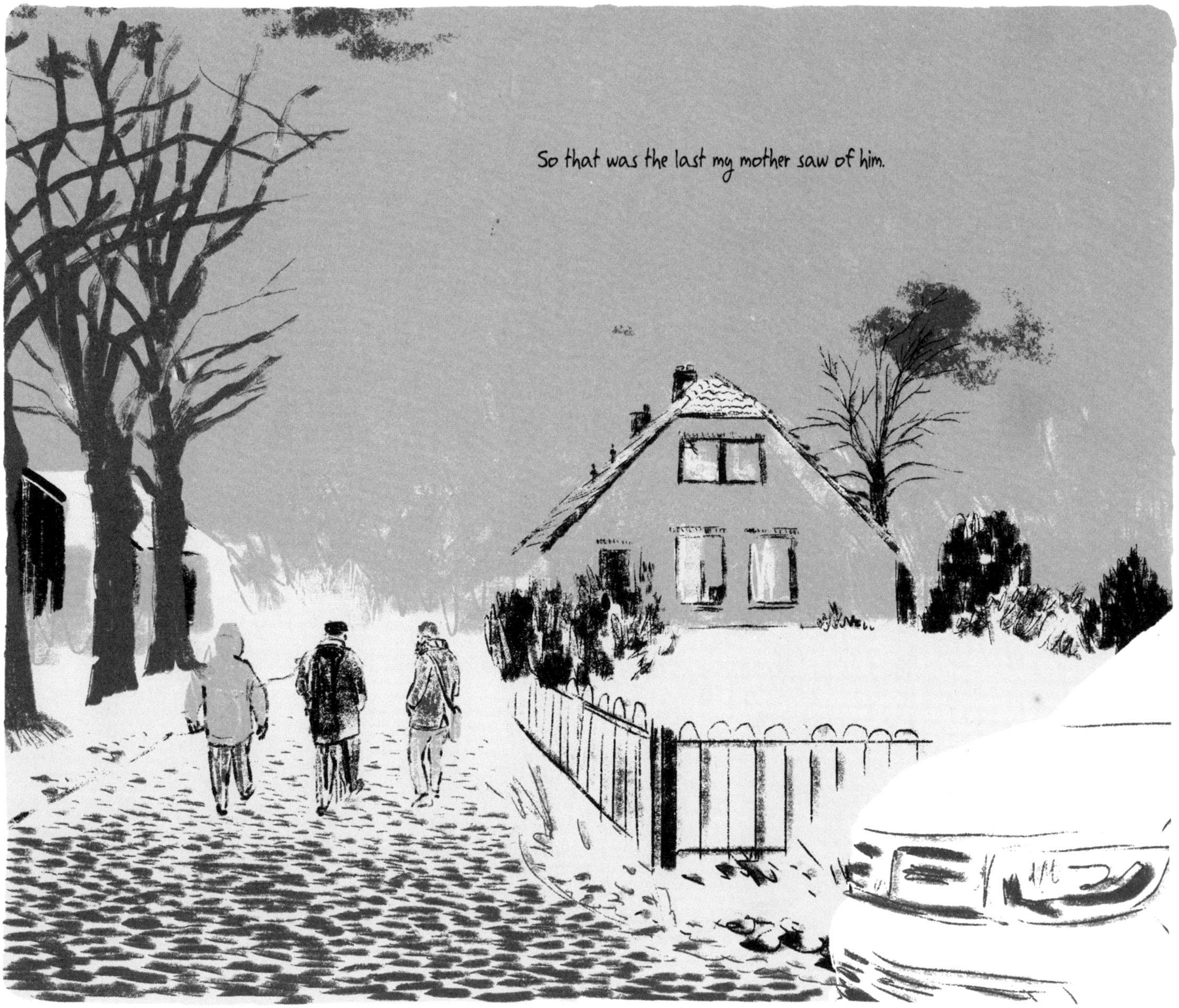
So that was the last my mother saw of him.

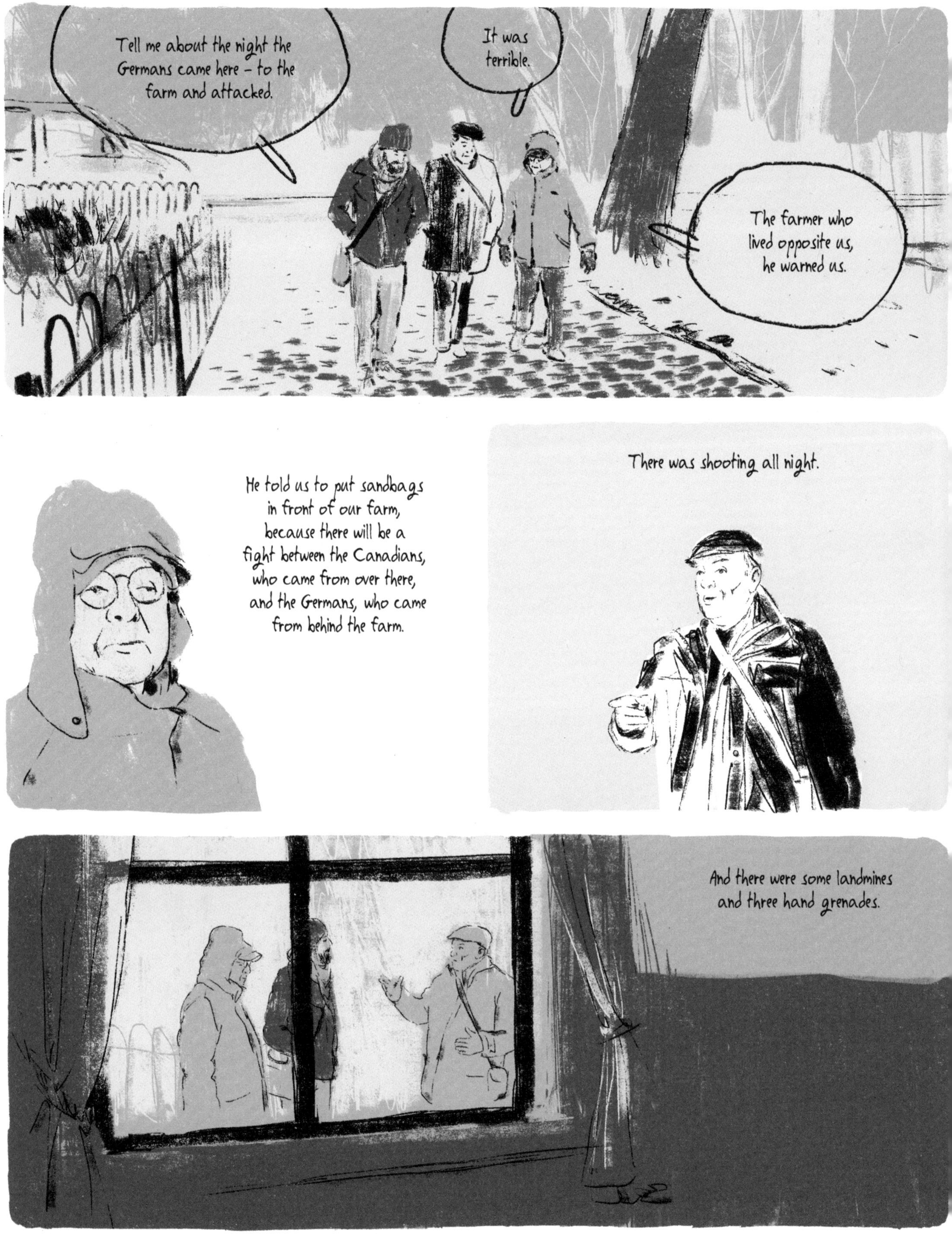
Tell me about the night the Germans came here – to the farm and attacked.
It was terrible.
The farmer who lived opposite us, he warned us.
He told us to put sandbags in front of our farm, because there will be a fight between the Canadians, who came from over there, and the Germans, who came from behind the farm.
There was shooting all night.
And there were some landmines and three hand grenades.

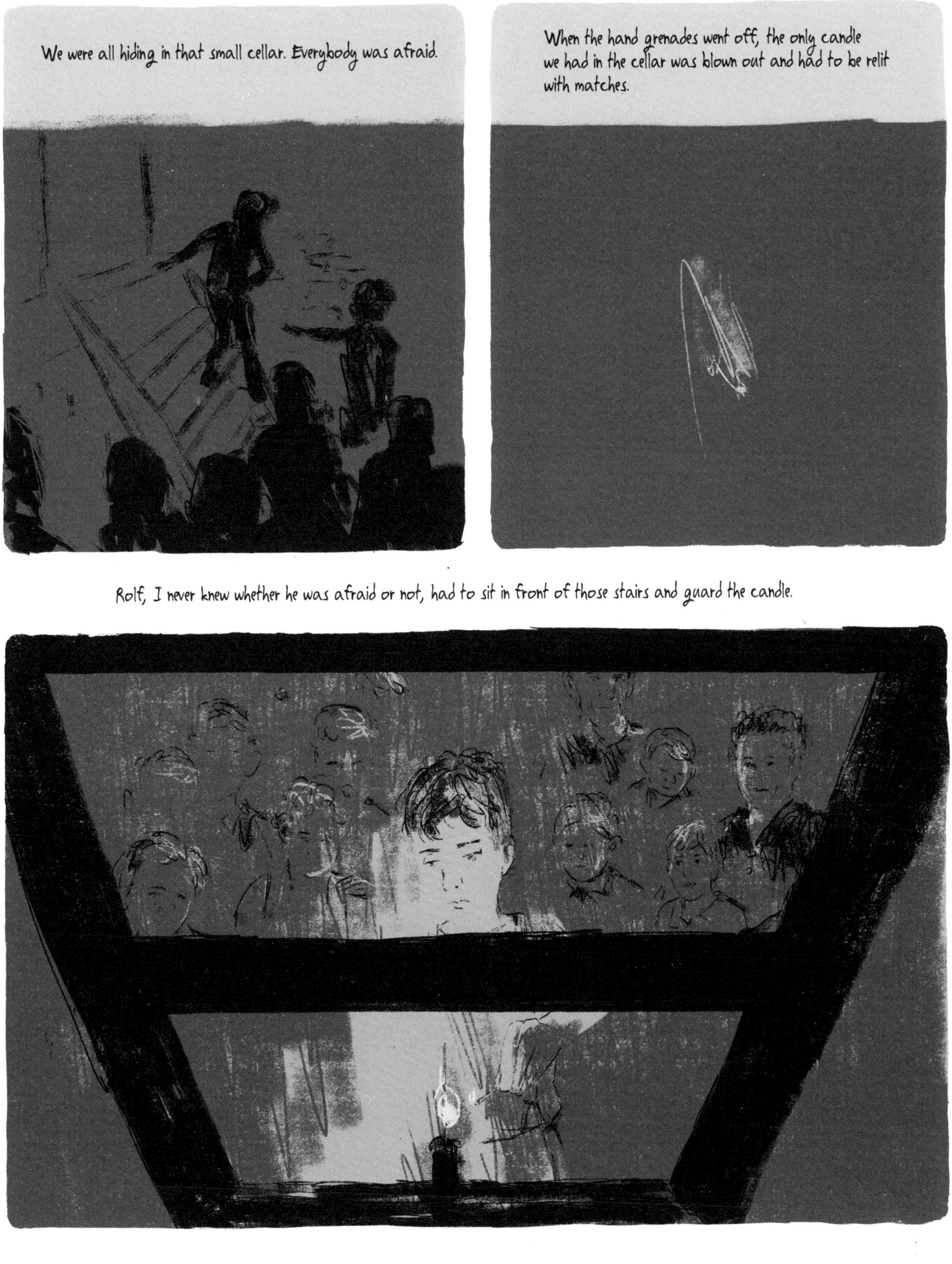
We were all hiding in that small cellar. Everybody was afraid.
When the hand grenades went off, the only candle we had in the cellar was blown out and had to be relit with matches.
Rolf, I never knew whether he was afraid or not, had to sit in front of those stairs and guard the candle.

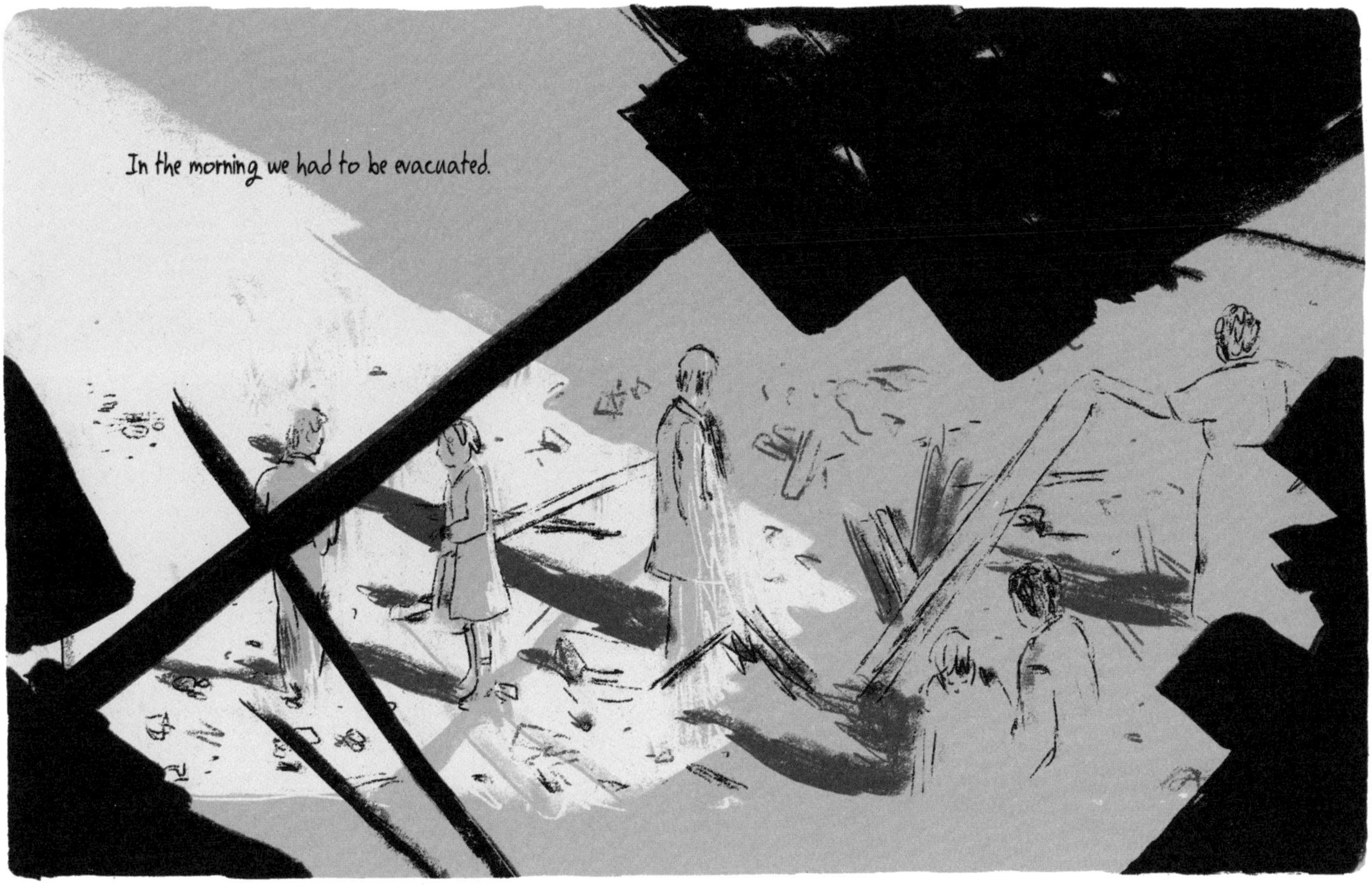
In the morning we had to be evacuated.

The Germans had confiscated the horse the farmer had. Now we had a cart but no horse. This cart was possibly pulled by the farmer and the man that was hiding from the Germans. And he put food and blankets and stuff like that on the cart.

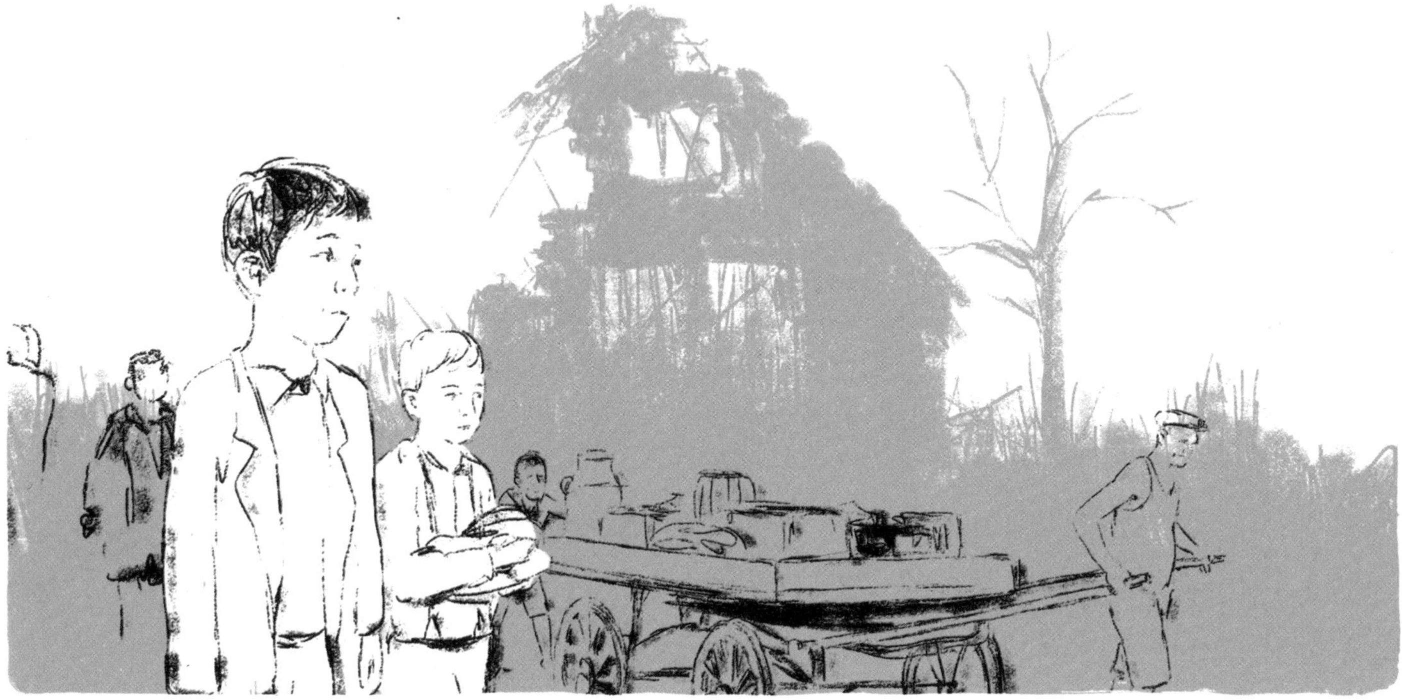

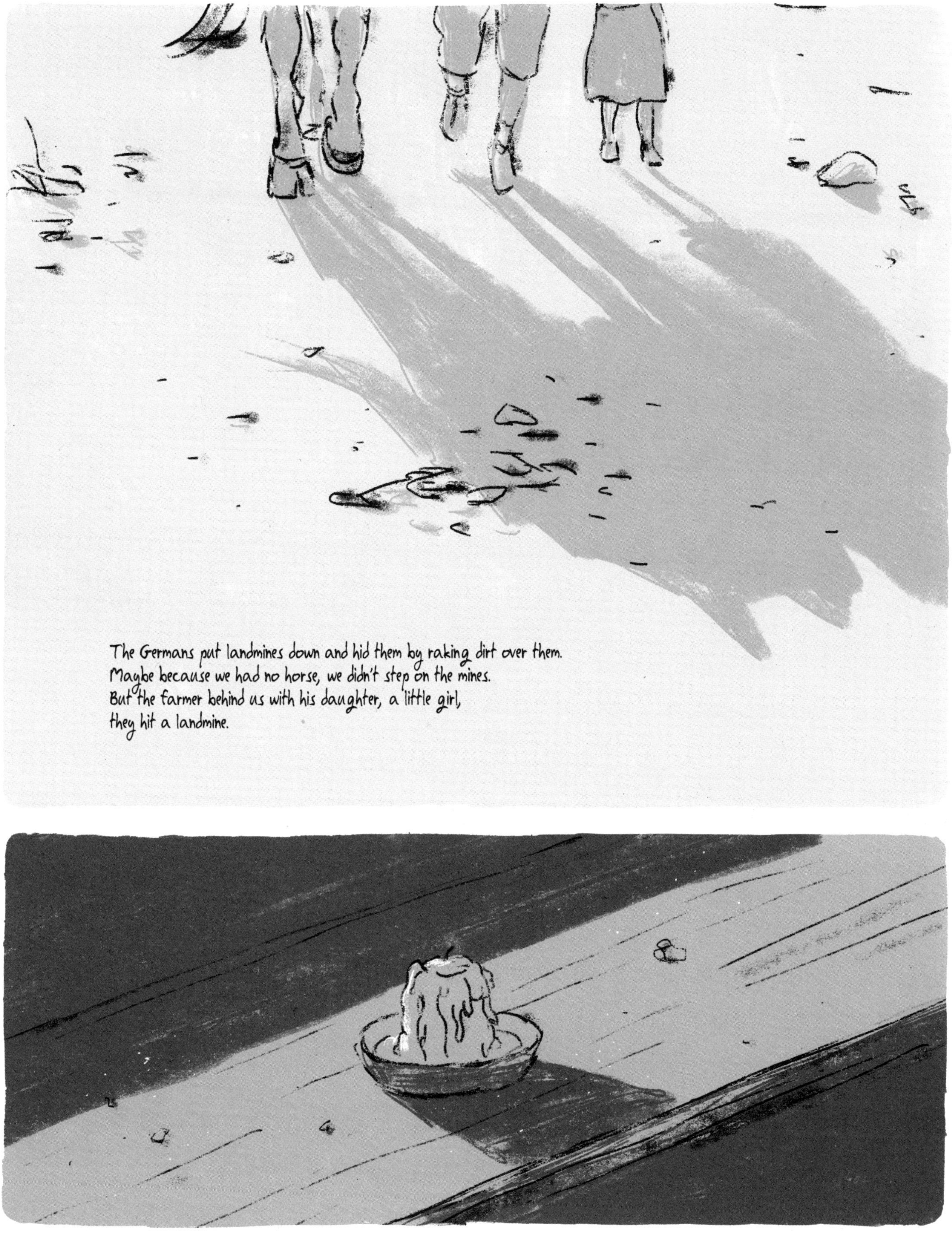
The Germans put landmines down and hid them by raking dirt over them.
Maybe because we had no horse, we didn't step on the mines.
But the farmer behind us with his daughter, a little girl,
they hit a landmine.

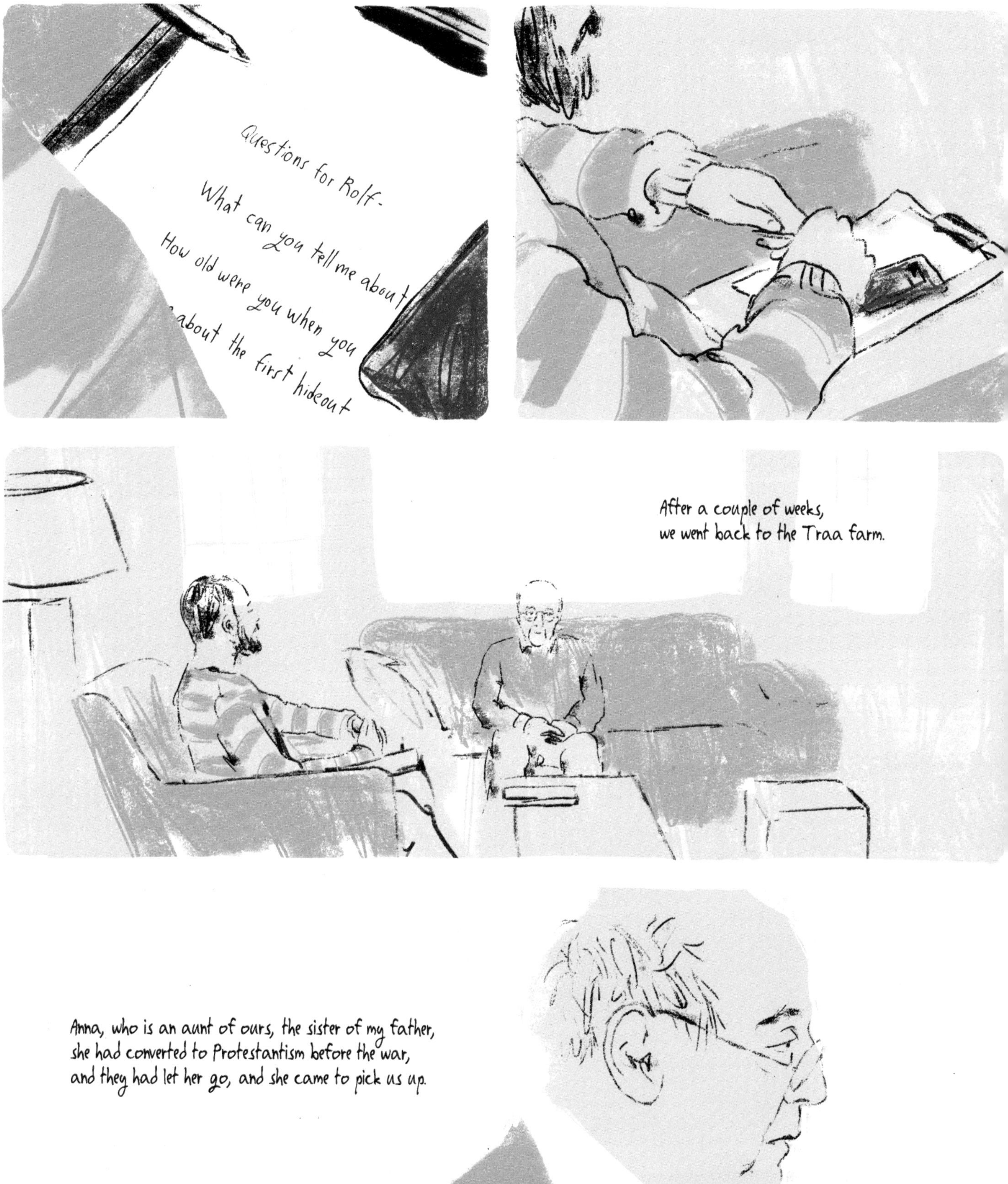
Questions for Rolf-
What can you tell me about
How old were you when you
about the first hideout
After a couple of weeks, we went back to the Traa farm.
Anna, who is an aunt of ours, the sister of my father, she had converted to Protestantism before the war, and they had let her go, and she came to pick us up.

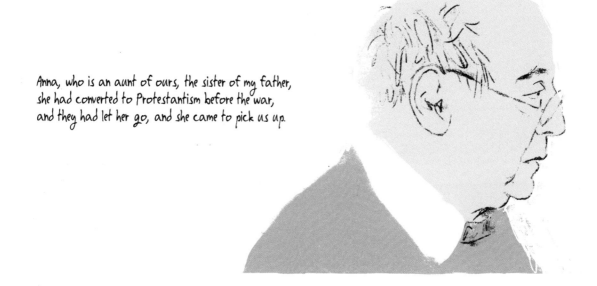

On the 13th of June, we found back our mother.

She was very thin — lost her weight. I think she was one meter, seventy-two centimeters tall, and she weighed like thirty-four, thirty-five kilos ...

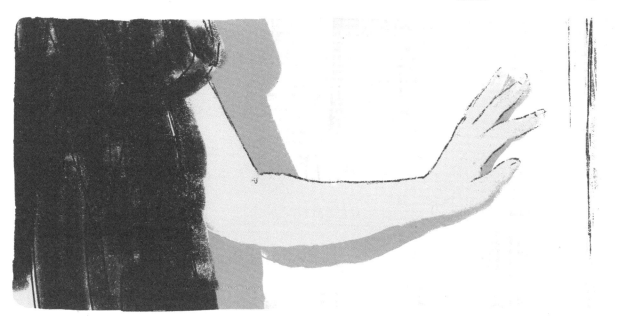

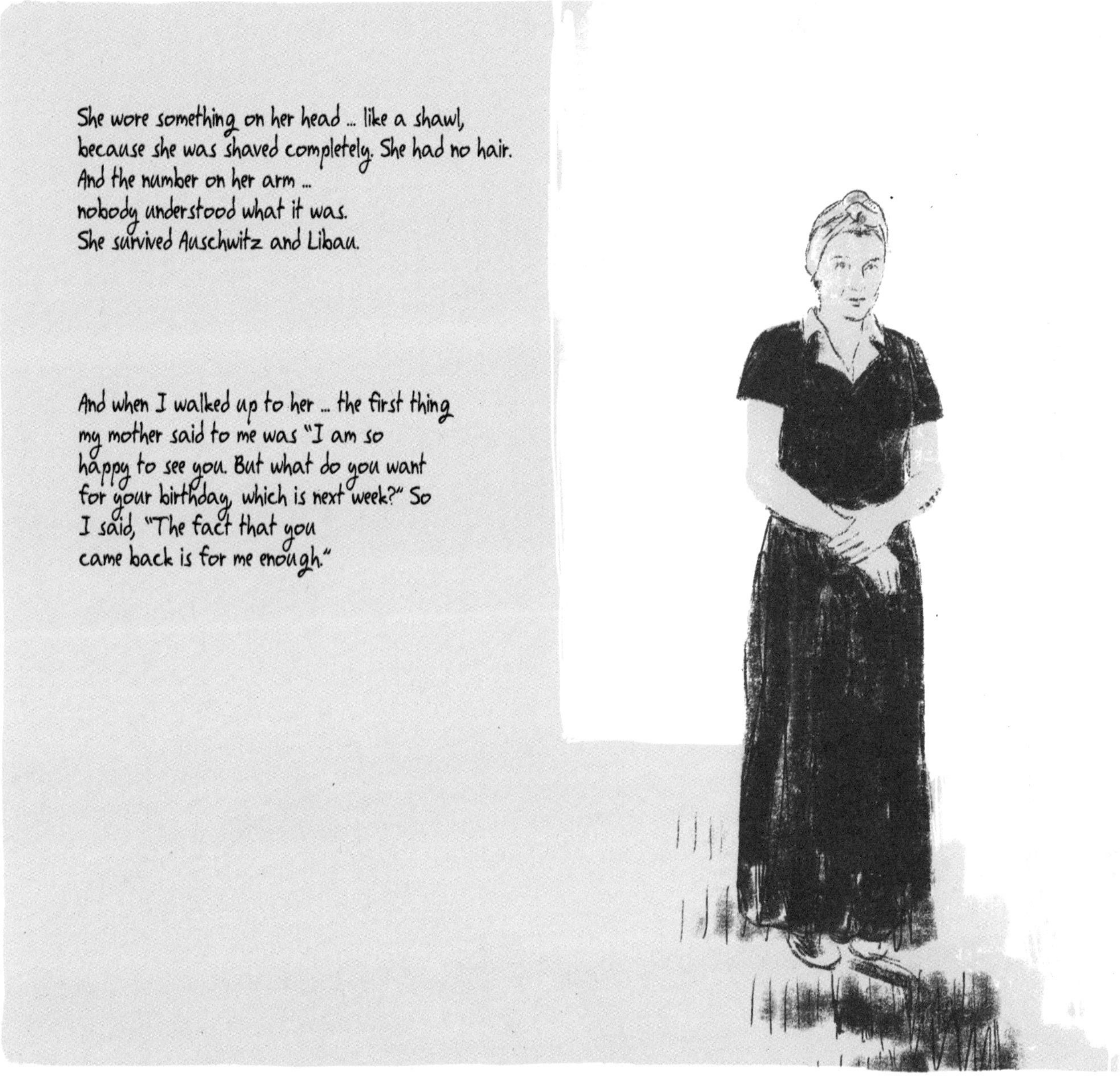
She wore something on her head ... like a shawl,
because she was shaved completely. She had no hair.
And the number on her arm ...
nobody understood what it was.
She survived Auschwitz and Libau.
And when I walked up to her ... the first thing
my mother said to me was "I am so
happy to see you. But what do you want
for your birthday, which is next week?" So
I said, "The fact that you
came back is for me enough."

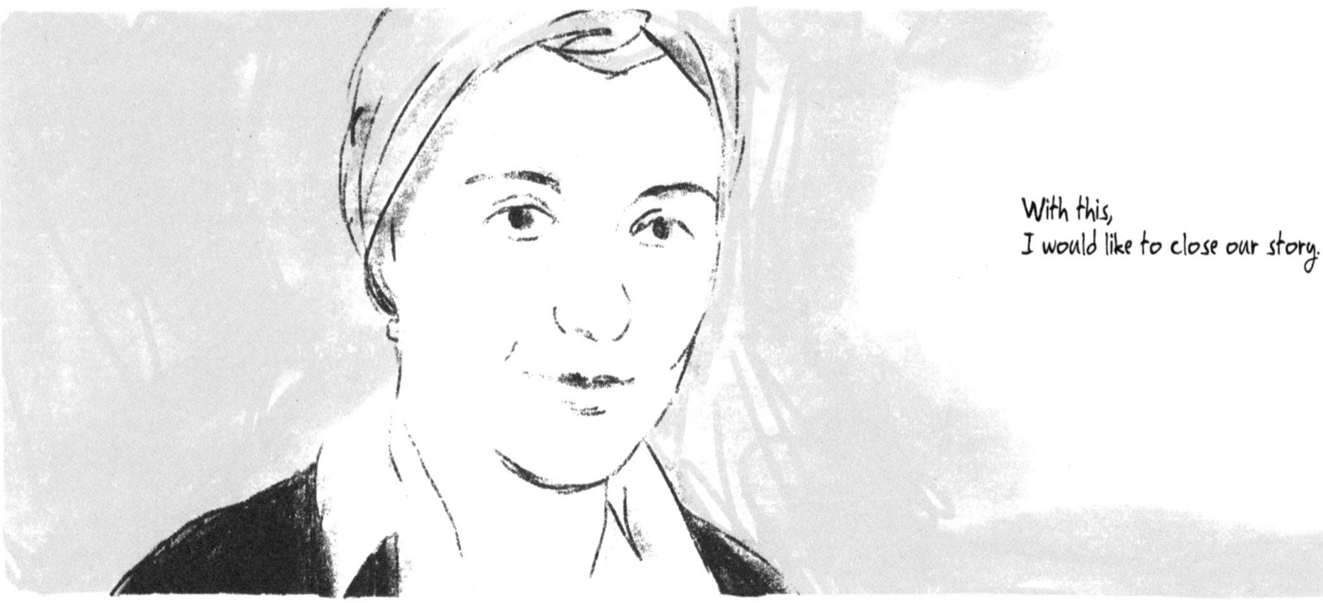
With this,
I would like to close our story.

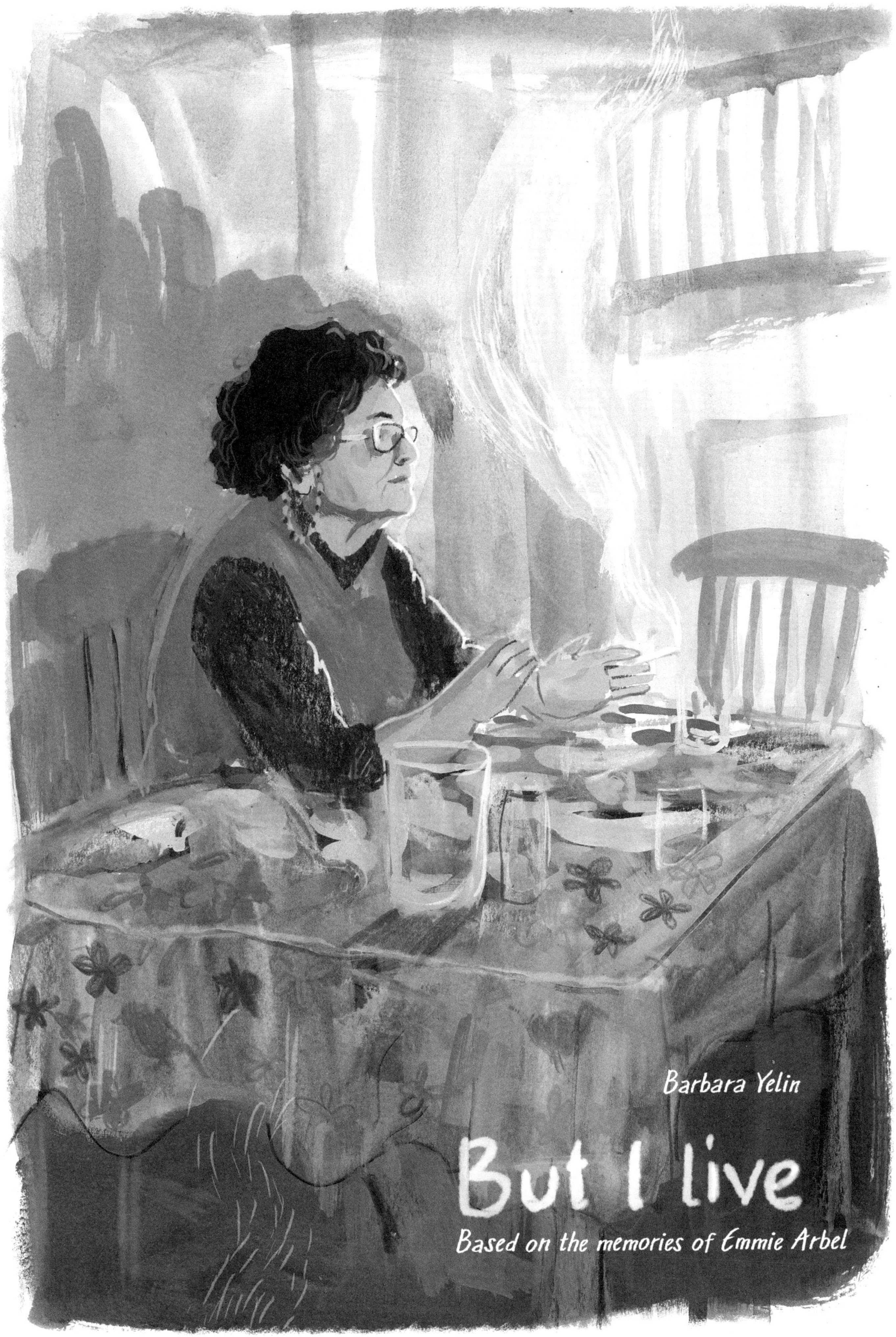
Barbara Yelin
But I live
Based on the memories of Emmie Arbel

In early Spring 2020, I visited Emmie Arbel in Kiryat Tiv'on, Israel, to interview her about her memories of the Holocaust. We spent four days together.

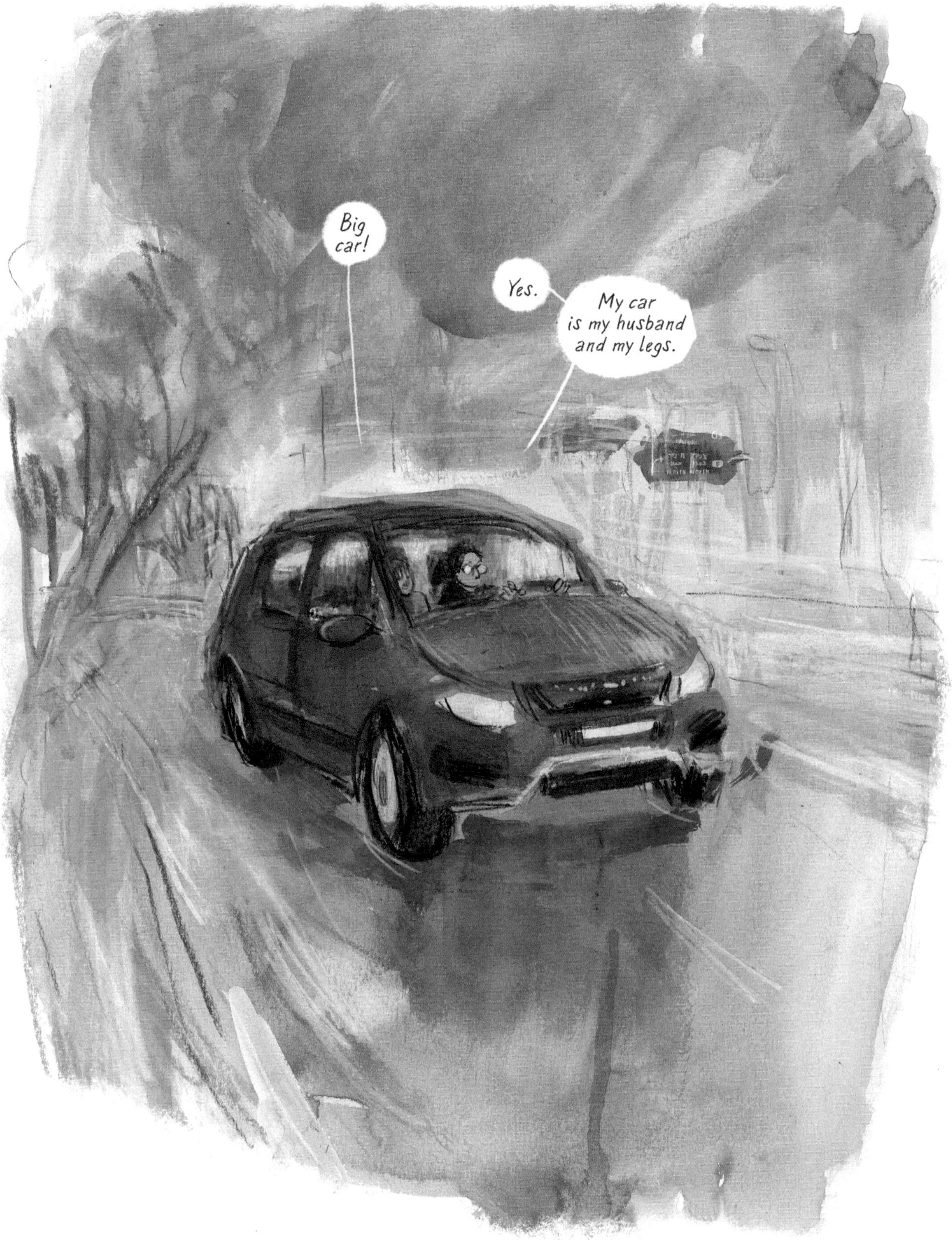
Big car!
Yes.
My car is my husband and my legs.

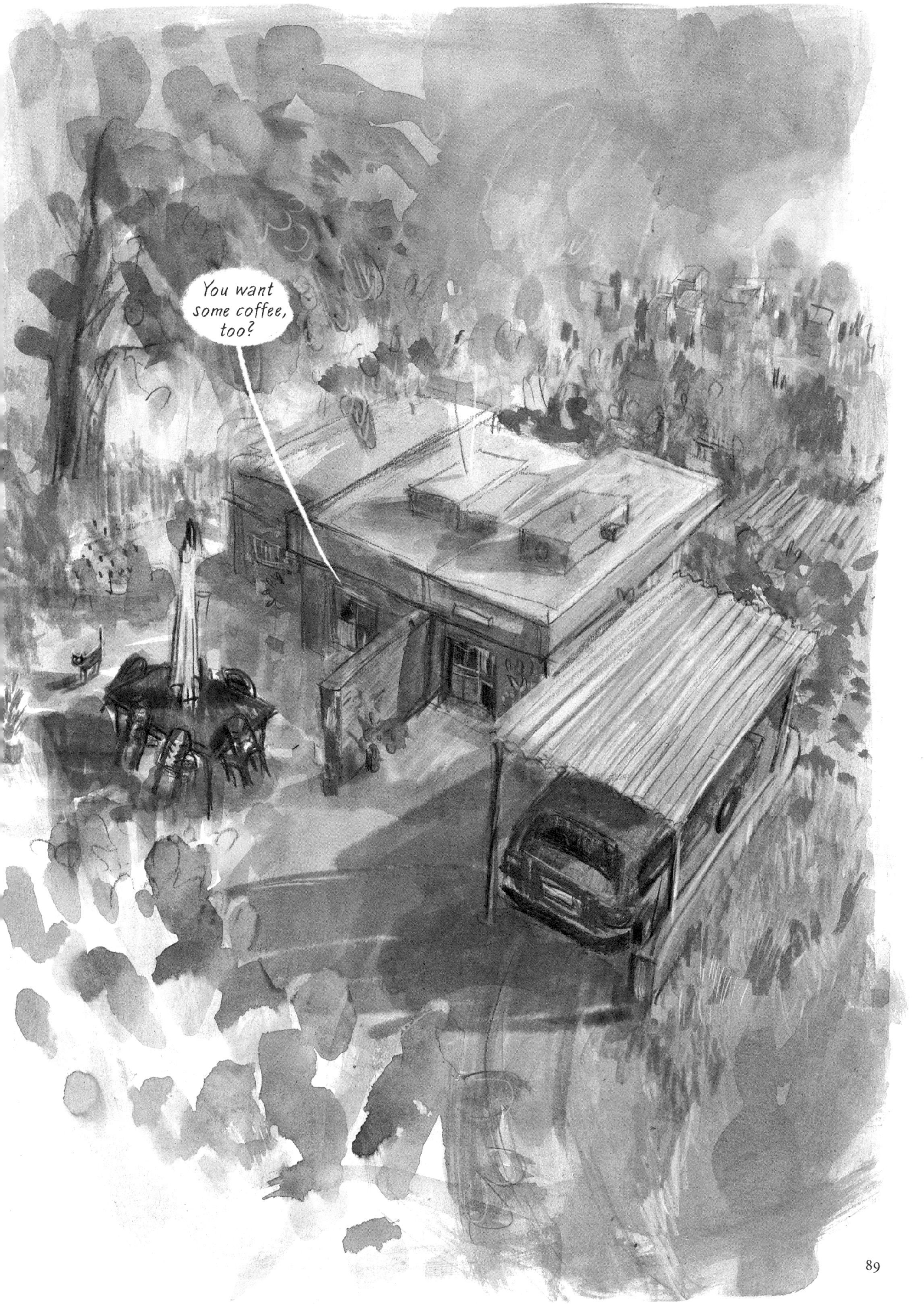
You want some coffee, too?

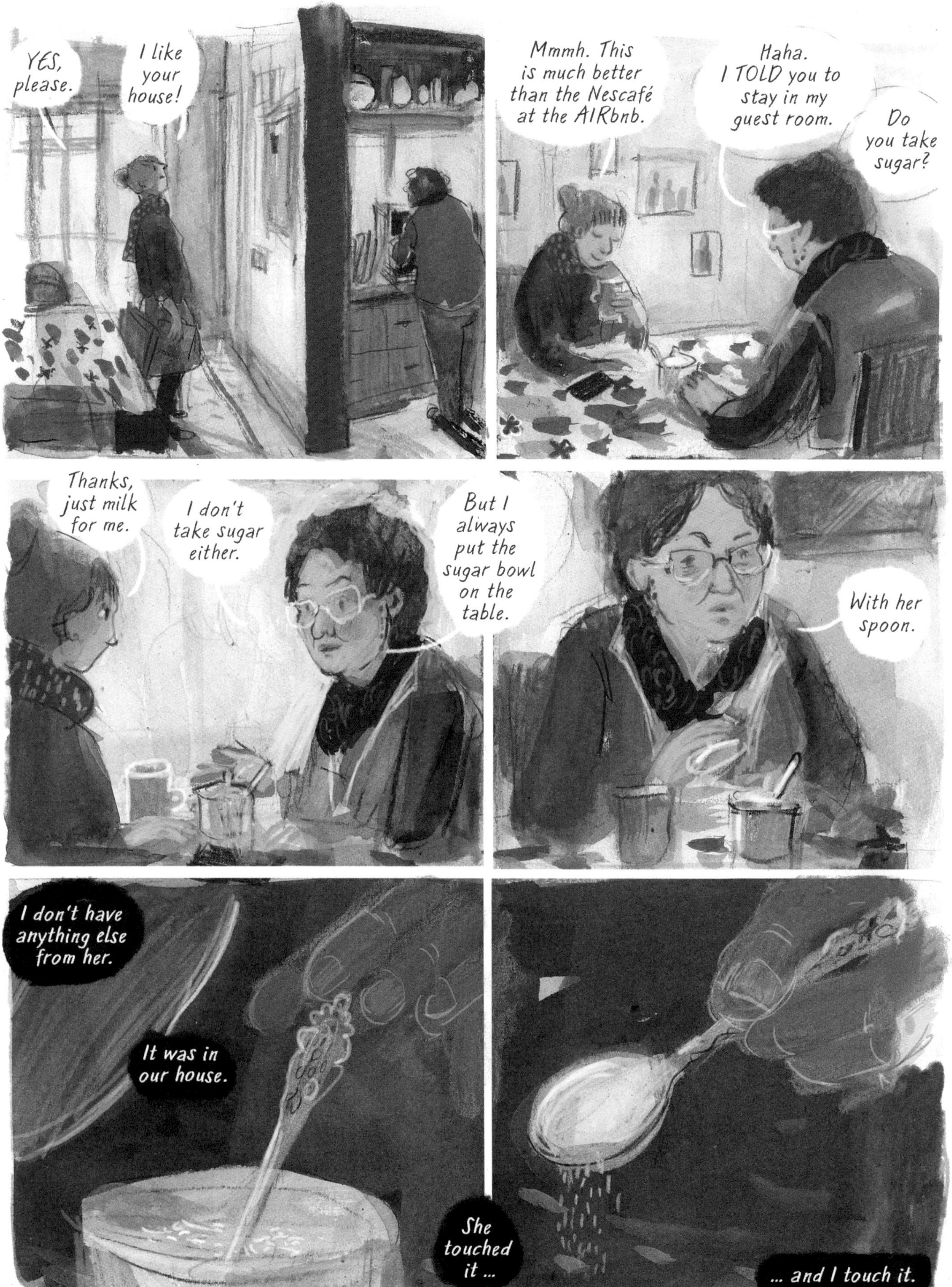
YES, please.
I like your house!
Mmmh. This is much better than the Nescafé at the AIRbnb.
Haha. I TOLD you to stay in my guest room.
Do you take sugar?
Thanks, just milk for me.
I don't take sugar either.
But I always put the sugar bowl on the table.
With her spoon.
I don't have anything else from her.
It was in our house.
She touched it ...
... and I touch it.

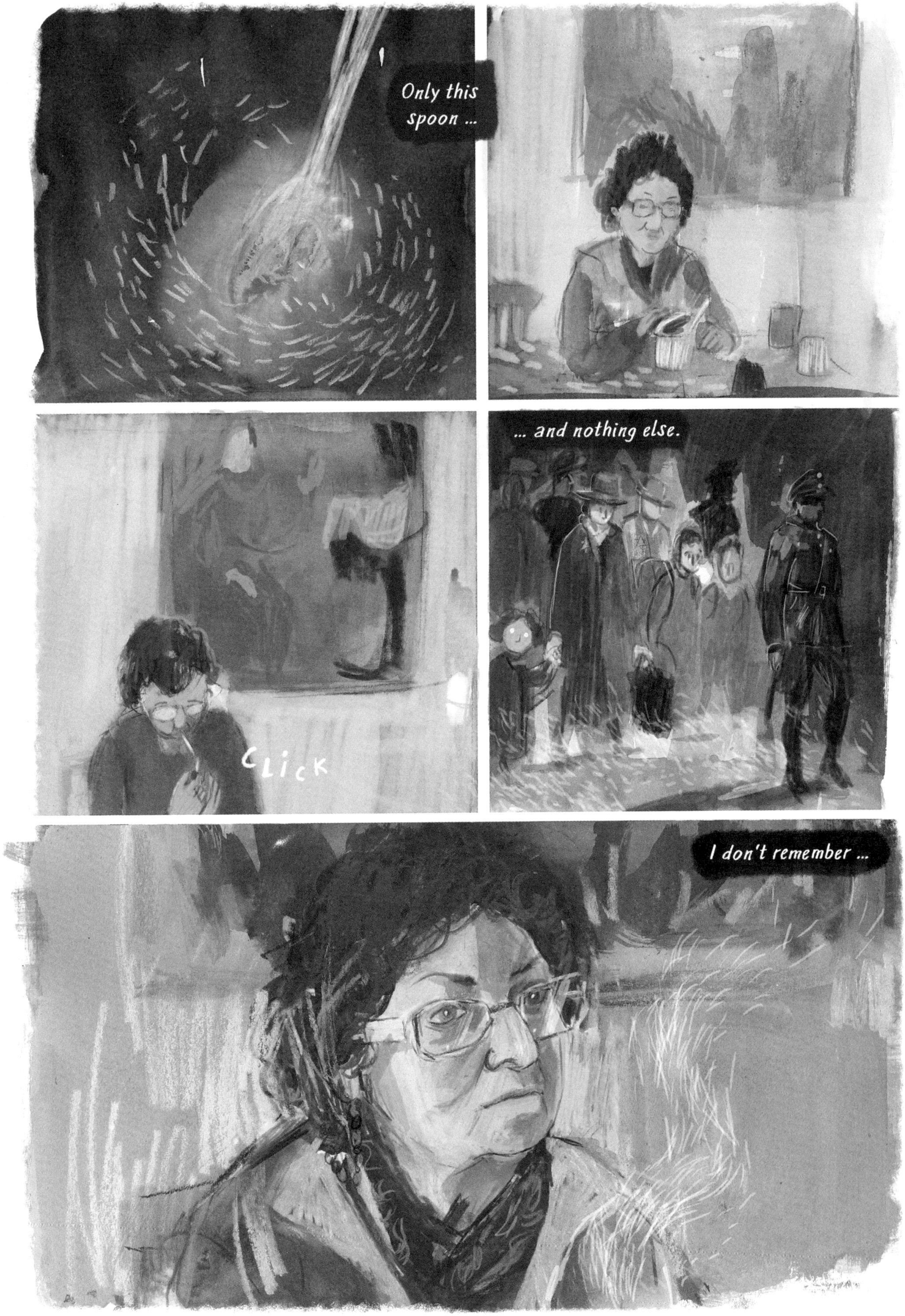
Only this spoon ...
CLICK
... and nothing else.
I don't remember ...

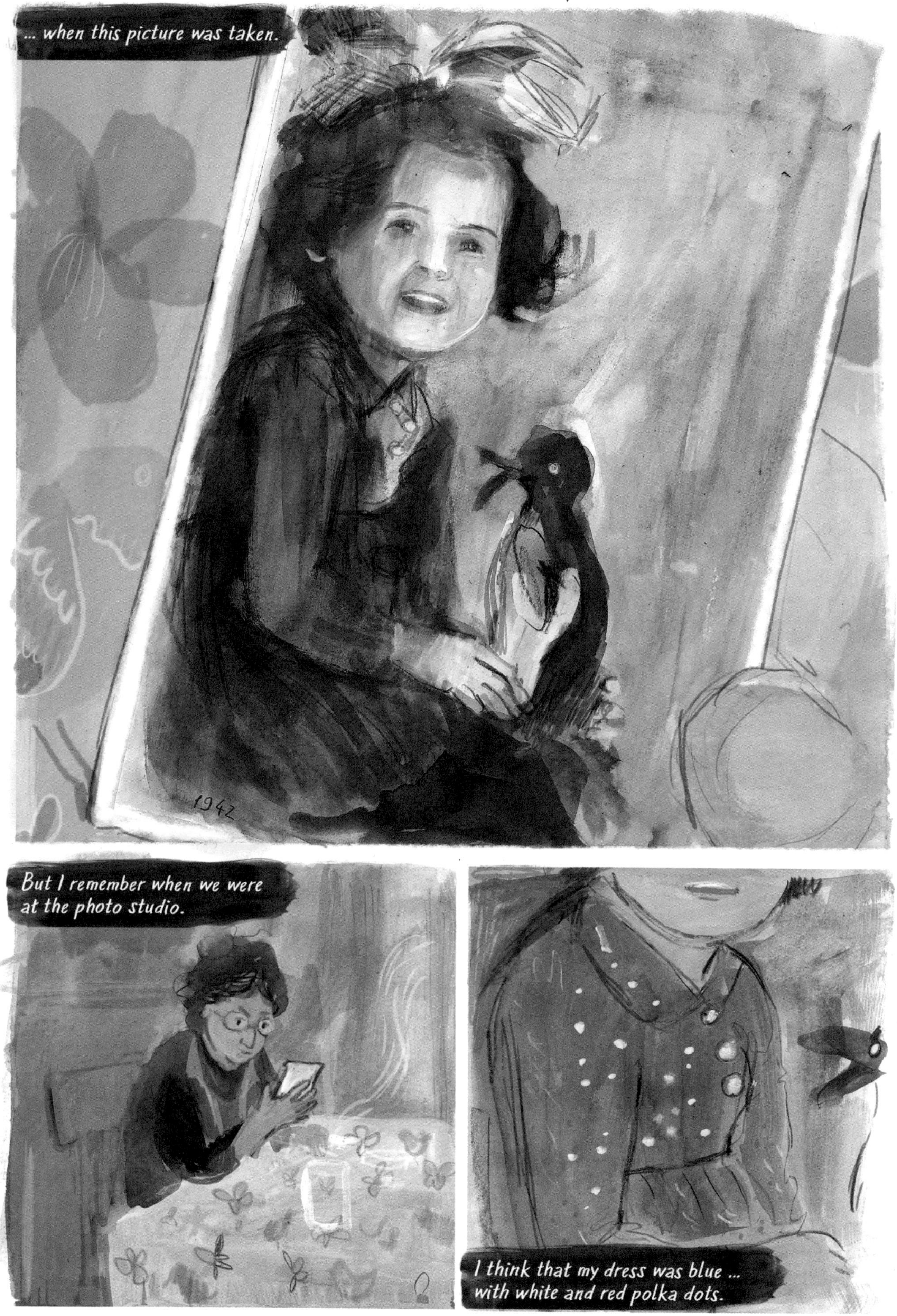
... when this picture was taken.
1942
But I remember when we were at the photo studio.
I think that my dress was blue ... with white and red polka dots.

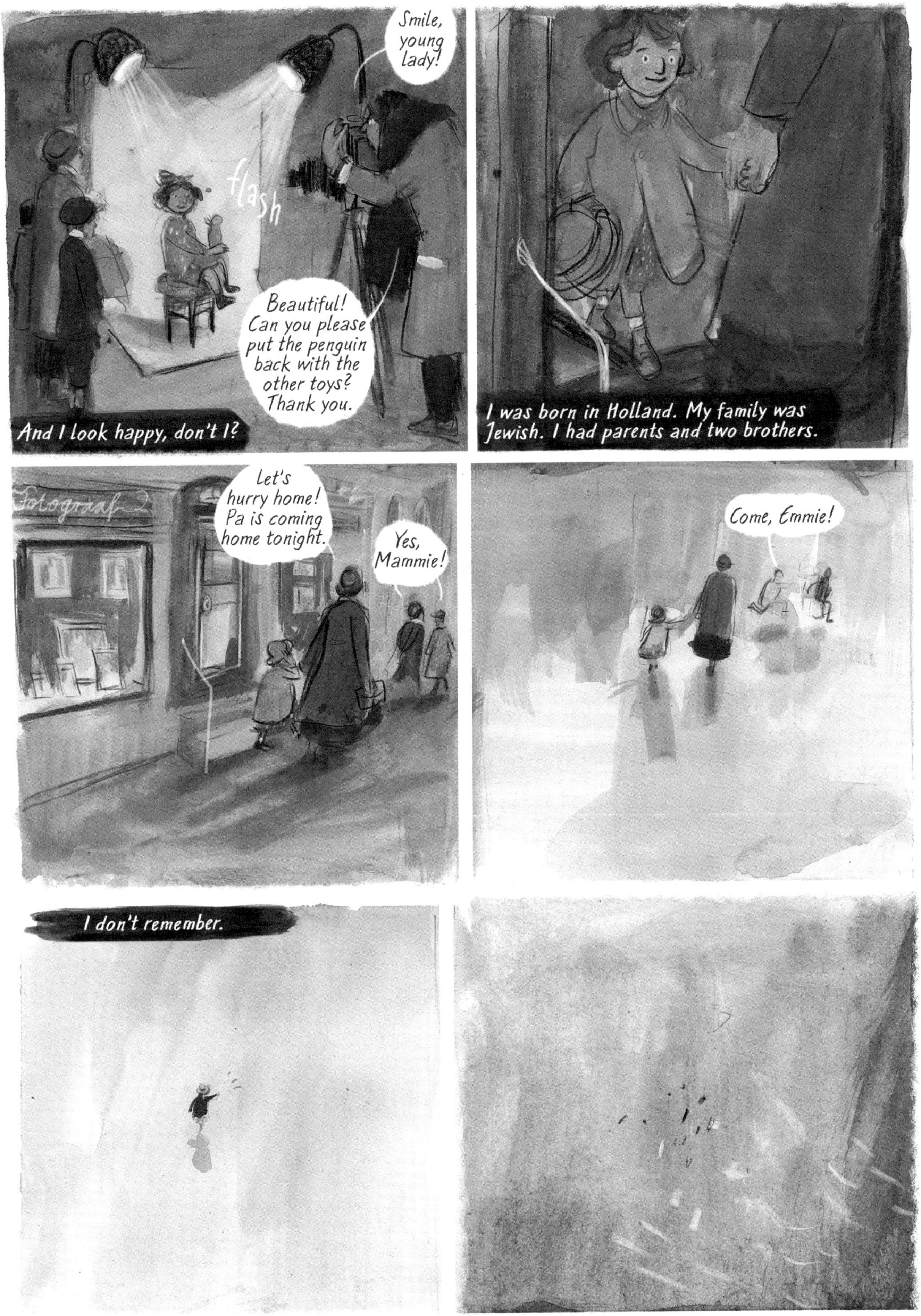

Smile, young lady!
flash
Beautiful! Can you please put the penguin back with the other toys? Thank you.
And I look happy, don't I?
I was born in Holland. My family was Jewish. I had parents and two brothers.
Fotograaf
Let's hurry home! Pa is coming home tonight.
Yes, Mammie!
Come, Emmie!
I don't remember.

I was four and a half, when two policemen came to our house and took us to Westerbork transit camp.

There were many people and we had no privacy. My mother put up a ... how do you call it, a "Laken"... a sheet? We were there a long time. I don't remember much from there.

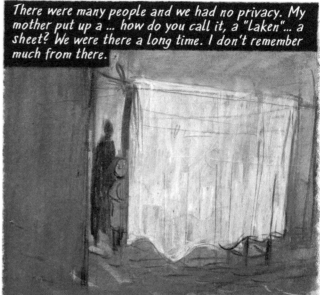

But I recall the weekly fear about who would be deported next to other camps. I don't remember the day when they took our father.

Then, the rest of us were deported to Ravensbrück. My oldest brother was later separated from us. Rudi and me stayed with our mother.

I saw many, many women. They all wore the same clothes. Strange clothes. In blue and white. And they looked at us. I think they talked about food.

I remember all kind of voices in the night, all kind of women who were crying OOH, OOOH.

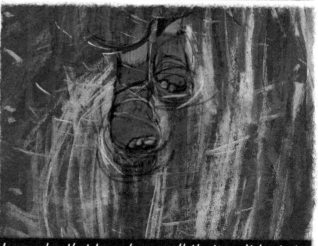

I remember that I was hungry all the time. It hurts to be hungry. It really hurts. It hurts in your stomach. I remember that it was cold and rain and snow. I had lost my shoes and my mother made me some from jute.

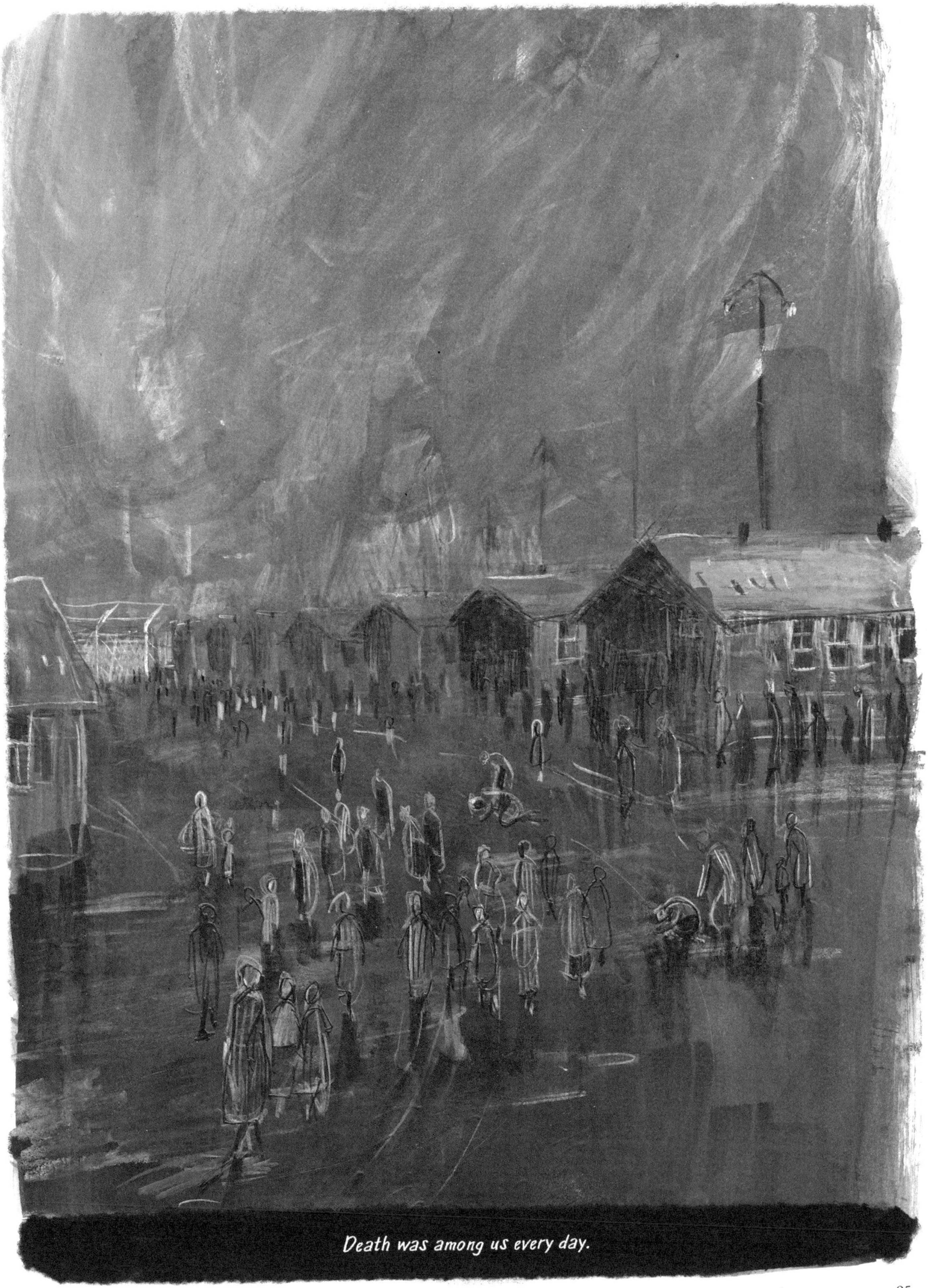
Death was among us every day.

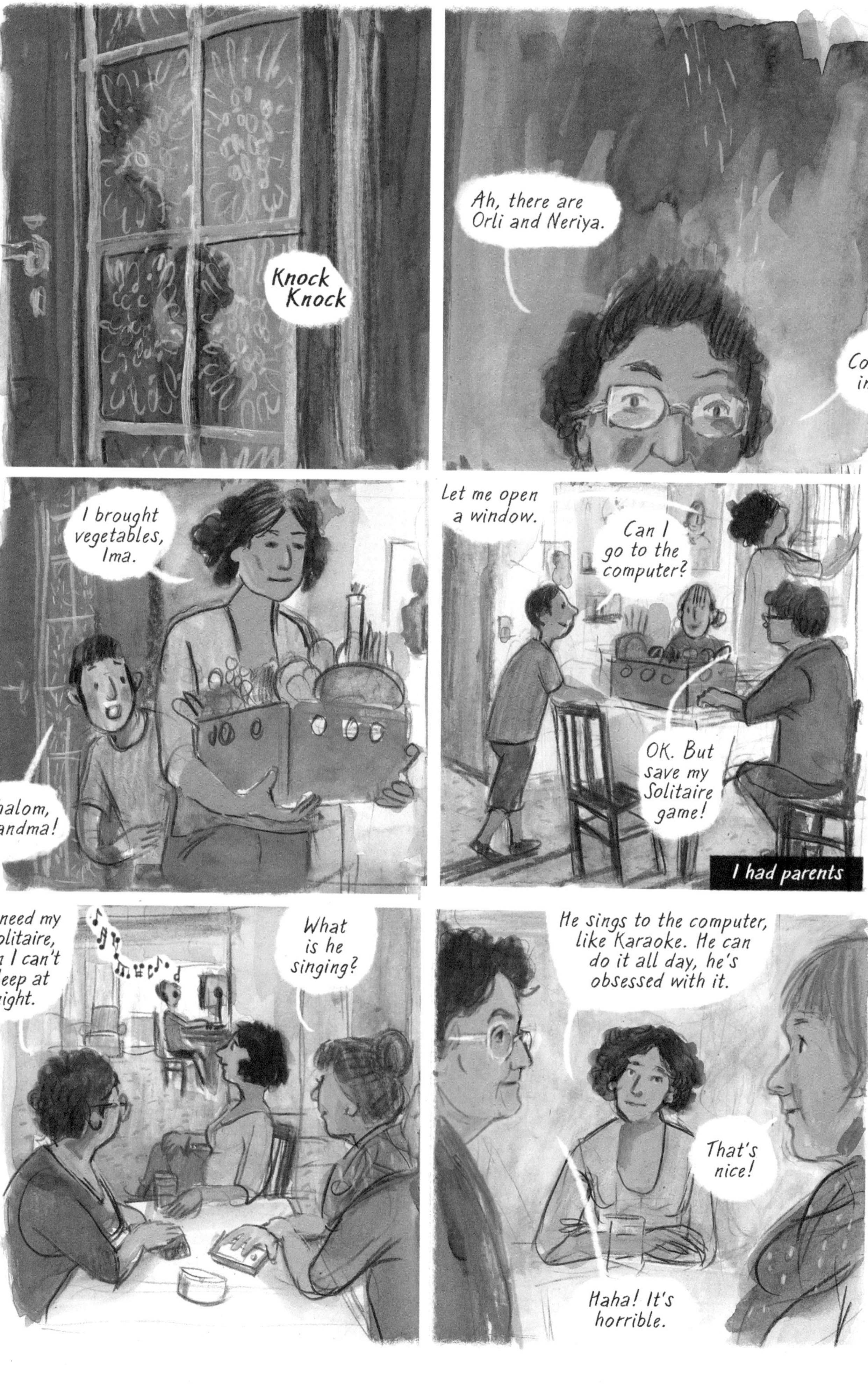
Knock Knock
Ah, there are Orli and Neriya.
Come in!
I brought vegetables, Ima.
Shalom, Grandma!
Let me open a window.
Can I go to the computer?
OK. But save my Solitaire game!
I had parents
I need my Solitaire, when I can't sleep at night.
What is he singing?
He sings to the computer, like Karaoke. He can do it all day, he's obsessed with it.
That's nice!
Haha! It's horrible.

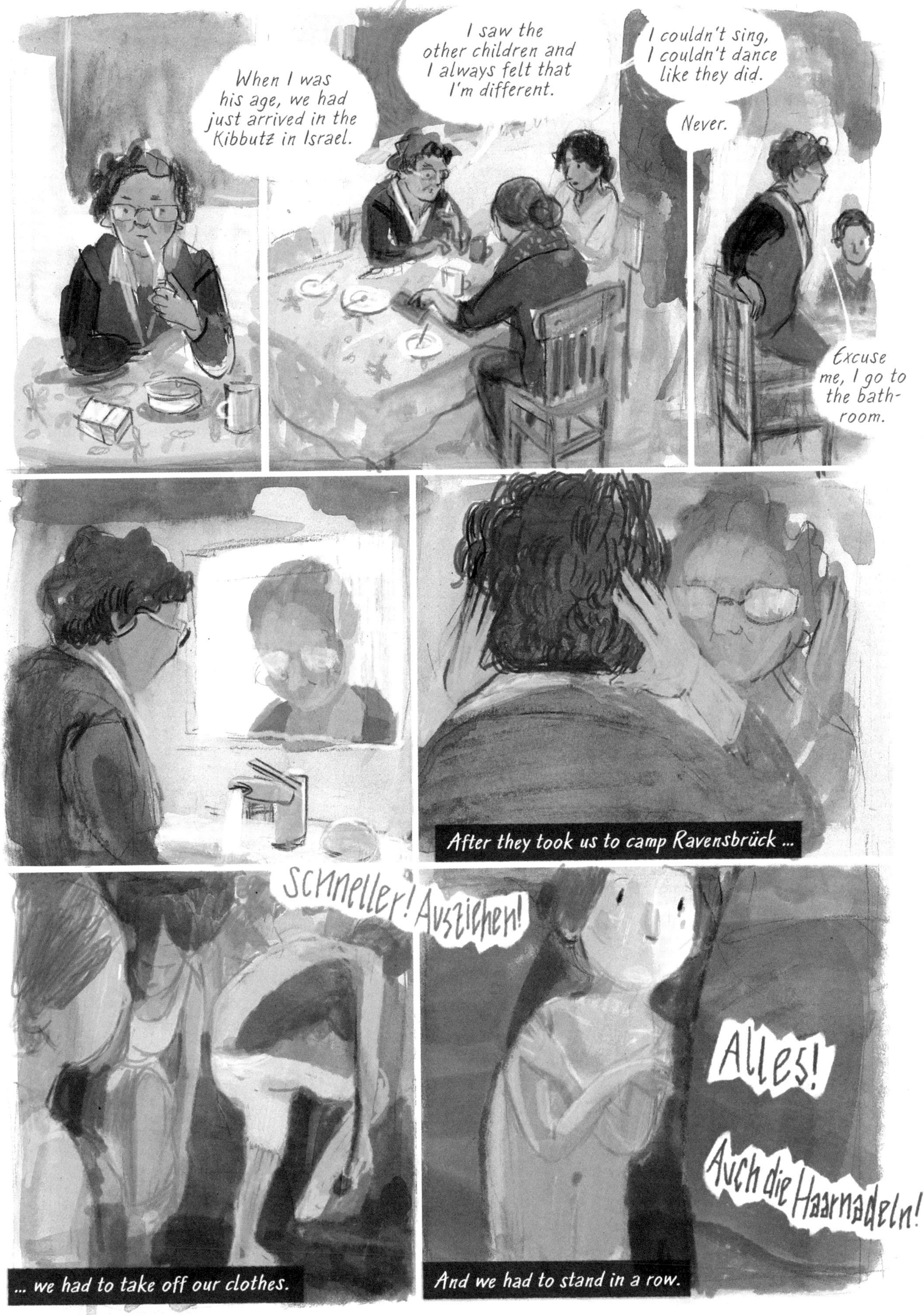
When I was his age, we had just arrived in the Kibbutz in Israel.
I saw the other children and I always felt that I'm different.
I couldn't sing, I couldn't dance like they did.
Never.
Excuse me, I go to the bath-room.
After they took us to camp Ravensbrück ...
Schneller! Ausziehen!
... we had to take off our clothes.
Alles!
Auch die Haarnadeln!
And we had to stand in a row.

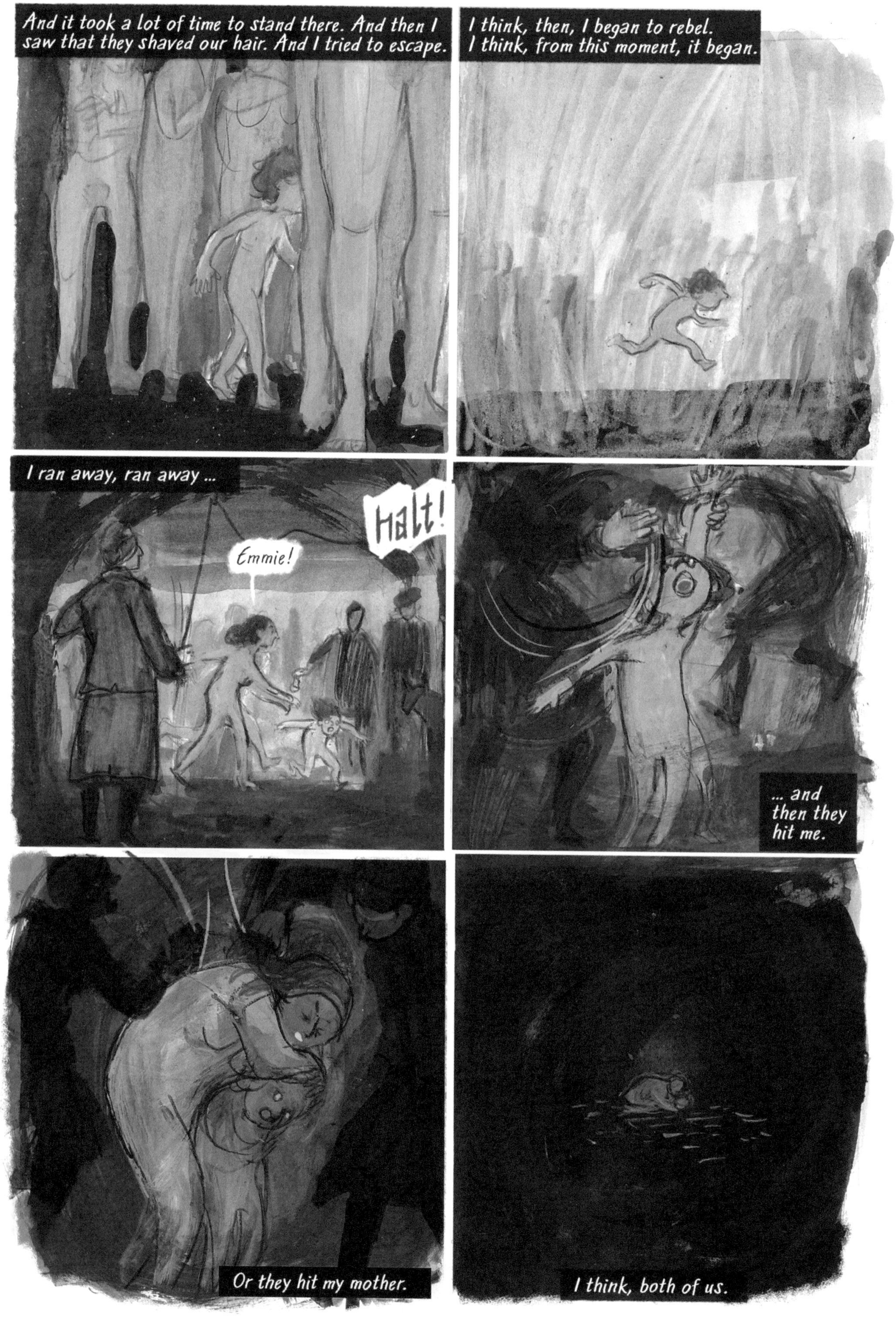
And it took a lot of time to stand there. And then I saw that they shaved our hair. And I tried to escape.
I think, then, I began to rebel. I think, from this moment, it began.
I ran away, ran away ...
Halt!
Emmie!
... and then they hit me.
Or they hit my mother.
I think, both of us.

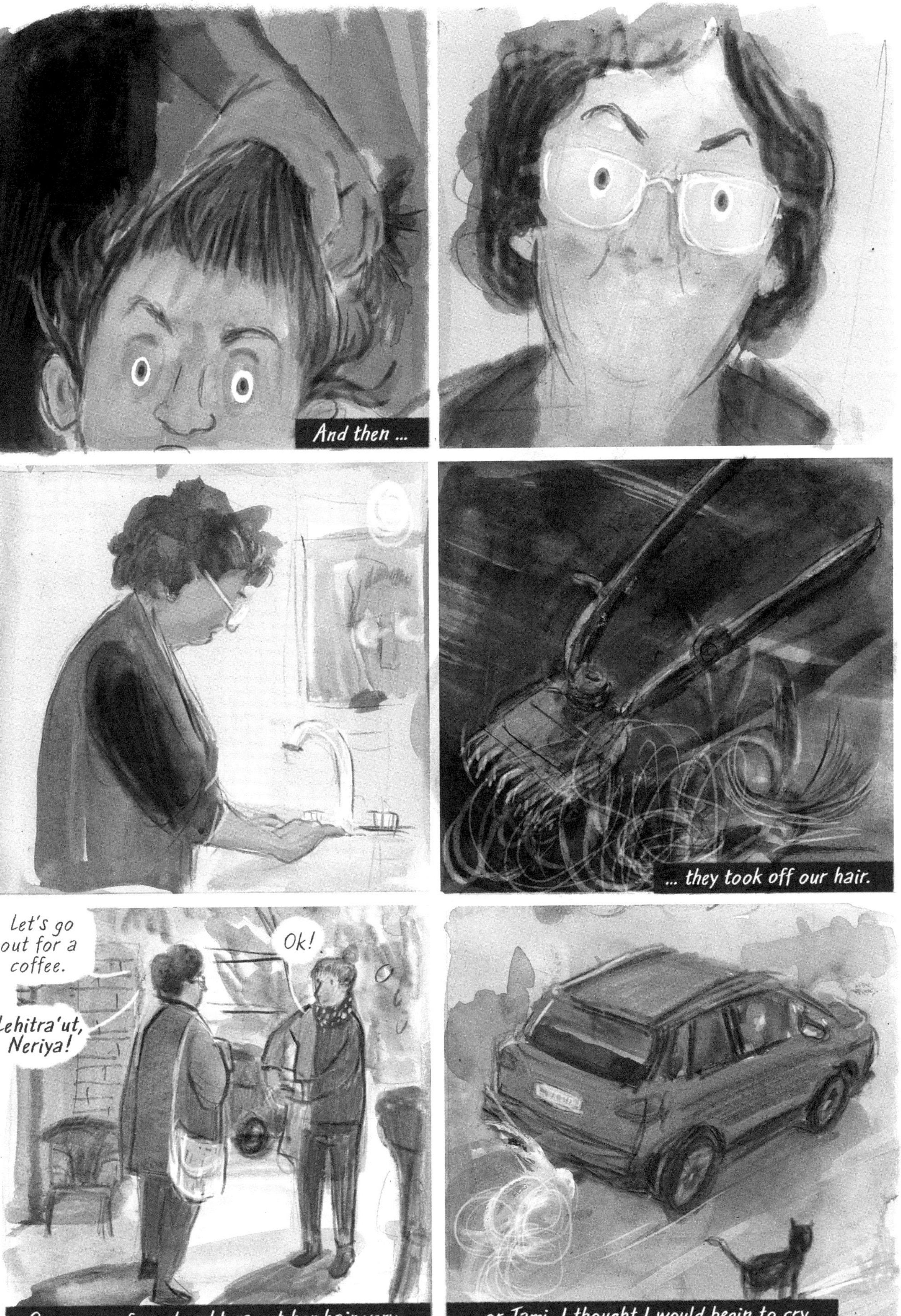
And then ...
... they took off our hair.
Let's go out for a coffee.
Ok!
Lehitra'ut, Neriya!
Once, one of my daughters cut her hair very, very short. I don't remember if it was Orli ...
... or Tami. I thought I would begin to cry.

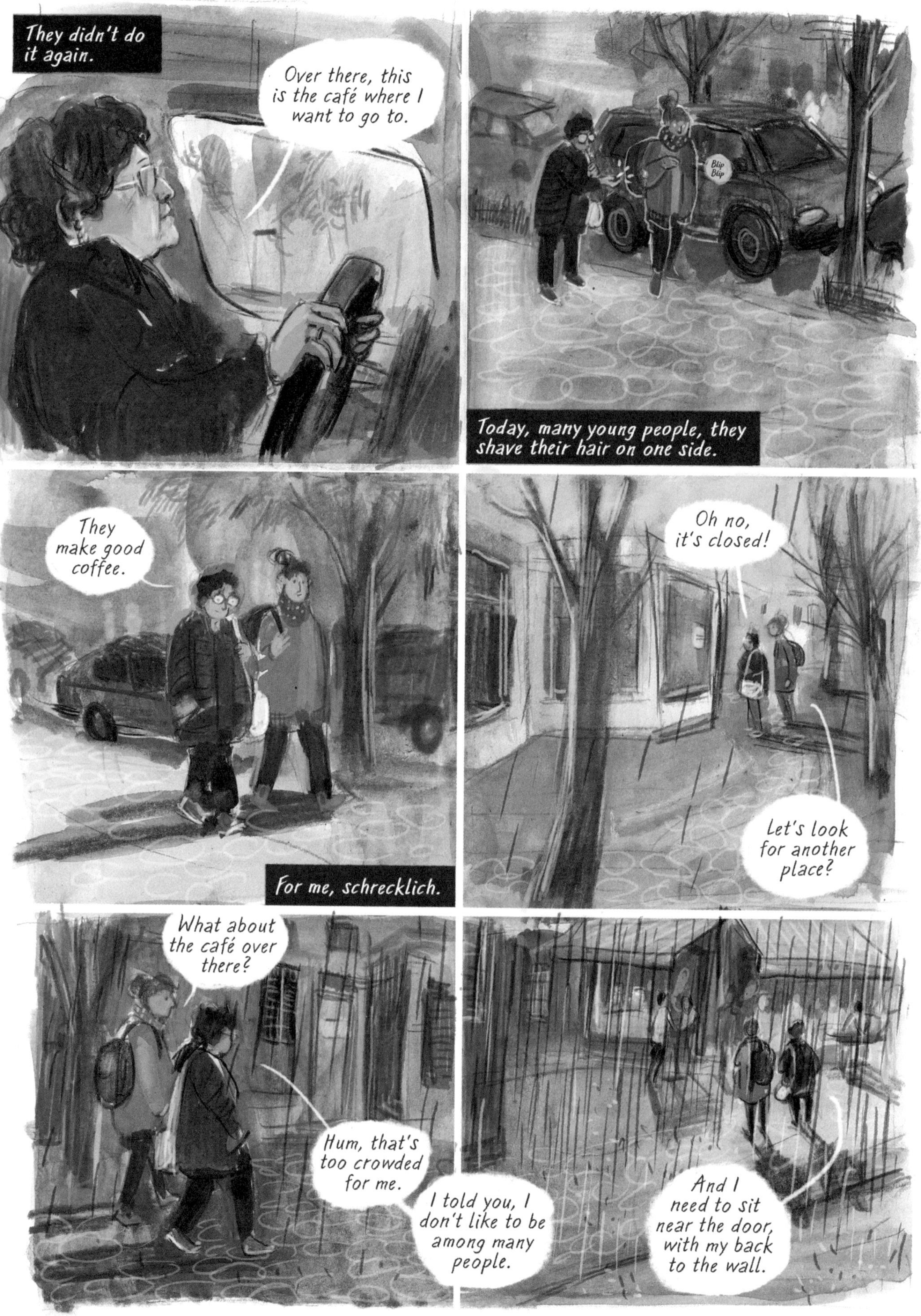
They didn't do it again.
Over there, this is the café where I want to go to.
Blip Blip
Today, many young people, they shave their hair on one side.
They make good coffee.
For me, schrecklich.
Oh no, it's closed!
Let's look for another place?
What about the café over there?
Hum, that's too crowded for me.
I told you, I don't like to be among many people.
And I need to sit near the door, with my back to the wall.

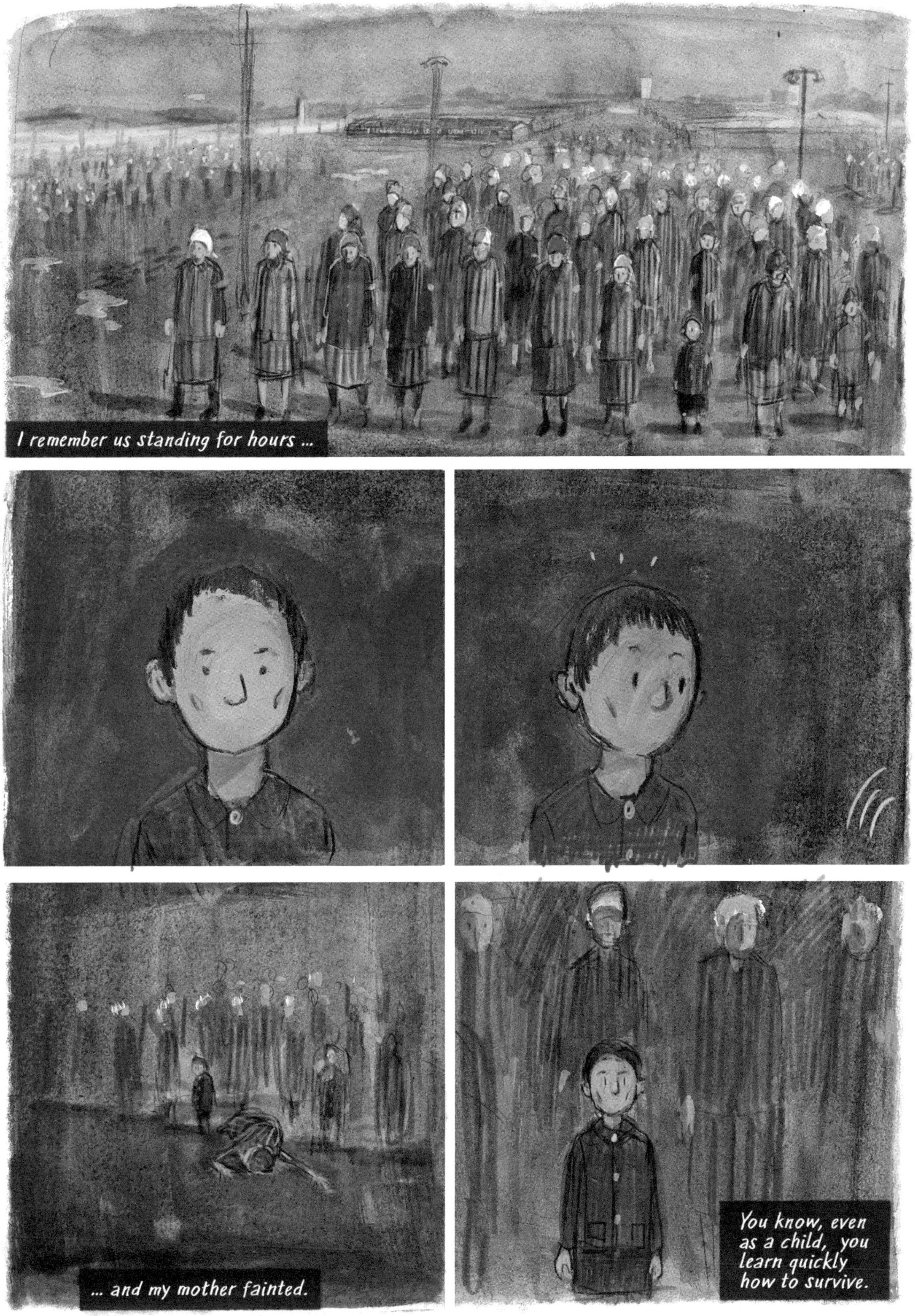
I remember us standing for hours ...
... and my mother fainted.
You know, even as a child, you learn quickly how to survive.

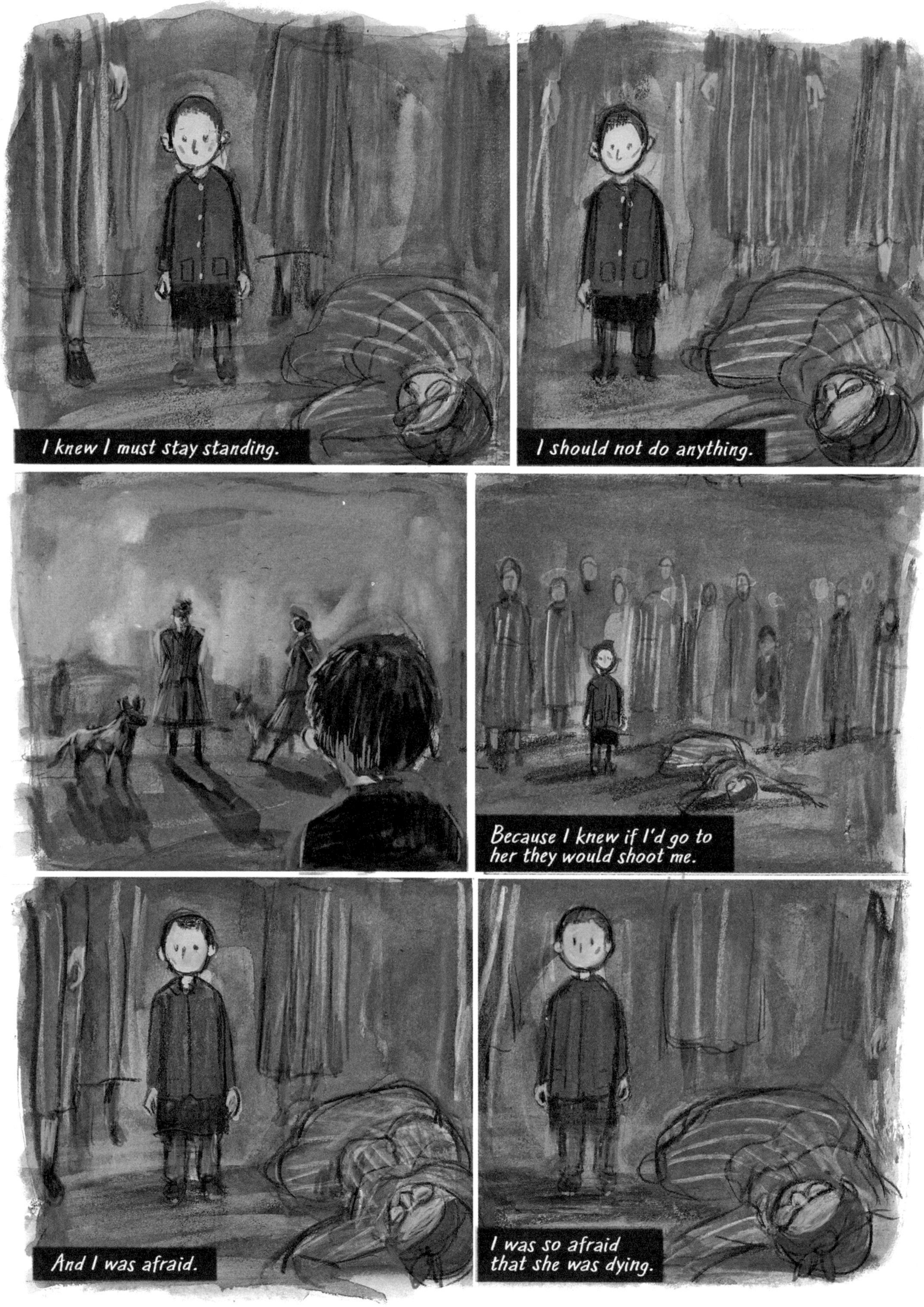
I knew I must stay standing.
I should not do anything.
Because I knew if I'd go to her they would shoot me.
And I was afraid.
I was so afraid that she was dying.

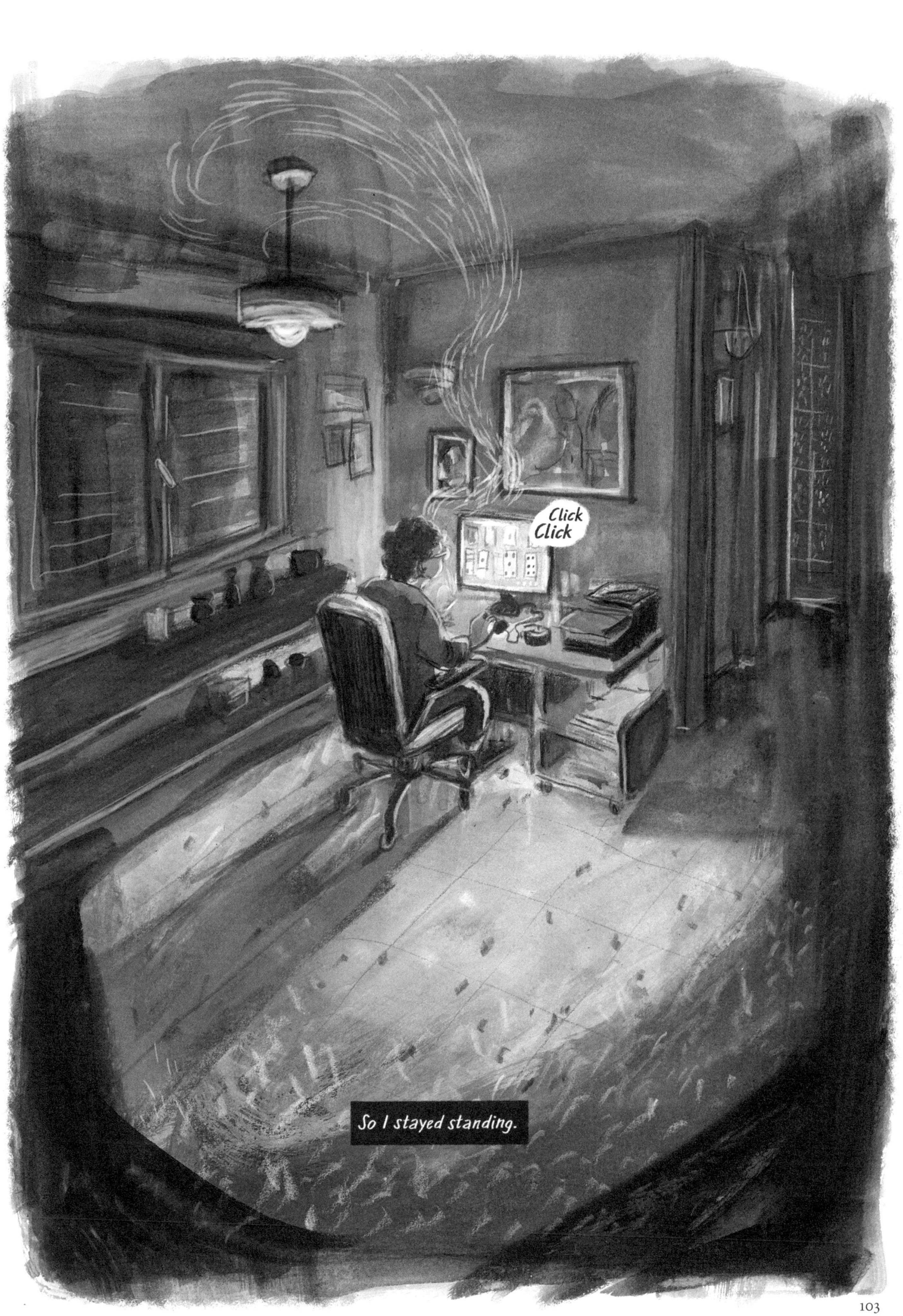
Click
Click
So I stayed standing.

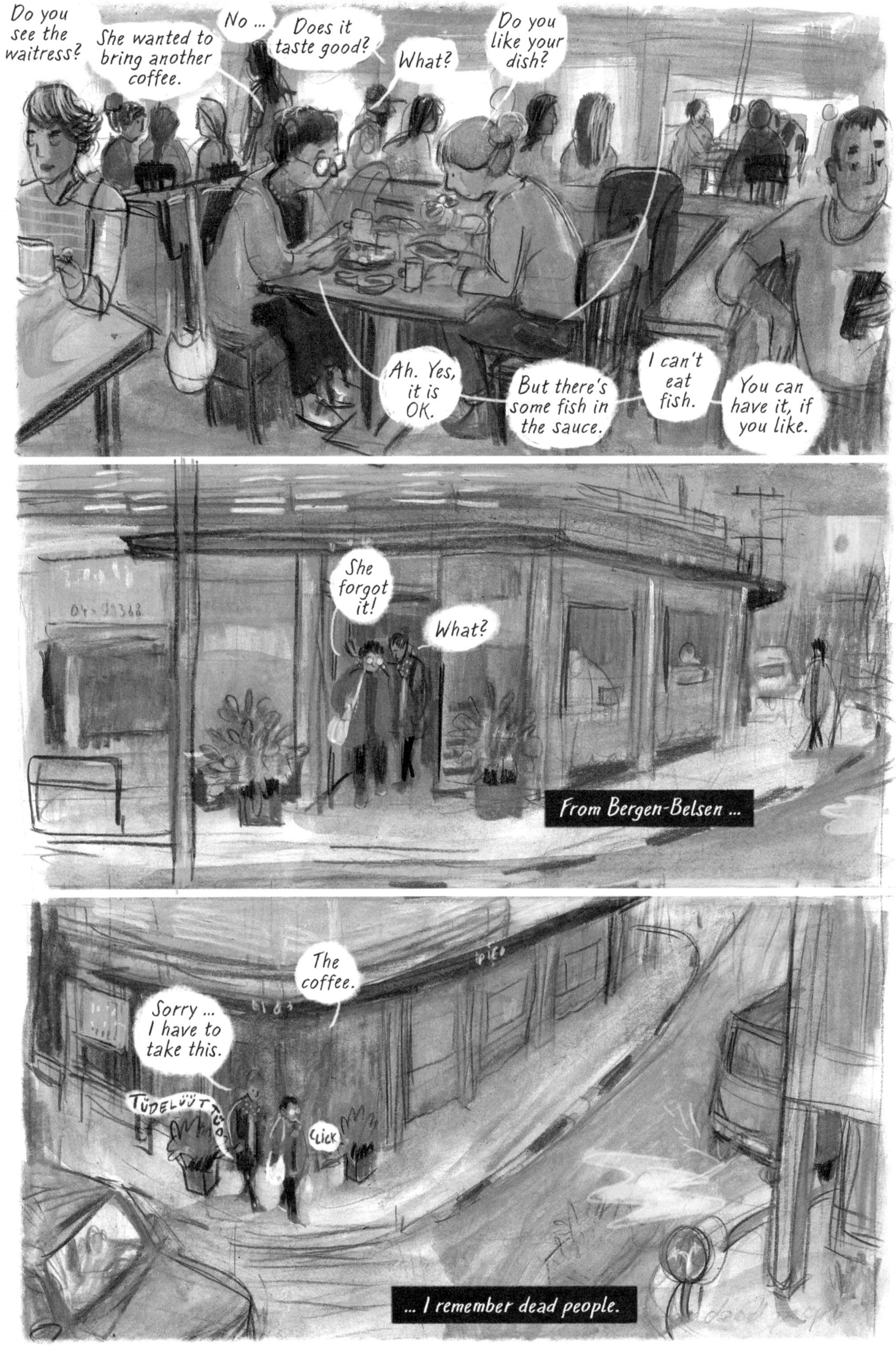
Do you see the waitress?
She wanted to bring another coffee.
No ...
Does it taste good?
What?
Do you like your dish?
Ah. Yes, it is OK.
But there's some fish in the sauce.
I can't eat fish.
You can have it, if you like.
She forgot it!
What?
From Bergen-Belsen ...
The coffee.
Sorry ... I have to take this.
TÜDELÜÜT
CLICK
... I remember dead people.

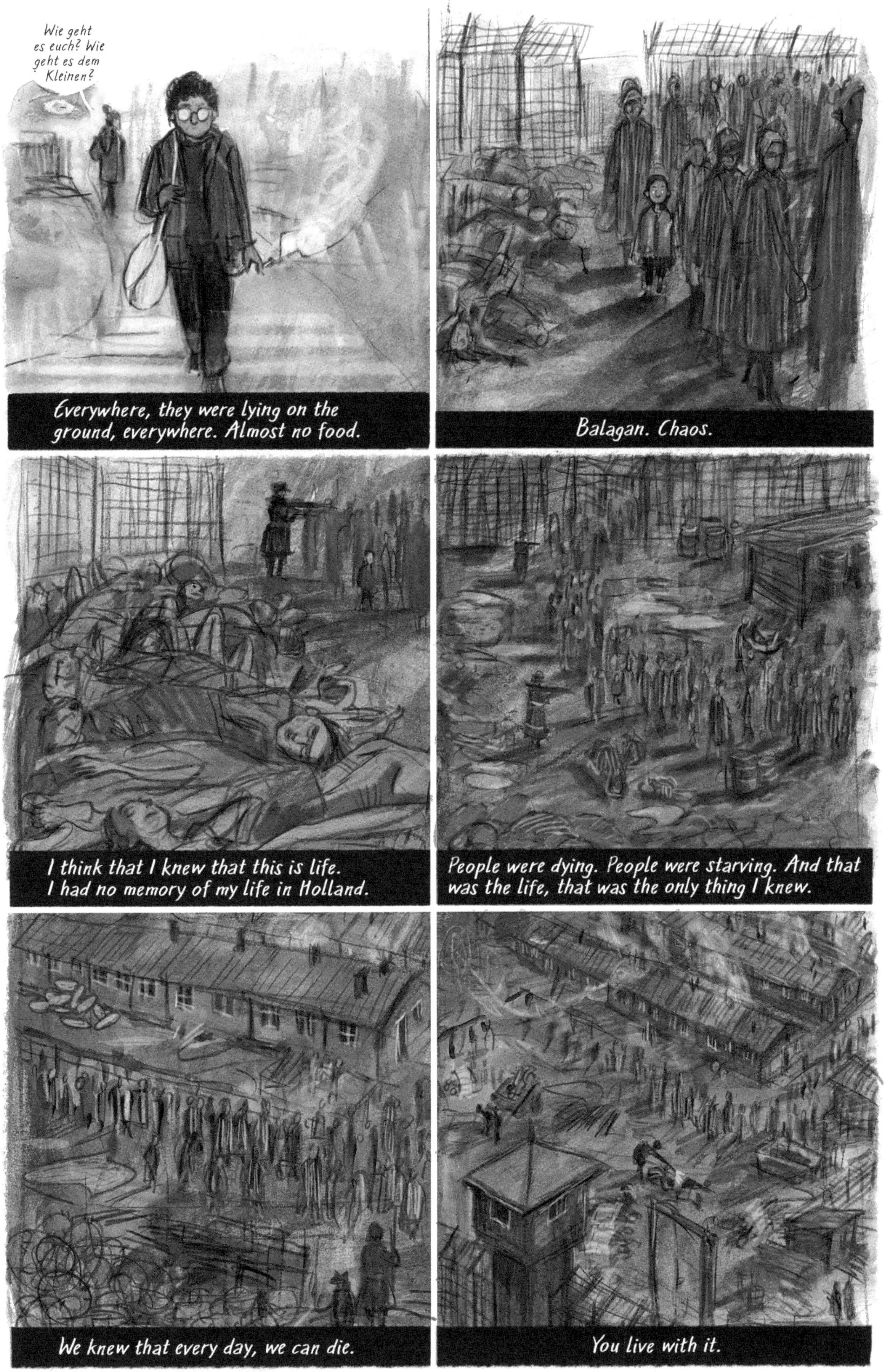
Wie geht es euch? Wie geht es dem Kleinen?
Everywhere, they were lying on the ground, everywhere. Almost no food.
Balagan. Chaos.
I think that I knew that this is life. I had no memory of my life in Holland.
People were dying. People were starving. And that was the life, that was the only thing I knew.
We knew that every day, we can die.
You live with it.

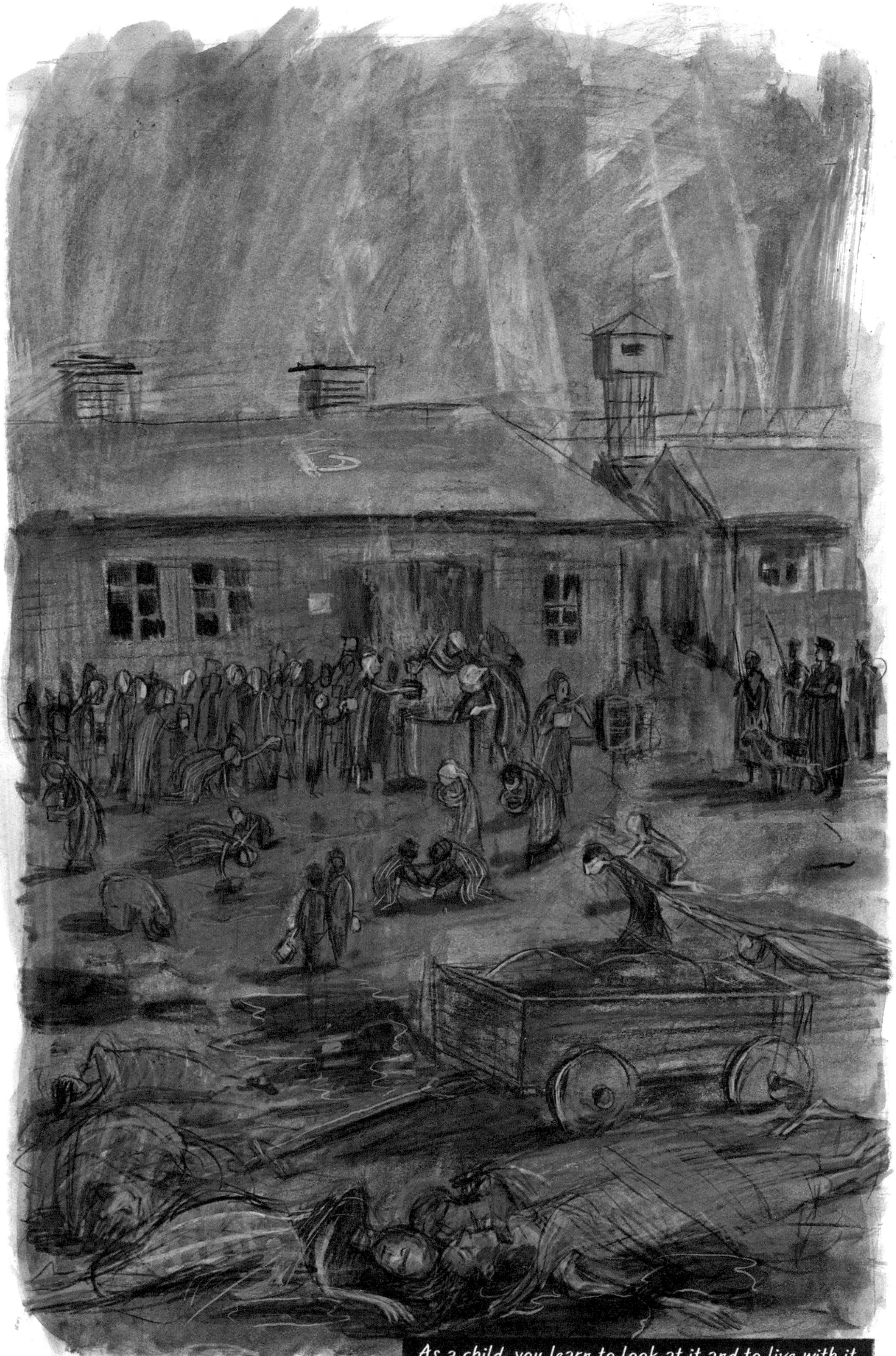

As a child, you learn to look at it and to live with it.

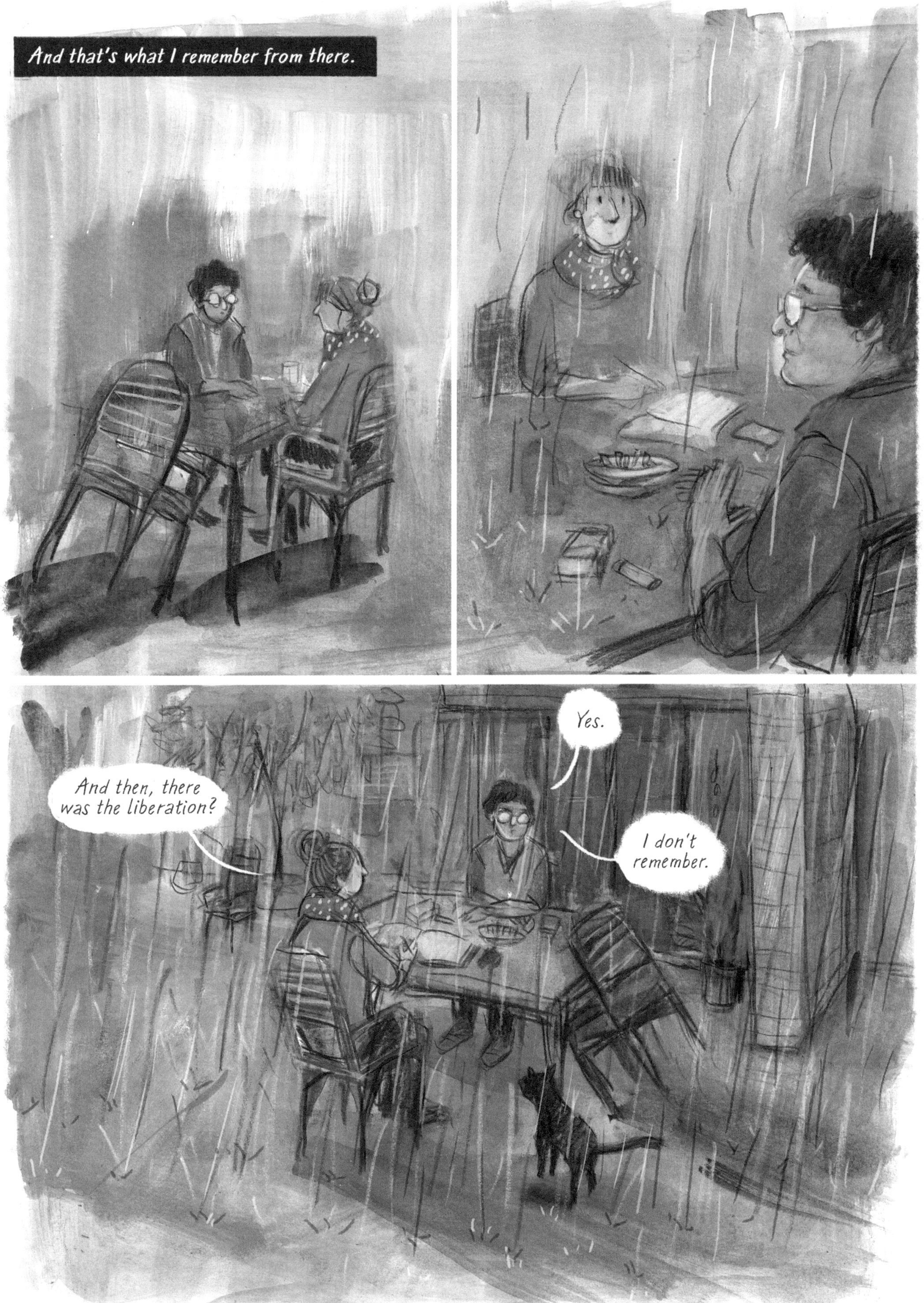

And that's what I remember from there.
And then, there was the liberation?
Yes.
I don't remember.

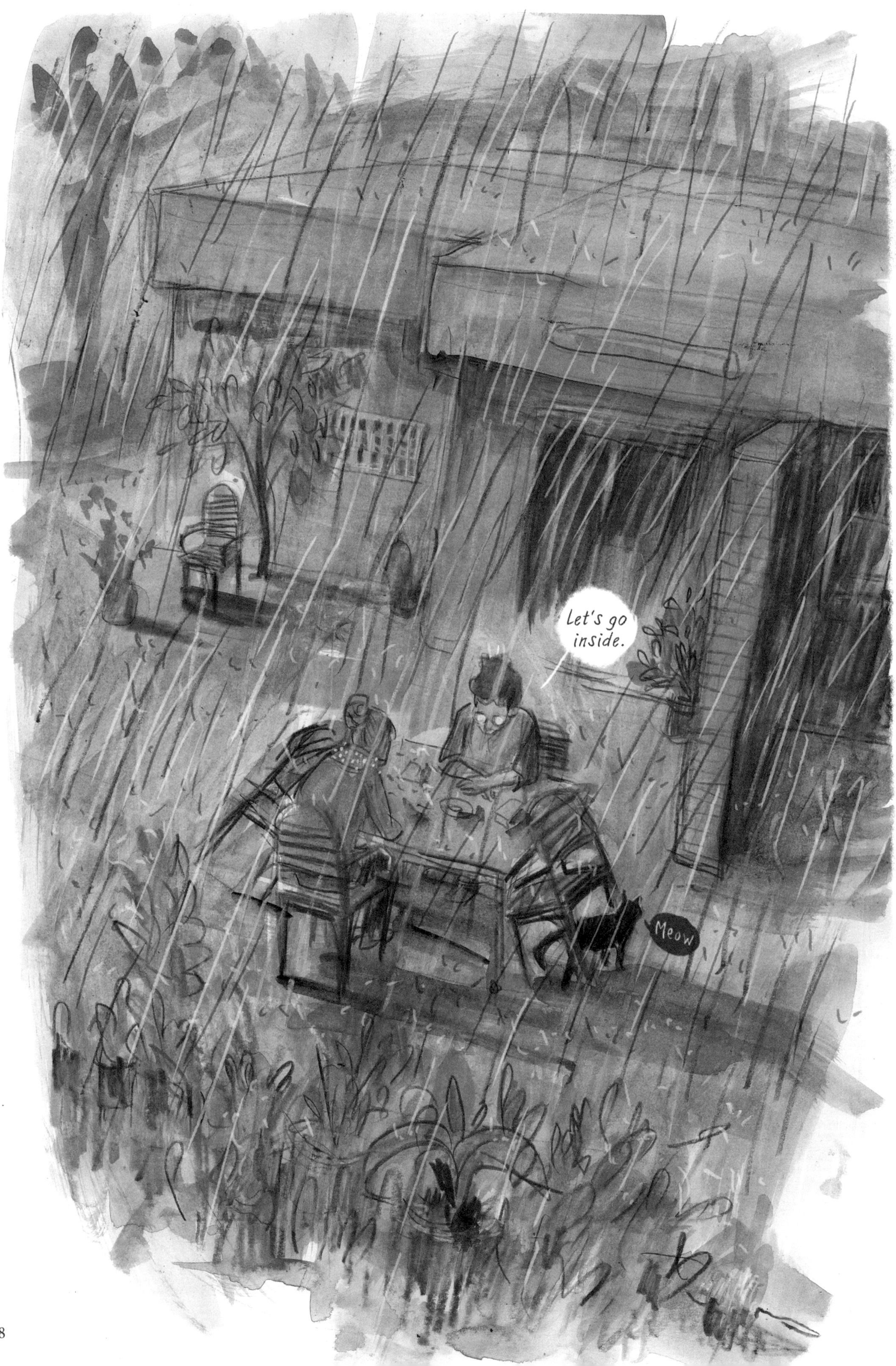
Let's go inside.
Meow

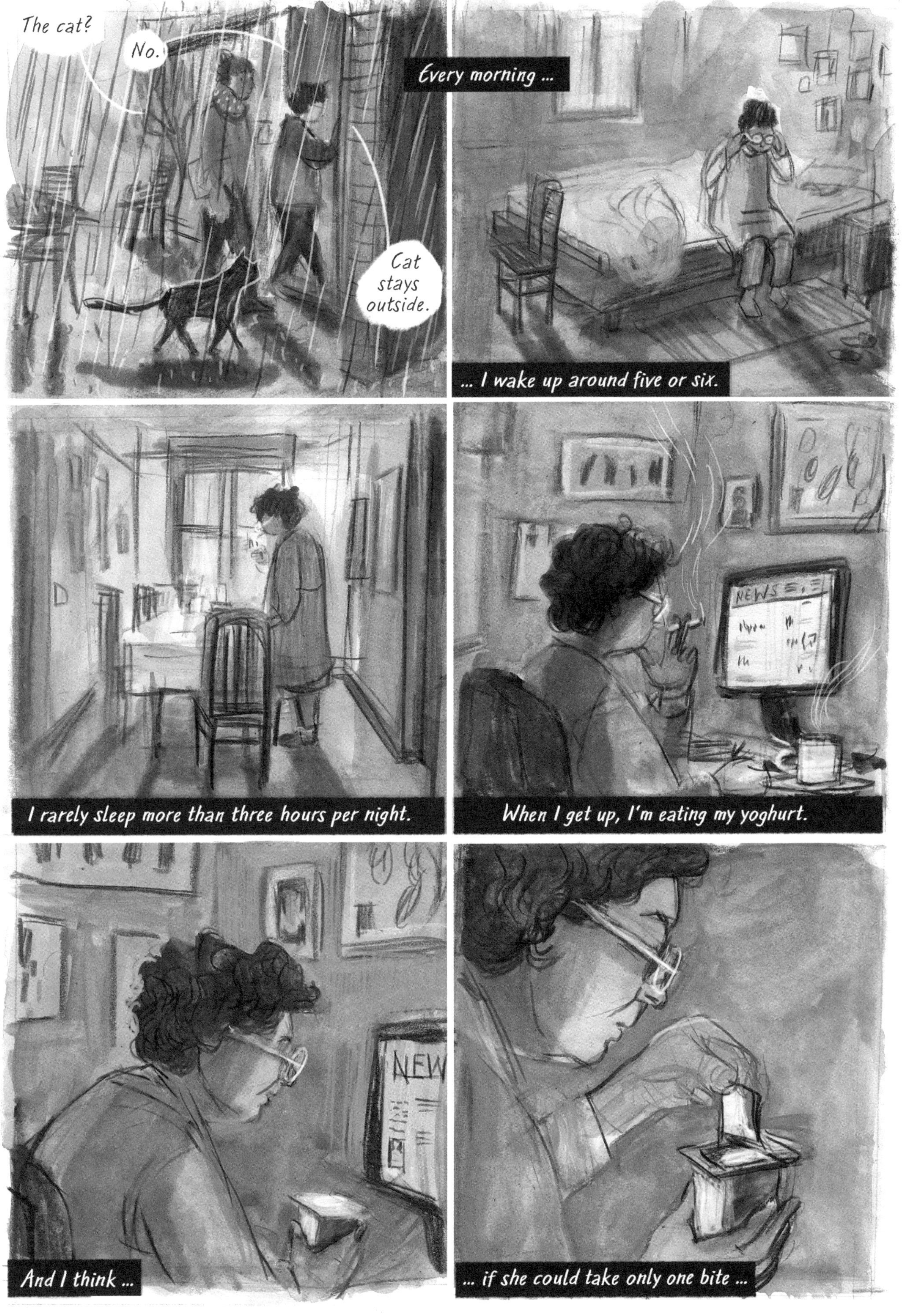

The cat?
No.
Cat stays outside.
Every morning ...
... I wake up around five or six.
I rarely sleep more than three hours per night.
When I get up, I'm eating my yoghurt.
And I think ...
... if she could take only one bite ...

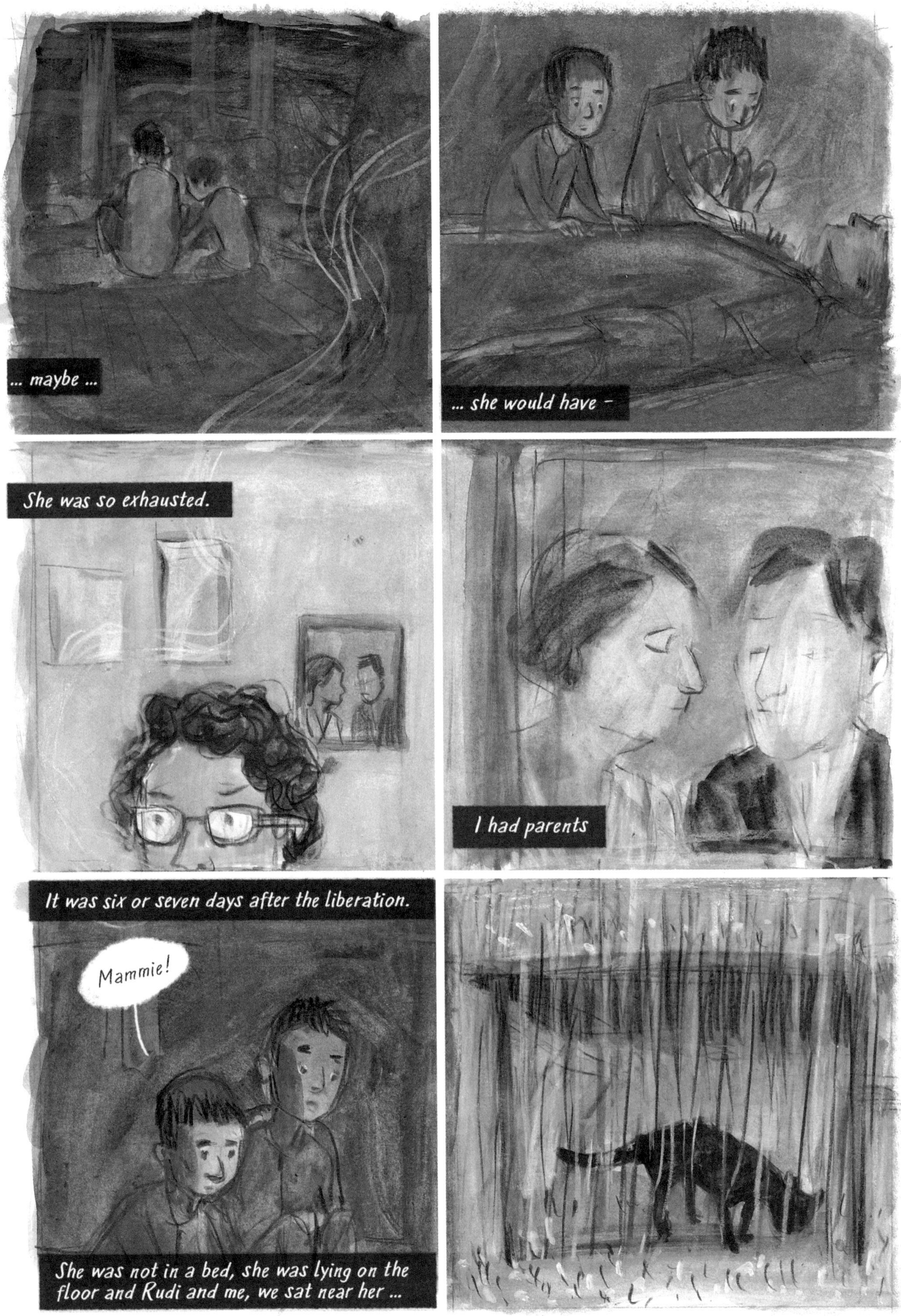
... maybe ...
... she would have -
She was so exhausted.
I had parents
It was six or seven days after the liberation.
Mammie!
She was not in a bed, she was lying on the floor and Rudi and me, we sat near her ...

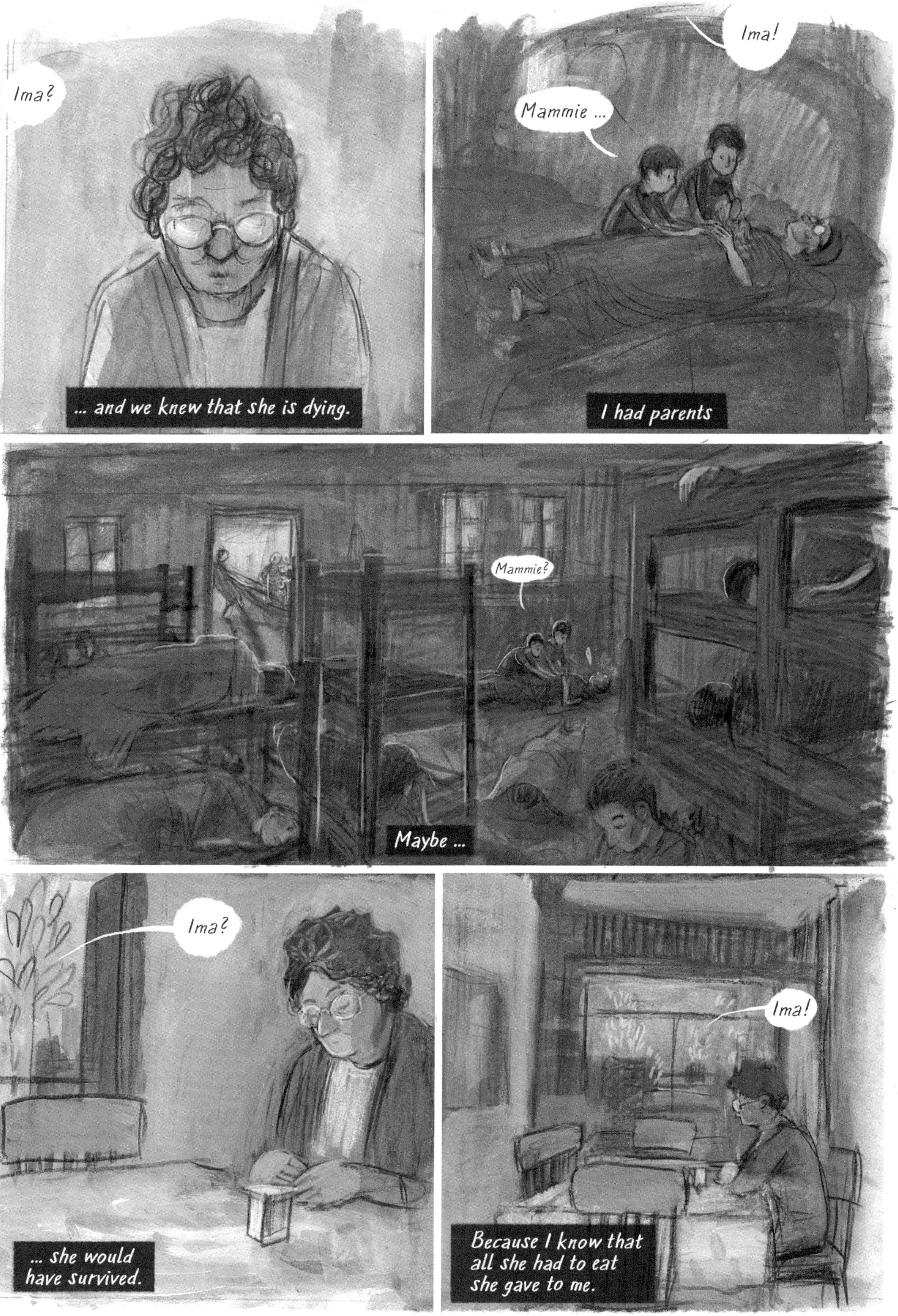
Ima?
... and we knew that she is dying.
Ima!
Mammie ...
I had parents
Mammie?
Maybe ...
Ima?
... she would have survived.
Ima!
Because I know that all she had to eat she gave to me.

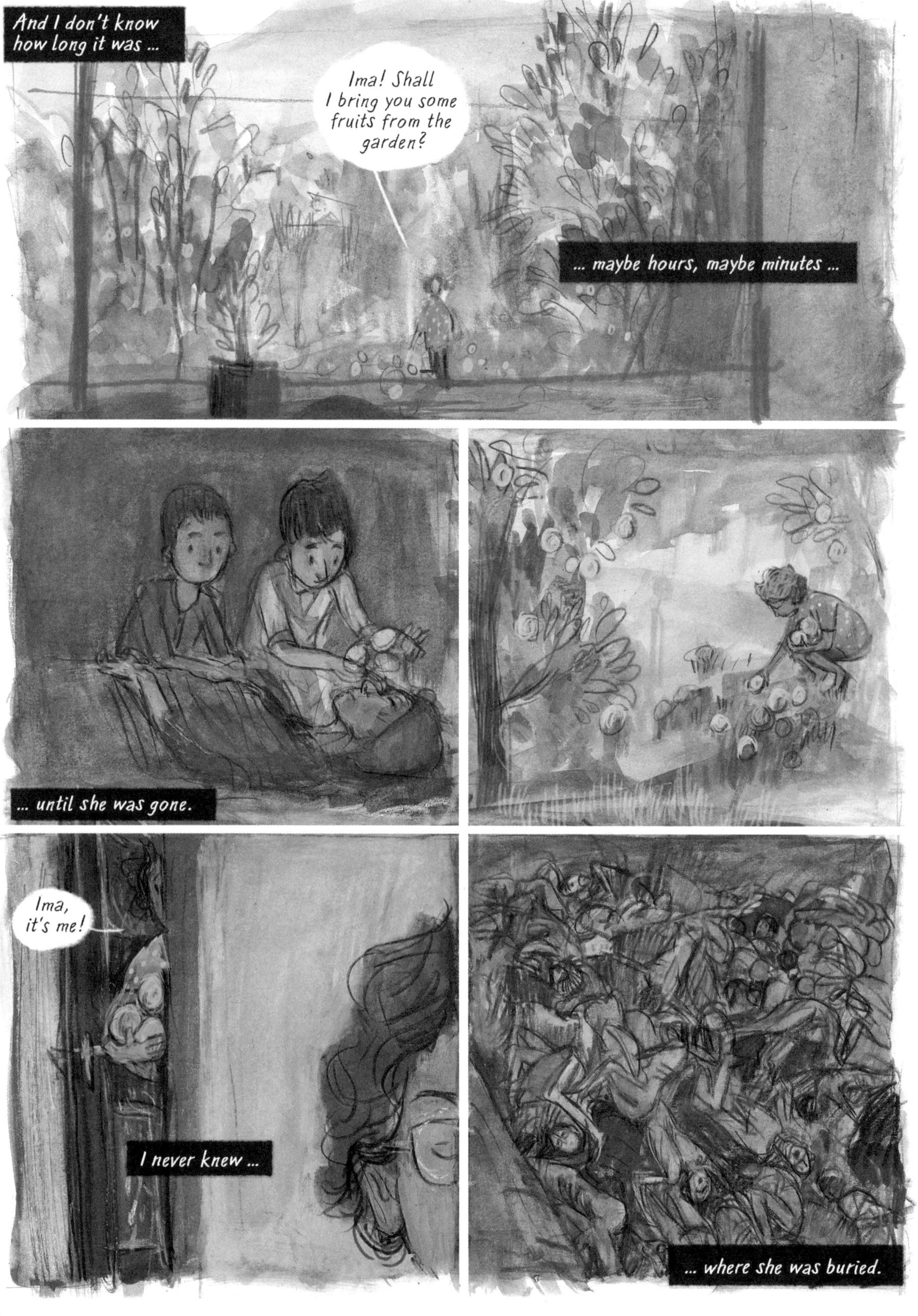

And I don't know how long it was ...
Ima! Shall I bring you some fruits from the garden?
... maybe hours, maybe minutes ...
... until she was gone.
Ima, it's me!
I never knew ...
... where she was buried.

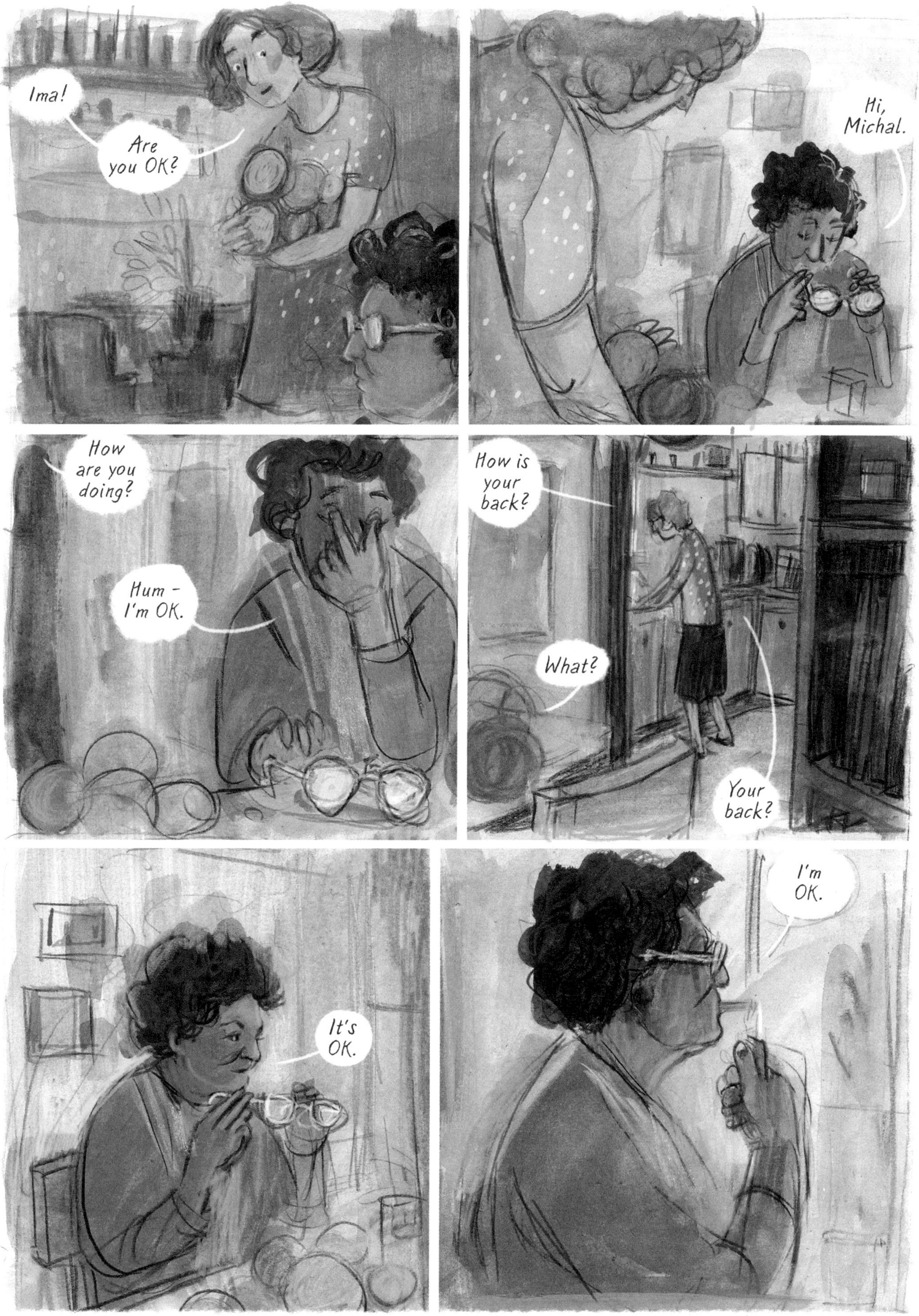
Ima!
Are you OK?
Hi, Michal.
How are you doing?
Hum - I'm OK.
How is your back?
What?
Your back?
It's OK.
I'm OK.

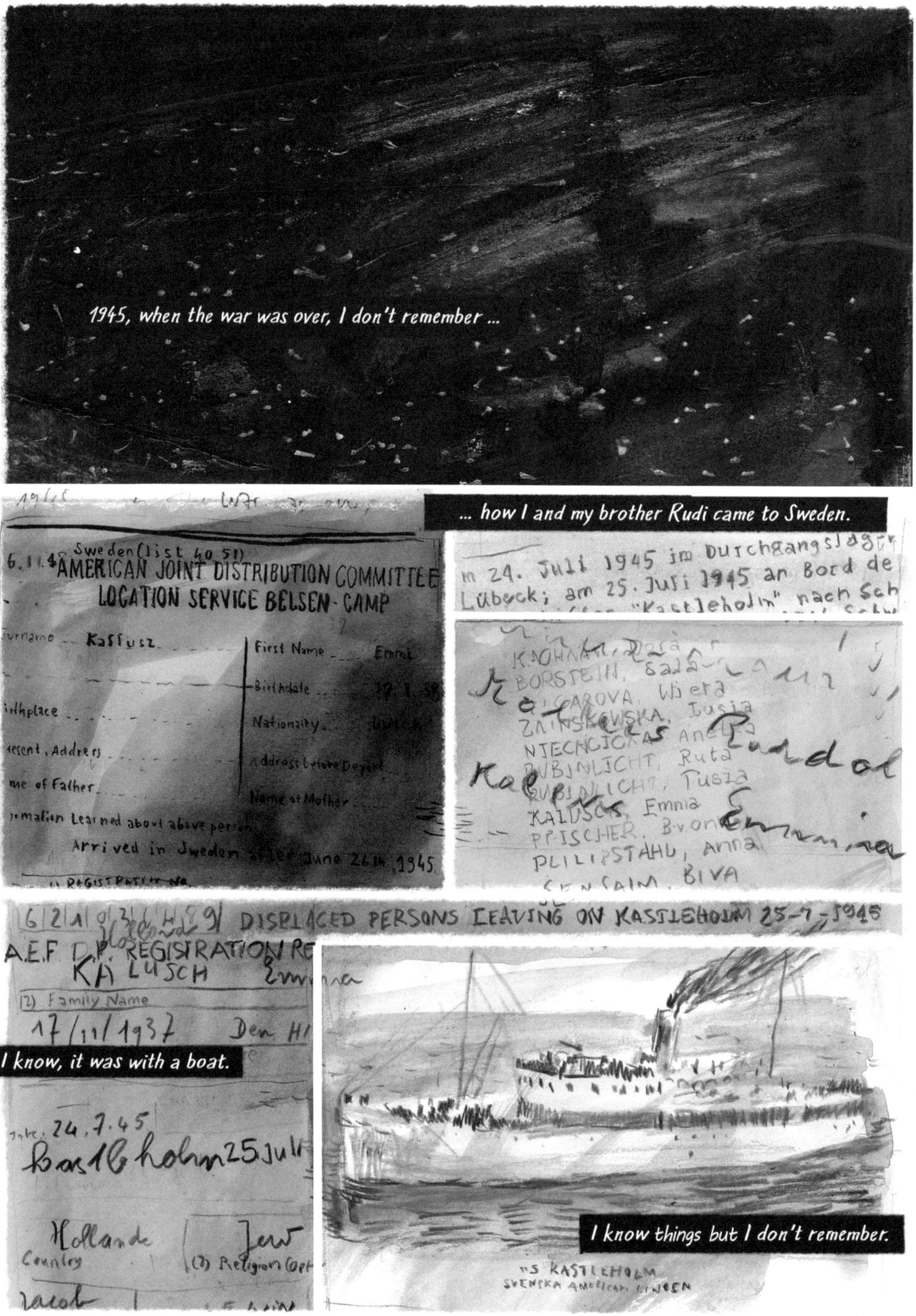
1945, when the war was over, I don't remember ...
... how I and my brother Rudi came to Sweden.
Sweden (list 40 51)
AMERICAN JOINT DISTRIBUTION COMMITTEE
LOCATION SERVICE BELSEN-CAMP
First Name
Birthdate
Nationality
Address before Deport
Name of Mother
Arrived in Sweden after June 26th 1945
m 24. Juli 1945 im Durchgangslager
Lübeck; am 25. Juli 1945 an Bord de
DISPLACED PERSONS LEAVING ON KASTLEHOLM 25-7-1945
A.E.F. D.P. REGISTRATION
(2) Family Name
17/11/1937
I know, it was with a boat.
Hollande
Country
Jew
(7) Religion
I know things but I don't remember.
MS KASTLEHOLM
SVENSKA AMERICAN LINIEN

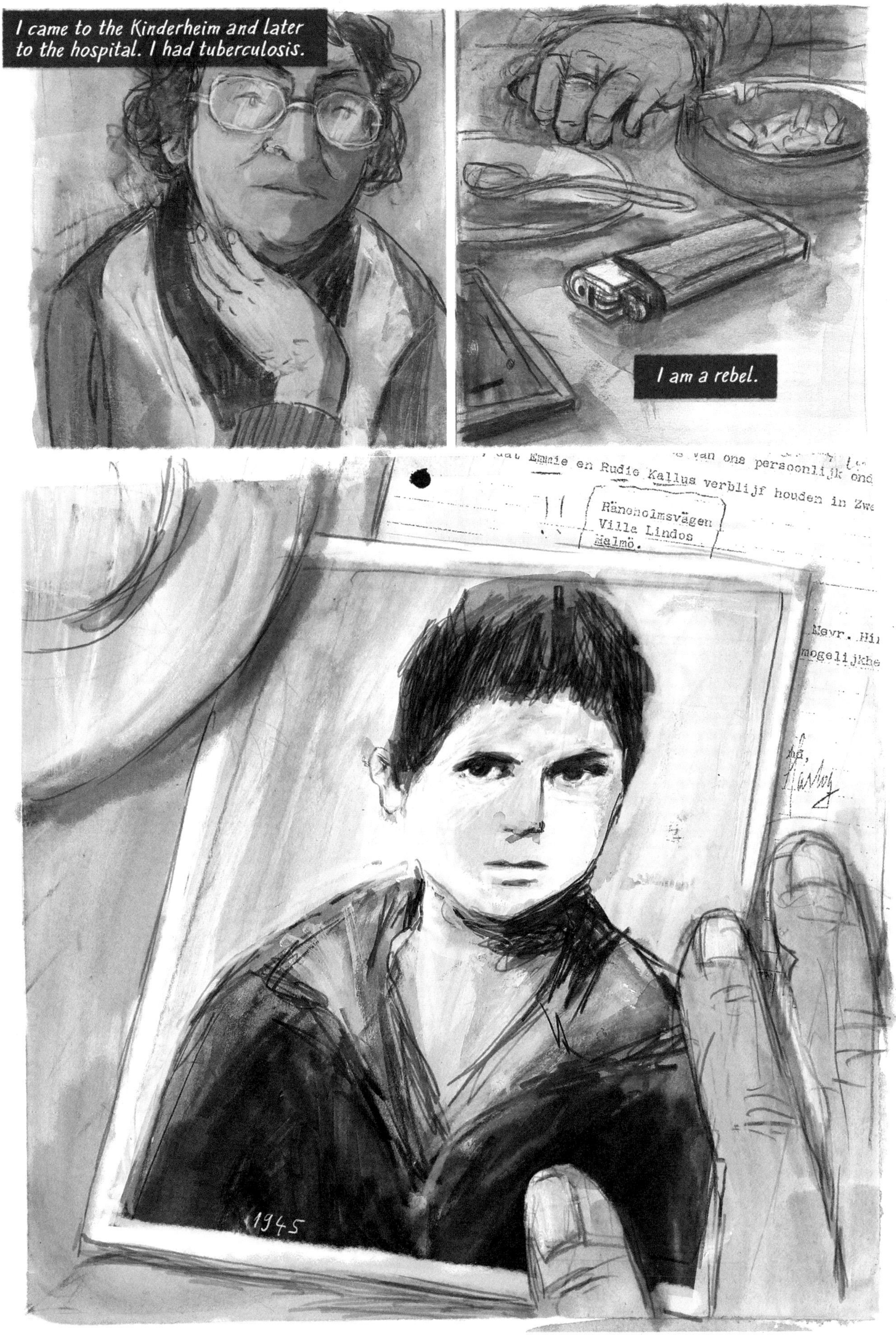
I came to the Kinderheim and later to the hospital. I had tuberculosis.
I am a rebel.
Emmie en Rudie Kallus verblijf houden in
van ons persoonlijk
Ränoholmsvägen
Villa Lindos
Malmö.
Mevr.
1945

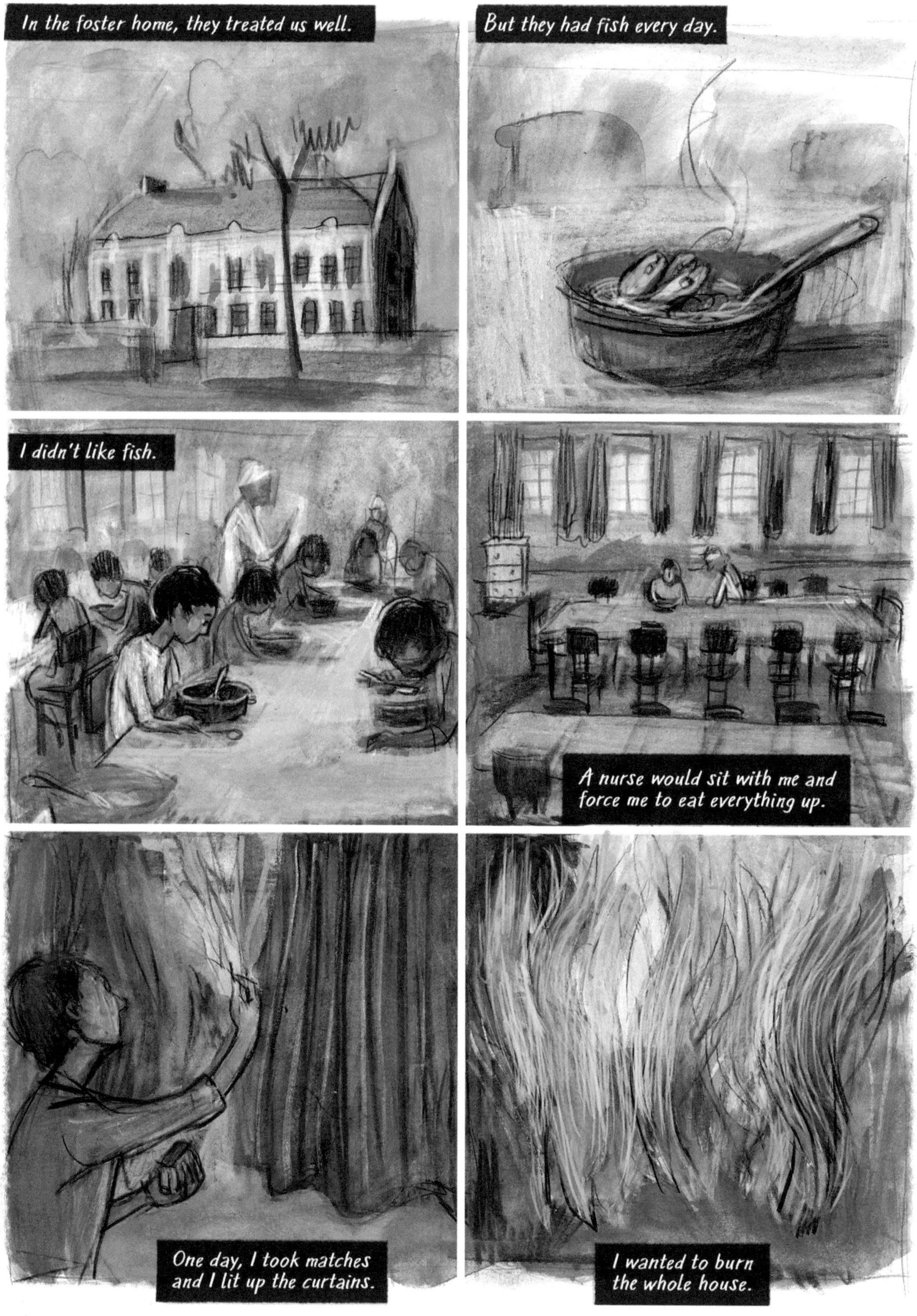
In the foster home, they treated us well.
But they had fish every day.
I didn't like fish.
A nurse would sit with me and force me to eat everything up.
One day, I took matches and I lit up the curtains.
I wanted to burn the whole house.

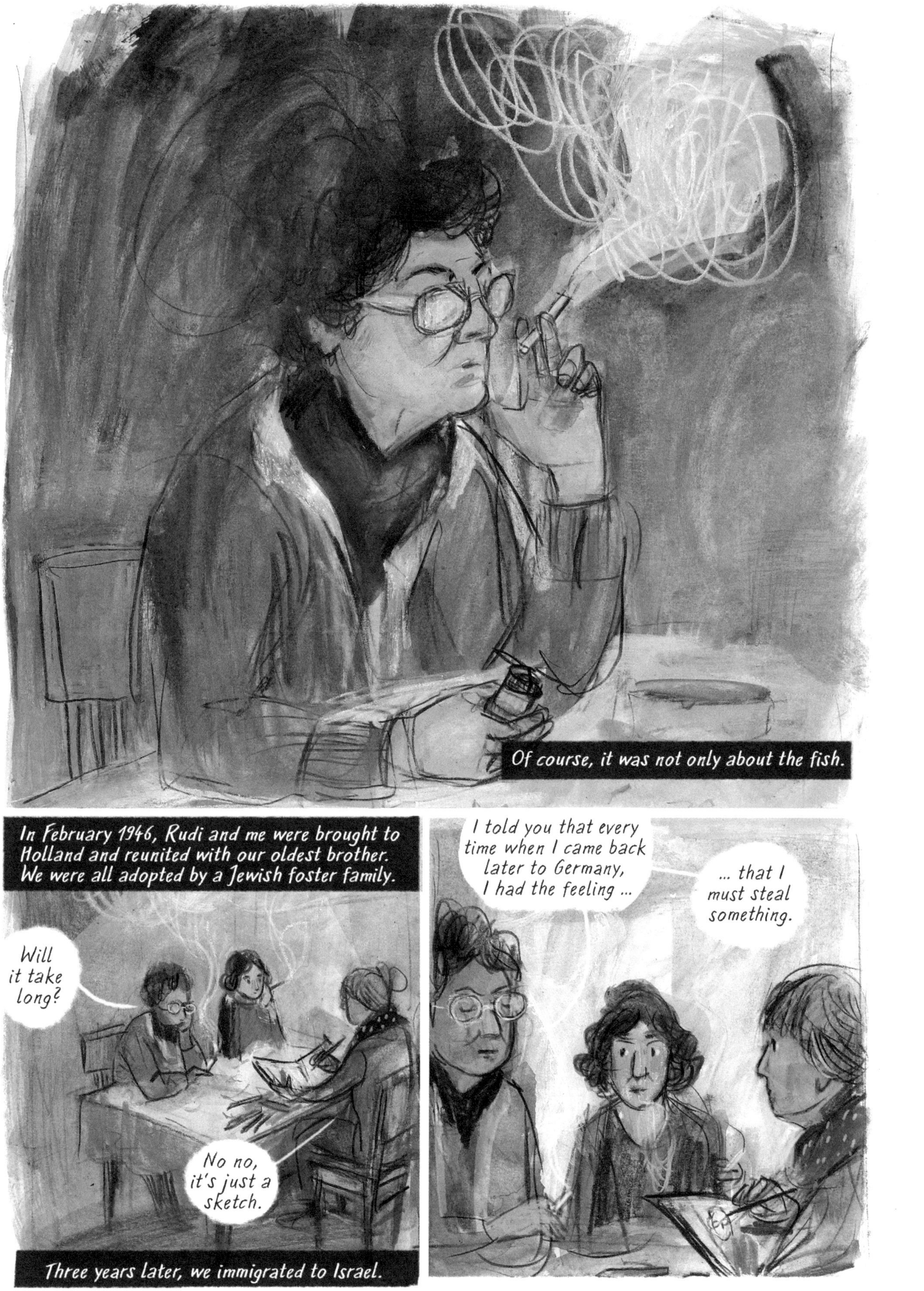
Of course, it was not only about the fish.
In February 1946, Rudi and me were brought to Holland and reunited with our oldest brother. We were all adopted by a Jewish foster family.
Will it take long?
No no, it's just a sketch.
Three years later, we immigrated to Israel.
I told you that every time when I came back later to Germany, I had the feeling ...
... that I must steal something.

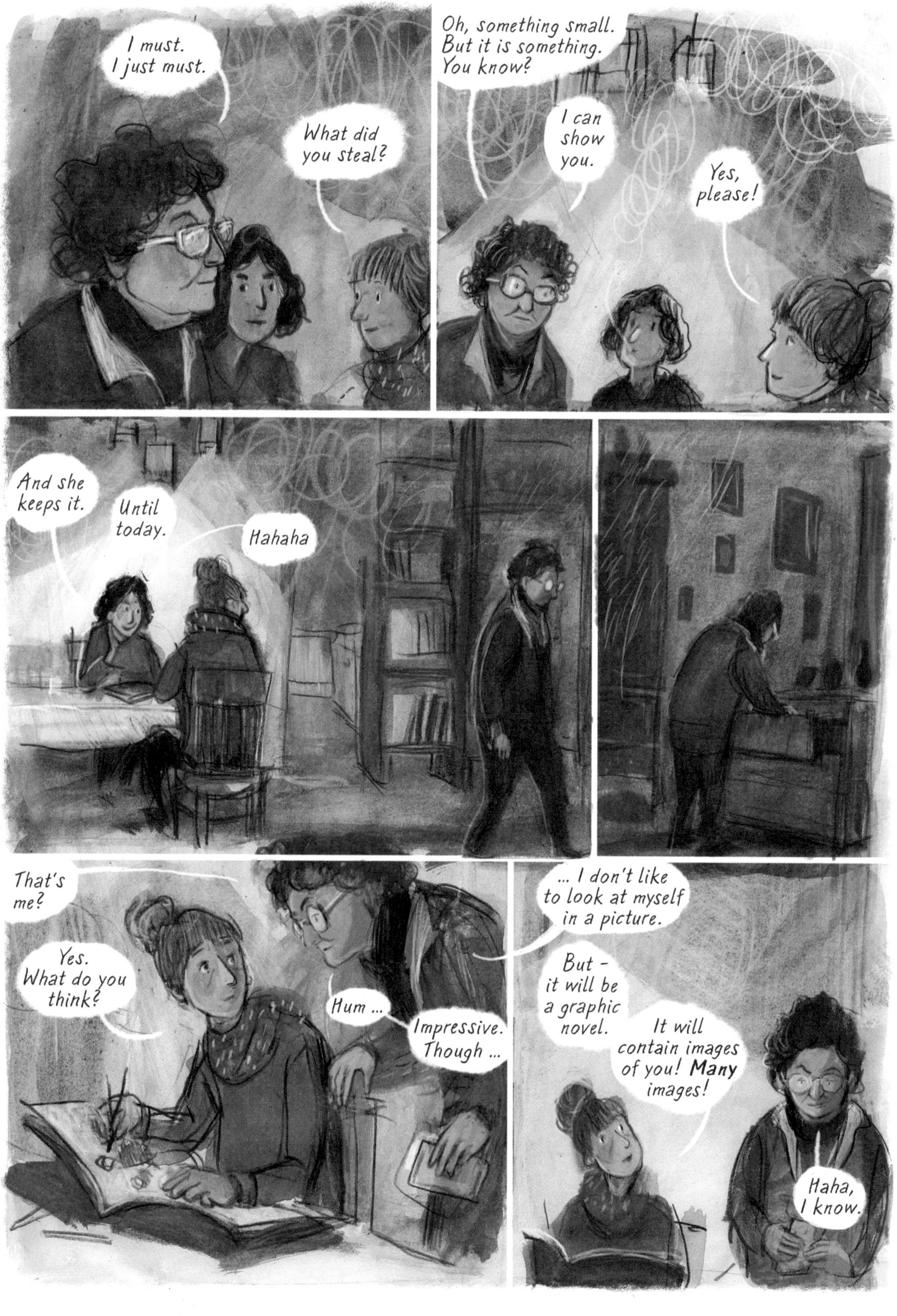
I must.
I just must.
What did you steal?
Oh, something small.
But it is something.
You know?
I can show you.
Yes, please!
And she keeps it.
Until today.
Hahaha
That's me?
Yes.
What do you think?
Hum ...
Impressive.
Though ...
... I don't like to look at myself in a picture.
But - it will be a graphic novel.
It will contain images of you! **Many** images!
Haha, I know.

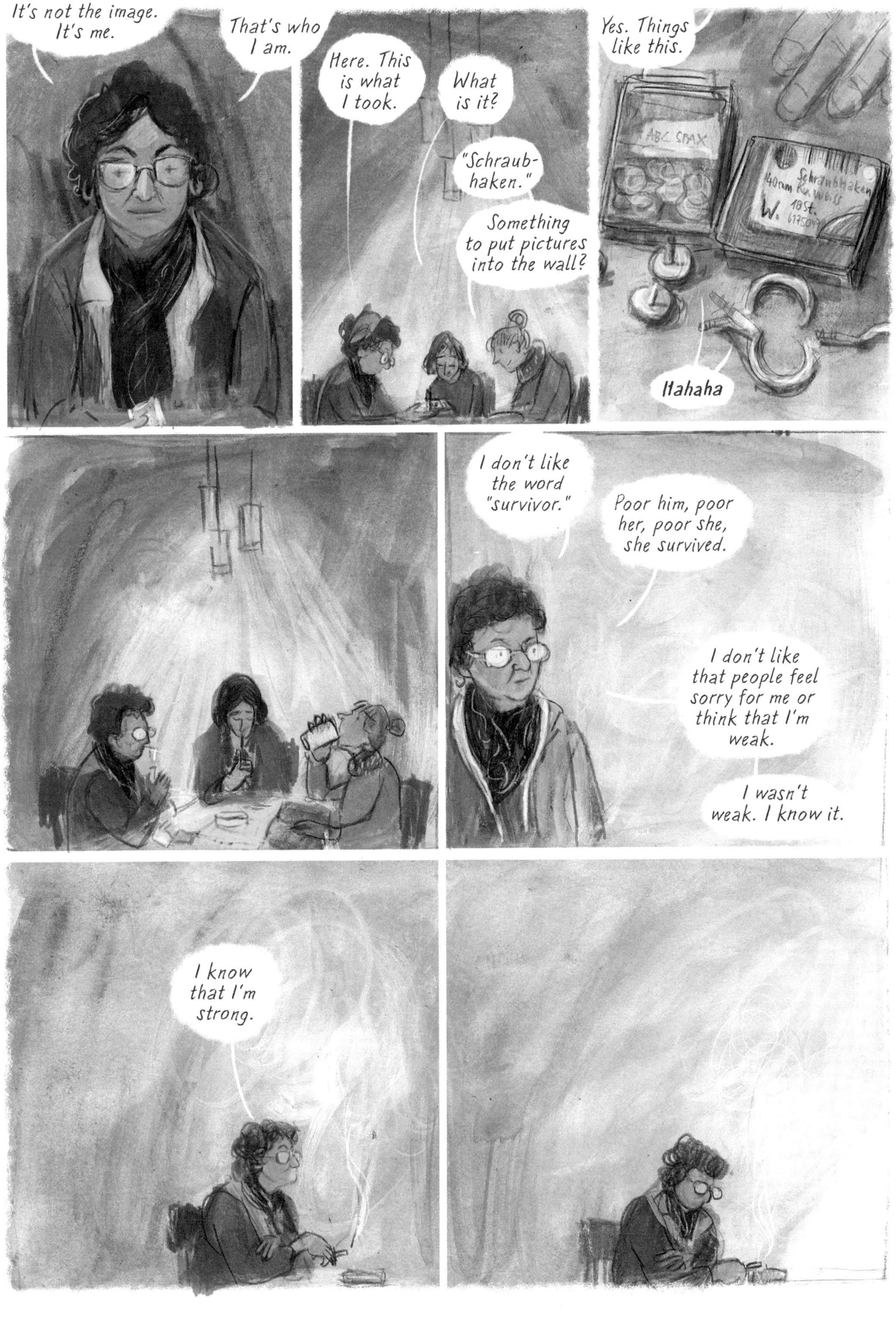
It's not the image. It's me.
That's who I am.
Here. This is what I took.
What is it?
"Schraub-haken."
Something to put pictures into the wall?
Yes. Things like this.
Hahaha
I don't like the word "survivor."
Poor him, poor her, poor she, she survived.
I don't like that people feel sorry for me or think that I'm weak.
I wasn't weak. I know it.
I know that I'm strong.

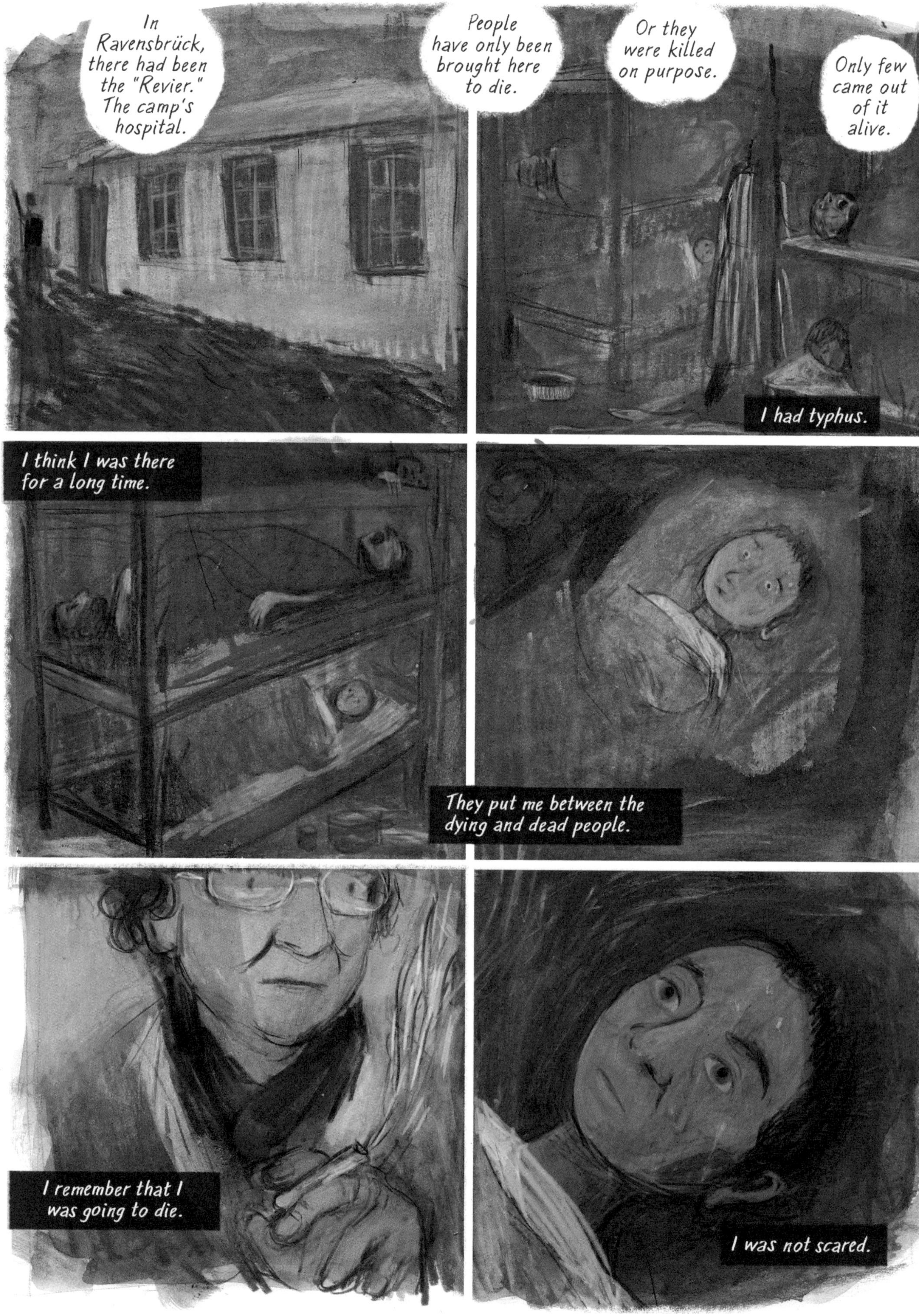
In Ravensbrück, there had been the "Revier." The camp's hospital.
People have only been brought here to die.
Or they were killed on purpose.
Only few came out of it alive.
I had typhus.
I think I was there for a long time.
They put me between the dying and dead people.
I remember that I was going to die.
I was not scared.

I think I remember ...

... the feeling of going to die.

It was a very good feeling.

I had no pain, no hunger, no noise.

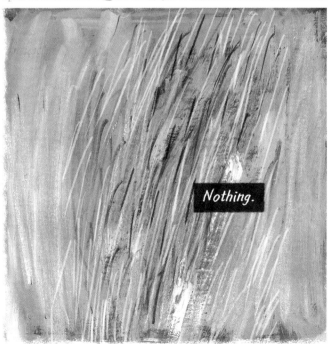

Nothing.

It was quiet and good.

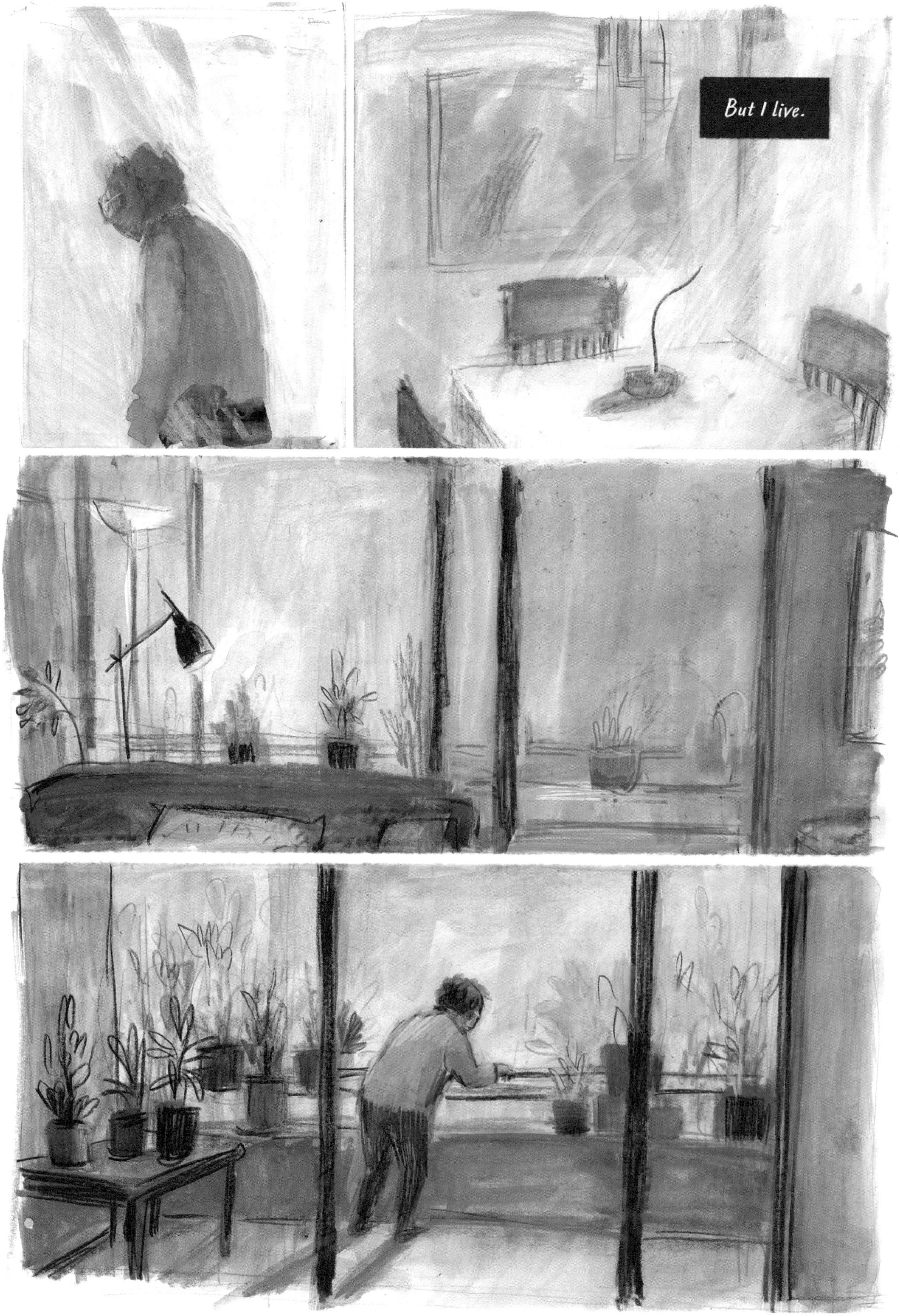
But I live.

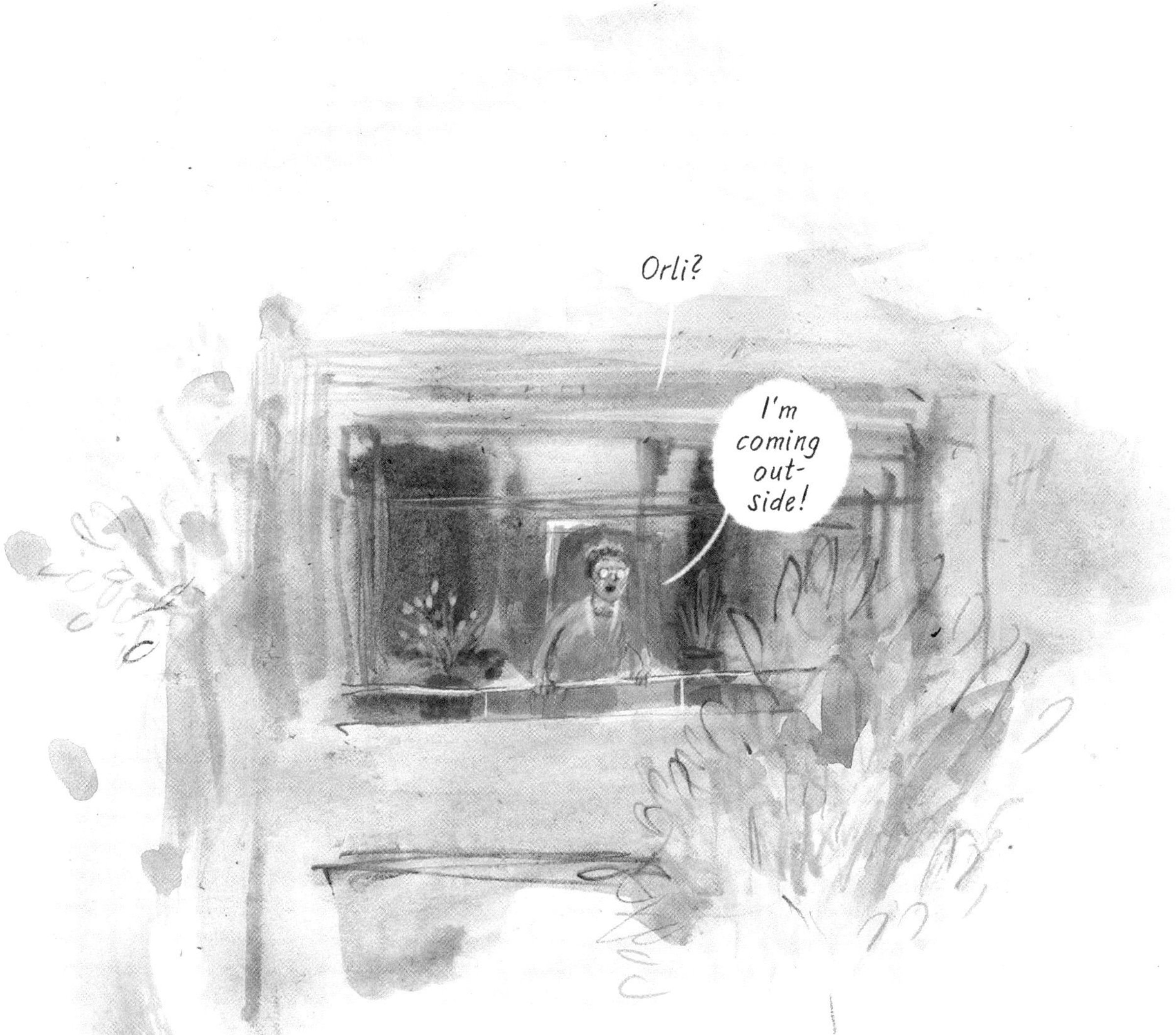
Orli?
I'm coming out-side!

The Histories

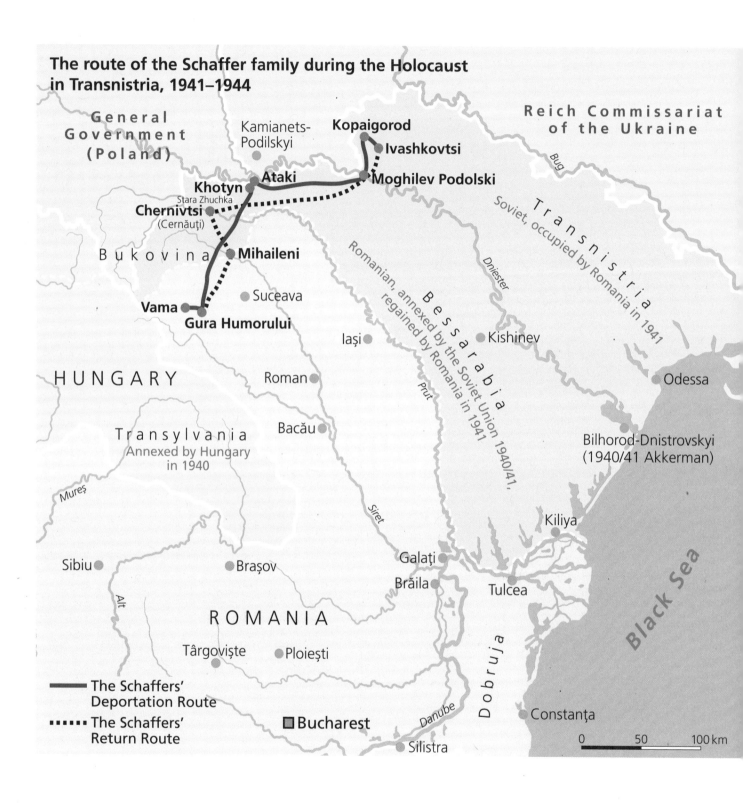

The route of the Schaffer family during the Holocaust in Transnistria, 1941–1944

General Government (Poland)

Reich Commissariat of the Ukraine

Kamianets-Podilskyi

Kopaigorod

Ivashkovtsi

Ataki

Khotyn

Stara Zhuchka

Chernivtsi (Cernăuţi)

Moghilev Podolski

Bug

Transnistria

Soviet, occupied by Romania in 1941

Bukovina

Mihaileni

Dniester

Vama

Gura Humorului

Suceava

Bessarabia

Romanian, annexed by the Soviet Union 1940/41, regained by Romania in 1941

Iaşi

Kishinev

Odessa

HUNGARY

Roman

Prut

Transylvania

Annexed by Hungary in 1940

Bacău

Bilhorod-Dnistrovskyi (1940/41 Akkerman)

Mureş

Kiliya

Sibiu

Braşov

Galaţi

Brăila

Siret

Tulcea

Black Sea

Alt

ROMANIA

Târgovişte

Ploieşti

Dobruja

The Schaffers' Deportation Route

The Schaffers' Return Route

Bucharest

Danube

Constanţa

Silistra

0   50   100 km

THE HOLOCAUST
IN TRANSNISTRIA

Alexander Korb

Associate Professor in Modern European History
at the University of Leicester

David Schaffer was born in 1931 in the village of Vama in the Bukovina region in northern Romania, known as "the land of the beech trees." Bukovina had belonged to the Austro-Hungarian Monarchy up until 1919. According to a census in 1910, 34 per cent of the population spoke Romanian as their first language, 38 per cent Ukrainian, and 27 per cent either German or Yiddish. Roughly 13 per cent of the population was Jewish. Some towns and even cities like Rădăuți and Gura Humorului had Jewish majorities. The region's capital is Chernivtsi and is now part of Ukraine. Bukovina's beauty and diversity are often romanticized. Poet Paul Celan called the region a place "where people and books lived together."[1] This refers to the old Francisco-Josephina University in Chernivtsi and to the huge number of coffee shops, where people gathered and read newspapers from all around Europe, but also to the Jewish love for the written word that was so abundant in the region's synagogues and schools. Yet there were ethnic conflicts before, during, and after World War I, even though Bukovina had been one of the calmest regions of the Austro-Hungarian Empire. These conflicts fueled antisemitism. The end of the war and the collapse of the Austro-Hungarian and Russian Empires led to a series of pogroms (anti-Jewish riots). Across Eastern

---

1   Paul Celan, Ansprache anlässlich der Entgegennahme des Literaturpreises der Freien Hansestadt Bremen (1958), in *Prosa I* [Gesammelte Werke 15,1] (Frankfurt/Main: Suhrkamp, 2014), 23.

Europe, nationalists killed thousands of Jews and tens of thousands fled to Western Europe and to countries overseas.

Romania had been amongst the winners of World War I and had been awarded substantial territories, including Bukovina. But by the 1930s, Romania had turned into an authoritarian and unstable state. The Great Depression was raging, and the country was politically divided. Persecution against the Jews escalated further in 1938. David's story shows that Jewish families could no longer send their children to state schools, and the Romanian majority discriminated against the Jews wherever it could. David's family was forced to move from their village to the city of Gura Humorului when Jews were no longer tolerated in the countryside. Even though Romania had not yet joined Germany's side in the war, German troops and personnel were everywhere. The strong fascist movement, the Iron Guard, was trying to come to power through violence and attacks on the Jewish population. King Carol II and his regime, however, were more concerned with what they saw as a Communist threat from the Soviet Union. The country's elite was focused on sustaining Romania's territorial integrity. Most of the neighboring countries, namely Hungary, Bulgaria, and the Soviet Union, claimed Romanian territories to be theirs. The borderlands in Eastern and Southeastern Europe were ethnically and religiously very diverse. For the Romanian government this was a problem because the more diverse a region was, the harder it was to prove that it was historically and culturally Romanian. Romania launched a variety of "Romanization" programs throughout the 1930s with the aim to increase the country's population that was seen as Romanian by culture, religion, and race. That affected Jews and Roma, who were treated as societal outsiders, as well as the Slavic and the Hungarian minorities.

With the rise of German military, economic, and political power in the years after 1936, most Southeastern European states started accepting Germany as their lead power. However, Romania's place in the German-led "new European order" started with a blow. Hitler's promise to undo the Paris Peace Treaties that had ended World War I threatened a series of border changes that would affect Romania in a negative way. In June 1940, the Soviet Union, empowered by the

1939 Nonaggression Pact between Hitler and Stalin, occupied Romania's eastern province, Bessarabia, as well as Northern Bukovina. The south, where David's family lived, remained Romanian. Bessarabia had belonged to Russia until 1918, and Soviet Russia never accepted the region as Romanian. Northern Bukovina's occupation, however, was harder to justify.

On 30 August 1940, Germany and Italy declared that Romania would have to cede a substantial part of its northern territories (Transylvania) with its Hungarian-speaking minority to its Hungarian neighbor. In other words, during the summer and autumn of 1940, Romania lost about 30 per cent of its territory and population. These developments came as a shock to the country's political system and its people. King Carol II abdicated to his young son, Michael I. Politically, Romania turned into the National Legionary State, which was based on an authoritarian alliance between the military and the state's "leader" (*conducator*), General Ion Antonescu, on the one hand, and the radical fascist Iron Guard as its partner on the other. Judged by the number of victims, Romania turned into the most violent dictatorship on the European continent, except for Nazi Germany. The Iron Guard started killing former adversaries and targeted the Jewish community. The alliance between the military and the Iron Guard did not work, though, and led to an attempted *putsch* (a violent attempt to overthrow the government) by the Iron Guard in January 1941. That uprising went hand in hand with the killing of opponents and with a pogrom in Bucharest during which Iron Guardists murdered 125 Jews.

Surprisingly for Europe in 1941, the outcome of the insurgency was not a victory by the radicals but rather their destruction by the military. Many members of the Iron Guard were imprisoned, and their leadership fled to Nazi Germany. The Iron Guard did not have Hitler's support. He preferred to cooperate with the larger authoritarian forces throughout Europe, which he saw as more reliable, rather than with smaller radical movements, which he did not trust. Moreover, this strategy enabled German diplomats to put pressure on existing governments by threatening to support the radicals. For example, if a government resisted implementing anti-Jewish policies, the Germans would threaten the government with helping the radicals replace it. The Antonescu regime understood this arrangement clearly and became one of Nazi Germany's most faithful allies. Romania delivered the oil Germany needed for its war machinery, opened itself for German troops, and it helped prepare the German attack on the Soviet Union in June 1941, which offered a pathway to regain Bessarabia and Northern Bukovina.

On 22 June 1941, Germany attacked the Soviet Union. Launched from Romanian territory, the attack was carried out by the German 11th Army jointly with two Romanian armies of more than 325,000 troops and 200 war planes. This is when the Romanian Holocaust started. With the armies marched a German killing squad, "Task Force D" (there were four such "task forces," D being the most southern one), and with Romanian help, it started to massacre the Jewish population by shooting them in the territories now occupied by the Germans. Simultaneously, the Romanian regime started targeting the Jewish population living in its borderlands. Before entering Soviet territory, Romanian troops conducted a massacre in Romania's second largest city – Iaşi – killing 13,000 Jews. Romanian and German units systematically murdered the Jews of Bessarabia's capital, Chişinău.

Despite the German influence, the Romanian state bore the sole responsibility for the violence that unfolded in 1941. The Romanian obsession with ethnic homogeneity – which was typical for most Southeastern European states during the 1930s – led to a genocide of Jews and Roma. It is important to note, though, that this also explains the difference between the German "Final Solution of the Jewish Question," as the Nazis called their Holocaust, and the Romanian genocide of Jews and Roma. For the Antonescu regime, Jews and Roma were minorities it wanted to get rid of, but not necessarily exterminate. This also explains the higher survival rate of Jews and Roma who were living under the Romanian thumb. Nevertheless, Romania was responsible for the second highest number of Jewish deaths in a single European country after Germany, being responsible for the death of between 280,000 and 380,000 Jews and 11,000 and 25,000 Roma. It is hard to conceive what the Holocaust in Romania would have looked like had the more radical Iron Guard been in power throughout the war. During the 1930s, the government developed plans to ethnically engineer Romania's population and to cleanse the country's borderlands of its Jewish and Roma minorities. In contrast to Germany, however, the Romanian government did not deport the Jewish minority from the Romanian heartland, for example, from the capital, Bucharest.

The war provided Antonescu with the environment to pursue his plans, and Hitler's decisions in 1941 provided him with the assistance to carry out these plans. With the attack on the Soviet Union, Hitler gave his Romanian allies permission to reannex Bessarabia and Northern Bukovina – the regions lost to the Soviet Union one year before. Moreover, Romania could occupy another territory that had never been Romanian: Transnistria. The region of Transnistria is situated between the Dniester River and the Bug River. Its largest city is the famous port of Odessa. Its population was predominantly Ukrainian, with sizeable Jewish, Roma, Russian, German, Romanian, and other minority communities. Because it was not of economic or strategic interest, Transnistria became the dumping ground for Romania's "others" – Jews and Roma – as well as a buffer zone between Romania and Ukraine. The Romanian genocide of Jews and Roma had different layers. The fate of Jews and Roma was intertwined, but many Jews took no notice of the plight of the Roma, or, like David, did not come across any in Transnistria.

During the occupation of Bessarabia, Northern Bukovina, and Transnistria, Romanian police and army units murdered tens of thousands of civilians. Romanian nationalists made Jews collectively responsible for the loss of Bessarabia to the Soviet Union and carried out "revenge" killings. According to the antisemitic obsession of the time, all Jews were Communists. This was not true, although some Jews preferred the Soviets to the Antonescu regime because the Soviets were not as antisemitic as were many segments of the Romanian population.

The survivors of the massacres were herded into ghettos and transit camps. In September 1941, the Antonescu regime began to deport Jews. Altogether, 150,000 Jews and 25,000 Roma were deported to Transnistria. Jews were not only deported from newly occupied territories but also from Southern Bukovina. The makeshift deportation was organized chaos. David's family, along with Gura

Humorului's Jewish population, were sent by train to Ataki, a former border town, situated on the Dniester River. The local Jewish population had already been murdered, and signs of the genocide were everywhere. Blood remained on the walls of the empty, ruined houses. From Ataki, the Jews were transferred across the river in makeshift rafts to Moghilev Podolski.

Transnistria was a killing field: it was like entering hell on earth, as many survivors remember. Corpses were floating in the rivers and lying on the fields and along the roads. Jews were walked into Transnistria in large convoys. Autumn had started, and the roads turned into deep mud. Everything was cold and wet, and there was no food. The Romanian guards, the local population, and even nature was hostile. These were death marches before the Germans' infamous use of them. During the marches, the Romanian gendarmerie frequently robbed the Jews. Survivors reported that policeman sometimes shot indiscriminately into crowds to force everybody to hand over their valuables. The Jews could not believe what they witnessed. David's father expressed a widely shared sentiment: if the Germans only knew what was going on, they would make an end to this mess. "I have to find the Germans. They are educated people – they would not behave like this!" Of course, the Romanian Jews would later find out that the Germans were the masterminds of the genocide they had suffered. The violent interplay between the Germans and their local partners radicalized the persecution of Romania's Jews and Roma.

That said, what is so remarkable about David's story, and the stories of most survivors from the regions and countries ruled by German allies, whether Croatia, Hungary, or Romania, is that the Germans were somewhat invisible. David did not see any German soldiers until 1944, when they retreated, and the Holocaust in Transnistria was already over. The Romanian Jews were persecuted and killed by Romanian perpetrators. These were neither controlled nor guided by the Germans. And this is the reason why the Holocaust in Romania was so different from countries where the Germans were in control. Most of the Jews in the region died of hunger, cold, or exhaustion, except for those killed by the "Task Force D" operation in the summer of 1941. The less systematic manner of persecution, horrific as it was, provided the Romanian Jews with higher chances of survival, because there were ways to fight back and to disobey the rules. The survival of David's family makes that perfectly clear.

The Schaffers were marched from Moghilev Podolski to a city called Kopaigorod. All Jews who survived Transnistria remember these marches into the dark, cold unknown. Many had to be left behind by their relatives and died on their way, as did David's great-grandmother; others were shot by guards. Shelter was essential for survival during the cold nights, and often it was sheer luck whether a family found a place to stay, or not. Survivors were often nagged by the question why they survived and their loved ones did not. For the Schaffers, David's father was key to their survival. David remembers that, when they arrived at their destination, "father went out and investigated the area. When he came back, he had decided that Kopaigorod was bad news." During the night, the family separated from the large group of deportees, and walked away on their own. That probably saved their lives. Most Jews were herded into ghettos like Kopaigorod. In some ghettos, more than half of the Jewish inmates died in the first winter alone. The chances of survival for the elderly and for children, especially for orphans, were slim. Starvation and typhus (a deadly contagious disease) killed many. Houses had been taken apart in need of firewood. Jews had no shelter. Moreover, the inmates could not do much to improve their situation.

Only after 1943 did things get better. For one, the Jewish communities in Romania proper, which had not been deported, were highly active in humanitarian efforts to support their fellow Jews who were targeted by the Romanian genocide in Transnistria. Though many of the parcels they sent to the ghettos were stolen, the help from outside started easing the plight of the Jews in Transnistria. A second factor was that after the battle of Stalingrad, most of Hitler's allies realized that Germany would lose the war, and that continuing to support the German war effort was a lost cause. They started to look towards their own future, which meant that they were less preoccupied with the Jews. Fortunately, the region was quickly liberated by the Red Army in the spring of 1944 before the Germans could take the mass murder of Jews into their hands, as they did in Hungary.

In contrast to most Jews who spent their years in Transnistria's ghettos, David's family reached a smaller village called Ivashkovtsi, where they found shelter. It was sort of a ghetto without a fence. Life was easier than in the real ghettos, even though the inmates were harassed by Romanian patrols that were stationed in the area. Two other reasons contributed to their survival. First, the Schaffers teamed up with another family, the Landaus, to create a support system where everybody contributed their skills and strengths. Second, they lived in a – relatively – nonhostile environment, because the Ukrainian population was also being victimized by the Romanian authorities and was therefore more helpful to the Jews. The history of collaboration among local populations during the Holocaust is complicated. Everywhere in Eastern Europe, locals contributed to Jewish persecution, and benefited from it. That sometimes led to a simplistic and one-sided image of "the Ukrainians" who supported Hitler during the Holocaust. Yet, for David, the Ukrainians were a big help to his family. Indeed, these two Jewish families in hiding lived for more than two years, during the Holocaust, in that village and peacefully coexisted with their Ukrainian neighbors. There was very little interaction, but the common motto was "live and let live."

It is the sad truth that such a lack of hostility in wartime Europe requires explanation. Transnistria had belonged to the Soviet Union since the end of the First World War. In other regions, where borders and governments had changed more frequently, the local degree of violence was much higher. In the Romanian, Polish and Baltic regions that had lost their independence to the Soviet Union after the Hitler-Stalin-pact in 1939, only to be conquered by the Germans in 1941, local attacks on Jews including deadly pogroms were very widespread. The reason is that the social fabric had taken damage in those years, and that most local authorities like mayors, priests and teachers had been deported or killed either by the Soviets or the Germans. That was not true for the regions further east like Transnistria. Unlike in, say, Bessarabia, the Jews were not associated with the Soviet Occupation, hence there were no "revenge" attacks. Moreover, the Soviet authorities did not tolerate antisemitism before the war, which certainly influenced the local level, too.

David took notice of another factor that played a role in their relationship with local Ukrainians and the fact that they were willing to trade food: In 1933, Ukraine had been devasted by a man-made famine caused by Stalin and his forces known as the Holodomor. Hundreds of thousands of peasants in the country, most of which were Ukrainian, died. David puts the effect of the famine on the locals' behavior this way: "Their people had been through famine before, so they had compassion."

The changes in the Germans' war fortunes were felt in Ivashkovtsi, too. David remembers that "there was a kind of uneasiness amongst the soldiers; they weren't so quick to shoot us anymore." The Romanian gendarmerie started retreating to larger cities, and Soviet partisans became increasingly active in the area. It was empowering for David to see Jewish partisans among them. This is also the time when the first Germans came to Ivashkovtsi. David's account is typical for how Jews experienced the Holocaust in that region: the only Germans David ever saw were not strongmen in shiny uniforms who abused Jews but haunted soldiers in rags who were losing the war. The partisans managed to kill most of them once they entered the village. Usually, the moment when the war ended for Holocaust survivors is called "liberation," but that would be an exaggerated term for what the Schaffer family experienced in the spring of 1944. The Germans and the Romanians were beaten and gone, but the war in Europe, including the Holocaust, continued for another year. Of the nine members of the Landau and the Schaffer families, two individuals – David's great grandmother on the transport, and the Landau grandmother, who succumbed to typhus – died. Seven survived. The Schaffers walked back all the way from Ukraine to Romania. How they managed to start a new life in Romania, Israel, and Canada after the war is another story.

SURVIVING IN HIDING FROM THE NAZIS

Dienke Hondius

*Assistant Professor of History at Vrije Universiteit Amsterdam
and staff member in the Department of Educational Projects,
Anne Frank House*

Rolf and Nico Kamp's history starts in Germany, where they were born in the city of Krefeld. Rolf was born in 1934, and Nico in 1937. The family was Jewish, and their life was threatened by the Nazis who were in power from 1933 onwards. In 1938, they fled with their father, Fritz, and their mother, Inge, across the border to the Netherlands. By then, Jewish refugees had a very hard time finding ways to escape Nazi Germany. All European and also many non-European countries flatly refused to take in Jewish refugees. They said their countries were already full. In the summer of 1938, an international conference was held in the town of Evian, on Lake Geneva. The topic was the refugee crisis in Europe, particularly regarding Jewish refugees. In a beautiful area with luxury accommodations and food, diplomats from many countries came together to discuss what to do. However, the conference became a shameful affair, when country after country declared that they had no room for refugees. This lack of international solidarity was seen by the Nazis as a sign they could continue their plans.

A few months later, in early November 1938, an explosion of violence against Jews broke out. Across Nazi Germany, Austria, and the recently occupied

Sudetenland, Jewish shops, houses, synagogues, and community buildings were attacked, set on fire, the windows smashed. Many Jews were beaten up and arrested. The police and the fire brigades were instructed by the Nazi headquarters in Berlin that they did not need to hurry to stop the fires or the attacks. The night of 9–10 November became infamous as Kristallnacht (the Night of Broken Glass). Again there was virtually no solidarity shown by the non-Jewish population. Many Jews who until then had remained hopeful, now decided the danger was so enormous that they had to leave their homes and find a place in another country. However, not many Jews succeeded in fleeing.

Leaving Germany, Entering the Netherlands

Fritz Kamp, the father of Nico and Rolf, was arrested in September 1938 in Krefeld. He was set free quickly, but it felt very unsafe, and the family began making plans to leave Krefeld. This was suddenly accelerated on the morning after Kristallnacht. The night before, the family had traveled to the city of Düsseldorf on their way to the Netherlands. In the morning, they were woken up by a colleague from the Netherlands. He told them, Inge Kamp remembers, "that we had to flee immediately because the synagogue and the cultural center of the Jewish community was on fire and there was unrest in the city."[1] They had not yet heard about the wave of violence and destruction. They even visited a factory as they had planned. Then the Gestapo arrived. Because their passports gave 10 November 1938 as the official day they were traveling, they were allowed to leave. Had they waited much longer, they would not have been allowed to travel. The family arrived in the Netherlands that day.

Thirteen Secrets illustrates the family's life in the Dutch city of Amersfoort, but they lived in other places too. In 1938 they were still very young. Nico was one year old and Rolf was four years old, and they do not remember exactly

---

1   Inge, Rolf, and Nico Kamp, *De laatste trein naar Auschwitz* [The last train to Auschwitz] 2nd ed. (Amsterdam: Uitgeverij Van Praag, 2018), 21. Inge Kamp also gave her testimony to the USC Shoah Foundation. All translations are by Dienke Hondius.

where they lived. Their mother, Inge, who survived the war and the extermination camps, later told them where they had been. Crossing the border, they first went to Roermond, then to Venlo, and after that to Dinxperlo, a village on the German-Dutch border. There, the family lived for one year. A work permit helped them to move to Amersfoort.[2]

In the Netherlands, the attitude towards Jewish refugees was also unwelcoming. Their experiences in Germany had made the Kamp family alert – a skill that they needed in the Netherlands as well. When the Netherlands was occupied by the Nazis on 10 May 1940, some of the German Jewish refugees were arrested. Inge Kamp remembers that men and women were separated in an army barracks. With Nico and Rolf, she was brought to a small town in North Holland, Heerhugowaard. Her husband, Fritz, and his father were arrested and taken to The Hague. After a while, they were set free and returned to Amersfoort where they organized the return of the rest of the family. From the summer of 1940 onwards, Inge writes that they had a "rather quiet life" in Amersfoort,[3] but not for long. In the Netherlands, 1941 was the year when most anti-Jewish decrees were announced. The deportations to camps began in July 1942. There were very few options to escape deportation; having a job at the Jewish Council offered temporary protection, as could being in a mixed marriage, but nothing was certain. Going into hiding was a radical act, a jump into the unknown, a move into illegality. Very few people had experienced illegal life before, and many hesitated. Where to go? Who to ask? For how long?

Finding Hiding Places

From the summer of 1942 onwards, many Jews tried to go into hiding. Inge and Fritz were already preparing and searching hiding places not only for themselves and their two sons but also for Fritz Kamp's parents, the grandparents of Nico and Rolf. They found three separate addresses, all close to Amersfoort. How did

---

2 Ibid., 19–21.
3 Ibid., 21.

they manage to do this? According to Nico Kamp, the advice to split up and look for three hiding places came from a member of the Dutch resistance who lived next to his grandfather. They called him "Uncle Piet." His real name was Wouter van Egdom.[4] The boys were the first to go to a hiding place in June 1942. Nico Kamp mentions a second helper, "Aunt Gijsje," whose name was Gijsje van Garderen. She and Wouter van Egdom took the two boys with their small suitcases on the back of their bicycles to the train station, and Gijsje van Garderen took them to their first hiding place. She also arranged later moves to other hiding places, according to Nico. Rolf remembers that "a mysterious man came to our house who spoke with my parents,"[5] and that this man took them to the train station. The brothers were first in hiding in Ommen near Zwolle, then in Lunteren, then in Stoutenburg, and then in Oud-Leusden, very close to "Aunt Gijsje," and also close to the hiding place of their parents. By then it was 1943.

Inge and Fritz decided to leave their house in Amersfoort when they heard that there would be a *razzia* (roundup of Jews, arrested one house after the other). Quietly, they left the house on Voltastraat 55 and walked for miles to their first hiding place, a few kilometers from Amersfoort. It was important to try to be as invisible as possible. From then on, they were in hiding as well. At some moment in 1943, the sons and parents found themselves in two different hiding places that were only a few kilometers apart from each other. Now the parents took the risk to visit their sons by foot. "We visited our children once per week, but only when it was dark," writes Inge.[6]

Which resistance network helped the Kamp family? Nico and Rolf mention that the families they stayed with varied in many ways, that they were often small farmers from protestant Christian backgrounds, and that the family Traa where they stayed longest, until the liberation, was Roman Catholic. Gijsje

---

4 Ibid., 58. Yad Vashem is currently researching the case of Wouter van Egdom. A photo of him and his wife appeared in 2019 and reports that they were running a children's home at the time where they could sometimes take in some extra children. Wichard Maassen, "Amersfoorts stel postuum geëerd" [Amersfoort couple honored posthumously], *Algemeen Dagblad*, 7 March 2019, https://www.ad.nl/amersfoort/amersfoorts-stel-postuum-geeerd~a9154221/.
5 Inge, Rolf, and Nico Kamp, *De laatste trein naar Auschwitz*, 83.
6 Ibid., 23.

van Garderen remained their main contact. Recent information suggests that Wouter van Egdom and Gijsje van Garderen may have been related, perhaps they were siblings or cousins, because Gijsje's maiden name was van Egdom. She was arrested as a political prisoner and deported to the notorious concentration camp, Vught, in July 1944. From there, she was taken to the Ravensbrück and Dachau concentration camps, and survived.[7] It is likely that Gijsje van Garderen, Wouter van Egdom, and their families were a small, careful, independent network of helpers. Whether they were connected to larger resistance organizations is not yet known.

Fritz and Inge Kamp were arrested in hiding on 23 May 1944 on a farm owned by a man named J. Kok in Stoutenburg. They were arrested by four Dutch policemen who were actively collaborating with the Nazis: Jan Johannes Cabalt, Jacob Tol, Diederik Lutke Schipholt, and Lubbertus Beumer. They received their order to search the farm from their superior, Jacob Breugem.[8] Of these five Dutch Nazi men, three were brought to justice and interrogated after the war: Cabalt, Beumer, and Tol. Breugem died in a shooting incident at the end of November 1944, and Schipholt was killed by resistance fighters on 14 May 1945.

Fritz and Inge Kamp and J. Kok were first taken to the Amersfoort police station, and from there the next day to Amsterdam. The Amersfoort police made a report of the arrest, which noted that a radio was confiscated from the hiding place, as well as clothing, money, and other possessions.[9]

---

7 Gijsbertha van Garderen-van Egdom was born in Stoutenburg on 4 September 1902, and arrived first at the Vught concentration camp on 6 July 1944, at Ravensbrück on 9 September 1944, and at Dachau on 15 October 1944. She survived and was liberated there on 29 April 1945. See Arolsen Archives, https://collections.arolsen-archives.org/en/archive/357103 /?p=1&s=garderen-van%20egdom&doc_id=357105; Dachau Archives, https://www.oorlogslevens.nl/tijdlijn/Gijsberta -van-Garderen-van-Egdom/24/1786w; for Ravensbrück information, see Resistance Museum Archives, https://www .verzetsmuseum.org/dachau/gijsbertha-van-garderen-van-egdom.

8 Kees Ribbens, *"Zullen wij nog terugkeeren …": De jodenvervolging in Amersfoort tijdens de Tweede Wereldoorlog* [Will we ever return … The persecution of the Jews of Amersfoort during World War II] (Amersfoort: Uitgeverij Bekking, 2002), 100, 137n243. Archival sources: City Archives Amersfoort (Gemeentearchief); Archives of the City Council (Archief Gemeentebestuur), Dossier 1021: IV 07, Daily Police Reports, and Municipal Police Archives (Archief Gemeentepolitie), Police Report 23 and 24 May 1944; National Archives, The Hague (Nationaal Archief); Archief Bureau Juridische Zaken / Zuivering van de Afdeling Politie en Taakvoorganger, Dossier 643, Dossier 5978. These archives contain interrogation reports of the policemen Beumer and Tol in 1946–7. The name of the NSB member who betrayed the hiding place is not mentioned. Additional information may be searched at Nationaal Archief, Centrale Archieven Bijzondere Rechtspleging.

9 Ribbens, *"Zullen wij nog terugkeeren…,"* 100.

Inge Kamp has spoken and written about their experiences several times. She remembers severe questioning by the Gestapo in the Amsterdam Nazi headquarters in Euterpestraat. The questions focused on the whereabouts of her children. Where were they hiding? Who helped them? She stuck to her story that she had no idea, and that she had not heard from them or seen them for a long time. "My husband was so terribly afraid that he could not speak. They kept asking about our children. I said that I had no idea where they were, and that I thought they had been arrested and taken long ago. They wanted us to believe that if we told them the hiding place of our children, we would all be able to live together in a place for families. I hung on to my story."[10] It worked, and there was no further questioning.

What they experienced here is similar to what happened to many other Jews arrested in hiding. For example, Anne Frank and her family were taken to exactly the same places after their hiding place in the secret annex of a house they rented as an office and a warehouse in Amsterdam was discovered. Rolf and Nico's parents were taken to a prison on Kleine Gartmanplantsoen near Leidseplein in Amsterdam's city center. There were two large cells there, one for men, one for women. After two days, they were taken to Amsterdam Central Station and by train to the Westerbork camp. J. Kok, the farmer who had hidden them, remained in prison in Amsterdam much longer. Though he was repeatedly interrogated for many weeks, he too did not mention the hiding place of Nico and Rolf Kamp.[11]

Moments of Extreme Danger and Survival

Surviving the Holocaust meant enduring a long list of situations, unexpected events, and moments of extreme danger and relative safety. This was very true for the Kamp family. Both the parents and the children managed to act quickly and escape from extremely dangerous situations first in Krefeld, then in Amersfoort, and then in various hiding places.

---

10 Inge, Rolf, and Nico Kamp, *De laatste trein naar Auschwitz*, 24.
11 Ribbens, *"Zullen wij nog terugkeeren …,"* 100. Whether J. Kok gave information about other aspects of the resistance group and events is not mentioned by Ribbens.

The decision to leave Krefeld in 1938 enhanced their chances of survival. The *Encyclopaedia Judaica* writes that in 1933 there were 1,481 Jews in Krefeld. Anti-Jewish violence was seen as early as 5–6 February 1933: the synagogue windows were smashed. During Kristallnacht, the synagogue and other Jewish community buildings were burnt to the ground. Later, 1,374 Jews were deported from Krefeld, and in 1946 there were only 56 Jewish people left.[12]

The Kamps' decision to leave Amersfoort and go into hiding was wise too. Historian Kees Ribbens writes that in August 1941 there were – according to the Nazi definition of who was Jewish – 731 Jews in Amersfoort. Among these, 115 Jews were German Jews like the Kamp family, who were all robbed of their German citizenship in November 1941 and became stateless. The Nazis counted 632 people in Amersfoort whom they regarded as *Volljuden* or Jews (people with three or four Jewish grandparents). Deportations started in July 1942.[13] The situation for stateless Jews had become very dangerous even before the deportations began. On 17 June 1942, two Amersfoort police officers, on the orders of the Nazi leaders in Amsterdam, arrested two stateless Jewish people who lived in Amersfoort: Joseph Adamski, forty-three years old and born in Warsaw, and his twelve-year-old son, Isidoor. Joseph was taken to Westerbork, a Dutch concentration camp near the German border, and deported from there on the first train to Auschwitz, where he was killed on 30 September 1942. His son, Isidoor, managed to survive until 3 May 1943 when he was killed in Sobibor.[14]

From the Netherlands as a whole, 107,000 Jews were deported to the extermination camps between July 1942 and September 1944. From Amersfoort, of the 632 so-called full-Jews, 353 were killed. Of the 133 Jews with non-Dutch nationality whose situation was similar to the Kamp family, 85 were killed: about 64 per cent.[15]

---

12 Chasia Turtel, "Krefeld," *Encyclopedia Judaica*, accessed 9 November 2021, https://www.encyclopedia.com/religion/encyclopedias-almanacs-transcripts-and-maps/krefeld.
13 Ibid., 31.
14 Ibid., 49–50.
15 Ibid., 124.

Return from Hiding, Finding a Voice

The period around the liberation, the return from hiding and from the concentration camps, was very difficult for most Jewish survivors. Many were confronted with disbelief and with forms of antisemitism from non-Jews. Very often, the Jewish survivors found that their houses had been taken, their possessions were robbed, and quite often goods they had given to neighbors to keep safe were not returned.[16] Jewish children who had lost one or both parents were sometimes taken in by other surviving family members. Others went to orphanages, and some were able to stay with foster families. There were many tensions and conflicts that resulted in post-war wounds and trauma.[17] In the early 1990s, a movement of child survivors of hiding was established through international conferences and initiatives in Canada, the United States, and Europe. They found a voice through self-help and support circles, writing groups, journals, and newsletters, and they remain active today.[18]

When we read the book by Inge, Rolf, and Nico Kamp, and listen to their testimonies in interviews, there are many very frightening moments.[19] They were in highly dangerous situations for a long time, and yet were able to somehow remain children, too, playing with the children of the families where they were hiding, adjusting again and again to quickly and unexpectedly changing circumstances. It took a long time before they were able to share some of their memories. However, they were among the first hidden children who returned to Krefeld, their city of origin in Germany, when they were invited for a week by the city in 1987. On this occasion, their mother, Inge, as well as Rolf's father-in-law joined them. It became a gathering of 100 Jews originally from Krefeld.[20]

---

16 Dienke Hondius, *Return: Holocaust Survivors and Dutch Anti-Semitism* (Westport, CT: Praeger/Greenwood, 2004).

17 Diane L. Wolf, *Beyond Anne Frank: Hidden Children and Postwar Families in Holland* (Berkeley: University of California Press, 2007). In the Netherlands, Bloeme Evers-Emden and Bert Jan Flim have published about the relations between hidden children and their helpers.

18 For example, Robert Krell initiated meetings of survivors of hiding in Canada in Vancouver, and in New York the Hidden Child Foundation and *The Hidden Child* newsletter started in the early 1990s. These initiatives have resulted in impressive collections of testimonies.

19 The Netherlands edition: Inge, Rolf, and Nico Kamp, *De laatste trein naar Auschwitz*, 2nd ed. (Amsterdam: Uitgeverij Van Praag, 2018). The German edition: Karin Kammann, Coen Hilbrink, Inge, Nico, and Rolf Kamp, *Die Geschichte der jüdischen Familie Kamp aus Krefeld* (Amsterdam: RVP Publishers, 2017).

20 Karin Kammann, "Das Wiedersehen der jüdischen Bürger mit Krefeld 1987" [Jewish citizens meet again in Krefeld in 1987], in Karin Kammann, Coen Hilbrink, Inge, Nico, and Rolf Kamp, *Die Geschichte der jüdischen Familie Kamp aus Krefeld* [The History of the Jewish family Kamp in Krefeld] (Amsterdam: RVP Publishers, 2017), 266–72.

Later, following questions from their grandchildren, they began to speak in public more often.

Getting to know Nico and Rolf Kamp and their wives, Hélène Kamp-van Dam and Marion Kamp-Berets, has been a moving experience for my husband Jan Erik Dubbelman (director emeritus of international educational projects at the Anne Frank House, Amsterdam) and me. We were particularly interested in the fact that not only the men but also both the women survived in hiding in the Netherlands. Marion was born in Amersfoort and her family was also from Krefeld. She, too, was in hiding, with her parents and brother, first in Amersfoort and later near the rural city of Voorthuizen. There, her father made a cabin, near a farm. One day the farmer came to warn them that Germans were on their way and they had to leave immediately. Marion remembers: "We ran into the woods! … We stayed there for three days and three nights."[21] They slept, she continues, "in the woods, on the leaves. It was end of March. Cold. We had nothing to cover us. Later the farmer came and gave us some blankets. He brought us wood too. My father dug holes for our family. We could not lay in the hole, we could only sit. Not very deep. Deep enough that we could sit and you could not see our heads."[22] After some time, an underground network found something else, a chicken coop. There were other people there too, and they had to take turns sleeping. "I remember sleeping on the floor. It was very crowded of course. We developed skin problems."[23] She does not remember whether it had a real roof. "There were eight of us. Each of us was allowed to sleep for two hours. Sleep on the floor. With blankets he brought us … Birds shit many times on us. We stayed there until after the end of the war."[24]

By contrast, Hélène's hiding history was a very urban one; she stayed in Amsterdam with one family throughout the war. The emotional toll of her hiding experiences was high, in spite of the fact that her adoptive family was generally

21 Interview with Marion Kamp on 16 May 2007 by Hilde Gattmann and Anne Grett Saldinger, JFCS San Francisco Holocaust Center, Bay Area Holocaust Oral History Project, USHMM Oral History Collection, Number 1999.A.0122.1491; RG Number: RG-50.477.1491, https://collections.ushmm.org/search/catalog/irn47804.
22 Dienke Hondius, interview with Marion Kamp-Berets, 15 December 2019, Amsterdam.
23 Interview, Marion Kamp, 16 May 2007.
24 Interview, Marion Kamp-Berets, 15 December 2019.

loving. She was mostly in the care of a strict nurse while the other children went to school. Hélène remembers: "The nurse was very stiff. I missed the tenderness and the love of my mother. They were wonderful, but they were distant. It was different from what it was like at home … You have no freedom ... that was very, very difficult. I had to stay in the house."[25] The loss of freedom remains a sad memory, and after the war living with her biological parents was not easy either. The relationship with her adoptive family remained friendly. She says it is important for her to talk about it more now. "Yes I think it is very important. Because the older you get, the more it comes to the surface."[26]

In their own ways, Marion and Hélène, Nico and Rolf each carry a heavy weight with them. Together, their stories contain many elements that are known from other hiding histories and the difficult postwar memories these stories have produced. Many child survivors remained silent for decades. Child survivors were often overlooked or silenced. Robert Krell, himself a hidden child in the Netherlands and a noted child psychiatrist, remarks, "A hierarchy had already formed as to who had survived the worst. Child survivors did not even find a place on that unofficial list … We were first-generation Holocaust survivors, too young to have had advocates for our existence and experiences."[27]

Given these significant postwar obstacles, we are very grateful that Nico and Rolf, Hélène and Marion are willing to share their stories. It is clear to me that the histories of Jews in hiding contain a wealth of historically significant information and insight that has not yet been collected and analyzed enough.[28] Thankfully, there are still many families with memories of hiding, making much more research possible.

25 Dienke Hondius, interview with Hélène Kamp-van Dam, 15 December 2019, Amsterdam.
26 Ibid.
27 Robert Krell, "30 Years of Friendship, Healing and Education – Our Legacy," in *Mishpocha! World Federation of Jewish Child Survivors of the Holocaust and Descendants* (Spring 2013), quoted in Marcel Tenenbaum, *Of Men, Monsters and Mazel: Surviving the "Final Solution" in Belgium* (Montreal: Xlibris Publishers, 2016).
28 Dienke Hondius, "Mapping Hiding Places," Research Project, Vrije Universiteit Amsterdam, accesssed 9 November 2021, www.mappinghidingplaces.org.

SURVIVING RAVENSBRÜCK AND BERGEN-BELSEN AS A CHILD

Andrea Löw

*Deputy Head of the Centre for Holocaust Studies
at the Institute for Contemporary History, Munich
Translated from German by Rebecca DeWald*

Emmie Arbel, whose childhood name was Emmie Kallus, survived the concentration camps Ravensbrück and Bergen-Belsen when she was just a little girl. Her family had already experienced persecution and imprisonment in a camp, when she was still living in her home country, the Netherlands. On 10 May 1940, the German Wehrmacht attacked the Netherlands, which led to a short battle culminating in the Dutch capitulation five days later. The country was then occupied by Germany, which resulted in an especially threatening situation for its Jewish population, including numerous people who had already fled the German Reich as refugees. Beginning in the summer of 1940, the German administration gradually began to exclude Jews from public life in the Netherlands, followed by increasingly harsher anti-Jewish measures. From early 1942 onwards, the German authorities banished the Jewish population from their provinces and either gathered them in the capital city of Amsterdam or transported them straight to the Dutch concentration camps: Westerbork and Vught. This measure made it easier for the authorities to identify the Dutch Jews when deportations from the Netherlands began in the summer of 1942. On 15 July 1942, the first train departed from Westerbork to Auschwitz.

Emmie and her family had been living in their hometown of The Hague until they were arrested and taken to Westerbork in November 1942. Emmie's brother Menachem remembers: "We left the world of ordinary people with their houses, jobs, and worries."[1]

Westerbork concentration camp had been set up in the autumn of 1939 as a central refugee camp for the internment of about 700 Jews who had fled Germany. In 1942, the German occupation's Security Police took over its administration. From July 1942, Westerbork served as a "transit camp," holding Jews to be deported to the death camps. Some of them lived there for several years. By the end of 1942, the camp was already overcrowded and there was no privacy in the barracks. Although subordinate to the German commander of the camp, Albert Gemmeker, there was a Jewish Council in Westerbork. Besides taking on various organizational tasks, this body also had to carry out orders, including the announcement of deportations. Those detained at Westerbork lived in constant fear of finding their names on one of the next deportation lists. With time, rumors about the true destinations of the deportations began to circulate in the camp. The final destination of many of their journeys was Auschwitz-Birkenau or Sobibór in German-occupied Poland, where most Jews were murdered upon their arrival.

Their deportation in February 1944 took Emmie, her two brothers, and her mother to Ravensbrück. Her father had been deported to the concentration camp Buchenwald near Weimar earlier, where he was killed. Deportation to Ravensbrück increased their chances of survival, especially for little Emmie. In Auschwitz-Birkenau, she would have been classified as a child "unfit for work" and most likely gassed immediately upon arrival.

Auschwitz served as both a concentration and an extermination camp. Those who were deemed too weak, too old, too young, or too ill were immediately selected for the gas chambers at Birkenau. The rest had to suffer forced labor for as

---

1 Menachem Kallus, *Als Junge im KZ Ravensbrück* [A boy in the Ravensbrück concentration camp] (Berlin: Metropol, 2005), 39.

long as they had enough strength to work. In Sobibór, survival was nearly impossible. Located in occupied Poland, Sobibór's sole purpose was the extermination of people, just like Treblinka, Bełżec, and Chełmno (Kulmhof). It is important to note the distinction between extermination and concentration camps. Two camps were used as concentration and extermination camps at the same time: Auschwitz and Majdanek, near Lublin.

The Nazis' camp system was gigantic. It was their central means of terror and was employed to exercise limitless power over those not wanted in German society for political or "racial" reasons. The role of these concentration camps changed between 1933 and 1945, and new camps were being built continuously. Initially set up for the primary reason of suppressing political opponents, over time the concentration camp system developed into an instrument of Nazi Germany's racial policy.

At the end of 1938, the November Pogroms (Kristallnacht) resulted in the mass detention of Jewish men in concentration camps. The start of the war saw a considerable increase in persecutions, and more and more prisoners from countries annexed or occupied by the German Reich were deported to these concentration camps. At the same time, the SS (Schutzstaffel, or Protection Squads) began building camps in these newly annexed territories. The German authorities used concentration camps more and more often as places of ruthless exploitation of the prisoners' labor force. Including the additional "subcamps," which were often located near manufacturing facilities, there were soon over 1,000 camps across Europe. From 1933 to 1945, around 2.3 million people were deported, around 1.7 million of these died in the camps.

The two concentration camps Emmie Arbel survived, Ravensbrück and Bergen-Belsen, also performed different functions at different times, while the types of inmates changed there as well.

The Ravensbrück concentration camp near the health spa Fürstenberg in the German state of Mecklenburg was in operation from the spring of 1939 until the end of April 1945. Beside Auschwitz-Birkenau, Ravensbrück housed one of the largest women's camps in Nazi Germany's concentration camp system. Around 120,000 women and children were interned here. Part of the camp complex was, from April 1941, a smaller men's camp, as well as the "juvenile protective custody camp" (*Jugendschutzlager*) known as Uckermark, which opened in June 1942. The camp also featured a "factory courtyard" that included various workshops, factory buildings belonging to the company Siemens & Halske located next to the camp grounds, and over forty subcamps. The camp underwent different phases, which resulted in a different prisoner makeup. The year 1944, when Emmie arrived at Ravensbrück, was a year of large-scale mass deportations to the camp, with 70,000 new prisoners arriving all in all. The camp was more crowded than ever before. The lack of space and the abundance of women in the camp needed for forced labor meant that the danger for each individual woman increased. In the cynical eyes of the commandant and the female guards, only those considered to be useful were deemed worthy enough to live.

Upon arrival at the camp, the prisoners had to undergo a humiliating procedure typical of concentration camps and designed to dehumanize them. Guards made them take off their clothes, their hair was shaved off, they were assigned prisoners' numbers and given prisoners' clothing, and forced to turn in the last of their belongings, including photographs of their loved ones. Menachem Kallus describes the scene: "Our entire lives were spread out on the ground, all those things that had made us the family we were."[2] All of this was accompanied by insults, acts of intimidation, and beatings. These people lost more than their individuality upon arrival in the concentration camp: they lost all of their rights. They were at the mercy of the guards and their tyranny. Emmie remembers: "In Ravensbrück is where the feeling of fear and humiliation set in."[3]

Since she was a young girl, Emmie was allowed to stay in the same barracks as her mother and her brother Rudi, and did not have to work like the other inmates. Her brother Menachem, however, was separated from them after a little

---

2 Kallus, *Junge*, 59.

3 Emmie Arbel, unpublished manuscript, 2018.

while and transferred to the men's camp. Their mother was obliged to carry out forced labor all day long, during which time the children were left unsupervised.

The living conditions in Ravensbrück were atrocious. The wooden barracks were extremely cramped. Multiple women were forced to share a mattress in one of the bunk beds. It was filthy, lice-infested, and it stank. There was never enough food. Women and children went hungry and became ever weaker. These catastrophic conditions meant that the inmates fell ill, and yet had to try and hide their illness to avoid being sent to their death in the next round of "selections." Being sent to the infirmary, known as the "Revier" (short for the German word for infirmary, *Krankenrevier*), was virtually a death sentence as well. Even critically ill prisoners dragged themselves to work to avoid being sent to the Revier. Emmie, too, suffered from a bad case of typhoid in Ravensbrück and found herself in the Revier. Yet she was lucky enough to have a Polish woman take her under her wing. This woman's friend worked at the infirmary and helped her to get better, so Emmie managed to escape this dangerous situation. Survival in the camps depended on many things: coincidence was one of them; having the right connections to draw on in the right moment was another. Emmie survived, albeit weakened and bone thin, but she survived.

The threat of death was omnipresent in Ravensbrück. SS doctors performed medical experiments on the prisoners, many of whom died or were mutilated as a result. Time and again, women and children were shot without warning. In early 1945, an impromptu gas chamber was set up in which selected women died a painful death by asphyxiation. Approximately 25,000 to 26,000 people died in Ravensbrück, either as a result of the terrible living conditions or as victims of murder.

Weakened prisoners dreaded the roll calls in particular, when guards walked through the ranks to assess who was still "fit for work" and therefore allowed to go on living for a little while longer – and who was not. Sometimes, as a mere means of torturing people further, the guards forced the prisoners to stand still for hours on end. The most minute of movements put one's life in danger. Emmie recounts such a situation and already understood as a young child that she had to stand still even though her mother had just fainted. From the autumn of 1944 onwards, prisoners who were considered "unfit for work" because they were simply too weak, were systematically "selected," that is, selected to be murdered. The youngest prisoners, unable to do any heavy labor, were permanently in danger of death.

More than 4,300 women and children were moved from Ravensbrück to Bergen-Belsen in the spring of 1945, shortly before the end of World War II, including Emmie, her brother Rudi, and their mother on 1 March 1945. This is where they had to endure the last weeks leading up to the liberation. Bergen-Belsen concentration camp near the German city of Celle was in operation from spring 1943 to April 1945. It was preceded by a prisoner of war camp on the same spot. It housed an "exchange camp" for Jewish hostages with the intention of trading them for money or German prisoners of war. The initial purpose of the camp was broadened by the SS in March 1944: it also became a kind of reception center for exhausted and ill prisoners, who were more or less left on their own to die. It was then split into a men's camp for prisoners no longer "fit for work" who had been transferred from other concentration camps, and a women's camp. Mothers and their children were housed here, as well as unaccompanied minors who had been deported from other camps. For women "fit for work," Bergen-Belsen was a transit camp; they were eventually sent on to other forced labor camps.

Among the more than 120,000 prisoners in this concentration camp, there were close to 3,500 children under the age of fifteen. It is not possible to determine exactly how many of them died in the camp, as the SS burned all documentation relating to the camp shortly before the end of the war. In total, an estimated 52,000 people – almost half of the inmates – died as a result of the atrocious conditions at Bergen-Belsen. The final phase, when Emmie arrived here, proved fatal for many. The living conditions were catastrophic. From the end of 1944, Bergen-Belsen became the destination of the so-called Death Marches and transports from other concentration camps, especially from those in the East, which had already been evacuated before the advance of the Red Army. At least 85,000 additional prisoners arrived at the camp. One of them was

Anita Lasker-Wallfisch. She was deported from Auschwitz to Bergen-Belsen in November 1944 and later described how the exhausted survivors of these Death Marches reached the camp: "Thousands upon thousands of prisoners were made to march – the famous Death Marches had begun. The sight of these poor people arriving in Belsen, some of them on their knees, defies description. Thousands had perished on the way."[4]

At the time when Emmie, Rudi, and their mother arrived at Bergen-Belsen, the camp was helplessly overcrowded; the only little food left was of poor quality. People were starving. This left the prisoners extremely weakened and they, including many children, died in mass numbers. The prisoners lay packed together on plank beds in crowded, cold, and dirty barracks. Diseases and epidemics spread easily. The state of care worsened increasingly over the final months and even weeks. Just as in Ravensbrück, life in Bergen-Belsen was characterized by a constant confrontation with death. Here, too, the prisoners feared hours-long roll calls, and even children from the age of four were forced to take part. Anita Lasker-Wallfisch recalled the spring of 1945: "Conditions deteriorated more and more, bodies became so commonplace that one just simply ignored them. The watery so-called soup we got became irregular and eventually stopped all together. Typhus raged and people dropped dead like flies. The mountains of corpses grew higher and higher ..."[5]

In this camp, too, children were often left by themselves during the day, since all adult prisoners, which included anyone over the age of fifteen, were forced to work. Children who were still strong enough to play did so, though they were permanently under threat and lived in constant fear of what could happen next. A guard's foul mood could mean arbitrary punishment. The children witnessed brutal violence and saw people die – in some cases even their own parents. The youngest ones knew no other world than that of the camp. They were small adults who had already learned how to behave during roll calls or in other threatening situations. These children were confronted with death and dying on a daily basis,

---

4 Anita Lasker-Wallfisch, "A Survivor's Memories of Liberation," *Holocaust Studies* 12, no. 1–2 (2006): 24.
5 Ibid.

and so their games reenacted the cruel reality of the camp. Some played that they were prisoners, others acted as guards. Children learned sums by counting the dead, and tried to guess who would die next. Teacher Hanna Lévy-Hass wrote in her diary while in Bergen-Belsen: "The children are unleashed, wild, famished. They feel that their existence has taken an unusual and abnormal turn and they react brutally and instinctively."[6]

The youngest inmates were particularly dependent on the help of adults. They needed to feel part of a family and relied on the support that only a close relative can provide. Mothers, in particular, tried to protect and care for their children. They often gave them some of their own inadequate rations, in the hope that at least some of the children would survive. That is also what Julia Kallus did, mother of Emmie and Rudi, resulting in her waning strength. The siblings had to watch this process, powerlessly.

When British troops reached Bergen-Belsen on 15 April 1945, they encountered approximately 10,000 bodies scattered around the camp. Around 55,000 prisoners, including 800 children, were still alive at this point. They were sick, lice-infested, and starving. Another 12,500 of them died within the next four weeks as a direct result of their camp detention. Emmie's mother also died a few days after the liberation. Emmie and Rudi could do nothing to save her.

Emmie and her brother Rudi were brought to Sweden, where they found shelter in a refugee home for rescued children, and were cared for in a hospital for a long time. Their brother Menachem also survived and reconnected with his younger siblings with the help of the Red Cross. All three were eventually reunited in the Netherlands.

Of the 140,000 Jews living in the Netherlands at the start of the war, 107,000 were deported to various concentration and extermination camps. Only about 5,000 of them survived. Menachem, Rudi, and Emmie Kallus were three of these

6 Hanna Lévy-Hass, *Diary of Bergen-Belsen, 1944-1945*, trans. Sophie Hand, ed. Amira Hass (Chicago: Haymarket Books, 2009), 45.

survivors. But they carried their trauma throughout their entire lives. In 1949, they immigrated to Israel. Emmie felt like a foreigner in the kibbutz. She was assigned to a school class according to her age but did not cope at all because she had simply missed too many classes. While the other children had spent their first years learning in school, Emmie had struggled to survive in German concentration camps. She remembers: "I was a sad girl, introverted and rebellious."[7]

Like many other survivors, Emmie tried for a long time to repress her experiences. It was not until many years later that she collapsed and eventually sought psychological help. What she was unable to forget now hit her with all its might: "The whole Holocaust suddenly resurfaced, the separation from my parents, which I had never mourned, all these difficult events I had endured during the war."[8] Emmie slowly began to engage with her past and to even talk about it – something she finds difficult to this day. For the survivors, the Holocaust was never over, which is reflected in Emmie Arbel's story. When the surviving children recall their time in German concentration camps, disease and violence, hunger and death are the dominant themes. These experiences shaped their lives after their survival. When Emmie and many other child survivors decided to finally tell young people about their experiences, they did so to send a key message: a crime like the Holocaust must never happen again.

---

7 Arbel, unpublished manuscript.
8 Ibid.

In Their Own Words

DAVID SCHAFFER

I survived the Holocaust by silently disobeying the rules and decrees proclaimed by the fascist authorities.

Under the leadership of Professor Charlotte Schallié, artist Miriam Libicki and I created a graphic novel describing how my family was deported to Transnistria in the Ukraine and how we struggled to survive. In March 1944, we were liberated by the Russian forces. My family and I walked back towards our home in Vama, Bukovina. We walked from Ivashkovtsi, in the Ukraine, to Mihaileni, a city in Romania. With minimal food, clothing, or footwear, we had a difficult and long journey.

We finally settled in an empty house in Mihaileni. It was not possible to continue on to Vama, Bukovina, as there was fighting in the area.

Before the war, I had finished Grade 1, but by the time we were liberated, I had forgotten most of the reading and writing skills. In Mihaileni, my parents developed an intense program of teaching me these skills again. Nearby, there was a courthouse, and outside was a pile of legal documents. I used the clean backside of the documents to write out the alphabet and then sentences.

My homeschooling ended as the number of displaced persons increased in the area and an "elementary school for the evacuated" was opened. I was thirteen years old and my parents registered me in Grade 4. I impressed the teacher with my quick and accurate math skills and he switched me to Grade 5. After several months at the school, I completed my exams and received a certificate proving I completed the fifth grade. Around this time, the fighting in Bukovina had moved on, but my parents decided not to return to our home.

We decided to settle in Gura Humorului. We struggled to procure food and basic necessities. Our relatives from Canada helped us by sending packages.

The city center was all in ruins from the fighting in the area. There were numerous areas where mines were planted and people were killed or injured. We were told to walk in the middle of the streets to stay safe. There were also large quantities of guns and ammunition left over in the area. My friends and I used live ammunition as toys, which really upset my mother. We also found a tire from a military vehicle made from foam rubber, which we cut into balls to play soccer barefoot.

The Jewish community of Gura Humorului opened a special fast-track school to educate the children who had survived. In Suceava, a larger nearby city, the government set up monthly exams to enable students to do several grades in one year. I registered in Grade 6, but they looked at my Grade 5 certificate and concluded it was not valid. They set up a special one-day exam session at a high school in Cimpolung, a nearby city. Through this one-day exam, I got a second certificate for Grade 5 and was admitted to Grade 6. I studied in the fast-track programs and graduated Grades 6, 7, and 8 in one year. After Grade 8 I had to pass an exam called "Small Baccalaureate" and present all of my certificates. They looked at my second Grade 5 certificate and concluded again it was not valid. I had to redo the exams AGAIN!

I started Grade 9 but, after a few months, they closed the school. My family lost their business and did not have the means to send me to a high school in a nearby city. I worked alongside my father, loading and unloading railroad cars by hand. It was a strenuous job with infrequent work and low pay.

When I was eighteen, I got a job at a cardboard factory as a helper to a blacksmith. The day began with bringing in a wheelbarrow loaded with coal, then banging the hot iron all day. I completed high school while working.

After graduating high school and working in an office job, I decided to study engineering. I failed the entrance exam and worked for one more year preparing. I passed the entrance exam and, in 1955, enrolled as a student at Polytechnic Institute in Bucharest. The first semester was very difficult for me. I failed some exams, but I studied hard and passed remedial exams to complete the first year.

The 31st of December 1956 was a memorable day. A friend invited me to his home to celebrate the New Year. There I met Sidi, my future wife. We connected right away.

My studies went well until the 24th of December 1959, when I was expelled with no given reason. I went on to get a job as a designer in a shipyard, designing machinery to be installed on various ships. The manager was a knowledgeable engineer and a very good person. He guided me and supervised my activities. I worked in the shipyard for three years until I got a phone call from my father that we had finally received permission to immigrate to Israel.

Sidi and I got married. I learned Hebrew and began working in a shipyard in Haifa. But I really wanted to complete my engineering degree. I passed a set of exams and finally received my engineering degree from the Israel Institute of Technology.

Sidi and I were very happy and had three sons together.

In 1975, I was invited to a family event in Edmonton, Alberta. There, I had an interview with an engineering company. They gave me a good job offer and my family and I moved to Edmonton where I was employed as a Supervising

Preassembly Engineer. Years went by and I worked on different jobs as a Consulting Engineer, Project Engineer, Project Manager, and even a Deputy Director. I really enjoyed my career as an engineer.

Eventually, I retired and settled down in Vancouver, British Columbia, where I currently reside with my wife. We have been blessed with nine grandchildren, all born in Canada.

Through reading my story, I hope to inspire you to be alert, learn from history, and take action when necessary to protect our freedom and way of life.

Vancouver, BC, Canada, May 2021

NICO KAMP

My neighbor, Betty Rosa van Os, was only four and a half years old when she was deported together with her parents to Auschwitz on 21 August 1942. Betty and her mother were gassed upon arrival.[1] Children often had to line up sometimes in icy cold weather until they were gassed. The image of curly-haired, little Betty waiting in such a line is an image I cannot let go of.

I want to tell readers about the fate of children – Jewish and non-Jewish. This is very personal for me because I am a Jewish child survivor. We now know that in those years a total of 1.5 million Jewish children from Europe under the age of twelve were murdered. These murdered children were young and they were innocent, just like many of the younger readers of this book. They had their whole lives ahead of them. They were just kids.

The killing of both Jewish and non-Jewish children began in 1939 in Nazi Germany and Austria. Between 1939 and 1945, the Nazi regime murdered hundreds of thousands of children with disabilities or chronic conditions, as part

---

1 Betty's father was selected for forced labor. He died five weeks later, 30 September 1942, in Auschwitz.

of the so-called Euthanasia Program. The Nazis referred to them as *Reichsausschusskinder* (Reich Committee Children) because they were diagnosed by the "Reich Committee for the Scientific Registering of Serious Hereditary and Congenital Illnesses," but one could also understand the term *Ausschuss* here to imply something faulty or defective, something meant for the garbage.

At least 275,000 German Jewish and non-Jewish children were victims of this program. Shortly after arriving at specific killing wards in children's hospitals or psychiatric clinics that were euphemistically called *Kinderfachabteilungen* (children's wards or children's departments), these innocent children were killed with poisonous injections, or by starvation in so-called starvation houses, where they died a slow and painful death of malnutrition.

These children had conditions like schizophrenia, epilepsy, paralysis, encephalitis, or physical limitations – conditions that today are accepted and treated. But then, Nazi doctors decided who was allowed to live and who was not. The murder of these children was central to Hitler's vision of a pure German state.

From the Netherlands, Jewish children, with or without disability, were deported and murdered. Some of them were deported from specific children's organizations and institutions, but many others were caught during raids or were found in hiding. My brother and I are among the lucky ones who survived, but we faced a lot of danger in our thirteen hiding places.

About Betty Rosa van Os I always keep thinking …

Amsterdam, the Netherlands, April 2021
Translated from the Dutch by Jan Erik Dubbelman

ROLF KAMP

My motivation to participate in this graphic novel is to share with present and future generations the story of what happened to me during World War II in the Netherlands.

First of all, the good experiences …

My mother, who survived three concentration camps and died at the ripe old age of ninety-eight, used to say that after the war there were three of us: two little boys and her. Now, we are a new family of twenty-two people!

My brother and I were hidden in thirteen different places, which varied from a few days in a chicken coop to living on a small farm with farmer Hendrik Traa, his wife, Regina, their ten children, and some others in hiding. I learned a lot during those years: the weather, planting and harvesting, farm animals, and all the work that needs to be done on a farm. I had a new Dutch-sounding name and had to learn the local dialect of our hiding places.

We liked to play in the hay storage area above the animals. This area was also a hiding place. One day, when a Jewish teenager was chased by Dutch Nazis, he came to the back of the farm and asked if we could hide him. In less than a minute, I showed him the ladder to the hay stack. I covered the hole in the hay, he went through and I quickly laid the ladder on the floor. The Dutch Nazi collaborators came in and asked the farmer if he had seen a fugitive. He said no and they believed him and went away. The Jewish teenager was allowed to stay with us for a few days and then went on to another hiding place. I was happy to find out that he survived and later worked for the Israeli Air Force.

After the war, my mother returned from the camps. We tried to lead a normal life. My brother and I went to school, received our diplomas, and went to work. We did not think too much about our wartime traumas, since we were busy. When her grandchildren were teens, my mother had long conversations with them about the war and her experiences. Our sons visited the Auschwitz-Birkenau Memorial and Museum to learn more about where their grandmother had been.

I missed three years of school during the war, but it didn't prevent me from becoming what I always wanted to be: a mechanical engineer. My family lived in the Netherlands, the USA, Israel, and then moved back to the Netherlands. As a result, our children can speak three languages. We are happily married, have three children and six grandchildren.

My granddaughter was the first to ask me to speak about my experiences in hiding at her school in New Jersey, and I agreed. Since then, for about fourteen years now, I have been a guest speaker, telling school children of our war experiences. I want students to recognize the beginning of evil and prevent it from spreading.

A few years ago, my brother located the Traa family in Canada. In June 2018, we visited them in Winnipeg. They are now a family of 183 people. We renewed our friendship and have been in contact ever since.

Now for the bad experiences ...

Among the 102,000 Jewish children, women, and men from the Netherlands who were murdered by the Nazis – out of the 140,000 prewar Jewish population – were my father who was gassed in Auschwitz and my paternal grandparents who died in Bergen-Belsen. With the help of Dutch betrayers, the Dutch police found my parents and grandparents in hiding. They arrested my parents first and several weeks later my grandparents and handed them over to the Nazi murderers. Not only did the Nazis ruin my youth, they continue to hurt me in my old age because I often think about the atrocities that they caused during the Holocaust. I cannot forget.

I want to end on a positive note …

I am excited that this book is in the form of a graphic novel. I want to thank Charlotte Schallié who initiated this project, and Gilad Seliktar who drew our story. I am grateful to all the people who helped us survive and made our lives and families and this book possible.

Amsterdam, the Netherlands, April 2021

EMMIE ARBEL

What happened during the Shoah (Holocaust) is difficult to comprehend. Sometimes, I cannot believe that I stayed alive. I came out of the war sick, weak, and lonely, but also very rebellious. I know what I want and what I don't want. I am not afraid of anyone or anything. The events I experienced in the camps taught me to be brave and to be strong, and have influenced me to this day.

I see my contribution to Holocaust education as a mission. There are fewer and fewer of us survivors still alive. I know that it is very important to share this horrible story with the world so nothing like this happens again. I never thought I would ever work with a comic artist. But I did. Barbara Yelin is an amazingly talented artist and a very kind and sensitive person. I have learnt so much from her, and I have gained a dear friend.

For many years I remained silent to protect my daughters and myself. I didn't want my children to be worried about me or to be sad. I accompanied my older brother Menachem on trips to Germany, where he told his story in schools for many years. I came along to strengthen and support him. But I remained silent. Over the years, he became weaker and his health prevented him from traveling. I was asked if I would continue on for him, and I agreed.

I was born in the Netherlands, in The Hague, in 1937. My father escaped from Hungary because he didn't want to join the Hungarian army. My mother was born in the Netherlands. I had two older brothers, Menachem and Rudi.

The war began for my family in 1942 when three policemen came to take us to Camp Westerbork in the Netherlands. I was about four and a half years old. Camp Westerbork was a transit camp. Every week, a train arrived there to take people to concentration camps in Germany and Poland. My grandfather and grandmother were also with us in Camp Westerbork, but a week after our arrival they were sent to Auschwitz where they were gassed. We were in Westerbork for a year and a half. My father was sent to Buchenwald in Germany and never returned. My mother, brothers, and I were sent to a large women's camp in Germany called Ravensbrück. There, we experienced real fear, which Barbara and I describe in my story.

Something that we didn't include was a time when my older brother got a skin disease and was sent to the Revier (the prisoners' sickbay). I missed him very much and, although it was absolutely forbidden, I went to see him. I was about six years old then. When the Kapo (concentration camp prisoner who was selected to oversee other prisoners) came in, I tried to hide behind the back of Menachem who was lying on an upper bunk bed. The Kapo threw me down from the bed and began beating me with a stick until I fainted. I still feel these beatings in my ears, and I don't hear as well as I should. Somebody brought me back to my mother.

Barbara and I describe in the graphic narrative how I almost died in the camps. When I was first asked to participate in the graphic novel project, and was told my story would appear as a comic book, I didn't like the idea. I thought that comics are only for children. But the more I thought about it, the more I understood why comics are effective. Now, I think it is a wonderful and creative idea to reach adults and especially children, who don't like to read books. Additionally, comics can help teachers explain this painful topic to their students. For these reasons, I decided to join the project.

After Ravensbrück, my mother and my younger brother Rudi were sent to Bergen-Belsen. My older brother Menachem was no longer with us. He was sent to the men's camp at Ravensbrück, since he was already a "man" at eleven years old. Barbara captured the chaos in her drawings. We were lucky to be there for only a few months, or I would not have survived. We were there until we were liberated by the British army. My mother died in Bergen-Belsen a week after liberation.

From Bergen-Belsen we were sent with Polish children to Malmö in Sweden to recuperate.

We were in Sweden for nine months, until Menachem, who also survived the war and returned to the Netherlands, found us through survivor lists created by the Red Cross and helped bring us to him back to the Netherlands.

We arrived at a large house where a couple and their three children took in Jewish children whose parents didn't survive the war. We were fifteen children. There I experienced some good and some not so good things. I had to lie in bed for a year because I had tuberculosis, and I felt very lonely when all the other children went happily to school. When I was nine and a half, I started at a Montessori school where each child had a lot of freedom and individual attention. This system suited me very well, but we left for Israel after one year and a half. I very much wanted to stay in the Netherlands, but I was too young to make my own decisions.

In Israel, we arrived to Kiryat Shmuel on 17 February 1949, a former British army camp, where they brought the new immigrants. I felt bad there, it reminded me of a concentration camp.

About a month later, we moved to a kibbutz. I felt a huge disappointment after the stories we heard about the beautiful land of Israel. We arrived on a grey winter day, there was mud everywhere, and many people came to see "the large family who survived the Shoah."

I felt like being in a zoo and I decided then and there that when I grew up, I would leave this place. I was eleven years old at the time.

I had many problems at school. I felt that nobody understood me. There were teachers whom all the children were scared of and I didn't understand why. I knew they would not kill me, so what was there to be afraid of? After repeating fifth grade, I decided to stop learning. Sometimes I entered the class, but mostly I went outside and read a book. I learned the language quickly and I loved to read. I acquired most of my knowledge from books and not from school. Sometimes, when I went to school, I would sit in the classroom quietly even when spoken to. I never did homework or tests. This is where I've learned how to be quiet, and also I don't like to be amongst many people.

At the end of my school years, I had to work. I didn't like other people deciding for me where to work or what to do. This issue caused me many troubles until I decided to leave the kibbutz.

I moved to Haifa and made my own decisions. In 1961, I wanted to see the world and left for Brazil. There I married my boyfriend whom I had met during my army service in Israel. When Menachem left for Africa for three years, he asked me if I wanted to return to Israel and stay in his house. We decided to go back in 1962 and moved into Menachem's house in a small town. Even though we are no longer together, my ex-husband and I still live in this place. We had three daughters. My daughter Tammi, who was born in 1968, passed away in 2005.

I started working as a secretary in a large mental health clinic and, after a few years, I became the administrative manager until my retirement. This shows you that with determination you can succeed even without a high school diploma or a university degree. From the moment I retired, I started to volunteer in many places with people who need help or who are in need.

My words are especially meant for you, the younger generation: Accept people who are different. And spread good in the world, not bad.

Kiryat Ti'von, Israel, April 2021
Translated from the Hebrew by Noga Yarmar

Behind the Art – by Miriam Libicki, Gilad Seliktar, and Barbara Yelin

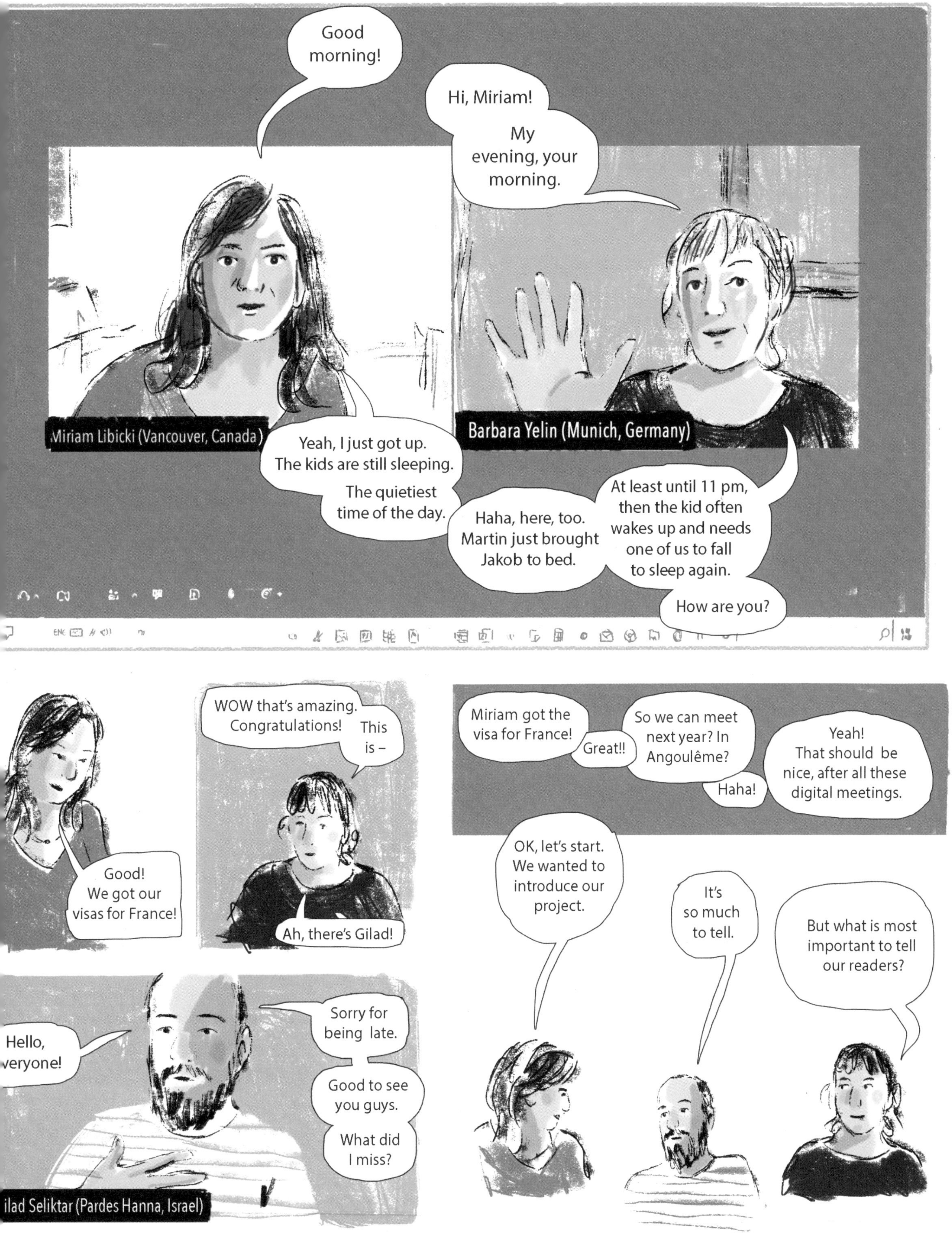
Good morning!
Hi, Miriam!
My evening, your morning.
Miriam Libicki (Vancouver, Canada)
Barbara Yelin (Munich, Germany)
Yeah, I just got up. The kids are still sleeping.
The quietest time of the day.
Haha, here, too. Martin just brought Jakob to bed.
At least until 11 pm, then the kid often wakes up and needs one of us to fall to sleep again.
How are you?
Good! We got our visas for France!
WOW that's amazing. Congratulations!
This is –
Ah, there's Gilad!
Hello, veryone!
Sorry for being late.
Good to see you guys.
What did I miss?
ilad Seliktar (Pardes Hanna, Israel)
Miriam got the visa for France!
Great!!
So we can meet next year? In Angoulême?
Haha!
Yeah! That should be nice, after all these digital meetings.
OK, let's start. We wanted to introduce our project.
It's so much to tell.
But what is most important to tell our readers?

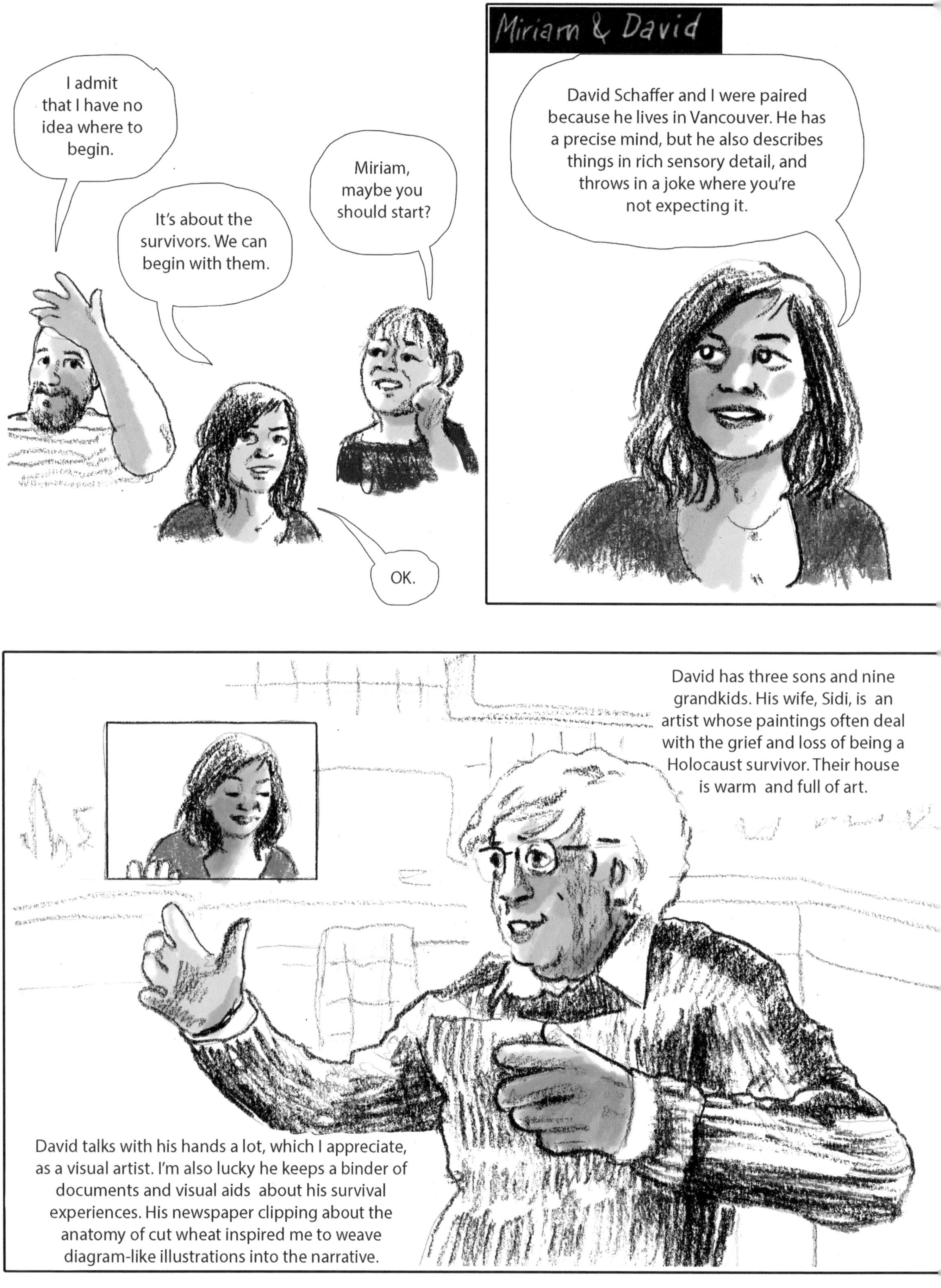
I admit that I have no idea where to begin.
It's about the survivors. We can begin with them.
Miriam, maybe you should start?
OK.
Miriam & David
David Schaffer and I were paired because he lives in Vancouver. He has a precise mind, but he also describes things in rich sensory detail, and throws in a joke where you're not expecting it.
David has three sons and nine grandkids. His wife, Sidi, is an artist whose paintings often deal with the grief and loss of being a Holocaust survivor. Their house is warm and full of art.
David talks with his hands a lot, which I appreciate, as a visual artist. I'm also lucky he keeps a binder of documents and visual aids about his survival experiences. His newspaper clipping about the anatomy of cut wheat inspired me to weave diagram-like illustrations into the narrative.

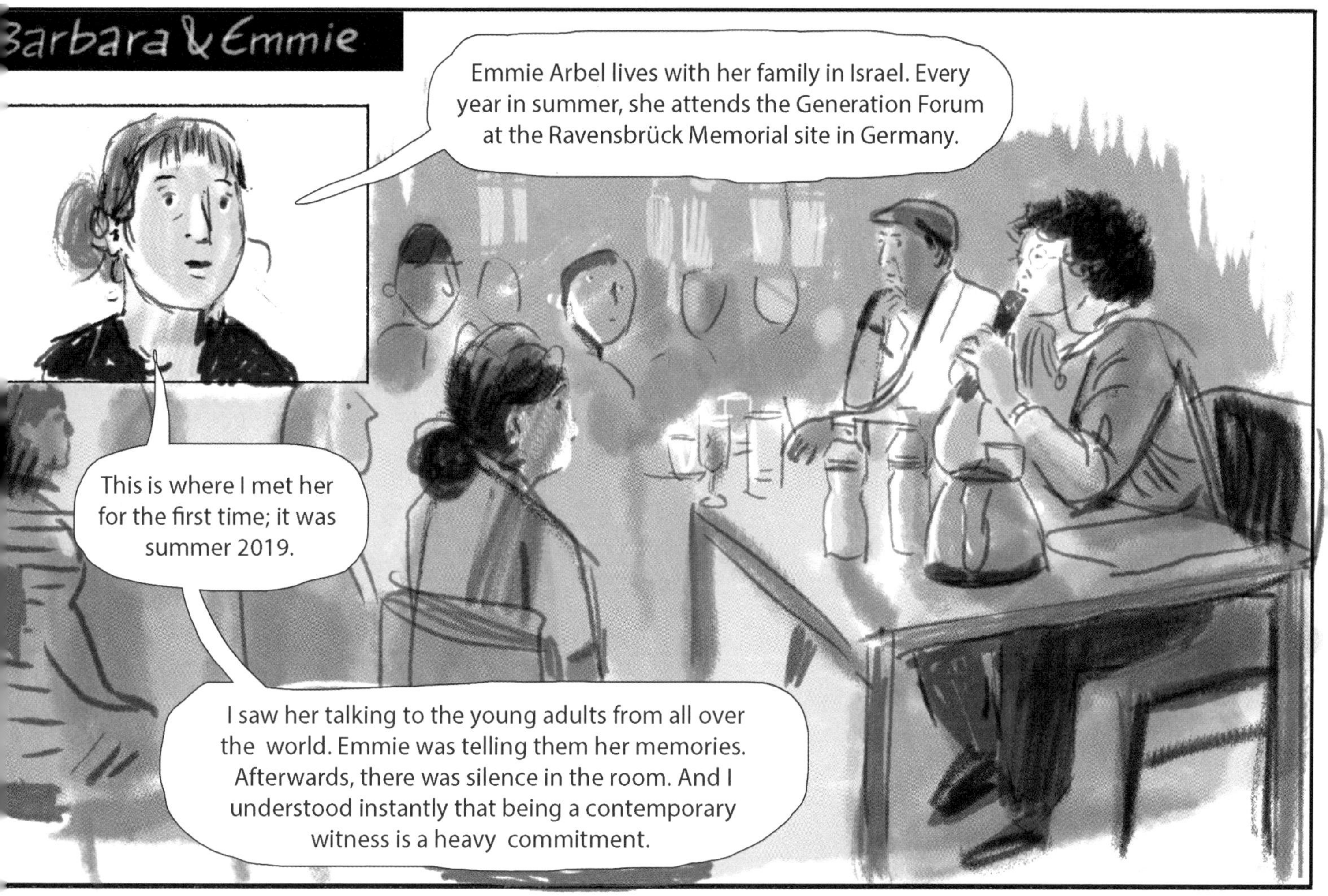
Barbara & Emmie
Emmie Arbel lives with her family in Israel. Every year in summer, she attends the Generation Forum at the Ravensbrück Memorial site in Germany.
This is where I met her for the first time; it was summer 2019.
I saw her talking to the young adults from all over the world. Emmie was telling them her memories. Afterwards, there was silence in the room. And I understood instantly that being a contemporary witness is a heavy commitment.

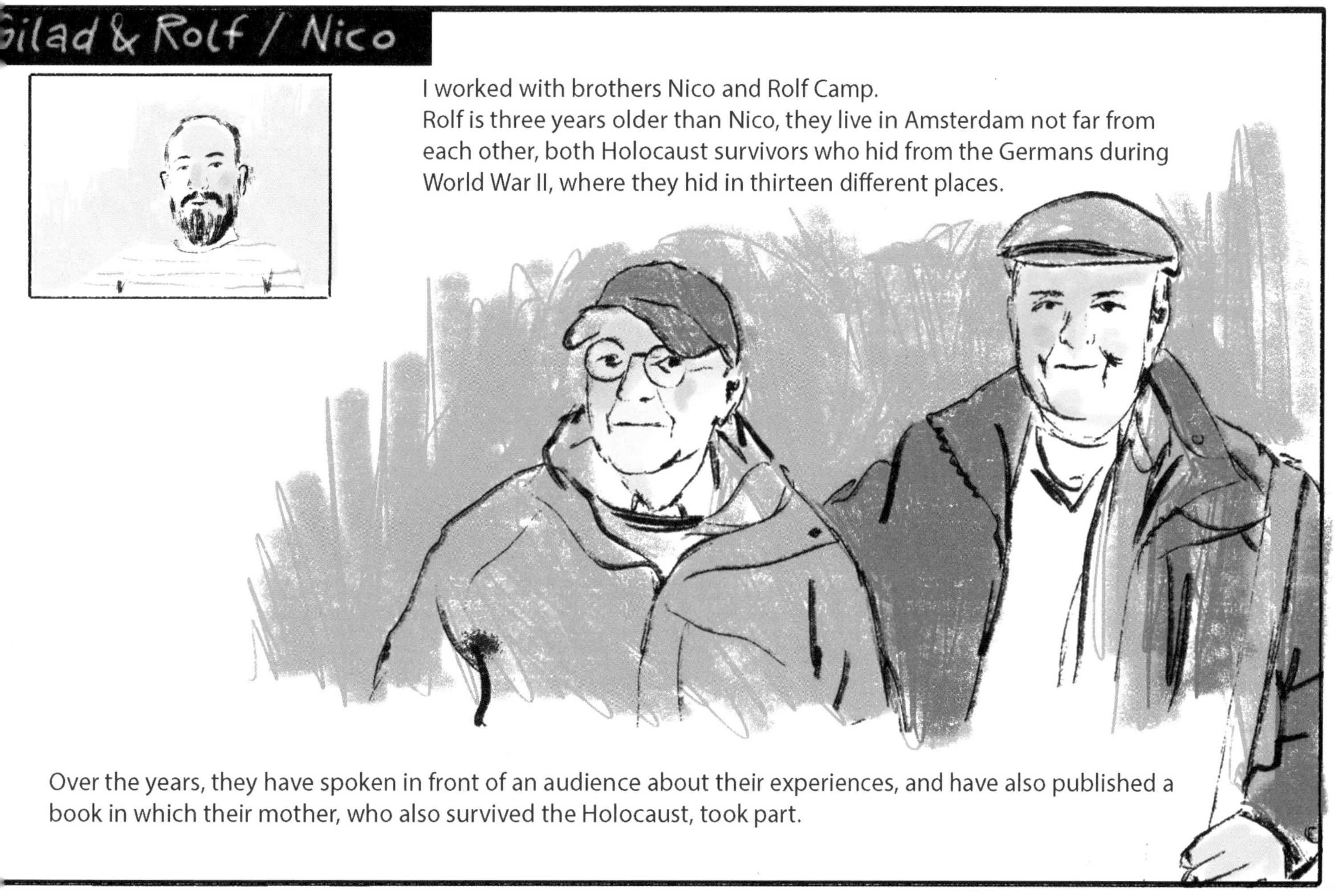
Gilad & Rolf / Nico
I worked with brothers Nico and Rolf Camp.
Rolf is three years older than Nico, they live in Amsterdam not far from each other, both Holocaust survivors who hid from the Germans during World War II, where they hid in thirteen different places.
Over the years, they have spoken in front of an audience about their experiences, and have also published a book in which their mother, who also survived the Holocaust, took part.

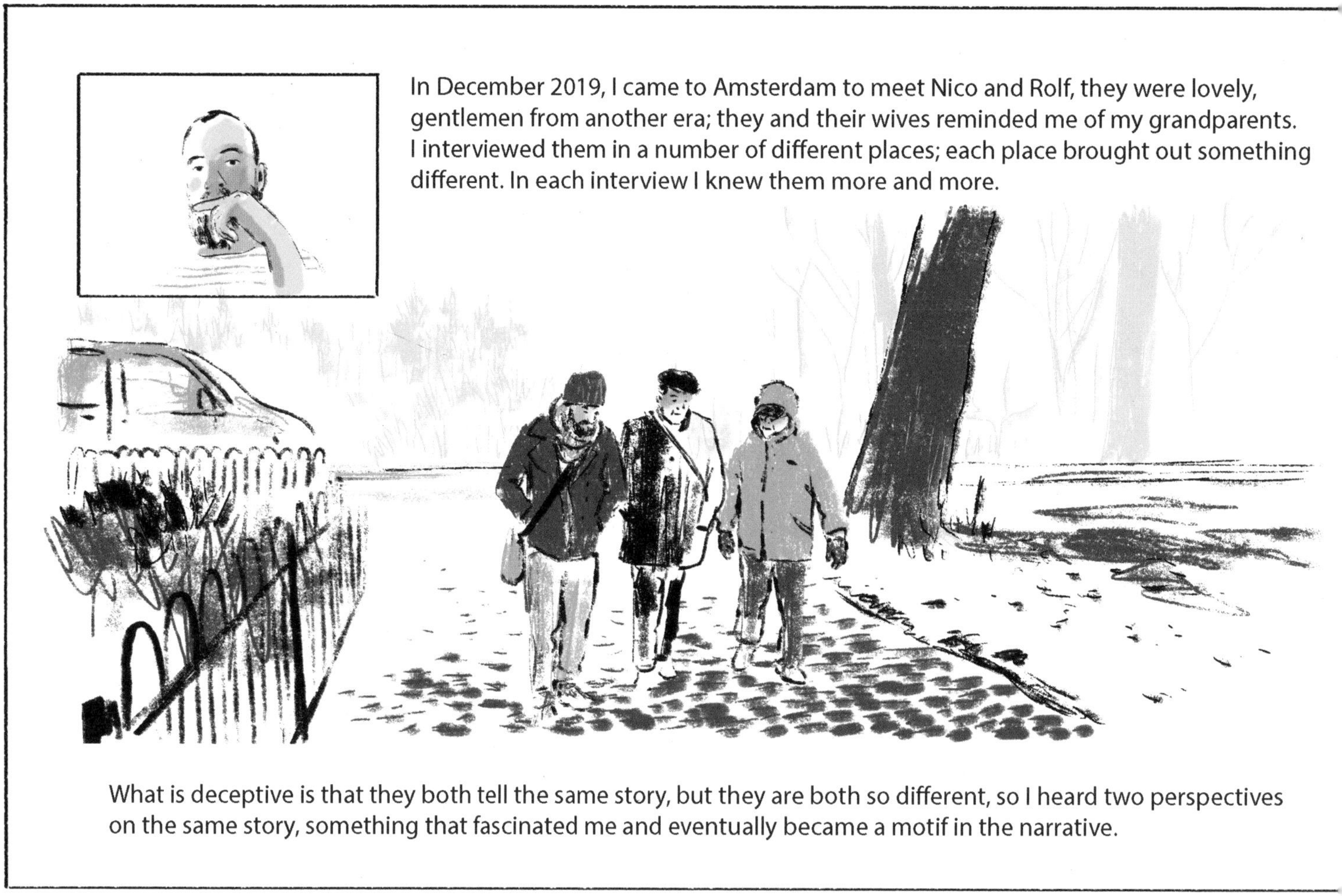
In December 2019, I came to Amsterdam to meet Nico and Rolf, they were lovely, gentlemen from another era; they and their wives reminded me of my grandparents. I interviewed them in a number of different places; each place brought out something different. In each interview I knew them more and more.
What is deceptive is that they both tell the same story, but they are both so different, so I heard two perspectives on the same story, something that fascinated me and eventually became a motif in the narrative.

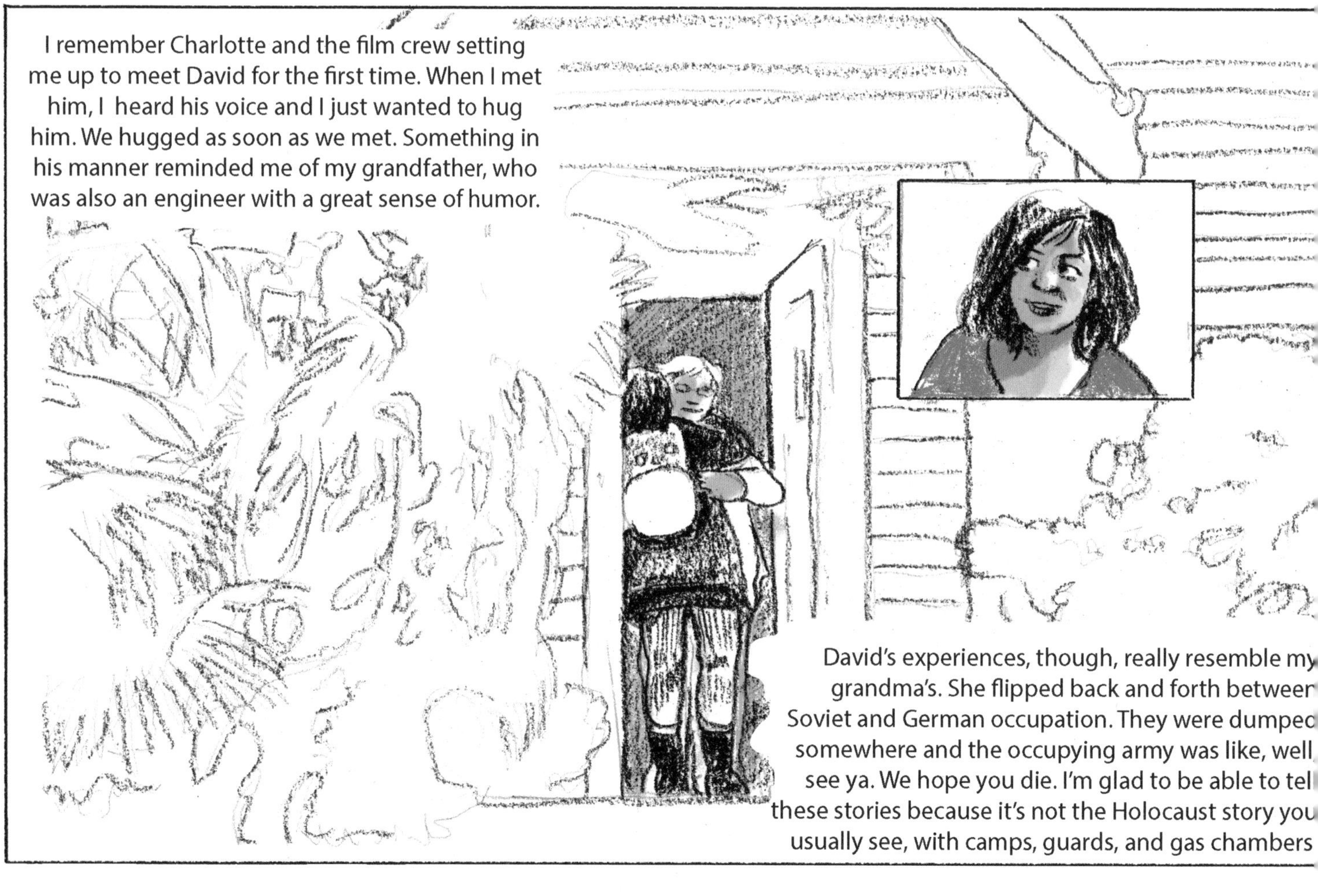
I remember Charlotte and the film crew setting me up to meet David for the first time. When I met him, I heard his voice and I just wanted to hug him. We hugged as soon as we met. Something in his manner reminded me of my grandfather, who was also an engineer with a great sense of humor.
David's experiences, though, really resemble my grandma's. She flipped back and forth between Soviet and German occupation. They were dumped somewhere and the occupying army was like, well, see ya. We hope you die. I'm glad to be able to tell these stories because it's not the Holocaust story you usually see, with camps, guards, and gas chambers

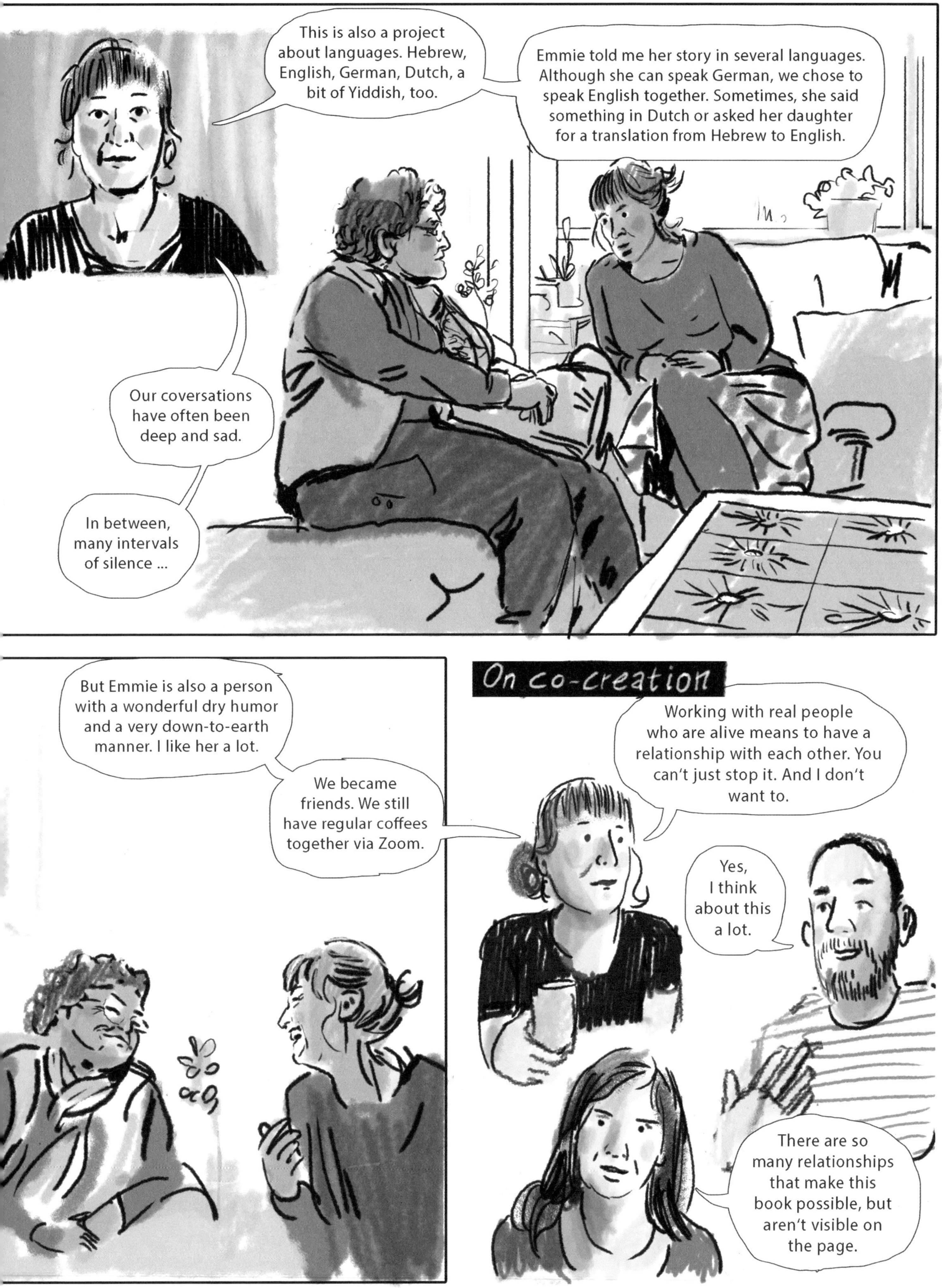
This is also a project about languages. Hebrew, English, German, Dutch, a bit of Yiddish, too.
Emmie told me her story in several languages. Although she can speak German, we chose to speak English together. Sometimes, she said something in Dutch or asked her daughter for a translation from Hebrew to English.
Our coversations have often been deep and sad.
In between, many intervals of silence ...
But Emmie is also a person with a wonderful dry humor and a very down-to-earth manner. I like her a lot.
We became friends. We still have regular coffees together via Zoom.
On co-creation
Working with real people who are alive means to have a relationship with each other. You can't just stop it. And I don't want to.
Yes, I think about this a lot.
There are so many relationships that make this book possible, but aren't visible on the page.

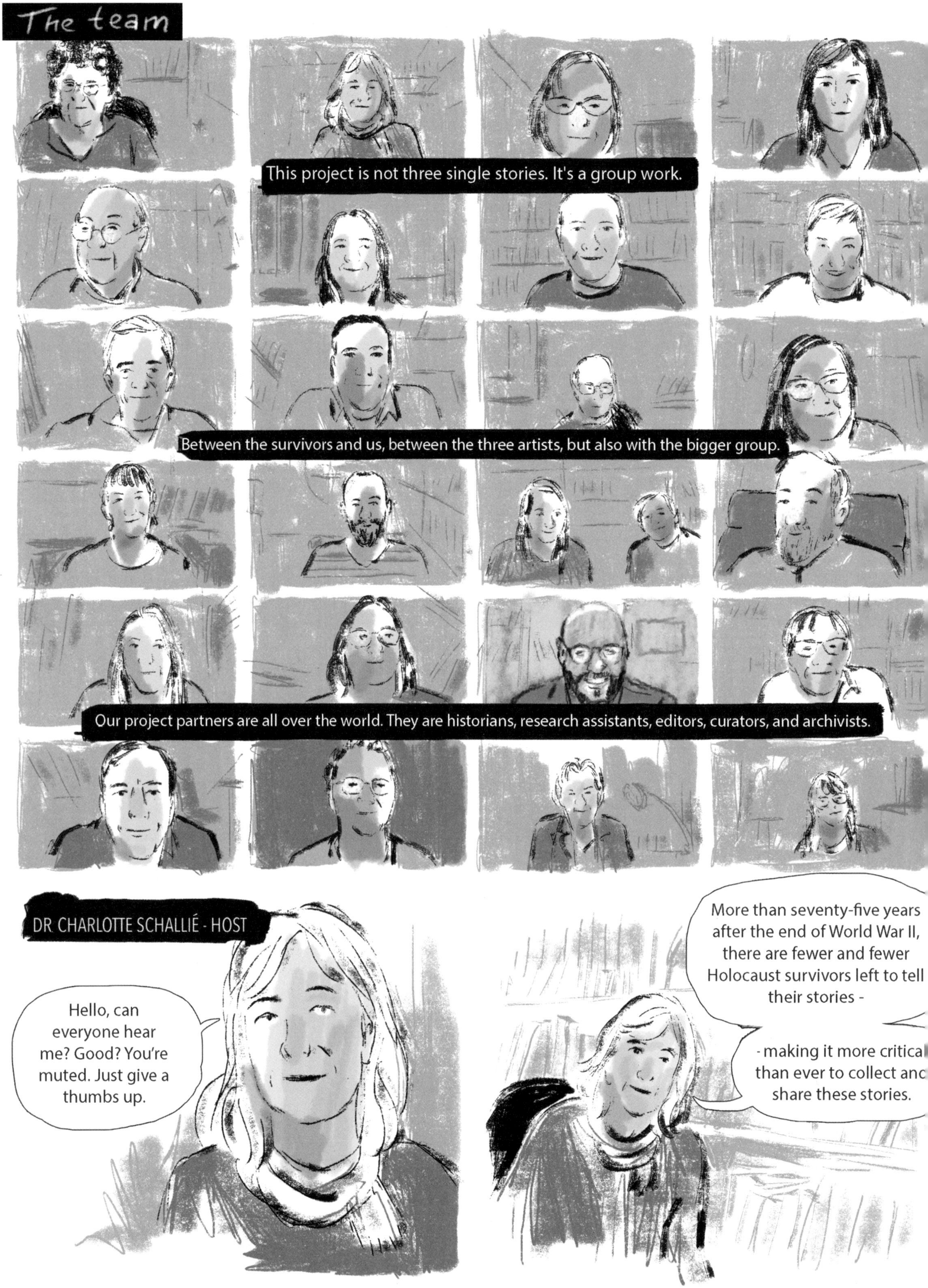
The team
This project is not three single stories. It's a group work.
Between the survivors and us, between the three artists, but also with the bigger group.
Our project partners are all over the world. They are historians, research assistants, editors, curators, and archivists.
DR CHARLOTTE SCHALLIÉ - HOST
Hello, can everyone hear me? Good? You're muted. Just give a thumbs up.
More than seventy-five years after the end of World War II, there are fewer and fewer Holocaust survivors left to tell their stories -
- making it more critica than ever to collect anc share these stories.

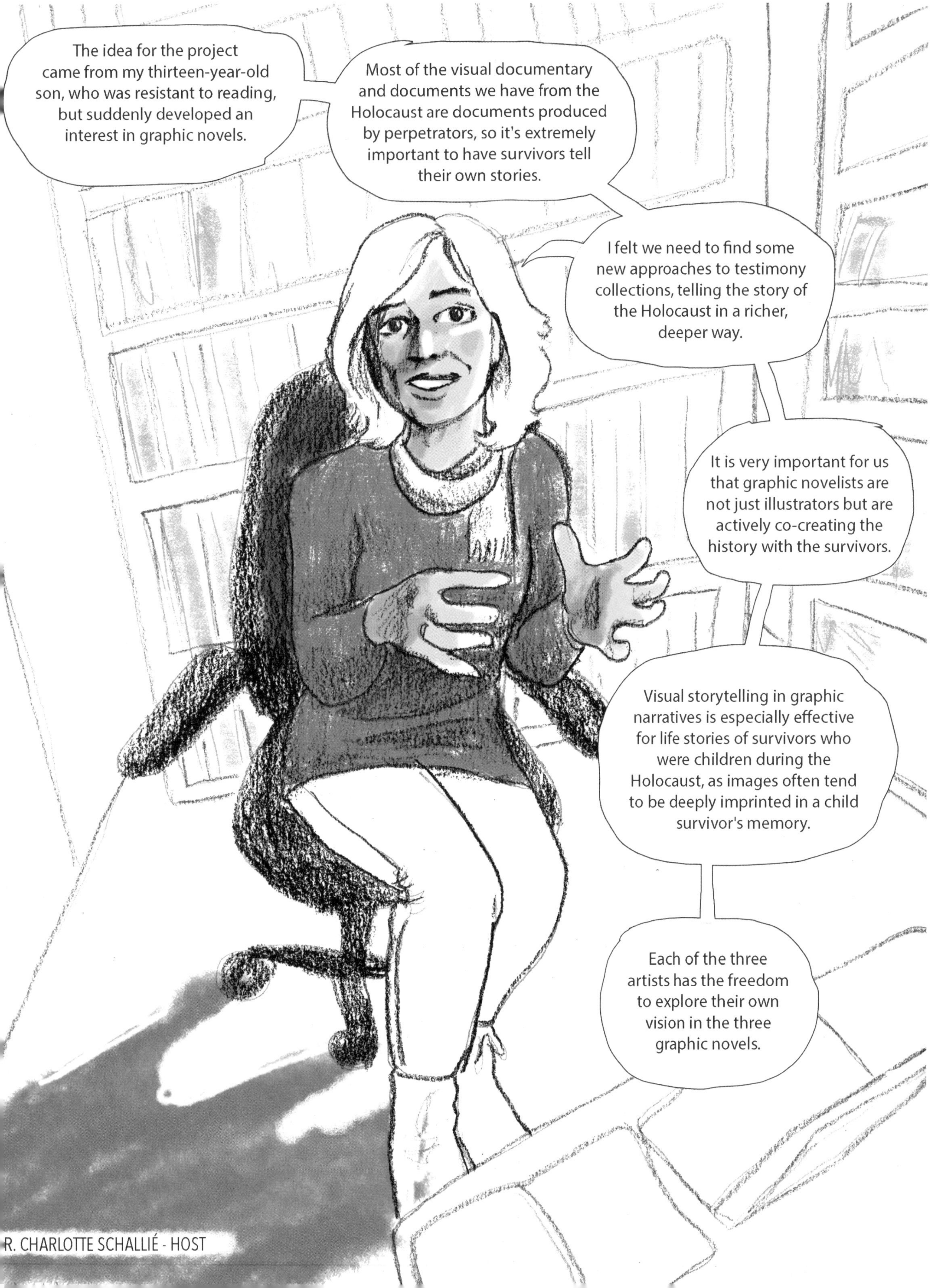
The idea for the project came from my thirteen-year-old son, who was resistant to reading, but suddenly developed an interest in graphic novels.
Most of the visual documentary and documents we have from the Holocaust are documents produced by perpetrators, so it's extremely important to have survivors tell their own stories.
I felt we need to find some new approaches to testimony collections, telling the story of the Holocaust in a richer, deeper way.
It is very important for us that graphic novelists are not just illustrators but are actively co-creating the history with the survivors.
Visual storytelling in graphic narratives is especially effective for life stories of survivors who were children during the Holocaust, as images often tend to be deeply imprinted in a child survivor's memory.
Each of the three artists has the freedom to explore their own vision in the three graphic novels.
R. CHARLOTTE SCHALLIÉ - HOST

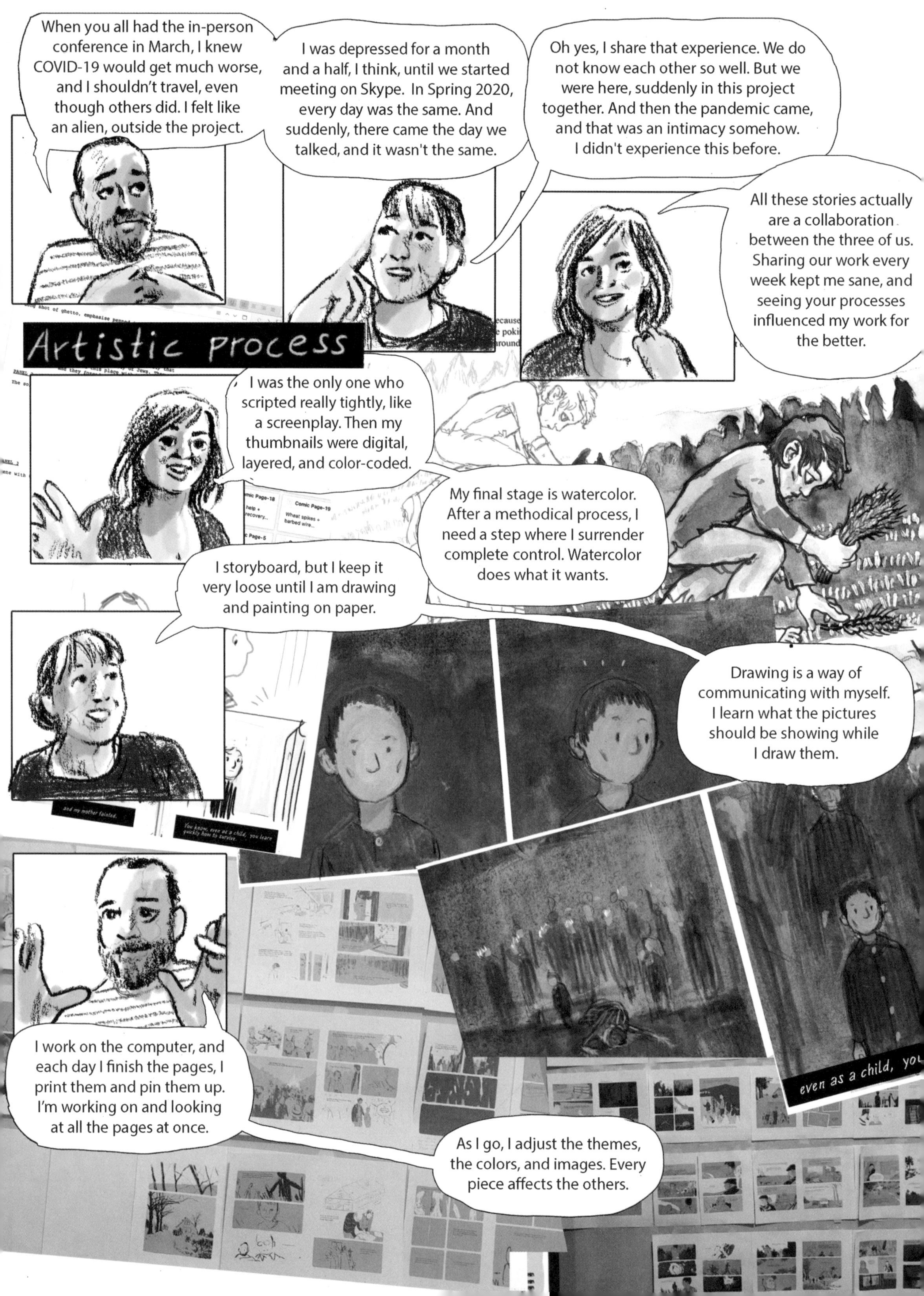
When you all had the in-person conference in March, I knew COVID-19 would get much worse, and I shouldn't travel, even though others did. I felt like an alien, outside the project.
I was depressed for a month and a half, I think, until we started meeting on Skype. In Spring 2020, every day was the same. And suddenly, there came the day we talked, and it wasn't the same.
Oh yes, I share that experience. We do not know each other so well. But we were here, suddenly in this project together. And then the pandemic came, and that was an intimacy somehow. I didn't experience this before.
All these stories actually are a collaboration between the three of us. Sharing our work every week kept me sane, and seeing your processes influenced my work for the better.
Artistic process
I was the only one who scripted really tightly, like a screenplay. Then my thumbnails were digital, layered, and color-coded.
My final stage is watercolor. After a methodical process, I need a step where I surrender complete control. Watercolor does what it wants.
I storyboard, but I keep it very loose until I am drawing and painting on paper.
Drawing is a way of communicating with myself. I learn what the pictures should be showing while I draw them.
and my mother fainted.
You know, even as a child, you learn quickly how to survive.
even as a child, you
I work on the computer, and each day I finish the pages, I print them and pin them up. I'm working on and looking at all the pages at once.
As I go, I adjust the themes, the colors, and images. Every piece affects the others.

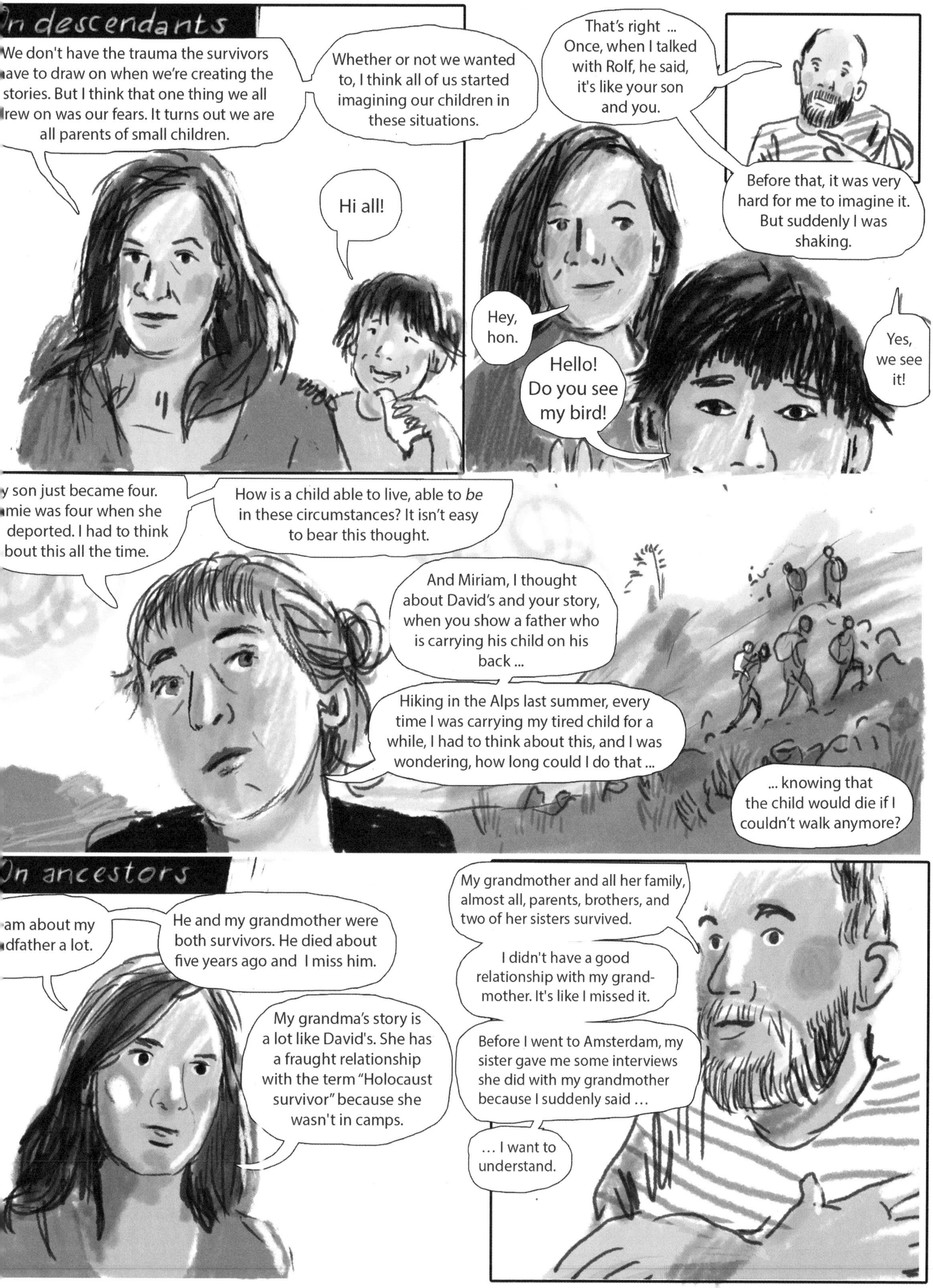
On descendants
We don't have the trauma the survivors have to draw on when we're creating the stories. But I think that one thing we all drew on was our fears. It turns out we are all parents of small children.
Whether or not we wanted to, I think all of us started imagining our children in these situations.
Hi all!
That's right ... Once, when I talked with Rolf, he said, it's like your son and you.
Before that, it was very hard for me to imagine it. But suddenly I was shaking.
Hey, hon.
Hello! Do you see my bird!
Yes, we see it!
y son just became four. mie was four when she deported. I had to think bout this all the time.
How is a child able to live, able to *be* in these circumstances? It isn't easy to bear this thought.
And Miriam, I thought about David's and your story, when you show a father who is carrying his child on his back ...
Hiking in the Alps last summer, every time I was carrying my tired child for a while, I had to think about this, and I was wondering, how long could I do that ...
... knowing that the child would die if I couldn't walk anymore?
On ancestors
am about my dfather a lot.
He and my grandmother were both survivors. He died about five years ago and I miss him.
My grandma's story is a lot like David's. She has a fraught relationship with the term "Holocaust survivor" because she wasn't in camps.
My grandmother and all her family, almost all, parents, brothers, and two of her sisters survived.
I didn't have a good relationship with my grand-mother. It's like I missed it.
Before I went to Amsterdam, my sister gave me some interviews she did with my grandmother because I suddenly said ...
... I want to understand.

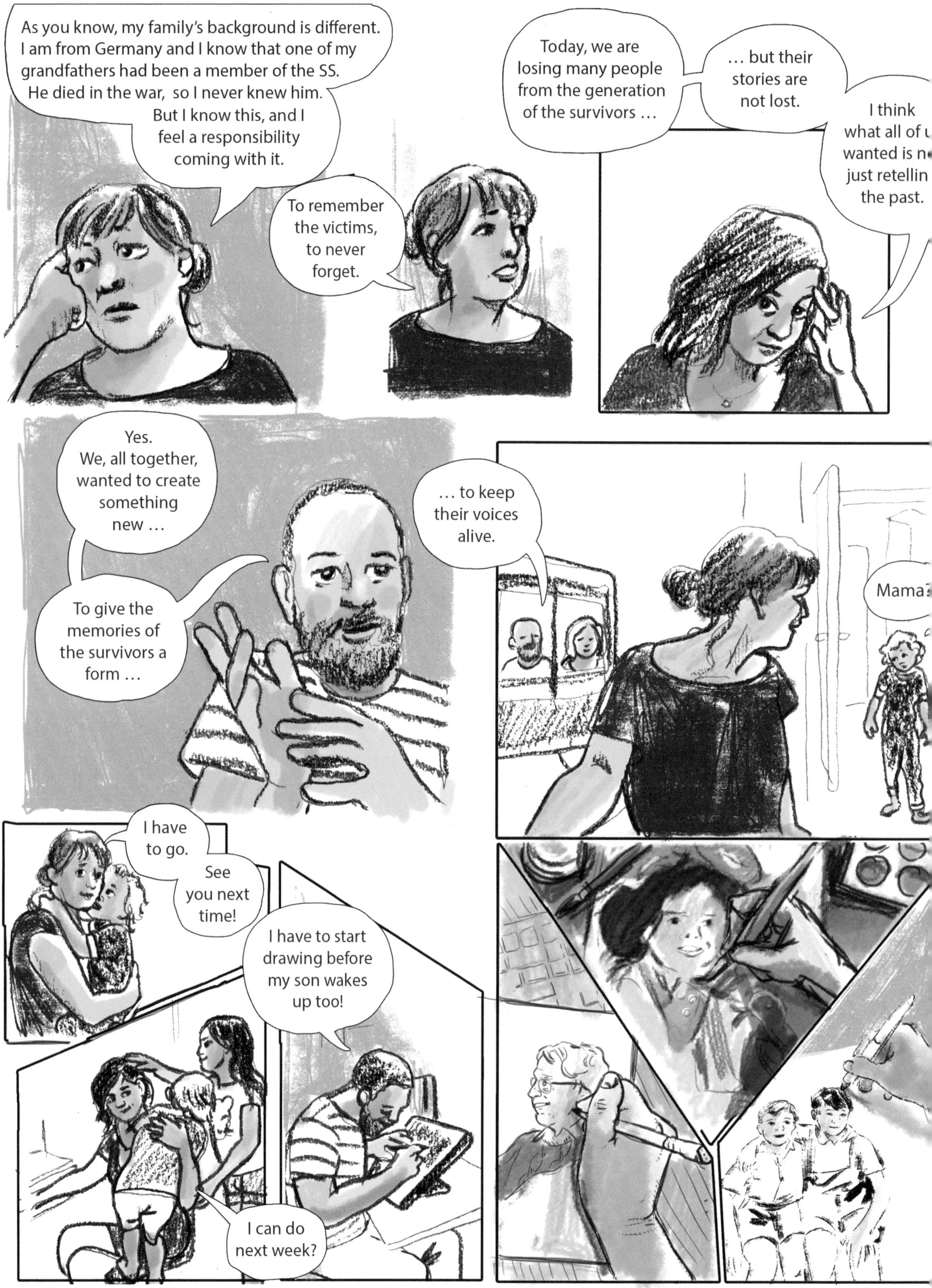

As you know, my family's background is different. I am from Germany and I know that one of my grandfathers had been a member of the SS. He died in the war, so I never knew him.
But I know this, and I feel a responsibility coming with it.
To remember the victims, to never forget.
Today, we are losing many people from the generation of the survivors …
… but their stories are not lost.
I think what all of u wanted is n just retellin the past.
Yes. We, all together, wanted to create something new …
To give the memories of the survivors a form …
… to keep their voices alive.
Mama?
I have to go.
See you next time!
I have to start drawing before my son wakes up too!
I can do next week?

AFTERWORD

Charlotte Schallié, Matt Huculak, Ilona Shulman Spaar, and Jan Erik Dubbelman

The three graphic narratives collected in this book were created as part of a collaborative research project that brought together Holocaust survivors, graphic novelists, Holocaust and Human Rights education professionals, historians, student teachers, high school teachers, librarians, and archivists over the course of three years. The three graphic novelists were invited to meet with four Holocaust child survivors both in person (between December 2019 and February 2020) and on Zoom when it was no longer possible to connect face to face due to the COVID-19 pandemic. We paired each artist with one child survivor – in one case we paired one artist with two brothers who survived together in hiding – asking them to jointly explore storylines, settings, and themes. Based on these collaborative creative sessions, Miriam Libicki, Gilad Seliktar, and Barbara Yelin developed the initial sketches and storyboards rendering the memories and reflections of David Schaffer, Nico and Rolf Kamp, and Emmie Arbel into visual narratives that respect the integrity, individuality, and dignity of the survivors' lived experiences. As each survivor holds unique knowledge not only of the mass atrocity itself but also of the process of sharing and shaping their life memories, it became imperative for the artists to anchor their visual narratives in the voices of the four child survivors. Thus, when we read *But I Live*, we hear the voices of the survivors as they are visually reimagined in multilayered narratives that, at times, seamlessly connect the past with the present.

Testimonies are key to understanding our past and present, but they are traumatic for those who share as well as for those who hear them. As our project elicits memories of human suffering, we were committed to engage practices and uphold standards responsive to the fluid and emergent needs of the survivors, their families, and the artists with whom we engaged in this critical work. Once the project was underway, we also discovered that our arts-based approach helped survivors recall new memories and take new agency over testimonies they had given many times before. We were reminded that visual storytelling in graphic narratives is especially effective for life stories and memories of child survivors as they recall their memories in a vivid associative context, which intuitively lends itself to visual representation. Whereas written and video-recorded testimonies tend to constrict engagement with survivors and, too often, treat testimony as a static document, visual storytelling – such as in the form of graphic art – foregrounds the interplay between interviewee and interviewer, thus highlighting the full range of the testimony sharing and receiving process. We thus contend that a shift towards a broader inclusion of visualizing techniques in storytelling has the potential to create innovative pathways in testimony collection – this is especially important as we are approaching the post-witness era without living survivors.

The project also speaks to the question of how does one represent the Holocaust? The testimony of the survivor, and we should say "testimonies" to evoke the iterative nature of memory in the collaboration between the artists and survivors, is mediated both graphically and verbally in multiple voices and visual styles. These stories show that there was not one generic experience of the Holocaust. The multiplicity of experiences is expressed through graphic style, color, and even the individual accents of the speakers. Each unique voice and experience is framed and represents one less voice lost to time.

These illustrated stories are a physical, graphic medium of embodying old memories conveyed and captured through drawing in the present, and as such, they create a new archive for future readers to consult that go beyond the collections created by perpetrators; they also gesture towards the countless silent voices and memories already gone. Through the support of libraries and archives, the work surrounding this project (drafts of drawings, film, and audio files) will be preserved at the University of Victoria Libraries for future researchers to consult. The stories of the survivors, however, live on through this publication.

There is an interplay at work in these graphic documents that this project cannot theorize or anticipate: the effect it has on the reader. The graphic narratives not only communicate the reciprocity between interviewee and interviewer, but also offer a new medium through which we as readers witness and imagine the experiences of David, Emmie, Nico, and Rolf. These stories are in our heads and hearts, and the embodied memories of the survivors, visually represented by the artists, are brought to life in our imaginations. We carry them forward, hand in hand, together in time.

We are profoundly grateful to Emmie Arbel, Nico Kamp, Rolf Kamp, and David Schaffer who entrusted their experiences of the Holocaust not only to the artists but also to the project team at large whose members are based in Europe, Israel, and North America. As none of the survivors had any previous experience working with graphic novelists, we applaud their curiosity, and willingness to engage in a collaborative creation process that might have seemed radical at first. Likewise, we would like to express our sincerest appreciation to Miriam Libicki, Gilad Seliktar, and Barbara Yelin. Without their deeply felt and enacted empathy, compassion, and generosity, which in so many ways powerfully defied the constraints of the conventional testimony genre, our project would not have come to fruition.

As real-time in-person Holocaust testimonies will soon be no longer available to us, we are challenged to explore new channels to access, understand, and contextualize the individual experiences of genocide survivors. Visually narrated stories – especially graphic narratives – help students acknowledge multiple perspectives and develop critical thinking skills. Although our graphic novels encourage students to reflect on the singularity of Holocaust survivor experiences, they also challenge students to critically respond to present-day human rights violations. Reading the survivors' essays collected in this volume, it becomes apparent that David, Emmie, Nico, and Rolf are role models for how we can integrate learning about the Holocaust into broader questions of human rights protection. We contend that learning *about*, *through*, and *for* human rights enables critical reflection on the use and abuse of power, the roles and responsibilities of individuals and states when faced with collective violence.

For use in the high school classroom, *But I Live* is supported by human rights-centered educational materials, short documentaries, interviews, and archival resources that are freely available on our project website for in-class and remote learning around the world (www.holocaustgraphicnovels.org). Under the leadership of Andrea Webb, education scholars and museum professionals in Canada, Germany, Israel, and the United States have been working with our three graphic novels developing multilingual educational resources that align Holocaust teaching and learning with social justice and anti-racism education. By leading with empathy and leveraging a global network, we hope to inspire and train the next generation of scholars, educators, curators, and human rights advocates. High school students are also the inheritors of Holocaust survivor memories, and their stewardship of those memories is essential to preserving the dignity of the experiences and the prevention of gross human rights violations.

ACKNOWLEDGMENTS

We gratefully acknowledge the indispensable hands-on assistance of our editors, Natalie Fingerhut (New Jewish Press) and Ulrich Nolte (C.H. Beck). Both Natalie and Ulrich were curious, attentive, and deeply engaged readers providing astute insight and feedback. Natalie and Ulrich were also open to working in a collaborative fashion, giving us the time and space to consult broadly with survivors, artists, scholars, and community partners prior to making any final decisions. We also wish to thank Lynn Fisher (University of Toronto Press) and Jonathan Beck (C.H. Beck) who reached out to us early on in the project. These were much-appreciated signs of encouragement signaling that we were on the right track. Thank you! We especially want to thank Dienke Hondius, Alex Korb, and Andrea Löw who provided critical historical context to each graphic novel. Dienke, Alex, and Andrea consulted with the survivors and the artists, ensuring that their own historiographical essays complemented the graphic narratives in the best way possible. Moreover, we are very thankful for the invaluable support of Wilhelmina Mensing (Traa) and Caroline Siegers-Boyd who shared photographs from the Traa family's personal collection with Gilad Seliktar. We would also like to thank Kristin Semmens who reviewed the historical contributions, providing important additional feedback.

As our arts-based community-engaged approach created synergies across disciplines, sectors, languages, and cultures, we would like to extend our deepest gratitude to our project partners (in alphabetical order): Frank Bajohr, Gillian Booth, Anna Bucchetti, Mark Celinscak, Tim Cole, Randa El Khatib, Stefanie Fischer, Martin Friedrich, Matthias Heyl, Andrea Hopp, Akim Jah, Kobi Kabalek, Chorong Kim, Arie Kizel, Fransiska Louwagie, Noa Mkayton, Lise Pinkos, Kees Ribbens, Christoph Sturm, Maja Sturm, Katarina Türler, and Andrea Webb. We also gratefully acknowledge the support of Dorothee Wierling, Michael Groenewald, Anna Fuchs, and Susanne Hellweg. Likewise, the work of our student researchers was integral to our collaborative creation process. Our heartfelt thanks go to Janine Wulz, Betsy Inlow, Maria Dechant, Patricia Piberger, Franziska Uhl, Giles Bennett, and to our translators Rebecca DeWald and Noga Yarmar. Special thanks are also due to the Community Field Experience (CFE) students in the Teacher Education Program at the University of British Columbia, teacher candidates at the University of Haifa, and the teacher candidates at the University of Osnabrück who created trauma-informed educational resources under the expert guidance and mentorship of Andrea Webb (Education team lead), Arie Kizel, Maja Sturm, and Christoph Sturm. We would also like to acknowledge the educators around the world who took part in piloting the materials in their classrooms and learning environments.

At the University of Victoria, we are grateful to have received the dedicated support of many colleagues, partners, and staff members: Jonathan Bengtson, Philip Cox, Alexandra D'Arcy, Stephanie Harrington, Lytton McDonnell, Rosemary Omner, Jennifer Sauter, Ray Siemens, Jennifer Swift, Emmanuelle Guenette, the Faculty of Humanities, UVic Libraries, the Electronic Textual Cultures Lab, the Legacy Art Galleries, and the Centre for Global Studies. We are also greatly indebted to the invaluable contributions and support of our community and university partners: the Vancouver Holocaust Education Centre (Vancouver, Canada), the Canadian Museum for Human Rights (Winnipeg, Canada), the Anne Frank House (Amsterdam, the Netherlands), Arolsen Archives (Bad Arolsen, Germany), the Ravensbrück Memorial Museum

(Fürstenberg/Havel, Germany), the Stanley Burton Centre for Holocaust and Genocide Studies (Leicester, UK), the Centre for Research on Antisemitism (Berlin, Germany), Yad Vashem – International School of Holocaust Studies (Jerusalem, Israel), the Faculty of Education (University of British Columbia, Canada), the Faculty of Education (University of Haifa, Israel), the Faculty of Education (University of Osnabrück, Germany), and The Sam & Frances Fried Holocaust & Genocide Academy (University of Nebraska Omaha, USA). The Social Sciences and Humanities Research Council of Canada (SSHRC) supported all of our research, knowledge mobilization activities, and creative endeavors. Without this generous and vital support, our collaborative work (*Narrative Art and Visual Storytelling in Holocaust and Human Rights Education*) would not have been feasible. And finally, without a young boy's love of graphic novels, the first seeds of this project might never have been planted. Thank you, Sebastian Schallié.

BIOGRAPHIES

Miriam Libicki is the creator of the Israeli Army memoir *jobnik!*, a book of graphic essays *Toward a Hot Jew* (recipient of the 2017 Vine Award for Canadian Jewish Literature), and many short nonfiction comics. She holds an MFA in Creative Writing and lives in Vancouver, Canada.

Gilad Seliktar wrote and illustrated four graphic novels. In 2018 he received an Honourable Mention in the Israel Museum Ben-Yitzhak Award for the Illustration of a Children's Book. He is a lecturer at the Bezalel Academy of Arts and Design in Jerusalem and lives in Pardes Hanna-Karkur, Israel.

Barbara Yelin studied illustration in Hamburg, Germany. She created several research-based books about women in history. In 2014, Yelin published the award-winning graphic novel *Irmina*, and in 2016, she was Best German-language Comics Artist at the International Comic Salon, Erlangen. She lives in Munich, Germany.

Charlotte Schallié is a professor and chair of the Department of Germanic and Slavic Studies at the University of Victoria.

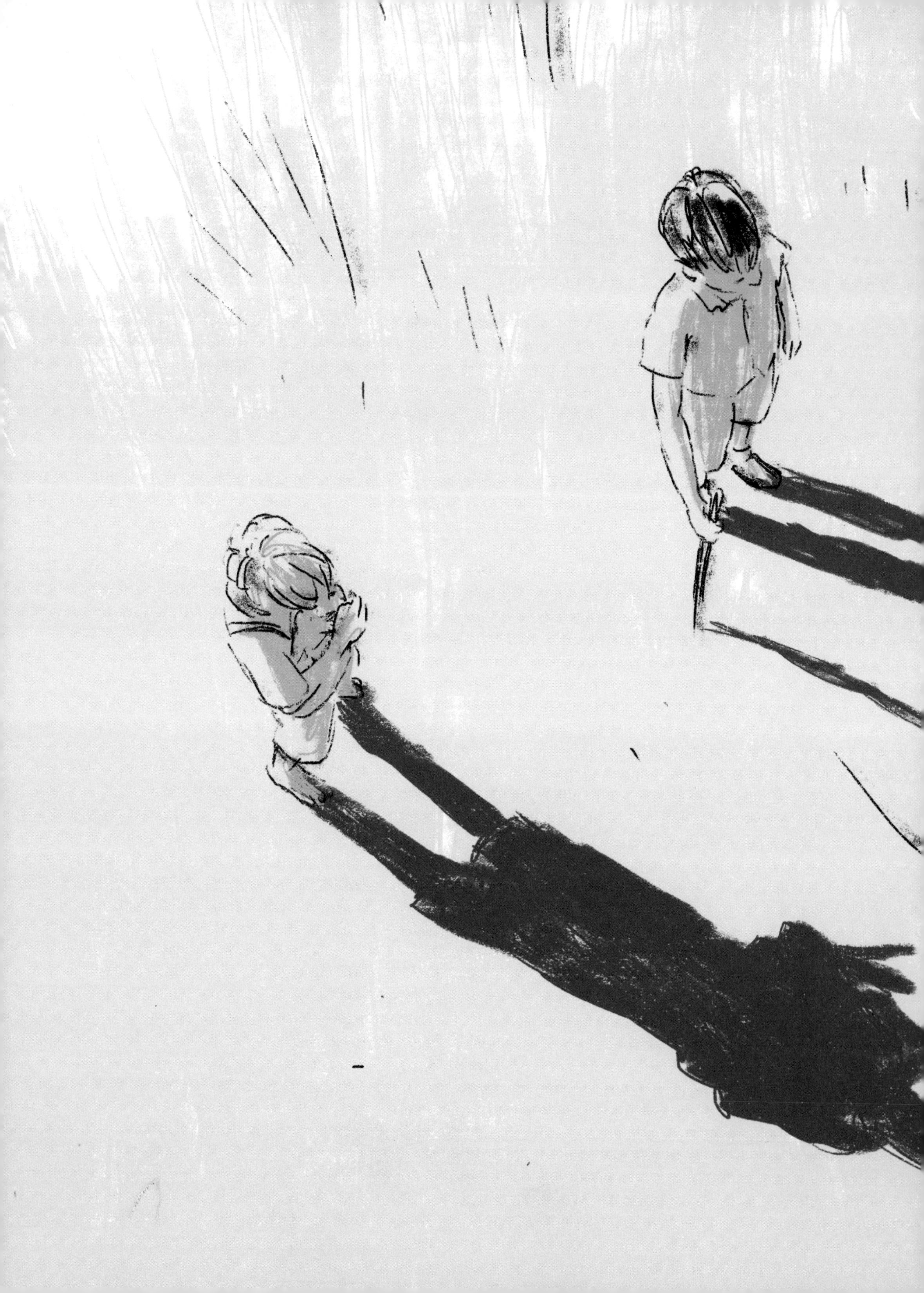